AF729726

# Human Rights and Comparative Foreign Policy

# Attention Authors

Manas Publications is fighting a war to tell the world that India can win the battle not only by bullet but also by pen. We are converting fighters into writers since our country is full of intellectuals but their knowledge is only confined to them. No sincere effort has been made by any publisher to give the right direction to their knowledge and the talent of intellectual is still hidden. An author always gives the raw material in the shape of manuscript and it is the sense of publisher to make it a finished product. We are motivating the intellectuals' mind and publishing their manuscripts for more than two decades and would like to publish your manuscript too. If you or your colleagues have any manuscript or are working on, please don't hesitate to contact us with detailed synopsis and contents for its publication. We take utmost care in production and give a wide publicity to the book and its author. We can also suggest you the title for writing related to your subject since we are the publishers who believe more in quality than in quantity.

# Human Rights and Comparative Foreign Policy

**David P. Forsythe**

*(Published in collaboration with United Nations University Press)*

**Manas Publications**
**New Delhi - 110 002 (India)**

**MANAS PUBLICATIONS**
(Publishers, Distributors, Importers & Exporters)
4858, Prahlad Street,
24, Ansari Road, Darya Ganj,
New Delhi - 110 002 (INDIA)
**Ph.: 23260783, 23265523 (O); 23842660(R)**
**Fax: 011- 23272766**
**E-mail: manaspublications@vsnl.com**

Published in collaboration with United Nations University Press
© United Nations University Press

2006

ISBN 81-7049-295-5
Rs. 695/-

Authorised edition for sale in India, Pakistan, Afghanistan, Nepal, Bhutan, Sri Lanka, Tibet, Bangladesh, Myanmar, Maldives only. Export of this edition to any other unauthorized territories/countries is strictly prohibited.

No part of this book can be reproduced, stored in a retrieval system, or transmitted in any form, by any means, including mechanical, electronic, photocopying, recording, or otherwise, without the prior written permission of the publisher.

*Printed in India at*
Salasar Imaging Systems, Delhi
and Published by Mrs. Suman Lata for
**Manas Publications**, 4858, Prahlad Street,
24, Ansari Road, Daryaganj,
New Delhi 110002 (INDIA)

# Contents

List of tables and figures ........................................ vii

Acknowledgements ........................................ viii

1 Introduction ........................................ 1
*David P. Forsythe*

**Part I: Some liberal democracies of the OECD** ........................................ 19

2 US foreign policy and human rights: The price of principles after the Cold War ........................................ 21
*David P. Forsythe*

3 Trials and errors: The Netherlands and human rights ........................................ 49
*Peter R. Baehr*

4 British foreign policy and human rights: From low to high politics ........................................ 87
*Sally Morphet*

5 Japan's foreign policy towards human rights: Uncertain changes ........................................ 115
*Yozo Yokota and Chiyuki Aoi*

**Part II: Some other states** ........................................ 147

6 Russian foreign policy and human rights: Conflicted culture and uncertain policy ........................................ 149
*Sergei V. Chugrov*

7 India's human rights diplomacy: Crisis and transformation .... 178
*Sanjoy Banerjee*

8 Iran and human rights ........................................ 206
*Zachary Karabell*

9 Human rights and foreign policy in Central Europe: Hungary, the Czech Republic, and Poland ........................................ 224
*Gábor Kardos*

10 Human rights and foreign policy in post-apartheid South Africa ........................................ 250
*Tiyanjana Maluwa*

11 Latin American foreign policies and human rights ............ 276
*Cristina Eguizabal*

12 An overview ........................................ 310
*Jack Donnelly*

Postscript: The Kosovo crisis ........................................ 335
*David P. Forsythe*

List of contributors ........................................ 342

Index ........................................ 343

# Tables and figures

**Tables**

3.1 Amnesty International membership, 1996 .................. 58
11.1 Latin American countries' status vis-à-vis selected international human rights treaties .......................... 283
11.2 Inter-American human rights regime.......................... 284

**Figure**

12.1 National attitudes towards international human rights...... 320

# Acknowledgements

The United Nations University, an independent unit of the UN system located in Tokyo, approached me in 1995 about carrying out a study of human rights in comparative foreign policy. I was eager to do so, having long regarded human rights in foreign policy as an underdeveloped aspect of international human rights. We had many studies on human rights and international law, and quite a few on human rights and international organizations. But few authors had focused on human rights and foreign policy, and fewer still had shown any interest in this topic on a truly comparative basis.

I am grateful to the leadership of the UNU for their interest in, and support for, this project: Rector von Ginkel and his associates Takashi Inoguchi, Hideo Sato, and Ramesh Thakur. With much-appreciated funding from the UNU, I assembled a steering committee whose diverse members included Peter Baehr, Sanjoy Banerjee, Jack Donnelly, Cristina Eguizabal, and myself. With the help of the New York office of the UNU, and especially of its director Jacques Fomerand, we hammered out a framework of analysis that would be used by all authors. With the assistance of UNU headquarters in Tokyo, and especially of Chiyuki Aoi and Yoshie Sawada there, we assembled a multinational team of authors who agreed to utilize the common framework that had been established by the steering committee.

Many of the authors met in Washington in 1997 to review progress and compare approaches. Christopher Joyner and Tony Arend of Georgetown University facilitated some of our meetings, and they joined Jack Donnelly and myself in presenting extended critiques of the works in process. The American Political Science Association gave us a couple of panel slots on their programme at the 1997 annual meeting, which led to lively discussions. At a later stage, two independent referees gave us further critiques that helped us improve the manuscript.

Along the way various graduate students and support staff at the University of Nebraska-Lincoln provided invaluable editorial and other assistance: J. T. Smith, Barbara Ann Rieffer, Jennier Gutierrez, Helen Sexton, and Monica M. Mason. UNL's computer experts were also most helpful: John Teets and Gregg Frey.

The result is a book that breaks new ground in our understanding of internationally recognized human rights in comparative perspective.

David P. Forsythe
Lincoln, Nebraska, USA
April 1999

# 1

# Introduction

*David P. Forsythe*

A review of the literature in English on international human rights in the mid-1990s concluded among other things that more attention needed to be paid to state foreign policy and human rights, especially in comparative perspective.[1] At about the same time as that bibliographic essay appeared, an overview on human rights and foreign policy was published by a Dutch author which provided a useful primer.[2] Then a couple of years later a Canadian author published a study about whether human rights considerations affected the development politics of three industrialized states in their dealings with various lesser developed countries.[3] The present project marks a further step toward responding to the challenge of providing a relatively broad but reasonably detailed and advanced treatment of human rights and foreign policy in comparative perspective.

The subject is important. We live in an era in which there is much discourse about the demise of the state and the anachronism of state sovereignty. We chart the growth over time of intergovernmental organizations, many of which deal with human rights. We note the proliferation of private human rights groups, some of which are transnational in membership and scope of action. It has become commonplace to note the power and presumed independence of multinational or transnational corporations. The independent communications media are a factor of considerable importance. But the state remains central to all such developments. It is states that create intergovernmental organizations, defining their authority and perhaps loaning them some elements of power.

When the United Nations Security Council declares that to interfere with humanitarian assistance in Somalia is a war crime for which there is individual responsibility, states collectively take that decision. States provide legal and political space for private human rights groups to operate in the first place, give them access to international organizations, and decide whether to cooperate with them and to what degree. States decide whether private for-profit corporations can trade with Iraq, Libya, or Yugoslavia, and states implement economic sanctions and assign penalties for their violation. States regulate the media and seek to manipulate them beyond that point, even if in return the media pry into state behaviour and report what they can. It is certainly true that the state shares the world stage with a variety of other actors. But the state is hardly withering away, even if its de facto independence of policy-making is increasingly restricted by a variety of factors. Even in Europe, where the state is considerably restricted by the European Union and the Council of Europe, there is still the political reality of a Netherlands, for example, with a relatively independent foreign policy on many issues – including global human rights.

Any state's foreign policy is the result of a two-level game in which domestic values and pressures combine with international standards and pressures to produce a given policy in a given situation for a given time. This combination of domestic and international factors varies from state to state, from time to time, and from place to place, making generalizations difficult to fashion with reliability. The West European democracies are greatly affected on human rights by regional international developments, especially the workings of the Council of Europe and also the European Union. There is also the Organization for Security and Cooperation in Europe. By contrast, on human rights matters the United States is more insular, and thus relatively more influenced by domestic factors. Unlike its democratic partners in Europe, the United States is subject neither to a regional human rights court, nor to a regional economic court that also makes human rights rulings on labour rights and other subjects affecting economic activity.

Yet commonalities exist. One of the major themes of this book is to confirm that most nations, if not all of them, harbour a self-image.[4] This self-image affects attention to human rights, both at home and in foreign policy. National self-image may be part and parcel of a nation's political culture – the sum total of a people's attitudes toward political values and processes. This self-image may be fruitfully discussed in terms of the roles that states choose to play in international relations. Canada, seeing itself as a progressive and middle-range power, chooses to play the role internationally as a major peacekeeping nation and catalyst for treaties banning land mines or creating an international criminal court.

Dominant American political culture, for example, sees the United States as a global beacon and shining example of personal freedom, regardless of evident blemishes on its national record concerning slavery, racial and gender discrimination, and various forms of other bigotry. The dominant political classes in the Netherlands tend to see that state as a progressive actor with a special history of support for international law and free trade in peaceful international relations. The Dutch dominant self-image in modern times provides support for human rights concerns in foreign policy, whether as linked to development assistance to the poorer countries of the global south, especially former Dutch colonies, or as linked to second-generation UN peacekeeping that contains human rights dimensions.

Some countries may contain a fuzzy self-image or conflicted political culture, as yet not fully distilled into clear international roles. This is evidently the case in Russia. A strong Slavic tradition of authoritarianism and suspicion of the West, *inter alia*, competes with a weaker Petrine tradition (from the time of Peter the Great) endorsing cosmopolitan human rights and openness to the West. One result of this conflicted political culture is vacillation in Russian foreign policy on various human rights issues, especially those linked to cooperation with the West. Even when conflicted or less than fully distilled, the notion of self-image as part of political culture is a useful way to begin to discuss the domestic or national factors that affect a state's foreign policy on international human rights issues.

There are a few states such as Iran where reigning notions of self-image and the dominant political culture mostly reject secular universal human rights. As an Islamic theocracy, Iran at times makes two different arguments. It can be an outspoken advocate for cultural relativism and national particularism. Thus it argues that internationally recognized human rights, not being grounded in Islam, do not apply to it. It sees itself as a bulwark against the misguided notions of secular human rights, inspired by the despised United States. On the other hand, in its revolutionary phase, Islamic Iran argues for its version of Islamic universalism, and tries – if necessary by force and subversion – to compel others to follow its religious vision.

But there are not many states in the world today that reject the very notion of secular and universal human rights – at least at the level of principled debate. Even those states at the 1993 UN Conference on Human Rights at Vienna that raised questions about the applicability of the International Bill of Rights to their states in the 1990s eventually accepted Conference language reaffirming the universal character of human rights norms. By 1998 even China had ratified the 1966 International Covenant on Economic, Social, and Cultural Rights and had promised likewise to endorse the companion Covenant on Civil and Political Rights. Thus all states, regardless of national history and mythology, were compelled to confront the international law and diplomacy of human rights. Still, national history and resultant political culture affected the interaction between national self-image and international human rights.

National domestic factors beyond self-image were almost always supremely important in the making of foreign policy on human rights. In the United States, and most probably in other liberal democracies, public opinion polls showed that the general public endorsed protection of human rights and advancement of democracy abroad as legitimate and even important foreign policy goals. But at the same time the general public was not inclined to support a costly crusade for human rights abroad. It was not only the United States but also other Western states that had proven reluctant to engage in decisive – and perhaps costly – intervention to protect human rights in places such as Bosnia prior to 1995 and Rwanda during 1994. Even an evident pattern of gross violations of rights to personal security, including genocide and systematic rape as a weapon of war, had not moved these countries to decisive action.

Readily available evidence, in addition to polls where they existed, showed that Western publics might endorse human rights in the abstract and even support routine diplomacy for their advancement. But expending national blood and treasure in their behalf was another matter. Public and legislative clamour for an exit from Somalia after American casualties in the fall of 1993 was symptomatic of what the polls were telling us about American public opinion and support for costly foreign ventures. Since Western states were the motor to interventionary protection of human rights through the United Nations Security Council and other international organizations, the nature of Western – especially American – public opinion was an important brake on protective possibilities. Systematic sacrifice in behalf of international human rights could be sustained in the liberal democratic states only with the support of public opinion translated into legislative opinion. And, as noted, public support for costly foreign policy for human rights was not much in evidence – especially after about 1993. If this situation prevailed in the liberal democracies, it should not be so surprising if other states were less than daring and steadfast in their efforts to see internationally recognized human rights implemented.

A certain public reserve about sacrifice for the rights of foreigners, which in other terms meant that moral interdependence across nations seemed weaker than material interdependence, did not preclude action by private groups active in support of international human rights. Indeed, in all the liberal democracies numerous human rights groups, and other private groups such as labour unions and churches that became active on certain human rights questions, were an evident feature of civil society. While maintaining their "non-political" status, they tried to "educate" – or lobby – various state officials. Media coverage also provided an independent if spasmodic spur to attention to human rights issues.

In states without a strong tradition of civic society, and particularly in those states dominated in the past by illiberal governments, the activity of private human rights groups was weak. Economic difficulties also impeded the development of a vigorous human rights network in the private domain. Yet almost everywhere the historical trend was toward more rather than less education by human rights groups, and more rather than less media coverage of the subject. Mexico was an interesting case in point. Long hesitant about the role of international as well as truly independent domestic human rights groups, the Mexican government in the 1990s found itself more and more having to explain its human rights record to a transnational or intermestic coalition made up of churches, the media, and human rights actors.[5] The government finally agreed to meet with the Executive Secretary of Amnesty International from London, and then later with UN Secretary-General Kofi Annan.

This is not to say that private human rights groups always generated significant influence on the making of foreign policy in a particular state. The groups themselves regularly complained about their impotence. Other factors might be more important for a given time, place, or policy. Executive preferences, military opinion, business interests, or national moods and traditions might control policy at the end of the day. But the presence or absence, the number and resources, the emphases and orientations of private human rights groups were subjects worthy of analysis in understanding foreign policy and human rights.

Likewise, in a number of states the analysis of political parties and their position on human rights issues was an important topic. In some states, such as the Netherlands, perhaps because of coalition governments, it might be possible for the state to manifest a more or less enduring foreign policy on human rights across time and changes in the coalition. Professor Peter Baehr appears to suggest this in chapter 3. In presidential systems like that in the United States, institutional conflict between the executive and legislative branches was at least as important for foreign policy and human rights as differences between the Democratic and Republican parties. But in states like the United Kingdom and India, party differences on human rights abroad were clear and important. In chapter 4, Sally Morphet shows clearly that the British Labour Party was far more likely than its Conservative counterpart to take numerous initiatives on international human rights. And the rise to power of the BJP or Hindu nationalist party in India in the late 1990s carried with it the prospect of important departures from previous Indian positions on several human rights subjects both at home and abroad, as shown in chapter 7 by Sanjoy Banerjee.

Likewise the very structure of the state merits analysis for an in-depth understanding of human rights policy abroad. On the one hand, a small state such as Costa Rica, with no military establishment and a small foreign policy bureaucracy, might manifest a dominant presidency in foreign affairs. Cristina Eguizabal is very clear on this point in chapter 11 on Latin America. The structure of the state might not matter much in such countries. On the other hand, a superpower such as the United States, with a sizeable military-industrial complex, presented quite different influences on the making of foreign policy in general and foreign human rights policy in particular. In the United States in the late 1990s, difficulties in Somalia reinforced the Vietnam syndrome, leading the Pentagon to try to continue to avoid involvement in low-intensity armed conflict. The Pentagon clearly preferred operations like Desert Storm (1991) rather than "operations other than war" in which political restrictions and objectives other than the military defeat of an enemy might be important. Given the considerable influence of the Pentagon in Washington, a President such as Clinton – who had no personal military record – could deploy military force in places such as Haiti and Bosnia only with considerable political risk at home and strict rules of engagement abroad. This situation hampered any move toward quick and decisive protection of human rights abroad through military action. By comparison, in Japan, as shown by Chiyuki Aoi and Yozo Yokota in chapter 5, a strong foreign policy bureaucracy wedded to strictly economic pursuits might prove a formidable obstacle to the development of an active and broad national policy on human rights abroad.

On the other hand, the United States did manifest a human rights bureau in the Department of State, as of the late 1990s called the Bureau of Democracy, Human Rights, and Labor. There was also a standing subcommittee of the House of Representatives, the lower house of the Congress, with explicit mandates pertaining to international human rights. These permanent features of the policy-making process enhanced the probability of regular review of foreign human rights issues, while giving those interested in such issues a focal point for trying to influence legislative and executive decisions. Britain, by comparison, had no such specialized agents in either the Foreign Office or Parliament, as Sally Morphet shows in chapter 4. The Netherlands, by way of further comparison, manifested for a time a Citizens' Advisory Council on Human Rights, which reported to the Foreign Minister, discussed by Peter Baehr in chapter 3.

There were other features of state structure that could be important from time to time for international human rights. The constituent states of the federal United States occasionally developed their own unofficial foreign policies related to human rights. Many internal states, Nebraska being the first, developed disinvestment and other financial policies designed to impede economic growth in the Republic of South Africa under white minority government.[6] Cities, counties, and states within the United States eventually blocked some US$20 billion in resources that might have been otherwise transferred to South Africa during the era of apartheid. When the federal Congress voted economic sanctions on South Africa in 1986, it explicitly decided to let stand, and not pre-empt on the part of the federal government, this decentralized pressure on white authorities. Numerous sub-federal units in the United States enacted similar policies designed to promote equitable labour rights and non-discrimination in the private sector of Northern Ireland, a province of the United Kingdom. Also in the 1990s, some internal states of the United States, such as Massachusetts, enacted legislation designed to curtail trade with Burma/Myanmar because of the human rights situation there. Thus in some federal nation-states, the sub-national governments might take action on human rights abroad that was uncoordinated by the central or federal or national authorities. Such action was not possible in countries like Britain with a unitary or centralized foreign policy process.

In a number of liberal democracies the corporate sector showed increased attention to international human rights toward the turn of the century.[7] Heineken, based in the Netherlands, pulled out of Burma because of the military government's continuing refusal to honour the outcome of elections a decade earlier. Levi Strauss, based in San Francisco, refused for a time to utilize cheap Chinese labour in the making of blue jeans, citing labour and other rights violations in that massive market. Reebok, based in the United Kingdom, certified that its soccer balls were not manufactured using child labour in places such as South Asia. Consumer boycotts in a number of states, as well as lobbying efforts by private human rights groups, were closely linked to these corporate decisions.

It was certainly true that not all for-profit corporations showed the same sensitivity to human rights issues noted above. A coalition of American companies combined to challenge the Massachusetts law on Burma cited above, hoping that some court in the United States would strike down the law as a violation of the US constitution, under which regulation of foreign commerce is arguably a prerogative of the federal Congress. The Massachusetts law was also the subject of various challenges within the World Trade Organization. Be all that as it may, the fact remains that, in a number of states, the role of the corporate sector was changing. It could no longer be assumed that for-profit corporations would always oppose attention to international human rights, or would always lobby against human rights legislation at the state and federal levels of government. Indeed, some corporations were banding together, and working with governments, to adopt codes of conduct for all corporations doing business in a particular industry, country, or region.

A review of the various domestic factors that frequently impinged on foreign policy-making regarding human rights did not always lead to the conclusion that such factors were decisively controlling for the fate of that policy. In Latin America, for example, it might be the case that at least governments in small countries were more affected by relations with Washington than by their own domestic factors. Cristina Equizabal stresses this point in chapter 11. That is to say, Latin governmental concerns about both maintaining good relations with the hemispheric hegemon and resisting US tendencies toward hemispheric intervention might outweigh the impact of at least some domestic factors at least some of the time. To take another example, it might also be the case that the communications media and private human rights groups generated less pressure on British governments than was the case in other North Atlantic democracies. Sally Morphet suggests this interpretation in chapter 4. A British government with majority support in the House of Commons could hold to a given policy despite criticism from the public and interest groups. Also, British governments benefited from a long tradition of parliamentary rather than popular sovereignty, and from a considerable tradition of widespread deference to the government in foreign affairs.

Nevertheless, in general most foreign policy decisions on human rights usually reflected to some degree various domestic influences beyond the calculations of national interest held by foreign policy officials. In general, domestic politics beyond officials' preferences mostly mattered in the making of foreign policy.[8] A nation's self-image, current public opinion, extent and nature of bureaucratic in-fighting, legislative independence, political party platforms, authority of sub-federal units, and the like combined to affect national human rights policy abroad.

These factors complemented, and frequently complicated, more strictly international influences on human rights policy abroad that stemmed from other governments, international organizations, and multinational corporations. Indeed, the very condition of anarchic international relations, lacking as it does a supranational centre, generated its own structural pressures on foreign policy for human rights – making coordinated policy difficult but not impossible. The operation of the principle of state sovereignty meant that any given state might chart its own independent course, based on its own perceived interests, rather than support a general policy in the name of human rights. Almost all international efforts to apply economic sanctions in behalf of human rights, for example, were met by some "cheating" or "sanctions busting" in pursuit of national economic advantage. Or to take another example, almost all efforts to coordinate policy toward China on human rights issues in the 1990s floundered on the hard rocks of varying perceptions of *raison d'état.* It was the nature of the international relations, and its rule of state sovereignty, that gave rise to this persistent condition.

It is against this background of the interplay of domestic and international conditions and pressures that we can chart state foreign policy and human rights.

## I. Foreign policy and multilateralism

Very few states openly reject the International Bill of Rights and many of its supplemental treaties. No state has ever sought to adhere formally to the United Nations Charter but reserve against Articles 55 and 56 dealing with human rights. Almost all of the eight states that abstained in voting on the 1948 Universal Declaration of Human Rights have repudiated their position at that time – Saudi Arabia being the notable exception. There is something about the intrinsic attractiveness of the abstract notion of human rights that deters formal rejection – even by states prone to violate specific human rights rules in specific situations. This pattern may represent only the homage that vice pays to virtue. Nevertheless, we should recognize the hegemonic quality of the idea of human rights.

Yet there is variation among states in how seriously they take international human rights instruments, in which obligations they accept, and in the extent to which they attach reservations and other conditions to their acceptance. Whereas Hungary's constitution, for example, proclaims the superiority of international law, including human rights law, over national law, dominant legal tradition is otherwise in the United States. In the latter state, it is only with considerable difficulty that the state agrees to be bound by international human rights provisions, if at all. US subordination to the international law of human rights certainly does not happen by constitutional proclamation. Other comparisons are useful. Whereas almost all states accept economic and social rights in the abstract but treat them as "step-children" or "poor cousins" in practice, the United States has never officially accepted economic and social rights as real rights that the state is obligated to respect. Various states have appended various reservations to various human rights treaties, but only the United States has so qualified its formal acceptance of the International Covenant on Civil and Political Rights as to have other states call into question the validity of its original acceptance under the international law of treaties.

We can also compare states in terms of the importance of regional arrangements on human rights. In general, the states most affected by regional organizations on human rights are the European ones. While all of them are now subject to the human rights standards and application measures in the Council of Europe (CE) and the Organization for Security and Cooperation in Europe (OSCE), especially affected are the states that are members of the European Union (EU). These 15 states are subject to the supranational human rights rulings of the both the EU's European Court of Justice and the CE's European Court of Human Rights. The sum total of the effects of the EU, CE, and OSCE means that human rights issues have a higher profile in Europe than in other regions. Most of the states in the western hemisphere, Africa, the Middle East, and Asia do not have to face the prospect of binding judgments on human rights by international courts, as is true in regard to the European Court of Human Rights and the European Court of Justice. (There is the Inter-American Court of Human Rights, but it handles few cases compared with Europe – and the United States is not subject to its jurisdiction.) Some states such as Britain may be far more affected by the need to bring domestic laws and conditions into compliance with regional standards than by the need to adjust national law to domestic pressures, although this particular comparison is a difficult one to make with certainty.

It is also illuminating to compare the pattern of foreign policy regarding human rights in the international financial institutions (IFIs) such as the World Bank. Some states like Germany have obviously been in favour of some "political conditionality" in which some loans are made conditional on certain human rights developments. Other states, particularly the borrowing states like India, have objected. The latter group of states tends to see such international human rights conditionality as a violation of the original terms of agreement of the IFIs and as a violation of the state sovereignty and domestic jurisdiction of the borrowers. For those states in favour of linking developmental loans to human rights conditions, important questions can be raised about whether or not such conditionality is being pursued with clarity and consistency. The answer in general is almost assuredly in the negative,[9] raising the issue of whether those states with paramount influence in IFI circles need to revisit their policy on this question.

During the first decade after the end of the Cold War, an important question concerned the interaction of state foreign policy with the United Nations organs most active on human rights issues. Especially if states were permanent members of the UN Security Council or elected to it, were they in favour of expanding the scope of Chapter VII and peace and security issues to encompass human rights matters? Were they in favour of a new permissibility for "humanitarian intervention" and thus overriding state consent in the interest of protecting persons inside states from gross and systematic violation of their rights recognized in international law? Some states, such as India, were clearly opposed, fearing the use of the discourse on human rights in the cause of rather narrow interests by the permanent five members. After all, in the past several centuries it was difficult to discover very many, if any, cases of truly principled humanitarian intervention in which the stronger powers acted for the real rights of foreigners without pursuit of narrow commercial or strategic issues. Ironically, India had rationalized its forcible dismemberment of old Pakistan in 1981 by reference to humanitarian intervention – namely, the need to stop the slaughter of Bengalis. Other states, such as the United States, seemed supportive of new thinking on humanitarian intervention at least during the 1991–1993 period, but more cautious after the 1993 events in Somalia. Still other states, such as Japan, in places like Cambodia, had certainly participated in UN field missions with human rights components, but had sought to maintain as much deference to state sovereignty as efficient politics would allow. The Japanese, for example, were not in favour of trying to use force to secure the compliance of the Khmer Rouge with the human rights and other agreements they had signed. Thus the matter of state cooperation with a Security Council sometimes prone to take a broad interpretation of its rights under Chapter VII pertaining to "peace and security" remained an important point of analysis.

Another important question was whether or not states really supported international criminal prosecution for those who had engaged in grave breaches of the 1949 Geneva Conventions, genocide, and crimes against humanity. Which states were in favour of a standing UN criminal court, with an independent prosecutor capable of initiating a broad range of indictments stemming especially from events in armed conflicts? On the other hand, which states saw emerging international criminal law as a grave infringement of the prerogatives of state sovereignty and sometimes an impediment to the diplomacy that could put an end to atrocities by political rather than juridical means? Britain under a Conservative government in the mid-1990s publicly endorsed international criminal justice in the former Yugoslavia, but behind the scenes worked to block the operation of the relevant Tribunal. London preferred a diplomatic rather than a juridical agreement that would end most of the fighting and associated violations of human rights. The United States supported international criminal justice in the former Yugoslavia and Rwanda, but the Pentagon and key conservatives in the Senate vigorously opposed any notion that US personnel should be subjected to trial by a standing international criminal court. Thus the United States voted against the statute for such a court at a diplomatic conference in Rome during July 1998.

Yet another set of questions that was related to state foreign policy at the United Nations concerned the use states made of the General Assembly. What initiatives, if any, did they take on human rights issues in that forum? Costa Rica, for example, had initiated a draft resolution on human rights education. How typical was this? Other states in the 1990s had introduced resolutions with wording favourable to a collective international right to receive humanitarian assistance, especially in times of armed conflict and similar situations. Which states supported such measures, and which states voted in opposition in the name of traditional notions of state sovereignty? On the outcome of answers to such questions rested the prospects of codification of new humanitarian principles.

In the UN Human Rights Commission, the traditional hub of UN routine diplomacy on human rights, which states pursued which agendas with what results? Which states, for example, wished to adopt resolutions critical of China's human rights record in order to pressure that permanent member of the Security Council to liberalize or perhaps even democratize? Which states wanted to pursue dialogue with China on human rights through other, less confrontational means? And which states sided with China in wanting to reduce as much as possible the international dialogue altogether about China and human rights? What were the long-term trends regarding use of the UN Human Rights Commission to try to see international human rights standards applied? And which states were primarily responsible for these trends? Which states, for example, pressed for emergency Commission sessions on former Yugoslavia and also Rwanda, with what results? To take another example, which states led the move toward enhanced legal protections for indigenous peoples, and again with what results?

A closely related question focused on state policies toward the Office of the UN High Commissioner for Refugees (UNHCR). It was reasonably well known that the OECD states were the largest contributors to UNHCR's budget, which in the 1990s was more and more devoted to humanitarian assistance. The UNHCR increasingly sought to provide socio-economic help not just to conventional refugees fleeing persecution, but also to those who found themselves in a refugee-like situation regardless of legal niceties – such as displaced persons inside a country's borders and those fleeing disorder rather than individually targeted persecution. But beyond financial support, which states – if any – afforded the UNHCR remarkable influence in the awarding of refugee status and/or at least temporary asylum? Which states most closely and consistently followed UNHCR guidelines for decision-making on these delicate questions? Which states manifested considerable friction with the UNHCR, and over what issues?

Given that the promotion and protection of human rights increasingly constituted one of the main activities of the United Nations, which was entirely consistent with its Charter adopted in 1945, it was important to understand the intersection of state foreign policy with this principal purpose of the Organization.

## II. Bilateral policy and human rights

In the shrinking and interconnected world that exists as we prepare to enter the twenty-first century, it is frequently not possible fully to separate multilateral from bilateral foreign policy. The difference is frequently one of degree rather than an absolute kind. When a state seeks to undertake a foreign policy apart from formal international organizations, increasingly it often seeks to coordinate that policy with its political friends and usual allies. The old maxim about safety in numbers has some relevance to the subject at hand, since collective approval and support, even outside intergovernmental organizations (IGOs), confers some political legitimacy and otherwise helpful backing to a state's goals. Thus when, in the early 1990s, the United States took up the possibility of some sanctions on military government in Nigeria because of its continuing repression, Washington discussed matters with especially its European political allies. (Finding little support for its ideas, the United States was not able to maximize its objectives.) Nevertheless, states do pursue some foreign policy objectives largely on a bilateral basis, even if at some point these national initiatives may become entangled in multilateral developments or take place against the background of multilateral standards and organizations. This pattern certainly holds for human rights abroad.

One of the more important questions in contemporary international relations is the extent to which various states make the creation and consolidation of liberal democracy one of their salient foreign policy goals. By liberal democracy we refer to a polity manifesting free and fair elections for national office, on the basis of almost universal suffrage, with the winners actually governing the country; accompanied by the rule of law and constitutionalism (government limited by law); with protection of those civil and political rights that reasonably protect against the tyranny of the majority. Whether a liberal democracy is also a social democracy depends on its implementation of socio-economic rights. There are multilateral programmes on this subject, such as supervision of elections by the United Nations and the Organization of American States (OAS) and the OSCE. But here we are concerned with bilateral developments.

It can actually happen that an authoritarian state displays a foreign policy supportive of some type of democracy abroad. Nigeria under military rule has operated in some neighbouring countries to oppose coups that deposed elected officials (Sierra Leone), and to create elected governments out of failed states (Liberia). But surely this is an exception that tends to prove the general rule that authoritarian foreign policy is not much interested in the creation and consolidation of liberal democracy.

It is also unhappily true that liberal democracies do not always support democratic developments abroad – certainly in the short term. It is well known, and reiterated in most of the chapters that follow, that liberal democracies often perceive economic, strategic, and other reasons to support authoritarian and otherwise repressive leaders in foreign countries. Historically it was war and other threats to national security traditionally defined that caused democracies to support authoritarian states. Allied support for Stalin's Soviet Union during the Second World War is a classic example.

In the modern world, however, many liberal democracies at least articulate a desire to create and consolidate liberal democracy as part of their foreign policy. This may be because such a goal is seen to reinforce global peace; the proposition of the democratic peace – that liberal democracies do not war *inter se* – has received much attention. This articulation of support for democracy abroad may occur because liberal democracies are seen to reinforce business and trade objectives; limited governments with large private sectors and a free electorate may be good for business and international trade. Articulating a pro-democracy foreign policy may occur because liberal democracies, at least in their public pronouncements, find it difficult to practise democracy at home and not preach it abroad; states do like to be, and do tend to be, similar in their domestic and foreign policies much of the time.[10] After all, domestic and foreign policy are made by the same elected leaders in liberal democracies.

In any event, most of the Western liberal democracies go beyond rhetoric and take a position on liberal democracy abroad in two ways. States such as the United States have a proactive, programmatic approach to this subject, helping to fund various activities in foreign countries designed to promote "liberal market democracies." The question arises as to the record of other states in this regard. Secondly, when there is an attempted or real change of government abroad, Washington takes a position on whether to recognize and otherwise support the new situation. The presence or absence of liberal democracy informs US decisions on these matters. This is not to say that liberal democracy is the only question on the agenda. It is to say that a *discussion* of liberal democracy is part of Washington's decision-making process – whether the precise subject is an *auto-golpe* or attempt to seize excessive power by the President in Guatemala in 1993, a coup in Sierra Leone in 1997, a change of government in former Zaire in 1997, a grab for power by Hun Sen in Cambodia in 1998, and so on.

Given that liberal democratic rights are enshrined in the International Bill of Rights, as well as in various resolutions by the United Nations, OAS, CE, EU, OSCE, etc., it is important to enquire into state foreign policy and liberal democracy. International standards call for liberal democracy, whatever its impact on international peace or free trade and prosperity. To what extent does a state seek to advance stable liberal democracy abroad on either a programmatic or an ad hoc basis? What resources, if any, are devoted to this objective? What policies might substitute for this objective as a central goal of foreign policy, and why? What is the state's pattern in finding reasons for recognizing, tolerating, or even actively working with authoritarian and repressive regimes? Over time, does a state show more or less attention to the question of democracy abroad, and why?

A related question is the extent to which a state will try to alter its various foreign assistance programmes, and regulate foreign direct investment and/or trade by the private sector, because of human rights issues. Again if we take the United States as an example, since the mid-1970s the Congress has required that US economic and military assistance to foreign states be linked to several human rights considerations or to unspecified human rights in general. Because of this legislation, and indeed because of shifting executive desires, the United States has some 25 years of experience with trying to use the levers of foreign assistance to advance certain human rights concerns. This is in addition to collective economic measures taken through the United Nations and other IGOs in the name of human rights protection. Washington has also sought on occasion to manipulate direct foreign assistance and trade by the private sector because of human rights, although in general it is reluctant to do this. It did so, however, regarding Uganda under Idi Amin and the Republic of South Africa under white minority rule from 1986.

One would think a clear picture has emerged as to the relationship of foreign assistance and other economic measures to human rights, and vice versa. Alas, as shown in chapter 2 on US foreign policy, efforts to track these relationships have led to somewhat elusive conclusions. Other states, too, such as Britain and the Netherlands, have from time to time made clear to other states that the latter should not count on continued foreign assistance as long as certain human rights problems remain. In particular, chapter 3 by Peter Baehr on the Netherlands shows that it is not always easy for a state to manipulate a relationship involving foreign assistance into influence for the donor over human rights matters.

Nevertheless, states continue to try to manipulate foreign assistance and regulate foreign investment and trade in the light of their foreign policy goals, including advancement of human rights. To generate influence is arguably the main point of, especially, foreign assistance, pure altruism on the part of states being in rather short supply. It is frequently difficult to sell a purely altruistic foreign policy to many taxpayers at home, who demand or expect some expedient return. And in some situations, say US relations with Guatemala in 1993, or US relations with Croatia during most of the late 1990s, the US threat of or actual withholding of foreign assistance because of human rights issues did appear to have some effect on the recipient state. The *auto-golpe* was rolled back (although more factors were at work than just US foreign policy); the Tudjman government in Croatia did turn over some indicted and thus suspected war criminals to the UN ad hoc criminal tribunal at The Hague. Thus it is important to continue to make a comparative analysis of the extent to which states seek to protect human rights through foreign assistance, and with what results. Likewise, although there is a large literature trying to assess the effect of sanctions that interrupt investment and trade, there is much left to learn about, in particular, prohibition of investment/trade on a bilateral basis and advancement of human rights.

States, because of political culture, geographical position, or constructed national interests, may take a variety of essentially national initiatives on human rights in foreign policy. We would hypothesize that the number of such initiatives is growing by an ever larger number of states, given the extent to which the discourse on human rights, and at least diplomatic action in its behalf, has been institutionalized in international relations.[11] We need to test that hypothesis with careful enquiry.

## III. Conclusions

The chapters that follow, undertaken on the basis of the questions outlined in this introduction, should begin to give us a better picture of state foreign policy and human rights on a fairly broad scale. We should arrive at a comparative evaluation of real as opposed to pro forma state views of the International Bill of Rights and of the most important human rights treaties ancillary to that core standard. On the basis of our enquiries, we should be able to say something about the prospects of consistency and perhaps even coordination concerning human rights in foreign policy. Is it true that most states seek to address human rights problems abroad only in small or weak states, or those perceived to be unimportant to national interests – however defined? Is it true that most states, in so far as they take action on human rights abroad through their foreign policies, do so almost exclusively in relation to civil-political rights rather than socio-economic rights? Even with various problems and deficiencies in conceptualization and execution, is it not true that more states are taking more action for international human rights than ever before in their histories?

These are important questions. This volume seeks to make a first step in answering them. No doubt it will not be the last word on the subject. Improvements will no doubt be made in conceptualization, methodology, and substantive findings. Nevertheless, given the lack of studies of human rights and foreign policy in comparative perspective to date, we are confident that the current project will provide a useful foundation on which others can build.

With some 190 states in the world, it is unclear what a perfect sample would look like for the purpose of examining the place of human rights in contemporary foreign policy. We wanted to include some major powers, and thus we included the United States, Japan, the Russian Federation, and the United Kingdom. We wanted to include some liberal democracies, members of the OECD, and thus we included the Netherlands along with the United States, the United Kingdom, and Japan. We wanted to include some states in the process of transition from authoritarian to democratic rule, and thus we included Hungary and South Africa, along with Russia. We also wanted to include some states that were critical of universal human rights as recognized through the United Nations, or critical of the way in which the Security Council had acted in relation to these rights, and so we included Iran and India. We wanted to pay attention to equitable geographical representation, and thus we included states from Latin America, Africa, East Asia, South Asia, the Middle East, Eastern Europe, Western Europe, and North America. We wanted to include a collection of states that did justice to population factors, and thus we included India, the United States, South Africa, and Russia, while not ignoring the smaller or middle range states such as Costa Rica and the Netherlands. Our original plans included attention to Chinese foreign policy and human rights, but for personnel reasons we were reluctantly forced to change course.

With an unlimited budget and a multi-volume project, we could have added numerous states that merit study: France, Norway, Germany, Nigeria, Kenya, Mexico, Brazil, Pakistan, Israel, the Philippines, etc. Constrained by finances and also by a desire to produce a single monograph at a reasonable price, so that our analyses might indeed circulate relatively widely, a steering committee in consultation with UNU officials finally decided upon the present 10 states. As stated in the earlier pages of this introduction, we believe the results comprise a carefully considered advance in our understanding of human rights and foreign policy in comparative perspective.

## Notes

1. Jack Donnelly, "Post-Cold War Reflections on the Study of International Human Rights," *Ethics and International Affairs* 8 (1994), 97–118. See also Donnelly's very good review of the literature on human rights and foreign policy in his *International Human Rights* (Boulder, CO: Westview Press, 1998, 2nd edn.), 195–198.
2. Peter R. Baehr, *The Role of Human Rights in Foreign Policy* (London: Macmillan, 1994).
3. David Gillies, *Between Principle and Practice: Human Rights in North–South Relations* (Montreal: McGill-Queens University Press, 1996).
4. See further John G. Stoessinger, *Nations in Darkness/Nations at Dawn* (New York: McGraw Hill, 1994, 6th edn.).
5. See further especially Margaret E. Keck and Kathryn Sikkink, *Activists beyond Borders: Advocacy Networks in International Politics* (Ithaca, NY: Cornell University Press, 1998).
6. David P. Forsythe, *American Exceptionalism and Global Human Rights* (Lincoln: University of Nebraska-Lincoln, 1999, Distinguished Professor Lecture).
7. For an optimistic account see Debora L. Spar, "The Spotlight and the Bottom Line," *Foreign Affairs* 77/2 (March/April 1998), 7–12.
8. Margaret Hermann and Joe. D. Hagan, "International Decision Making: Leadership Matters," *Foreign Policy* no. 110 (Spring 1998), 124–137.
9. David P. Forsythe, "The United Nations, Human Rights, and Development," *Human Rights Quarterly* 19/2 (May 1997), 334–349.
10. Alain Noel and Jean-Marc Therien, "From Domestic to International Justice: The Welfare State and Foreign Aid," *International Organization* 49/3 (Summer 1995), 523–553.
11. David P. Forsythe, "The UN and Human Rights at Fifty: An Incremental but Incomplete Revolution," *Global Governance* 1/3 (September–December 1995), 297–318.

# Part I

# Some liberal democracies of the OECD

# 2

# US foreign policy and human rights: The price of principles after the Cold War

*David P. Forsythe*

The United States, like virtually all other states, has constructed a positive self-image. This self-image centres on defence of personal freedom, understood as civil and political rights. The notion of the United States as symbol of individual civil and political rights, an idea not without some relative and historical validity, has been problematic enough in a domestic context – given such historical facts as slavery and racial segregation, racist immigration laws, anti-Semitism, and gender discrimination, *inter alia*. But the question of whether the United States should champion civil and political rights through an activist foreign policy has been much more problematical, giving rise to considerable debate since the founding of the Republic. Moreover, the United States mostly rejects any necessary relationship between socio-economic rights and the classical civil and political rights so central to Western liberal philosophy – aside from a commitment to the economic (civil?) right to private property. After the Cold War, the United States has continued to identify with leadership for civil and political rights in world affairs. But it has not always, or even very often, been willing to pay even a moderate price, in either blood or treasure, to see these rights implemented in foreign countries – as seems true for other democracies as well. It has also continued to reject a clear, consistent, and meaningful endorsement of most socio-economic rights. The United States, although making some positive contributions to the advancement of internationally recognized human rights through its foreign policy, still struggles to institutionalize attention to human rights abroad, especially as defined in the International Bill of Rights, and especially when even moderate costs are entailed.

## I. Introduction

Rare is the ruling élite that does not manipulate national opinion to produce a positive self-image. The United States is no exception to this generalization. The United States sees itself as standing above all for personal freedom. In this view the American revolution from 1776 and especially its Constitution from 1787 represented the broadest and most practical endorsement of individual human rights then known to political man. Given the subsequent cultural, economic, and political accomplishments of the United States, most Americans accept the view that the country represents a shining city on a hill, a beacon to all others; in this view the United States has much to teach others about the proper conduct of public affairs.[1] That other countries like France make similar claims to being a universal model for human rights with a *mission civilitrice* has not diminished the United States' sense of itself as positively unique. The core conception of what it means to be American entails allegiance to the US Constitution and the personal freedoms entailed in that document and its Bill of Rights.[2] Thus dominant American political culture is inseparable from a conception of human rights within a rule of law. The notion of civil and political rights is intrinsic to US political history.

Obvious defects in American society have done little to undermine the dominant view that the United States stands for personal freedom and has constructed an admirable society based on this principle. Systematic and legally approved discrimination against racial minorities, women, and certain foreign nationalities trying to immigrate to the United States has not undermined an American informal ideology that sees the country as representing equal freedom and opportunity for all. Part of this amorphous ideology holds that, if an individual is assertive and works hard, individual freedom will produce material good things. Thus there is little need for socio-economic rights, such as the right to publicly provided national health care.[3] Dominant American opinion is not very sympathetic to the idea that there can be too much personal freedom, so that those with power and wealth exploit those without. The presence in the United States of inner cities and rural areas with a poor quality of life is mostly attributed to the deficiencies of the inhabitants, not to any failings of the society or the political–legal system as a whole. The alleged lack of an American sense of community, by comparison with countries such as

Canada, is not given much attention and is certainly not attributed to an excessive commitment to individualism.[4] Criticisms of American individualism from various foreign parties, whether Canadian, West European, or Asian, *inter alia*, have yet to make notable inroads on traditional thinking. After the Cold War the Democratic Party joined the Republican Party in reducing welfare benefits for the poor and vulnerable, while emphasizing the individual work ethic and the need to grow the economy through governmental support for the business sector. The Reagan revolution persists, entailing an emphasis on individual freedom and competition – and American greatness. At the 1997 Denver summit of the seven largest industrialized democracies, plus Russia, President Clinton trumpeted this belief in the superiority of the American example, to the obvious reserve of the other participants.

Despite this self-image of leadership for human rights, it is by no means clear that the United States is easily given to moral crusades for personal freedom abroad in actual policy. It is true that distinguished analysts such as George Kennan and John Spanier have identified a moral strain in American rhetoric about foreign policy, such as Woodrow Wilson's "crusade" to make the world safe for democracy after the First World War.[5] But the noted historian Arthur M. Schlesinger, Jr. has shown that from the beginning of the Republic there has been debate about whether it should have an activist foreign policy in behalf of individual freedom abroad, or should lead by the more introverted model of constructing the good society at home.[6] A few examples suffice to make the point historically. The United States did not actively support various democratic movements abroad, as in 1848, and was one of the last states of the Western world to abandon slavery at home and then oppose it elsewhere. Neither in 1914 nor in 1939 did the United States rush to defend its democratic partners in Europe, but rather clung to a commercially inspired neutrality until attacks on its shipping and military installations, respectively, brought it into the two world wars. During the Cold War the United States undermined a number of elected governments and engaged in other anti-humanitarian interventions in order to increase its power vis-à-vis the Soviet Union.[7] Although some authors feared that increased rhetoric in behalf of human rights during the 1970s would lead to a moral crusade in US foreign policy,[8] the overall evidence strongly suggests that US concrete support for human rights abroad is a matter to be demonstrated rather than assumed.[9] The United States, like other states with a relatively serious (but far from perfect) commitment to certain human rights at home, may sometimes not be inclined toward a rights-supportive foreign policy – as French policy toward various contemporary African states so clearly demonstrates.[10]

## II. Domestic factors

A variety of domestic factors in the United States combined after the Cold War to ensure some attention to human rights in foreign policy, but also to ensure that the government did not pay a high price to see those principles advanced in world affairs.

President Bush spoke of a "new world order" with increased attention to international law and human rights,[11] and President Clinton spoke of enlarging the global democratic community as one of the pillars of his foreign policy.[12] This was to be expected. Since the Nixon–Kissinger years (1969–1976), all Presidents have paid lip-service to advancing international human rights as part of a moral dimension to US foreign policy. Both principal political parties realized that a Kissinger-like emphasis on a realist or power politics approach to world affairs did not resonate well with American society.

Public opinion polls showed that the general public as well as opinion leaders did indeed list promoting and defending human rights in other countries, as well as helping to bring a democratic form of government to other nations, as "very important" goals of US foreign policy.[13] But in 1995 these goals were in 13th and 14th place, respectively, with only 34 per cent and 25 per cent of the general public listing them as very important. In contrast, 80 per cent or more of the general public listed stopping the flow of illegal drugs into the United States, protecting the jobs of American workers, and preventing the spread of nuclear weapons as much more important, *inter alia*. Analysts concluded that there was considerable American popular support for pragmatic or self-interested internationalism, but not a great deal of support for moral internationalism.[14]

There were many non-governmental organizations active in Washington on human rights questions. Two of the most prominent were Amnesty International-USA and Human Rights Watch. They were quite different. AI-USA used a general figure of 350,000 for its American membership, relied on public pressure to achieve its goals of specific protection on the ground, and manifested a restricted mandate focusing on prisoner matters – a mandate that had displayed "mission creep" over the years since its founding in the United Kingdom in 1961. Human Rights Watch relied on élite action rather than a mass movement, focused traditionally on a broad range of civil and political rights with some slight attention to socio-economic factors, and aimed more at affecting public policy than releasing specific prisoners. Legally oriented groups, such as the Lawyers' Committee for Human Rights, were especially numerous. Physicians for Human Rights frequently used forensic science to testify in Congress about such subjects as political murder in places like El Salvador and

Bosnia. American labour, ethnic, and religious groups also were active on international human rights issues. And foreign-based human rights organizations, such as Doctors Without Borders (Médecins Sans Frontières), were much in evidence in various policy debates. But Amnesty International, among others, bemoaned its lack of ability to orient US foreign policy toward more support for various human rights issues.[15]

The communications media based in the United States covered foreign human rights and humanitarian issues with such apparent influence sometimes that one spoke of "the CNN factor" in the making of US foreign policy. This was especially true after media coverage of the Kurdish plight in Iraq in 1991 and the plight of many starving Somalis in 1992 helped to produce US and international action on these issues. But the failure of media coverage to propel international involvement in Rwanda in 1994 and in eastern Zaire in 1997 showed the limits of the CNN factor. If an administration had a firm view of its interests, and especially of the dangers of involvement, it might not be much influenced by media coverage of foreign human rights problems.

The American business community is difficult to characterize on foreign human rights issues. Some American corporations, such as Levi Strauss, had a clear human rights policy. Strauss, based in San Francisco, refused to make blue jeans in China for human rights reasons. They were willing to pay whatever costs were involved in such decisions. The American garment industry was under increased pressure in the 1990s to do something about child labour and other issues about exploitation in its foreign operations. But most American corporations seemed not to support the interruption of business as usual for human rights purposes. Most American businesses interested in contracts in China, for example, came down on the side of delinking China's human rights record from questions of trade and especially questions about most-favoured-nation (MFN) status. Under heavy business lobbying, a majority in Congress pushed for a delinking of China's human rights record from MFN status, and the Clinton administration shifted gears to accept this orientation.

The Congress paid considerable attention to human rights in foreign policy from the mid-1970s, and on the House side – but not the Senate – there was a subcommittee of the Foreign Affairs Committee that tracked international human rights issues. The Congress acted in independent fashion on many foreign policy issues, relative to other legislatures. It had pushed the executive branch into action on a variety of human rights issues in the past in places such as Eastern Europe and South Africa. It had created a special bipartisan and bicameral Helsinki Commission to work for human rights in communist Europe during the Cold War. This Helsinki Commission continued its existence after about 1990 in efforts to promote democracy and the protection of national minorities in Europe.

But especially after 1994 the Republican-controlled Congress seemed to reflect a certain fatigue with many foreign policy initiatives, especially those involving expenditure of money. Forty years of Cold War produced a wave of budget-cutting on foreign spending that made it difficult to undertake costly human rights programmes.

Although the Department of State manifested a human rights bureau from the mid-1970s because of congressional instructions, this office – renamed the Bureau of Democracy, Human Rights, and Labor – had little special clout in most administrations whether Democratic or Republican. Foreign Service Officers preferred assignment in other parts of the State Department as a faster track to career advancement. The office did compile annual country reports on the human rights situation in all other countries of the world, which received considerable domestic and foreign attention when submitted to Congress each year. Under congressional pressure, itself generated primarily by American conservative Christian groups, the office also started putting out an annual report on the persecution of Christians abroad. This report contributed to the saliency of the issue of religious freedom, which had long enjoyed a special status in the United States, given that many early settlers came to North America to escape religious persecution in Europe.

More important was the general opposition at high levels of the Defense Department to involvement of the US military in operations other than war or in low-level irregular warfare where the full power of the US high-tech, industrialized military establishment could not be brought to bear. The Pentagon was more comfortable fighting the Persian Gulf War against Iraq than in deploying limited force for limited and complicated human rights purposes in places such as Somalia, Haiti, and Bosnia. Especially after Madeleine Albright became Secretary of State, the Clinton administration was the scene of much debate between a Secretary of State who favoured military deployment for human rights purposes on occasion, and a Secretary of Defense and military staff who agreed with Michael Mandelbaum when he wrote that foreign policy was not social work and the United States was not Mother Teresa.[16] The Pentagon's reluctance to engage itself in less than all-out warfare led one commentator to observe that, since the United States wanted no casualties except in defence of traditional and narrow national interests, which was true of major European states as well, there were no Great Powers any more.[17] No state wanted to pay any significant price to control the outcome of most controversies that arose in international relations.

Because of this mix of domestic factors, one can better understand why human rights remained a fixture on the agenda of US foreign policy, but also why there were no crusades for human rights abroad entailing even moderate, much less high, financial and human costs. One can thus understand why the United States was reluctant to engage decisively while killing raged in places such as Bosnia and Rwanda, especially after American loss of life in Somalia. One can equally understand why the Clinton administration was mostly hesitant to pursue the arrest of war criminals, especially in the former Yugoslavia, fearing costly retaliation that would undermine public, congressional, and military support for the presence of US military forces in that complicated and unstable situation. One could fashion moral, legal, and even pragmatic arguments for US activism on a number of human rights issues abroad. One could argue, for example, that it would have cost the United States less money to stop the genocide in Rwanda than it paid out in subsequent years to help care for the refugees from genocide. The Clinton administration did take politically risky action for human rights in Haiti, since there was little support for that action in Congress and the Pentagon, although it was also pushed toward military deployment by domestic political forces – i.e. the congressional Black caucus demanding attention to the plight of Haitians, and politicians from south Florida demanding an end to unwanted Haitian immigration. But the central fact remained. Important parts of the American body politic – the general public, the business community, the Pentagon, and the Congress – were highly pragmatic and prudent about any costly crusade for international human rights. Clinton himself, a capable domestic politician and one not much given to sustained interest in foreign affairs, demonstrated no great personal passion on the issue of internationally recognized human rights.

## III. Multilateral human rights policy

### *The International Bill of Rights*

Although the United States pictures itself as a leader for human rights in the world, it has long manifested an uneasy relationship with the International Bill of Rights, made up of the human rights provisions of the United Nations Charter, the 1948 Universal Declaration of Human Rights, the International Covenant on Civil and Political Rights, and the International Covenant on Economic, Social, and Cultural Rights. In 1945 the United States was in favour of general human rights language in the UN Charter, but opposed more specific language creating enforceable legal obligations. Likewise, the United States took the lead in the UN Human Rights Commission in pressing for the adoption of the Universal Declaration, but insisted it was only a statement of aspirations.

The two basic Covenants, and other UN human rights treaties like the one on genocide, have been especially controversial in Washington.[18]

American nationalists fear that the preferred status of the US Constitution will be superseded by treaty law. Those in favour of internal states' rights fear that treaty law will excessively empower the federal government. Conservatives fear that international human rights principles will weaken American individualism and respect for private property. Racists fear further attention to principles of racial equality and multiculturalism. Unilateralists fear the further enmeshment of the United States in international (read, foreign) decision-making.

The prominence of these views during the 1950s, reflected in lobbying by the American Bar Association, caused the Eisenhower administration to eschew ratification of human rights treaties and to abandon a leadership role in human rights within international organizations.[19] The Kennedy administration successfully obtained ratification of several non-salient human rights treaties. The Carter administration, after Congress partially reversed itself and began to emphasize human rights abroad in some of its legislation from 1974,[20] submitted the two basic Covenants to the Senate for advice and consent, but did not lobby effectively for them. Things began to change superficially thereafter.

The Reagan administration, despite being the most unilateralist administration since the Second World War, secured ratification of the 1948 Genocide Convention in 1989. The Bush administration secured ratification of the 1966 Covenant on Civil and Political Rights in 1992. Both formal adherences were accompanied by senatorial reservations, understandings, and declarations of a highly restrictive nature.[21] In fact, the Dutch government challenged US actions as being violative of international law. In the Dutch view, shared by others, the reservations, understandings, and declarations were incompatible with the basic purposes of the treaties in question. It appeared to these critics that the United States was trying to appear to accept the human rights treaties in question without actually having to incur any real and specific legal obligations. It was clear that, on the subject of civil and political rights, the United States did not want to expand on the provisions in the US Constitution and Bill of Rights. Moreover, the United States did not want to give the International Court of Justice at The Hague the jurisdiction to handle genocide petitions, or the UN Committee on Human Rights in Geneva the jurisdiction to receive individual complaints from Americans. The United States did finally agree, under the Civil and Political Covenant, to submit a report on its civil and political rights to the UN Committee on Human Rights and to respond to questions about that report. Such a process transpired for the first time during the Clinton administration. This exchange immediately led to conflict between the Senate Foreign Relations Committee and the UN Human Rights Committee. Senator Jesse Helms, the Chair of the Senate Foreign Relations Committee, challenged the right of the UN Human Rights Committee to make general statements about US policy decisions.

Although both the Carter and Clinton administrations have endorsed the UN Covenant on Economic, Social, and Cultural Rights, it remains especially controversial in Washington. Its values are in fact quite different from traditional American values, as noted above. The Republican Party and conservatives in general remain strongly opposed to the notion that the US government should be obligated, without the fundamental discretion to choose otherwise, to provide such things as food, clothing, shelter, and medical care to those who cannot purchase them in private markets. There is zero prospect, as of 1999, that the Senate Foreign Relations Committee would recommend to the full Senate that the latter give its advice and consent to this treaty. Even absent the Chair of that committee in 1997, Senator Jesse Helms of North Carolina, a strong critic of the United Nations and its human rights activities in general, Senate approval would be highly difficult to obtain.[22] Thus far no President, including Carter, wanted to use up limited presidential influence vis-à-vis Congress in fighting for ratification of this Covenant.

*Regional developments*

The United States is a member both of the Organization of American States (OAS) and of the Organization for Security and Cooperation in Europe (OSCE). In the former it has displayed sporadic diplomacy for human rights while avoiding as many legal obligations as possible under both the American Declaration on the Rights and Duties of Man and the Inter-American Convention on Human Rights. In the OSCE, including its predecessor diplomatic process, the Conference on Security and Cooperation in Europe (CSCE), the United States has been highly active on human rights. One sees in these two regional organizations the same US pattern in foreign policy that one finds more generally. The United States frequently pushes civil and political rights for others through diplomacy, but is reluctant to reconsider its domestic laws and policies under international human rights instruments.

The inter-American system for the promotion and protection of human rights is complicated.[23] The United States has not been, and is not in the 1990s, a hegemonic leader for human rights in this regional arrangement.[24] The same domestic factors that caused reserve toward the International Bill of Rights at the United Nations caused the United States to reject the Inter-American Convention on Human Rights, with its attendant Court, and to contest the judgment that the American Declaration of the Rights and Duties of Man was legally binding on members of the OAS. Also, the United States during the Cold War saw the OAS as primarily a security arrangement for the containment if not rollback of communism. This view required the United States to downgrade the importance of specific human rights in the hemisphere, since many of its security allies were also brutal authoritarians. Moreover, given the history of US military interventions in the hemisphere, many hemispheric states refused to defer to US leadership on a variety of issues including human rights, fearing US motivations and intentions.

From time to time the United States has utilized the OAS to advance human rights concerns. The Carter administration did so in its efforts to oust the dictator Anastasio Debayle Somoza from Nicaragua in the 1970s, supporting the Inter-American Commission on Human Rights in its critical reports and diplomacy. The Bush administration did so in supporting the Santiago Declaration that declared any attack on democratic government in states of the hemisphere to be an international, and not domestic, matter – meriting a regional response. The Bush and Clinton administrations utilized the OAS, along with the United Nations, for electoral assistance and expanded peacekeeping operations (which include additional human rights programmes) in such countries as Nicaragua, El Salvador, Guatemala, and Haiti. Although the OAS has few programmes on the ground in the hemisphere and is not an organization that one can rely on for either military security or sustainable economic development, its human rights programme is the bright spot of the organization. This programme the United States has supported as it sees fit, but without fully integrating itself into OAS human rights activities – much less being a hegemonic leader for human rights. If US deployment of force is contemplated in relation to hemispheric human rights, as in Haiti or El Salvador, for example, the United States normally acts via the United Nations. This is because of OAS sensitivity to past uses of force in the hemisphere as controlled by the United States.

The old CSCE from 1974 manifested a human rights focus as one of its three main areas for diplomacy between the European communist and democratic states (with the United States and Canada as honorary Europeans). The third section of the Helsinki Accord (Basket Three) on human rights was devised by certain West European states, with the United States, under the influence of Henry Kissinger, being reserved about the wisdom of discussing such "internal" questions as human rights violations by the Soviet Union and its allies.[25] Once established, Basket Three came to be warmly endorsed by subsequent US administrations, which, prodded by private human rights groups such as Helsinki Watch, found it desirable to press the European communists on their human rights records. Because the old Soviet Union wanted certain security and economic arrangements from the West, a number of Western parties found it logical and advantageous to press the communists on human rights as a quid pro quo.

From the mid-1970s to about 1990, the European communists obtained very little through the CSCE pertaining to security and economics. But, although scientific analysis is difficult, there is reason to believe that constant US and Western pressure for human rights via the CSCE helped erode the legitimacy of communist authority in Europe. It is plausible to argue that communist endorsement of the Helsinki Accord, with its human rights and humanitarian provisions, including an obligation to disseminate the accord in all CSCE states, encouraged dissent from communist authoritarian rule. Numerous observers and participants have concluded that the CSCE process encouraged East European defection from the Soviet alliance circa 1989, and helped undermine the very existence of the Soviet Union up to 1991.[26] Many factors were at work, not least the many defects of the communist systems. And the United States was only one of many actors involved in highlighting communist deficiencies. Nevertheless, US foreign policy should be given some credit for developments, even if the CSCE provisions on human rights and humanitarian affairs were of West European origin.

After the Cold War, the United States was hesitant to transform the CSCE into the OSCE, given US concerns about the growing number of international organizations, bureaucracies, and budgets. Once the OSCE was created, however, the United States supported its efforts to protect minorities and advance human rights more generally throughout member states. The OSCE was especially active on human rights issues in countries of the former Yugoslavia. These efforts drew strong US support, as Washington was the primary player trying to make effective the provisions of the 1995 Dayton Accord. The Clinton administration had brokered that accord and had self-interested reasons for making it work. It thus welcomed efforts by the OSCE, along with others, to secure a liberal democratic peace in especially Bosnia and Croatia.

Space limitations preclude analysis of two other regional developments. The North American Free Trade Agreement (NAFTA) included provisions affecting labour rights in the United States, Canada, and Mexico. And the US push for an expanded North Atlantic Treaty Organization (NATO) sometimes entailed human rights arguments, namely that such expansion would provide another international framework for advancing democracy and managing minority problems. Significantly, the argument was made in connection with an expanded NATO that international security ultimately meant the security of persons inside states through protection of their human rights.[27]

## *International financial institutions*

For anyone concerned with the implementation of internationally recognized human rights, one of the great problems has been the role of the

World Bank and the International Monetary Fund (IMF). These international financial institutions (IFIs) have historically seen themselves as strictly economic organizations that are precluded from acting on political grounds. Human rights, including socio-economic rights to adequate food, clothing, shelter, and health care, have been considered political factors by these two agencies, which control sizeable resources. The World Bank has come to accept that ecological concerns should be incorporated into its loan decisions as a regular part of its policy. The Bank has not come to a similar conclusion about various human rights. The Bank began to address issues of good governance, but tended to define this concept in accounting terms such as transparent economic decision-making. The IMF has been even more resistant than the Bank in addressing human rights issues, although some (inconsistent) shift might be taking place by the late 1990s. The United States has always been the most important state in these two IFIs and bears considerable responsibility for their record on human rights.

The crux of the problem is that the World Bank and the IMF may adopt loan policies that make it more difficult, rather than less, for a state to consolidate liberal democracy and protect a wide range of socio-economic human rights. The Bank and/or the IMF may insist on structural adjustment programmes (SAPs) that cause the state to shrink programmes and services to the people, particularly the most vulnerable people, for the sake of balancing the national budget, and thus increasing the private sector and particularly its exports. Such SAPs may cause popular dissatisfaction with, even riots or rebellions against, weak democratic governments. The Bank may make social assessments and provide some relief for social adjustments, but continues to resist the idea that it is obligated under international law to meet internationally recognized human rights. There is some evidence that IMF policies correlate with increased governmental repression in the short term, as governments under SAP conditionality seek to suppress popular discontent about harsh readjustment programmes.[28] If a weak democratic government, as in El Salvador, needs resources to carry out land reform and other costly programmes in order to satisfy various parties that have been in rebellion against past injustices, SAPs are definitely contrary to the implementation of socio-economic rights within a democratic framework.[29]

The United States has frequently pursued a contradictory foreign policy in a number of situations, working in general for civil and political rights but voting for SAPs in the two IFIs under discussion that undermine the prospects for implementation of international human rights standards. In some cases the United States has resolved this contradiction by using the Bank as leverage to advance civil and political rights. Thus, in a limited number of instances, the United States has joined some of its democratic partners in the Bank to bring pressure on governments in places such as China, Kenya, or Malawi to improve the implementation of these rights. Yet in other situations the United States and its democratic allies have not insisted on political conditionality via the Bank. The overall record of the Bank on these matters is thus highly inconsistent. The Bank staff, composed mostly of traditional economists, resists systematic linkage with internationally recognized human rights, being willing to address social assessment only in the form of increased public participation in Bank projects. In this connection the Bank has created an Inspection Panel that can be triggered by private complaint. Periodically, state members of the Bank, however, compel it to delay or suspend loans because of massacres, repression, or authoritarianism.[30] In 1997 the United States succeeded in blocking an IMF loan to Croatia, because of that state's failure to do such things as protect minorities and arrest those indicted for international crimes. The United States had previously held up a Bank loan to the Serbian Republic within federal Bosnia, for similar non-implementation of the Dayton Accord. Thus under US pressure the Bank and Fund addressed some human rights factors, but on an inconsistent basis. The fact that the United States has never accepted the Covenant on Economic, Social, and Cultural Rights contributes to this highly problematic situation.

The European Bank for Reconstruction and Development, which was supported by the United States diplomatically and financially, contained an explicit clause on human rights in its articles of agreement. Thus this European regional bank was always supposed to factor human rights considerations into its loan decisions. On the other hand, the Inter-American Development Bank, which was greatly affected by US policy, was similar to the World Bank, with only sporadic and inconsistent attention to human rights considerations.[31]

### *United Nations action*

We have noted the United States' ambivalent attitude toward the International Bill of Rights. There has been more general US ambivalence toward the United Nations as a whole, especially with the increased influence of conservative circles of opinion in Washington in the 1980s and 1990s.[32] This ambivalence toward the United Nations was deepened when, during the Cold War, the majority of states in the UN General Assembly used the language of human rights to try to undermine governments allied with the United States in South Africa, Israel, and Portugal and its colonial territories.

Since the ending of the Cold War, the United States has persistently sought to advance its views about human rights through the Security

Council, the General Assembly, and the Human Rights Commission. As the one putative superpower during this era, it has met with considerable success in its policy objectives at the United Nations, and has broken some new legal and political ground in the process. Although the United States has been *primus inter pares* in the Security Council, it has met with more opposition in the Commission. In this latter body a strong undercurrent of reserve about US human rights policy has surfaced, articulated primarily by non-Western critics.

In the Council during the first decade after the Cold War, the United States has pushed with some success for three changes of major importance involving human rights. First, it has led in expanding the scope of Chapter VII of the Charter, involving matters on which the Council can take a binding decision, if necessary entailing coercive measures. In the process, the Council has shrunk the domain of exclusive state domestic jurisdiction. In dealing with Iraq's repression of Iraqi Kurds in 1991, Somalian starvation in 1992–1994, the breakup of former Yugoslavia during 1992–1995, the nature of government in Haiti during 1993–1996, and genocide in Rwanda in 1994, the United States led the Council in adopting a very broad scope to the notion of international peace and security. In effect, many human rights violations essentially inside states came to be viewed as constituting a threat to or breach of international peace and security, permitting authoritative Council decisions including the deployment of force and sometimes limited combat action. The 1992 Security Council summit of heads of state officially endorsed this expanded view of international responsibility, declaring that international peace could be disrupted by economic, ecological, and social developments, not just by traditional military developments.[33] The consequences of these Council decisions are potentially quite far reaching, leaving much less subject matter to be essentially within the exclusive domain of supposedly sovereign states. The United States has been central to all these developments, taking the lead in dealing with Iraq, Somalia, and Haiti, and being supportive of broad-reaching Council resolutions in the other relevant cases.

Secondly, the United States has also led in expanding the notion of UN peacekeeping that occurs mostly under Chapter VI of the Charter pertaining to the peaceful settlement of disputes. At the end of the Cold War the Council began to authorize complex or second-generation peacekeeping missions in countries such as Namibia, El Salvador, and Cambodia. Lightly armed military contingents, deployed with the consent of the parties in conflict, were increasingly accompanied by civilian personnel, and entailed considerable human rights duties. In places like El Salvador, deployments of human rights monitors actually preceded cease-fire agreements and the deployment of cease-fire monitors. Especially in internal rather than interstate conflicts, where the behaviour of the preceding government was a major cause of unrest, UN peacekeeping was mostly directed to improvement of human rights conditions and the creation and consolidation of a liberal democratic peace. Electoral assistance in various forms was frequently a part of these field missions. Narrow military or quasi-military functions were only a small part of most complex peacekeeping operations, although some of the operations were expanded to limited enforcement operations under Chapter VII. While the United States might or might not provide military elements to these field missions, it was always a key player in the authorization of second-generation peacekeeping. It was still true that the UN Security Council had never in its history deployed military force without the support of the United States.[34] Thus in many situations the United States led the United Nations in seeking not just peace based on the constellation of military power, but a liberal democratic peace based on many human rights.

Thirdly, the United States led the Council into the creation of two international criminal courts, one for the former Yugoslavia and one for Rwanda, the first such courts since 1946 and the international tribunals at Nuremberg and Tokyo.[35] In using the Council to create the 1993 and 1995 ad hoc courts with jurisdiction to prosecute and try individuals for certain violations of international law, the United States displayed mixed motives. On the one hand the United States did not want to engage in a costly intervention into the complicated situations of former Yugoslavia and Rwanda, where people of ill-will showed little hesitation in committing gross violations of human rights. In October 1993, events in Somalia had demonstrated to the United States that good intentions could lead to further death and injury. The two courts were created precisely because the United States in particular eschewed more decisive action. Here was further evidence that the United States was not interested in a costly crusade for human rights. On the other hand, the United States led the way in believing that *some* response had to be made to the evident killing and abuse of civilians on a massive scale. Thus the United States rejuvenated the idea of individual criminal responsibility for violations of the laws of war, crimes against humanity, and genocide. It provided more financial and personnel support to the two courts than any other state did. The United States eventually but successfully got agreement that NATO, embodied as SFOR, should arrest indicted suspects in the former Yugoslavia from mid-1997.

At the same time, the United States as a whole displayed consistent caution about a permanent UN criminal court.[36] It participated in negotiations for such a court, but in July 1998 it voted against the draft statute for such a court, which was approved by 120 states. Only six other states, mostly repressive, voted in the negative. The United States had tried to weaken the projected court, and had engaged in heavy-handed lobbying in defence of its views. But Washington found itself isolated at the Rome diplomatic conference, much as it had been isolated at the 1997 Ottawa diplomatic conference that agreed to ban anti-personnel land mines. Clinton essentially caved in to a Pentagon that did not want an international criminal court pressing it to court-martial US military personnel who might commit war crimes. Clinton was also under pressure from the nativists in the Congress like Jesse Helms who refused to accept in principle that US personnel and policies should be subject to international review and control. Once again we see the United States using the United Nations when the issue is human rights for others, as in former Yugoslavia and Rwanda, but hesitant to put itself under UN human rights law and authoritative agencies.

Since the ending of the Cold War, the General Assembly has not been terribly important to US foreign policy. The United States prefers to focus on the Security Council, where it has a preferred position, where it has important allies making up a high proportion of members, and where it can utilize the authority of Chapter VII. From time to time the United States has supported certain initiatives in the Assembly, such as the attempt to have clarified a presumed right to humanitarian assistance for individuals in armed conflict and what at the United Nations are called complex emergencies. This initiative resulted in several Assembly resolutions whose combined effect was ambiguous. Whereas the United States and others succeeded in having adopted by consensus some language addressing humanitarian need in these situations, developing countries insisted on including language endorsing state consent before assistance could proceed.[37] The United States has supported other Assembly resolutions on human rights and humanitarian affairs, but their impact on world politics has been mostly marginal.

The United States used the Assembly to create the new office of High Commissioner for Human Rights during fall 1993. The United States lobbied hard for this position, but so did other actors both public and private. The United States was especially pleased when Secretary-General Kofi Annan named the former Irish President, Mary Robinson, as the second High Commissioner. However, the United States has not been a leader in efforts to increase the UN human rights budget, which remains at about 1 per cent of UN regular spending, or under US$20 million. Congressional pressures have sought to reduce, not increase, most UN finances.

In recent decades the United States had displayed a highly active diplomacy in the UN Human Rights Commission. In the 1940s and 1950s in the Commission, to which the United States has always been elected by the Economic and Social Council (ECOSOC), Washington was content with the Commission's self-denying ordinance by which it refused to take up specific human rights problems in specific states. The executive's policy was shaped by its attempt to appease a non-cosmopolitan Congress in the 1950s and 1960s, noted above. From about 1970 the United States was part of the bargaining that led the Commission to shift its orientation, as it agreed to address human rights issues not only in Israel, South Africa, and, somewhat later, Chile, but also in other countries such as Greece and Haiti.[38] From that time the United States has, in principle, led or supported efforts to create a focus on particular countries and subject matter through such mechanisms as rapporteurs and working groups. The United States cooperated with the UN rapporteur on racial discrimination when he paid an extended visit to the country, but the subsequent report resulted in very little American media coverage. The United States has also supported the 1503 resolution, by which ECOSOC authorized the Commission to process private petitions alleging a systematic pattern of gross violations of human rights, and eventually to give some sort of publicity to offending states. The main exception to this US record of support for Commission diplomacy of a specific nature occurred during the first Reagan administration when Washington sought to block attention in the Commission to some of its more brutal authoritarian allies in places such as Chile, El Salvador, and Guatemala.

If one looks at the list of countries during the Cold War targeted by way of Commission resolutions and decisions to create rapporteurs and working groups, that list is more or less balanced according to geography and ideology. This suggests some US success, along with the Western Group, in directing attention to a number of communist states and other adversaries. Since the Cold War, the overall list of states that has drawn Commission concern remains a reasonable one. However, the United States has been unable to get the Commission to adopt a resolution critical of China's human rights record. China has effectively mobilized a blocking coalition of states, appealing to a number of non-Western states with the argument that the United States and certain other Western states focus too much on individual civil and political rights, without sufficient attention to underdevelopment and cultural differences. In historical fact, the Commission *has* focused mainly on civil and political rights since about 1970, with relatively little attention to economic, social, and cultural rights. China has also utilized its growing economic leverage to threaten states with loss of business contracts if they vote for critical resolutions in the Commission. These threats were quite explicit with regard to Denmark and the Netherlands in 1997. While these and other states like Britain continued to align with the United States in efforts to censure

China, other European states such as France, Germany, Italy, and Greece refused to support the United States in the Commission during 1997 on the China question.

At the 1993 Vienna Conference on Human Rights sponsored by the United Nations, these same sorts of debates were played out.[39] The United States took the lead in trying to reaffirm the validity of universal human rights – while reserving to itself the discretion not to become a party to the Socio-Economic Covenant, not to allow individual petitions under the Civil–Political Covenant, not to ban the death penalty for common crimes, and not to give special protection to convicted minors under the age of 18. The Clinton administration did rhetorically endorse a right to development, although previous administrations had contested such a right in UN debates. A group of states led by China, Indonesia, Singapore, and Malaysia, *inter alia*, argued for a strong version of cultural relativism and national particularism, suggesting that universal human rights should yield to local conditions. At the heart of the public debate was the argument that the US conception of human rights was too individualistic and strictly Western, and thus inappropriate to, in particular, crowded Asian countries with a history of elevating duties to the community over individual rights. The final document of the Vienna Conference proved more satisfying to the United States than the Commission debates on China in the mid-1990s. The Vienna Final Act reaffirmed universal human rights for all, stating that all countries had the obligation to respect them. The universal nature of these rights and freedoms is beyond question. But some language in the Final Act indicated that national and regional particularities and various historical, cultural, and religious backgrounds must be borne in mind.

The United States, with the world's largest economy, is usually among the leading countries, or is the leading country, in supporting certain agencies that work for human rights and humanitarian progress. It is, for example, the largest contributor to both the International Committee of the Red Cross, which works for victims of war and of complex emergencies, and the Office of the UN High Commissioner for Refugees, which works with not only legal refugees but those who find themselves in a refugee-like situation. It should be noted, however, that the United States supports certain humanitarian programmes, which can be said to implement various human rights, precisely as a substitute for more decisive involvement. Some observers have estimated that it would have cost the United States less money to lead a military deployment in Rwanda in 1994 to stop genocide than it subsequently spent in helping to provide for the refugees from genocide. This type of analysis omits from the calculation of cost the probability of American military casualties from such an enforcement operation.

## IV. Bilateral policy

### *Foreign assistance*

From the mid-1970s the US Congress, in an ironic volte-face, required the executive to link US foreign security assistance, then later economic assistance, to internationally recognized human rights.[40] These laws were permissively written, with the executive able to utilize loopholes to avoid applying the statutes. Congress also lacked the will power, through follow-up oversight legislation, to compel various administrations to comply with the general standards that had been established in law. Congress then turned to more specific legislation. Perhaps the best known of these provisions was the so-called "Jackson–Vanik" amendment, requiring communist states desiring most-favoured-nation trading status with the United States to permit reasonable emigration. In addition to these and other congressional initiatives, various administrations on their own have manipulated US bilateral foreign assistance to reflect some concern with human rights.

Since 1981 a number of scholars have sought to establish the effect of human rights considerations in decisions about bilateral US foreign assistance. A general or summary effect has been difficult to prove. Some students of the issue have found that human rights concerns are evident in a first stage of decision-making, called the gate-keeping function, about which countries are eligible to receive foreign aid. Other studies looking at a one-stage process of foreign aid allocation have found little general and persistent influence from human rights considerations. A 1994 study covering Latin America found that human rights considerations did affect the disbursement of US economic and security assistance, as one factor among several, as long as a country was not deemed of major importance to the United States. But if a country, such as El Salvador in the 1980s, was considered highly important to US security, then other considerations like human rights fell by the wayside.[41] A 1995 study found that, with regard to US economic assistance to a broad range of countries, there was no correlation between levels of that assistance and the human rights record of recipient countries.[42] Likewise, a 1989 study showed no correlation between levels of US economic assistance and recipient countries' records on either political rights (democracy) or right to life (summary executions and forced disappearances).[43]

A study published in 1999 argued that "human rights considerations did play a role in determining whether or not a state received military aid during the Reagan and Bush administrations, but not for the Carter and Clinton administrations. With the exception of the Clinton administration, human rights was a determinant factor in the decision to grant economic aid, albeit of secondary importance ... Human rights considerations are neither the only nor the primary consideration in aid allocation."[44]

Moving away from macro or summary interpretations, one can easily observe that on any number of occasions the United States will at least temporarily link economic and security assistance to various human rights concerns – almost always pertaining to civil and political rights.[45] In 1997 the United States suspended foreign assistance to Cambodia after the Hun Sen coup that interrupted coalition government in a fragile and imperfect democratic political system. In that same year the United States made foreign assistance to the Kabila government in Zaire/Democratic Republic of the Congo dependent upon progress concerning several human rights issues, including an investigation into alleged massacres of refugees during fighting to oust the Mobutu government. As suggested by the broader studies, rarely is such US decision-making decisive in fully controlling a situation. Other states may not follow the US lead, thus lessening the impact of Washington's policy. The US aid programme may not be large enough to affect foreign decision-making. But in some cases the US impact is great enough to cause foreign leaders to think seriously about whether or not they wish to forgo Washington's support in order to continue their policies of the past. In 1993 the United States helped preserve movement toward liberal democracy and a winding down of civil war in Guatemala by suspending foreign assistance after an *auto-golpe* or attempt to seize excessive power by the existing President.

### *Humanitarian intervention*

Historically the United States has made claims to a unilateral right to humanitarian intervention in order, presumably, to protect lives and property in foreign states. Recent Presidents did so, for example, in 1965 in the Dominican Republic, in 1983 in Grenada, and in 1989 in Panama. President Carter, in authorizing the attempted rescue of Americans from Iran in 1980, made claims to self-defence rather than humanitarian intervention.[46] There being no codified right of humanitarian intervention in international law to rescue either one's own nationals or foreigners, owing to the widespread and well-justified fear of its misuse, the United States is left with consideration of controversial exercises of power accompanied mostly by claims of self-defence (Iran, 1980) and/or of invitation to act by the consent of the government (Grenada, 1983). President Bush's assertion of an additional right to use force to restore a properly elected government in Panama was met with widespread opposition. President Clinton later side-stepped this issue in Haiti by obtaining UN Security Council authorization to use all necessary means to remove an unelected government, which had deposed an elected one, because of an alleged threat to international peace and security. Some uses of the US military to rescue both US nationals and foreigners have not been controversial in places such as Liberia and Somalia, because US action was met by widespread deference.

## *Democracy assistance*

The United States has manifested a long history of concern with democracy abroad – at least via rhetoric.[47] Since the end of the Cold War the United States has stitched together a crazy-quilt of bits and pieces of legislation and executive decisions that with some overstatement can be called a programme of official democracy assistance.[48] Because of its disjointed nature, no one in Washington could give a firm figure of how much was being spent *in toto* to advance liberal democracy abroad. The Agency for International Development estimated that it was spending almost US$500 million per annum as of 1995. The State Department and the Justice Department also had their own programmes and budgets. Funding remained small relative to benchmarks such as the Marshall Plan of the late 1940s, or German spending on democracy in the area of former East Germany and its 17 million persons. The George Soros foundations spent more money for democracy and civic society in Russia than did the United States.

These official US activities were directed at three general targets: support for civic societies and the private groups found therein; support for state building, primarily via strong legislatures and independent courts; and support for free and fair elections with party competition. The absence of a compelling theory about what factors produced stable liberal democracy over time and place contributed to a lack of systematic governmental planning. The variety of conditions evident in Russia, Eastern and Central Europe, and the Western hemisphere, the principal areas of US interest, also led to a scatter-shot approach.

Evaluating the impact of the US democracy assistance programme is no easy task. The US role is intertwined with intergovernmental organizations such as the United Nations, the OSCE, and the OAS. The United States shares objectives with numerous private groups. US programmes are quite similar to those of the National Endowment for Democracy, a quasi-independent Washington-based agency funded by congressional appropriation. Other states have their own pro-democracy policies. Even in one country such as Romania, it is difficult to say what is the precise influence of US decisions for democracy, given the short time-frame so far, the plethora of other influences, and the absence of a proven theory of causation as a check-point.[49]

Several hypotheses suggest themselves for further enquiry. Particularly in the new states emerging from the former Soviet Union, and in much of Eastern Europe, US programmes in the name of democracy seemed more oriented to market restructuring for privatization than for democracy per se. Washington's semantics about market democracies seemed designed to legitimize this emphasis on economic reform. Some research suggests no automatic correlations between economic growth via markets and liberal democracy.[50] Absent a concerted push to make privately generated wealth compatible with democracy, private wealth can be easily combined with authoritarianism. This line of research and reasoning casts some doubt on the US emphasis on extensive privatization as a necessary precondition for liberal democracy. Although all stable democracies are based on some version of capitalism, a number of relatively stable democracies, such as France and Sweden, manifest relatively large public sectors.

In the Western hemisphere especially, relative lack of US attention to the economic resources of the public sector has hampered the consolidation of liberal democracy in places like El Salvador. This was noted above in the section on international financial institutions. US determination to shrink the public sector, in the name of an efficient private and for-profit sector, may not be what emerging democracies need in order to obtain popular support through expensive programmes of land reform, education, etc. In Eastern Europe, several electorates have returned to power a somewhat reformed communist party in protest against shrinking public services and in quest for a better quality of life. US democracy assistance may be driven as much by a bias against big government and in favour of big markets as by a programme that is appropriately tailored to the needs of the recipient. The fact that the United States is not a social democracy and does not recognize socio-economic human rights contributes to this situation.[51]

The amount of US spending for democracy abroad, and in general the real importance of this objective in US foreign policy, may be too small to generate profound influence in many countries. In a number of countries the United States may be more interested in traditional military security and economic arrangements advantageous to the United States than in liberal democracy. This hypothesis is difficult to test. Is the expansion of NATO to provide a check on the Russian Bear in the event of a more nationalistic and militarized government in Moscow, or is that expansion to provide an additional framework for the management of problems of democracy and other human rights in former European communist states? In any event, it is highly probable that, given the absence of congressional and public sentiment in support of further spending on foreign assistance, it would be desirable for the United States to concentrate on certain key or pivotal states. If the United States decides to leave the basic question of guaranteeing public order in Albania to an Italian-led coalition of European states, it is difficult to understand why the United States should have a democracy assistance programme in Albania rather than transferring that spending to Indonesia.

Finally, it should be noted that the United States takes many decisions in its foreign policy apart from official democracy assistance that have an impact on democracy abroad. We noted above the US reaction to Hun Sen's coup in Cambodia in 1997, and to the Guatemalan *auto-golpe* in 1993. We could also note US deference to French policy in supporting the cancellation of national elections in Algeria in 1992; or US support for controlled Algerian elections in 1997. These ad hoc or reactive decisions do not present one pattern in support of, or opposition to, free and fair national elections. In some cases, e.g. Syria or Saudi Arabia, the United States does not push for liberal democracy, giving preference to traditional security and economic interests. In other cases, e.g. Albania or Kenya, the United States does support electoral freedoms. In still other cases, e.g. Nigeria, the United States endorses liberal democracy in the abstract but does not much push for it in quotidian diplomacy.

## V. Conclusions

The United States professes to be a leader for human rights in the world but displays an ambivalent attitude toward the International Bill of Rights and numerous other international human rights documents. In American society there is much scepticism not only about international rights standards in general, as compared with US constitutional norms, but also about economic rights and a claimed collective human right to development in particular. Nevertheless, in the United Nations, the OAS, and the OSCE the United States has either initiated or supported much diplomacy at least for civil and political rights. And in Somalia President Bush took significant action to respond to starvation and malnutrition, even if he did not address the issues in terms of socio-economic rights. Somalia notwithstanding, however, by emphasizing civil and political rights to the almost total exclusion of socio-economic rights, US diplomacy tends to spotlight repression while mostly ignoring oppression.[52]

Particularly noteworthy was US leadership, at least during 1991–1993, for an expanded UN programme of complex peacekeeping with overtones of Chapter VII enforcement action on issues that were substantially human rights issues. In other words, the United States agreed that international peace and security could sometimes refer to the security of persons inside states. This latter view logically entailed a far-reaching consideration of human rights.[53]

The United States appears to be belatedly addressing the interplay of economic and political rights through a debate about policy toward the international financial institutions. The United States, like its democratic partners, appears to be slowly moving away from the view that the World Bank and the IMF, *inter alia*, should be strictly economic organizations without a human rights component. As noted, the United States has sought to link both the Bank and the Fund to its human rights concerns in the former Yugoslavia (where human rights are intertwined with security issues). The United States may even eventually recognize that in places such as El Salvador, shrinking the resources of the public sector in the name of private markets and export-led economic growth, under the umbrella of structural adjustment programmes, may in fact impede the consolidation of liberal democracy. On balance, US foreign policy makers in various administrations and political parties do not display a consensus on the relationship between economics on the one hand and civil and political rights on the other. The bias is toward the primacy of market restructuring. This is evident in US bilateral programmes for democracy abroad, where more funds have been spent on market reform than on civic society, state building, and electoral assistance. In part this lack of careful attention to the interplay of economics and democracy is because social scientists lack consensus on the same subject.

The most notable feature of US foreign policy on human rights after the Cold War, whether multilateral or bilateral, is the desire to avoid significant costs of either blood or treasure. This is quite evident in Washington's desire to avoid even small-scale casualties after its Somalian experience, and in spending for official democracy assistance that falls far short of the expectations generated by the accompanying rhetoric. It is one thing for the United States to engage in the easy diplomacy for human rights that is detached from finances and coercion. It is another thing to take rights so seriously in foreign policy that one's diplomacy on the subject is in fact linked to means of implementation, beyond jawboning, in the face of obstacles.

It is persuasive for moralists to argue that, in the twenty-first century, an age of rights should demand at a minimum that there be no mass murder and no mass starvation. Insofar as the 1990s are concerned, when we review US foreign policy in places such as Bosnia, Somalia, and Rwanda, we are forced to conclude that one cannot rely on US foreign policy consistently to help ensure this minimal respect for international human rights. Some countries, like Rwanda, seem beyond the scope of American humanitarian concern. Others, like Bosnia, seem not worth the candle – too costly in terms of American vested interests. A third problem, evident in places such as Turkey and China, is that American economic and security interests dictate a lower priority to human rights.[54]

This record cannot help but detract from a more positive US record, at least for civil and political rights, in some countries like Guatemala and Burma.

The most fundamental problem blocking a consistently progressive stand on international human rights issues stems from a lack of political will at home to pay the necessary price to see even American, much less international, rights principles realized abroad. The real problem is the danger not of moral crusade but of moral abnegation. In this sense the American self-image of a nation standing for individual freedom for all is at considerable variance with international reality. The world is still a large and imperfect place, but states can set priorities and distinguish between gross and more minor violations of human rights. Extensive rhetoric about universal human rights, however, generates its own pressures over time to close the gap between rhetoric and reality.

## Notes

1. T. Davis and S. Lynn-Jones, "City upon a Hill," *Foreign Policy*, no. 66 (1987), 20–38.
2. David Jacobson, *Rights across Borders* (Baltimore, MD: Johns Hopkins University Press, 1996), 102 and passim.
3. Contemporary public opinion polls indicate superficial popular support for national health care, but this opinion tends to dissipate when questions are asked about cost, less coverage for some, and a larger state bureaucracy, etc. See further Audrey R. Chapman, "The Defeat of Comprehensive Health Care Reform: A Human Rights Perspective," in David P. Forsythe, ed., *The United States and Human Rights: Looking Inward and Outward* (Lincoln, NE: University of Nebraska Press, 1999).
4. See further David P. Forsythe, *Human Rights and World Politics* (Lincoln, NE: University of Nebraska Press, 1984), chapter V, p. 168, quoting the novelist John Fowles. See also Rhoda Howard, *Human Rights and the Search for Community* (Boulder, CO: Westview Press, 1995).
5. George F. Kennan, *American Diplomacy 1900–1950* (Chicago: Chicago University Press, 1951); John G. Spanier, *American Foreign Policy since World War II* (Washington, DC: Congressional Quarterly Press, 1992).
6. Arthur Schlesinger, Jr., "Human Rights and the American Tradition," *Foreign Affairs* 57/2 (1979), 503–526.
7. See especially David P. Forsythe, "Democracy, War, and Covert Action," *Journal of Peace Research* 29/4 (1992), 385–395; and Jack Donnelly, "Humanitarian Intervention and American Foreign Policy: Law, Morality, and Politics," *Journal of International Affairs* 37 (1984), 311–328.
8. Ernst B. Haas, *Global Evangelism Rides Again: How to Protect Human Rights without Really Trying* (Berkeley, CA: Institute of International Studies, 1978). For an example of assumptions about a US crusade not substantiated by the facts, see Joshua Muravchik, *The Uncertain Crusade: Jimmy Carter and the Dilemmas of Human Rights Policy* (Lanham: Hamilton Press, 1986).
9. David P. Forsythe, "Human Rights and US Foreign Policy: Two Levels, Two Worlds," *Political Studies* 43 (1995), 111–130; also in David Beetham, ed., *Politics and Human Rights* (London: Blackwell, 1996). The Spanish–American War of 1898 constitutes one

of the better examples of American moralism in foreign policy, but even in this case the United States was driven as much by the quest for colonies and Great Power status as by the desire to liberate Cuba and the Philippines from Spanish tyranny. The United States did not grant Filipino independence until 1946.

10. Crag N. Whitney, "Paris Snips Ties Binding It to Africa," *New York Times*, 25 June 1997, p. A5. France had stuck with ageing African dictators too long in an effort to carve out a zone of French influence, had lost out in shifts of power, and was thus forced to realign its relations with various African governments.
11. *U.S. Department of State Dispatch*, 28 September 1992, pp. 721–724.
12. *Weekly Compilation of Presidential Documents*, 24 October 1994, pp. 2041–2044.
13. Chicago Council on Foreign Relations, American Public Opinion Report-1995, http://www.uicdocs.lib.uic.edu/ccfr/publications/opinion_1995/2-3html.
14. In addition to ibid., see Ole R. Holsti, "Public Opinion on Human Rights in American Foreign Policy," in Forsythe, ed., *The United States and Human Rights*, op. cit.
15. Ellen Dorsey, "U.S. Foreign Policy and the Human Rights Movement: New Strategies for a Global Era," in Forsythe, ed., *The United States and Human Rights*, op. cit.
16. Michael Mandelbaum, "Foreign Policy as Social Work," *Foreign Affairs* 75/1 (January/February 1996), 16–32.
17. Edward Luttwak, "Where Are the Great Powers," *Foreign Affairs* 73/4 (July/August 1994), 23–29.
18. See Natalie Hevener Kaufman, *Human Rights Treaties and the Senate: A History of Opposition* (Chapel Hill, NC: University of North Carolina Press, 1990). See also Lawrence J. LeBlanc, *The United States and the Genocide Convention* (Durham, NC: Duke University Press, 1991). And David P. Forsythe, "The Politics of Efficacy: The United Nations and Human Rights," in Lawrence S. Finkelstein, ed., *Politics in the United Nations System* (Durham, NC: Duke University Press, 1988), 246–273.
19. Tony Evans, *US Hegemony and the Project of Universal Human Rights* (London: Macmillan, 1996).
20. David P. Forsythe, *Human Rights and U.S. Foreign Policy: Congress Reconsidered* (Gainesville, FL: University Presses of Florida, 1988).
21. William Schabas, "Spare the RUD or Spoil the Treaty: The United States Challenges the Human Rights Committee on the Subject of Reservations," in Forsythe, ed., *The United States and Human Rights,* op. cit.
22. To date the International Bill of Rights generates almost no influence on US courts when they decide questions of treaty law, slight influence regarding questions of customary law, and some influence on constitutional law issues. With regard to the latter, international human rights norms sometimes inform US court decisions on such constitutional questions as the meaning of "cruel and unusual punishment," the definition of "minors," or the content of "due process of law," etc. Richard B. Lillich, "International Human Rights Law in U.S. Courts," *Journal of Transnational Law and Policy* 2/1 (1993), 1–22.
23. Scott Davidson, *The Inter-American Human Rights System* (Aldershot: Dartmouth Publishing Co., 1997).
24. David P. Forsythe, "Human Rights, the United States, and the Organization of American States," *Human Rights Quarterly* 13/1 (February 1991), 66–98.
25. William Korey, *The Promises We Keep: Human Rights, the Helsinki Process, and American Foreign Policy* (New York: St. Martin's, 1993).
26. See further David P. Forsythe, ed., *Human Rights in the New Europe: Problems and Progress* (Lincoln, NE: University of Nebraska Press, 1993).
27. US Congress Commission on Security and Cooperation in Europe, *Report on Human Rights and the Process of NATO Enlargement* (Washington, DC: The Commission, 1997).

28. Linda Camp Keith and Steven C. Poe, "The United States, the IMF, and Human Rights: A Policy Relevant Approach," in Forsythe, ed., *The United States and Human Rights*, op. cit.
29. Alvaro de Soto and Graciana del Castillo, "Obstacles to Peacebuilding," *Foreign Policy*, no. 94 (Spring 1994), 69–83.
30. David P. Forsythe, "The United Nations, Human Rights, and Development," *Human Rights Quarterly* 19/2 (May 1997), 334–349.
31. Charles A. Reilly, *Complementing States and Markets: The IDB and Civil Society* (Miami, FL: North–South Center of Miami University, 1996).
32. Robert W. Gregg, *About Face? The United States and the United Nations* (Boulder, CO: Lynne Rienner Publishers, 1993).
33. S/23500, 31 January 1992, "Note by the President of the Security Council."
34. In addition to David P. Forsythe, "Human Rights and International Security: United Nations Field Operations Redux," in M. Castermans et al., eds., *The Role of the Nation State in the 21st Century* (The Hague: Kluwer, 1998), 265–276, see also: Ramesh Thakur and Carlyle A. Thayer, eds., *A Crisis of Expectations: UN Peacekeeping in the 1990s* (Boulder, CO: Westview Press, 1995); Steven Ratner, *The New UN Peacekeeping* (New York: St. Martin's, 1995); Paul F. Diehl, *International Peacekeeping* (Baltimore, MD: Johns Hopkins University Press, 1993); William J. Durch, ed., *The Evolution of UN Peacekeeping: Case Studies and Comparative Analysis* (New York: St. Martin's, 1993); and Lori Damrosch, ed., *Enforcing Restraint: Collective Intervention in Internal Conflicts* (New York: Council on Foreign Relations, 1993).
35. A good overview of issues is found in Roger S. Clark and Madeleine Sann, eds., *The Prosecution of International Crimes* (New Brunswick, NJ: Transaction, 1996).
36. David P. Forsythe, "International Criminal Courts: A Political View," *Netherlands Quarterly of Human Rights* 15/1 (March 1997), 5–19.
37. See further David P. Forsythe, "Human Rights and Humanitarian Operations: Theoretical Observations," in Eric A. Belgrad and Nitza Nachmias, eds., *The Politics of International Humanitarian Aid Operations* (Westport, CT: Praeger, 1997), 37–52.
38. Vernon Van Dyke, *The United States, Human Rights, and World Community* (New York: Oxford University Press, 1970).
39. See further David P. Forsythe, "The UN and Human Rights at 50: An Incremental but Incomplete Revolution," *Global Governance* 1/3 (September–December 1995), 297–318.
40. David P. Forsythe, *Humcn Rights and U.S. Foreign Policy: Congress Reconsidered* (Dainesville, FL: University Press of Florida, 1988).
41. Steven C. Poe, et al., "Human Rights and US Foreign Aid Revisited: The Latin American Region," *Human Rights Quarterly* 16/3 (August 1994), 539–558, and the literature cited therein.
42. Patrick M. Regan, "U.S. Economic Aid and Political Repression: An Empirical Evaluation of US Foreign Policy," *Political Research Quarterly* 48/3 (September 1995), 613–628.
43. David P. Forsythe, "U.S. Economic Assistance and Human Rights: Why the Emperor Has No Clothes (Almost)," in Forsythe, ed., *Human Rights and Development: International Views* (London: Macmillan, 1989), 171–195.
44. Clair Apodaca and Michael Stohl, "United States Human Rights Policy and Foreign Assistance," *International Studies Quarterly* 43/1 (March 1999), 185.
45. David D. Newsom, ed., *The Diplomacy of Human Rights* (Lanham: University Press of America, 1986); Sandy Vogelgesang, *American Dream, Global Nightmare: The Dilemma of U.S. Human Rights Policy* (New York: Norton, 1980). US attention to human rights is highly problematical during times of revolution; see Sara Steinmetz, *Democratic Transition and Human Rights: Perspectives on U.S. Foreign Policy* (Albany, NY: SUNY Press, 1994).

46. For an overview see Kelly-Kate S. Pease and David P. Forsythe, "Human Rights, Humanitarian Intervention, and World Politics," *Human Rights Quarterly* 15/3 (May 1993), 290–314.
47. Tony Smith, *America's Mission: The United States and the Worldwide Struggle for Democracy in the Twentieth Century* (Princeton, NJ: Princeton University Press, 1994).
48. David P. Forsythe, with Michele Leonard and Garry Baker, "U.S. Foreign Policy, Democracy, and Migration," paper presented at the New School, New York City, April 1997.
49. Thomas Carothers, *Assessing Democracy Assistance: The Case of Romania* (Washington, DC: Carnegie Endowment, 1996).
50. Adam Przeworski and Fernando Limongi, "Modernization: Theories and Facts," *World Politics* 49/2 (January 1997), 155–183. Compare especially Samuel P. Huntington, *The Third Wave: Democratization in the Late Twentieth Century* (Norman, OK: University of Oklahoma Press, 1991).
51. See further William I. Robinson, *Promoting Polyarchy: Globalization, U.S. Intervention, and Hegemony* (Cambridge: Cambridge University Press, 1996).
52. Kathryn Sikkink, "The Power of Principled Ideas: Human Rights Policies in the United States and Western Europe," in Judith Goldstein and Robert O. Keohane, eds., *Ideas and Foreign Policy: Beliefs, Institutions, and Political Change* (Ithaca, NY: Cornell University Press, 1995), 159. See also Smith, *America's Mission*, op. cit.: the United States, while preaching civil and political rights, actually acted to shore up autocracy in places like the Philippines and the Western hemisphere during much history, through inattention to the effects of economic policies.
53. See further David P. Forsythe, "Human Rights Policy: Change and Continuity," in Randall B. Ripley and James M. Lindsay, eds., *U.S. Foreign Policy after the Cold War* (Pittsburgh, PA: University of Pittsburgh Press, 1997).
54. See further Aryeh Neier, "The New Double Standard," *Foreign Policy*, no. 105 (Winter 1996–7), 91–103.

# 3

# Trials and errors: The Netherlands and human rights

*Peter R. Baehr*

## I. Introduction

Certain West European countries have the reputation of pursuing an active human rights policy. They are often referred to as "like-minded" in their foreign policy. The Scandinavian countries – Denmark, Finland, Norway, and Sweden – are mentioned in this regard. The Netherlands has, for many years, had a similar reputation. The Norwegian human rights activist and present deputy foreign minister Jan Egeland once described this as follows:

> The Netherlands has probably become the most effective human rights advocate today, because she ambitiously combines her favourable image as small state with allocating considerable resources to the planning, implementation and follow-up to an innovative and ambitious policy.... In the UN Human Rights Commission, the General Assembly and other UN bodies, the Dutch are always in the forefront in initiating new substantive mechanisms to monitor, mediate or improve when human rights problems are on the international agenda.[1]

To what extent is Egeland's positive description – positive as seen from the perspective of the promotion and protection of human rights – still true?

This chapter does not pretend to cover the subject of Dutch human rights policy in its entirety. An effort has been made to present material that gives a picture that is representative of the subject. Inevitably, a selection had to be made. In the multilateral area, emphasis is put on activities in the United Nations, including the Netherlands' role in the former Yugoslavia under the auspices of the United Nations. Some attention is also paid to relations within the European Union, the Organization for Security and Cooperation in Europe, and the Council of Europe. The section on bilateral relations deals with Turkey and with the linkage between human rights and development assistance policy, with particular reference to the former Dutch colonies of Indonesia and Surinam.

## II. Historical background

The foreign policy of the Netherlands is characterized by a sense of international engagement. In the Netherlands – perhaps more than in other countries – there has always been a strong interest in events abroad. This phenomenon, which has been observed by many commentators at home as well as abroad,[2] has been explained in various ways. There is the physical location of the Netherlands on the shores of the North Sea, in the Rhine estuary, in the immediate neighbourhood of the three most important West European powers, Germany, France, and Great Britain. This location, with relatively few natural resources, in combination with a relatively large population in a small area,[3] led to an early emphasis on international trade as a source of income. This explains the great interest in the development of the rule of law in the world – a traditional feature of Dutch policy dating back to the time of Hugo Grotius (1583–1645). From time immemorial, the Dutch economy has been dominated by its dependence on international trade. This trade has always greatly depended on the freedom of the high seas – *mare liberum*. The development of international law was not only a fine principle, but also in the national interest of a small, militarily weak state such as the Netherlands. The seventeenth-century statesman Johan de Witt summarized the Dutch position in the following often-quoted sentence: "The interest of the State demands that there be quiet and peace everywhere and that commerce be conducted in an unrestricted manner." These words have remained a maxim of Dutch foreign policy ever since.

Since the seventeenth century, that maxim has been translated into the maintenance of international peace and the furtherance of international trade as tenets of Dutch foreign policy. The achievement of international peace and prosperity was seen as a national interest of the Netherlands. In modern times, this has received a new application in the form of furnishing development aid to poor countries and the promotion and protection of human rights. The long-standing international legal tradition and the desire to contribute to the improvement of international living conditions were mutually reinforcing factors that were expressed in the Dutch support of international organizations.[4] This idea has been given a legal foundation in the Netherlands Constitution (article 90): "The government promotes the development of the international legal order."

The implementation of these objectives has not always been easy. Dutch foreign policy has often been compared to a struggle between the clergyman and the merchant: although wanting to do good all over the world, commercial interests are never lost sight of. In the early 1960s, in political circles to the left of the political spectrum, it was customary to describe the Netherlands as a *gidsland*, a "guiding country," that was expected to provide guidance to the world.[5] In the end, however, commerce usually gained the upper hand.[6]

In 1947 and 1948, the Netherlands was confronted with its own principles regarding the establishment of the rule of law, when the question of Indonesian independence came before the United Nations. The Netherlands considered its two "police actions" against the newly established (but not yet internationally recognized) Republic of Indonesia as strictly a matter of domestic jurisdiction over which the Security Council had no authority. Furthermore, in the view of the Dutch government, the situation did not present a threat to international peace and security. The majority of the members of the Security Council were not, however, convinced by the Dutch arguments. Under considerable pressure from the United States and other Council members, the Netherlands was eventually forced to agree to the transfer of sovereignty over the Indies to Indonesia. For a number of years, it held on to Western New Guinea (nowadays called Irian Jaya), but in 1962 it was forced to give up its rule over this remnant of its former colony.

To this day, the events leading to Indonesian independence in the years 1945–1949 have remained an issue of controversy in the Netherlands. Not so long ago, proposals were launched (and subsequently rejected) to hold a "national debate" to come to terms with the issue. The immediate cause for the controversy was the granting of a visitor's visa to a former Dutch soldier who had defected to the Indonesian forces back in 1948 and who had subsequently adopted Indonesian nationality and become a well-known human rights activist in Indonesia. The discussions on this issue and the emotions it entailed illustrate that for the Netherlands the relationship with Indonesia remains a very special one.[7]

Voorhoeve has linked the internationalist attitude of the Dutch to "a tinge of Calvinist penance." He refers to similar attitudes in countries such as Sweden, Norway, and Denmark, which share with the Netherlands a Northern Protestant political culture that tells them to do good in the world.[8] In the case of the Netherlands, an additional factor is undoubtedly its colonial past. This has two aspects. On the one hand, next to hard-boiled commercial interests, there was always an aspect of moralism in the way the Dutch approached their colonial burden, fuelled not in last instance by the Roman Catholic and Protestant churches, which laid great emphasis on their missionary activities in the colonies. On the other hand, since the loss of the colonies, there has also been, at least in some circles, a certain feeling of guilt, of wanting to make up for the past, which is translated into efforts in the fields of development assistance and the promotion of human rights. The traditional Dutch interest in human rights policy stems from the same roots – what Voorhoeve has called the Dutch internationalist–idealist tradition.[9] This has been strongly pushed by national domestic actors. But before turning to these domestic actors, we shall discuss some basic elements of Dutch human rights policy.

## III. Basic elements of Dutch human rights policy

The government of the Netherlands has expressed its ideas about human rights in foreign policy in a formal policy document.[10] That document was issued in 1979 and updated in 1986, 1991, and 1997. According to the present Foreign Minister, it still contains the basic elements of government policy in this field.[11]

### *General principles*

The government of the Netherlands has stated that in "international relations the conduct of States may be examined in the light of their observance of the elementary rights of their own subjects."[12] This is based on the principle that "man does not exist for the state but that the state exists for man."[13] The government considers civil and political rights of equal importance to economic, social, and cultural rights: "A person who has material prosperity but no political freedom and who is defenceless against arbitrary action by the State does not enjoy an existence worthy of human dignity any more than does a person who is free in formal terms but has neither work nor shelter and is on the verge of starvation."[14] It has opted for evenhandedness and non-selectivity in applying the principles of its human rights policy: "A policy which seeks to counter specific human rights abuses should be impartial and non-selective in that it must not concentrate on abuses in countries of one particular political colour."[15] A final point of consideration is the extent to which Dutch economic, cultural, or other interests restrain the raising of human rights considerations. Although the government "regards the promotion of human rights as an essential part of its foreign policy," that "does not alter the fact that this is a part of its total policy and cannot under all circumstances enjoy priority over the other aims of that policy."[16] Such limitations are for instance (1) "the promotion of other values and interests the government has to care for," and (2) the political sensitivity of the issue, "because in principle human rights affect profoundly the internal affairs of all States. A policy which seeks to counter specific abuses abroad regarding human rights ought to avoid arrogance. One should have understanding for the problems that other countries are faced with. At the same time one should be free from moral complacency."[17]

The human rights discussed so far all refer to the rights of individuals. The Netherlands government, like most other Western governments, has been reluctant to accept the notion of collective rights, considering collectivities such as nations, peoples, or indigenous peoples as beneficiaries but not as bearers of human rights. In a letter to the Advisory Committee on Human Rights and Foreign Policy, which at his request had reported on the notion of collective rights,[18] the Foreign Minister explicitly rejected the notion of collective rights as human rights:

> I am not inclined to add the category of collective rights to the human rights catalogue.... [C]ollective actions to protect individual human rights can meet existing needs. Solutions should be sought departing from that approach. I prefer a strengthening of existing mechanisms to protect already existing human rights, giving specific attention to the position of collectivities.[19]

I have already mentioned the principle that man does not exist for the state, but that the state exists for man. From this principle the government concluded that "the individual as an autonomous entity [is] entitled to certain rights and freedoms" because "he is a human being and not from his being part of a larger whole such as a title, a class, a people or a State."[20] Therefore, when collective rights do not coincide with individual rights, the government will give priority to individual human rights.[21]

## *Development aid and human rights*

Should development assistance policy be used as a means for promoting human rights elsewhere? The government considered "that there is an indissoluble connection between human rights and development policy, as the aim of the latter is to create the basic preconditions for human development in the third world, both materially and spiritually."[22] The government has emphasized that human rights involve all the elementary preconditions for an existence worthy of human dignity, which "requires not only protection from oppression, arbitrariness and discrimination but also access to such matters as food, housing, education and medical care."[23] Should aid be used to reward countries that respect human rights and conversely withheld to punish countries that disregard such rights? In the shaping of development cooperation, one must consider in what ways development aid could be made to serve the best possible realization of human rights. In this respect it may be necessary to take account of the human rights situation in recipient countries, including the policy pursued by the authorities. The aid-giving countries should, however, "act with a certain restraint and without presumption in this delicate area. In cases where abuses derive directly from government policy, one should take care at any rate to ensure that aid does not contribute directly to the perpetuation of repression. Where there is a pattern of gross and persistent violations of fundamental human rights, non-allocation or suspension of aid may be considered, but other relevant policy considerations must be taken into account before such exceptional measures are taken."[24] In general, however, development aid will not be used "as an instrument for manipulating recipient countries" because "the government rejects the idea that aid should be used to reward countries which respect human rights and conversely withheld to punish countries which disregard those rights."[25] The human rights situation in the recipient country is on the other hand relevant at the moment of shaping development cooperation. The more positive a country's human rights policy, the greater the chance that it will be selected as a target country for development cooperation.[26]

Mr. Jan Pronk, who was the Netherlands Minister for Development Cooperation from 1973 until 1977 and again from 1989 until 1998, was one of the main architects of policy in this field. In his 1990 policy paper, *A World of Difference: A New Framework for Development Cooperation in the 1990s,*[27] human rights received a great deal of attention.[28] An explicit choice was made for freedom and human rights. Human rights were said to play an essential role as a guiding principle and moral foundation for democratization processes. Classic human rights are the basis of democracy and provide opportunities to the lower levels of society to present and, if possible, legalize their justified claims and interests.[29] The argument that governments must be allowed to restrict civil and political rights in order to make progress in the field of socio-economic rights is explicitly rejected: "There is no freedom without food, but freedom prevails."[30] Political and civil rights are seen as preliminary conditions for achieving social and economic rights. Poverty must be fought by strengthening the autonomy of marginal groups. An explicit choice is made in favour of "development of, for and by the people."[31]

At the same time, the paper noted the weak position of the state in many developing countries, which makes it impossible for governmental bodies to prevent violations of human rights. Therefore, a plea is made for strengthening institutional frameworks. In that respect, the training of judges and public prosecutors and support for human rights organizations should be given priority.[32]

The 1993 government paper, also written by Mr. Pronk, *A World in Dispute*,[33] stated that freedom and democracy are necessary to achieve manageable growth in the world. "Good governance" must be stimulated, which means support for governmental services and private organizations in developing countries that aim for sustainable growth of legal security and of civil and political liberties. "Furthermore," Mr. Pronk wrote, "it is justified on grounds of development policy, in case of a serious relapse of democratization or in case of sustained excessive military expenses, to cut or stop fully the giving of aid to the country in question."[34]

The two policy papers clearly emphasize the importance of promoting human rights on the one hand, and of emphasizing aid to poor countries on the other, and their mutual relationship. The Netherlands government directed its development aid policy in the 1980s to the promotion of human rights as well. It did not exclude that, in the case of serious violations of human rights, development aid might be decreased, suspended, or even fully terminated.

Economic relations may affect human rights in two major ways. They may have a direct negative effect on human rights in the country in question, or they may on the contrary be used to contribute in a positive way to improve that situation. In the end, international economic relations may be used to improve respect for economic, social, and cultural human rights in another country. That is especially true in the case of trade relations with developing countries. Seen from that perspective, there is indeed a direct relationship between economic relations and respect for human rights.

> Grave and systematic violations of human rights may under certain conditions constitute grounds for restrictions on economic relations with the country in question. One of those conditions is that other methods of improving the human rights situation concerned have proved clearly inadequate. Another condition is that economic restrictions can genuinely be expected to lead to improvements.... An interesting as well as very important observation is the caveat that the measures must not disproportionately damage Netherlands interests.[35]

## *Preconditions for action*

The government of the Netherlands tried to clarify in the 1979 memorandum when, where, at what time, how, and under what restrictions it would react to specific situations in which human rights are abused:

"Wherever possible the government wishes to help counter specific human rights abuses abroad, particularly in cases of gross and persistent violations."[36] Its efforts are "in principle concentrated on cases where there are grave violations of fundamental human rights, particularly when such violations appear to proceed from a systematic policy."[37] This can be considered a necessary condition for any Dutch reaction. To break diplomatic relations completely[38] or to refrain from customary export-promoting actions[39] are two instruments that the government has excluded from any reaction.

The next step in decision-making is "to take account of the other values and interests which the government has to promote" and "the repercussions on bilateral relations"[40] of any Dutch reaction to human rights violations. There is a constant need to examine the possibility of a reaction in relation "to other considerations of government policy."[41] The reaction "should be impartial and non-selective" and free from moral complacency.[42]

Considering all these constraints on a governmental reaction, the government prefers "to combine forces with other countries: this applies both to confidential approaches and to public action"[43] "through international organizations such as the Council of Europe and the United Nations."[44] Common action is preferred because "our country can exert only limited influence through bilateral channels,"[45] while "the chance of finding a positive response" when specific human rights situations are raised in confidential talks "is greatest in the case of governments with which the Netherlands had a certain relationship of trust as a result of cooperation between the two countries." A further consideration is "whether action by the Netherlands is likely to have any effect at all on the situation concerned"[46] and "it must not be counterproductive by unintentionally harming those whom one is trying to help."[47]

When all or most of these deliberations have resulted in an affirmative answer towards action, the action itself will be restricted, because only in "exceptional circumstances there may be reason to restrict diplomatic relations temporarily with the country concerned."[48] Economic sanctions will be applied only if "other methods of improving the human rights situation concerned have proved clearly inadequate" and these "economic restrictions can genuinely be expected to lead to improvements" whereas "it can be assumed that maintaining these relations would contribute towards a continuation or increase of the human rights violations."[49]

The most recent follow-up memorandum, issued in 1997, basically reaffirmed the principles listed in the 1979 paper. The government reiterated human dignity as the nucleus of the concept of human rights. It stated that it continued to subscribe to the equivalence of the different categories of human rights. In its policy, it would continue to emphasize the right to life and the inviolability of the human person. These rights were seen as specimens of the universality of human rights, which remained the point of departure. Thanks to the disappearance of the East–West conflict, human rights are now seen as one of the regular "tracks" of foreign policy: there is a responsibility to ensure that this human rights track has a content and is not marginalized in relation to other tracks of foreign policy. In addition, ways must be found to raise the issue of violations of human rights and to seek ways of cooperating to prevent violations.[50]

## IV. Domestic factors

### *Non-governmental organizations*

In the Netherlands, as in other countries, the issue of human rights has been put on the political agenda mainly thanks to the efforts of non-governmental organizations (NGOs). More than the traditional political parties, NGOs have stimulated activities in this field and reminded the government of its obligations in this area. It is not an overstatement to suggest that it is largely owing to their efforts that the Netherlands began to play a leading role in the international human rights debate.

In the period 1960–1980, activities in the field of human rights mainly concerned situations in particular countries, such as apartheid in South Africa, the struggle for liberation in the Portuguese colonies in Africa, the military junta in Greece, human rights violations by military regimes in Chile and Argentina, and the suppression of political opponents by the Suharto regime in Indonesia. In all of these cases, "country committees" were formed in the Netherlands that concentrated their activities on the political and human rights situation in their country of concern. Herman Burgers, who was at the time himself an official with the Foreign Ministry, even calls the Vietnam protest movement "essentially ... a human rights campaign, although it was seldom presented in those terms."[51]

The activities of NGOs that deal with human rights concerns of a more general nature, such as Amnesty International, date mainly from the late 1970s, when the Netherlands government issued its policy paper in which it set out the principles of Dutch human rights policy. Since then, NGOs have played an important role in the formation of Dutch human rights policy. They submit suggestions and proposals for strengthening human rights as part of foreign policy. The papers and memoranda of the Minister of Foreign Affairs are commented on. NGO representatives appear at hearings and approach officials of the ministry and members of parliament. The ministry usually pays a great deal of attention to the views

Table 3.1 **Amnesty International membership, 1996**

| Country | Population size | Size AI section |
|---|---|---|
| Netherlands | 15,800,000 | 185,000 |
| Belgium | 10,000,000 | 16,000 |
| Denmark | 5,000,000 | 29,000 |
| Sweden | 8,000,000 | 76,000 |
| Norway | 4,200,000 | 36,000 |

Source: *Amnesty International Membership Statistics*, AI Index: ORG 40/02/96, June 1996.

of these organizations. For example, the Dutch delegation to the 1993 World Conference on Human Rights in Vienna included two NGO representatives.

Among the non-governmental organizations in this field is the Dutch section of Amnesty International. This important organization has over 185,000 members in the Netherlands. In table 3.1, membership data are given for a few comparable West European countries.

Other important human rights organizations are the Netherlands Jurists Committee for Human Rights (NJCM), which is the Dutch section of the International Commission of Jurists, and the Humanist Committee on Human Rights (HOM). These and similar organizations[52] work together with organizations in the field of foreign policy in the Breed Mensenrechten Overleg (BMO, or "Broad Human Rights Platform"). This is a loose form of cooperation that meets periodically. Its activities become more intensive at times, for instance during the debates over the 1979 government memorandum (for which purpose it was actually established) and subsequent policy memoranda, in the preparation for the 1993 World Conference, and in the preparation of the activities on the occasion of the fiftieth anniversary of the Universal Declaration of Human Rights, in December 1998.

### *Advisory Committee*

Between 1983 and 1996, an Advisory Committee on Human Rights and Foreign Policy provided the Foreign Minister with advisory reports on human rights issues, at his request or on its own initiative.[53] The Advisory Committee had been the result of intensive lobbying activities on the part of human rights organizations. Its independent members came from the ranks of non-governmental organizations, former diplomats, labour unions, employers' organizations, and academics. The Committee published 23 advisory reports[54] plus a number of shorter advisory letters.

The Minister of Foreign Affairs issued written commentaries on most of the advisory reports, which sometimes led to further oral communications. The Committee acquired a position of its own by the quality of its reports as well as by serving as an intermediary between the ministry and non-governmental organizations.

In 1993, however, the government decided on a major reform of the entire system of policy advisory committees. Henceforth there would be only one advisory committee per ministerial department. For the Ministry of Foreign Affairs this meant that its three advisory committees (peace and security, development cooperation, and human rights) were merged. By the end of 1996, the advisory committees were replaced by a new Advisory Council on International Affairs, which was to be assisted by four consultative committees: peace and security, development cooperation, human rights, and European affairs. The result seems to be mainly an administrative downgrading of the previous system, basically maintaining the original advisory structure.

### *Political parties*

The four major political parties represented in parliament[55] emphasize their commitment to the place of human rights in Dutch foreign policy. The radical liberal party D66 devotes comparatively the largest segment of its electoral programme to human rights, while the more conservative Liberal Party (VVD) has the shortest text on the subject.

The Christian Democratic Party (CDA) states that the promotion of respect for human rights must have a central place in foreign policy. Human rights are universal, because the dignity of every human being is not related to his or her country or culture. The human rights situation in a country serves as a criterion for giving bilateral aid. Gross and systematic violations of human rights are a threat to international peace and security and may be reason for international intervention. Such intervention may vary from diplomatic steps to economic sanctions and in the last instance to military action.[56]

The Labour Party (PvdA) sees foreign policy as the promotion of not just national economic interests, but also pluriformity, tolerance, democracy, and openness. In view of changing international power relations, the promotion of human rights may cost an ever higher price. The recent conflicts with Indonesia and China serve to show that in order to promote human rights one needs allies. The Netherlands must make an effort to intensify European cooperation in the field of human rights as well. This is the only way to avoid becoming isolated.[57]

The Liberal Party (VVD) states that serious and continuing violations of human rights may lead to interference in the domestic policy of other countries. To achieve a positive outcome, caution is prescribed. Interference by a group of states is to be preferred.[58]

Finally, the draft electoral programme of the radical liberal party D66 devotes eight paragraphs of its section on foreign policy to human rights, the protection of which should be "fully integrated in foreign policy." It is the task of the Ministry of Foreign Affairs to raise human rights aspects with other ministries. Human rights policy should be conducted with the use of all national and international bilateral and multilateral instruments. Effectiveness should determine the selection of such instruments. Universal human rights should be valid always and everywhere and must not depend on culture-bound interpretations by national authorities. If in a certain country terror reigns against its own subjects and neither the use of customary diplomatic channels nor NGO activities result in sufficient progress, international isolation of such a country may be considered.[59]

### *Parliament*

Dutch members of parliament used to be very active in human rights matters. On the basis most often of information provided by non-governmental organizations or of what they had seen or read in the media, they questioned the Foreign Minister on such matters. As already noted, NGOs direct a considerable part of their activities toward maintaining contact with, and trying to influence, members of parliament. The 1979 policy paper on human rights and foreign policy was the direct result of a parliamentary request. Sometimes, parliament gets directly involved in the organization of the governmental machinery. When it debated the 1979 paper, it asked for the appointment of a high-level officer within the Ministry of Foreign Affairs to deal with human rights. From then on, the deputy director-general for international cooperation, later the director-general himself, was charged with human rights affairs. His "high-level" position meant that he had also to deal with a great number of other issues and therefore could not give human rights his undivided attention. Consequently, in day-to-day practice it was a deputy coordinator who dealt with human rights matters in the ministry.[60] Parliament was also instrumental in the reactivation of the defunct Advisory Committee on Human Rights and Foreign Policy. It was less successful in its efforts to have the ministry publish annual reports on the human rights situation in other countries, following the model of the US State Department. Then Foreign Minister Hans van den Broek rejected this request, because in his view enough public information was already available and Dutch diplomatic posts abroad should continue to provide him with confidential information. Public reports would expose them too much in their country of accreditation – something that the United States as a major power could afford, but the Netherlands could not.[61]

Under the Dutch constitutional system, government ministers are accountable to parliament. As no political party has ever achieved an absolute majority in the parliamentary elections, cabinets are always formed on the basis of party coalitions that reflect the composition of parliament. That makes their position relatively secure. Government ministers are seldom forced to resign during their term of office. The position of the Foreign Minister is even stronger, because it is recognized that he is often engaged in sensitive negotiations with other governments, which may not always make it possible for him to give a full account to parliament.[62] Members of parliament tend to give the Foreign Minister considerable political freedom. Although non-governmental human rights organizations tend to be critical of what they perceive as parliamentary weakness, it is in fact a reflection of the Dutch constitutional system. This having been said, it remains a fact that parliament seems to pay less attention to human rights matters now than it did in the late 1970s and early 1980s.[63]

### *Conclusion*

On the whole, it can be said that in the Netherlands domestic public opinion,[64] as expressed by political parties and NGOs, favours human rights. At times, pressure is put on the government to react strongly to human rights violations abroad or to take initiatives to extend the international promotion and protection of human rights. This means that the government could ill afford to ignore human rights altogether, even if it wanted to do so.

## V. Multilateral policy

### *The United Nations*

From 1980 until 1986 and again from 1992 until 1997, the Netherlands served as a member of the UN Commission on Human Rights. In that capacity it developed a considerable number of initiatives and proposals.[65] The Netherlands was active in the drafting of the Principles of Medical Ethics in Relation to Detained Persons. During the 1979 session of the General Assembly, it requested the Secretary-General to send these draft principles to the Member States for comment and then repeatedly requested consideration of the draft text. This led in 1981 to an unusual procedure: together with Sweden, Denmark, Portugal, and the United States, the Netherlands took the initiative to incorporate the comments that had been received into a new draft text. This revised text was again sent to the Member States for comment, and then discussed in a working group of the Third Committee under the chairmanship of the Dutch delegate. He succeeded in drafting a final version which was then adopted by the General Assembly.[66]

Another major initiative was its collaborative effort with Sweden to steer a draft Convention against Torture and other Cruel, Inhuman or Degrading Treatment or Punishment through the Commission. In the General Assembly, it was again the Dutch delegation, with considerable help from a number of third world countries, that managed to achieve agreement on a text that was adopted by consensus on 10 December 1984.[67]

Furthermore, the Netherlands was one of the countries that worked on drafting the (Second) Optional Protocol to the International Covenant on Civil and Political Rights on the Abolition of the Death Penalty as well as the draft principles on Conscientious Objection to Military Service. For many years the Netherlands has endeavoured to get included such principles in the right to freedom of conscience. In 1985, the Netherlands introduced a draft text that established the possibility of refusing to perform military service and of creating an alternative service. Faced with strong opposition from some of the East European states, the delegation proposed to adjourn the discussion of the proposal. In 1987, however, the Commission adopted a text, co-sponsored by the Dutch delegation, in which conscientious objection to military service was defined as a legitimate exercise of the right to freedom of thought, conscience, and religion.[68]

In 1979, a working group of the Commission on Human Rights was established to prepare a draft Convention on the Rights of the Child, originally a Polish draft. The Netherlands supported the adoption of such a Convention and made considerable contributions to the draft. It took until 1989, however, before the draft text was finally adopted by the Commission on Human Rights and referred to the General Assembly, which adopted it by consensus on 20 November 1989. It was ratified by the Netherlands as late as 1995. The Netherlands delegation also played an important role in the drafting of the Principles Relating to the Protection and Welfare of Children, with special reference to foster placement and adoption, nationally as well as internationally.

Another issue in which the Netherlands was actively involved was the Declaration on the Right to Development, in which it played the role of mediator between the third world countries on the one hand and the Western countries on the other. In 1979, the General Assembly adopted a resolution sponsored by a number of third world nations that named the right to development a human right. In following years, the Dutch expert Paul de Waart was one of the key negotiators in the drafting of the Declaration on the Right to Development, which was adopted by the General Assembly in 1986.

The Netherlands played a role in the drafting of the Declaration on the Elimination of All Forms of Intolerance and of Discrimination Based on Religion or Belief (1981). As early as 1962, the General Assembly had asked the Commission on Human Rights to draft such a declaration. Although there was still a considerable amount of opposition on the part of the East European countries, the Dutch delegation to the Commission on Human Rights introduced a draft resolution aimed at the adoption of the declaration. In the General Assembly, the Dutch delegation, acting as coordinator of the group of Western countries, succeeded, after intensive negotiations with the Islamic states, in getting the declaration adopted.

The Netherlands was also very active in further developing the role of UN organs in the supervision of respect for human rights. The proposal for a Special Rapporteur on Torture of the Commission on Human Rights was drafted by the Dutch delegation. The chairman of the delegation, Professor Kooijmans, was the first person to be appointed to that position.[69] In 1980, the Commission on Human Rights decided, on a proposal mainly developed by the Australian, Canadian, and Dutch delegations, to establish a Working Group on Involuntary Disappearances. Since its establishment, the Netherlands has actively supported the annual renewal of its mandate. A Dutch Foreign Ministry official, Toine van Dongen, served as a member of the Working Group between 1984 and 1993. Similar strong support was given to the establishment of a Special Rapporteur on Summary or Arbitrary Executions (1982). Dutch support for this organ received additional stimulus from the summary execution of 15 political opponents of the military regime in the former Dutch colony of Surinam in December 1982 (see further below).

On the whole, it can be said that the Netherlands government gave support to most of the proposals to strengthen UN supervision mechanisms. In 1996, it adopted and circulated among members of the UN Sub-Commission on the Prevention of Discrimination and Protection of Minorities a report from the Advisory Committee on Human Rights and Foreign Policy on "The Role of the UN Sub-Commission on Prevention of Discrimination and Protection of Minorities."[70] A second report from the Advisory Committee, which dealt with reporting procedures, complaints procedures, inquiry procedures, Charter-based procedures, and mechanisms,[71] was adopted by the government and circulated as a document of the UN General Assembly.[72]

## *Former Yugoslavia*

Since 1963, the Netherlands has put military units on stand-by to be used for UN peacekeeping operations. Between 1979 and 1985 Dutch military units participated in the UN peacekeeping operation in Lebanon (UNIFIL). After the end of the Cold War, the Netherlands contributed military units, observers, and police monitors to UN peacekeeping operations in Namibia, Angola, Cambodia, Uganda–Rwanda, and Mozambique. It was directly confronted with the practice of gross human rights violations[73] through its involvement in the United Nations peacekeeping efforts in the war in Yugoslavia. As part of its contribution to the United Nations Protection Force in Yugoslavia (UNPROFOR), the Netherlands government decided in early 1994 to station a lightly armed small military unit (630 persons, later reduced to 430) in the Bosnian enclave of Srebrenica, which had been named a "safe area" by the Security Council. The idea was that such a safe area should be free from any armed attack or any other hostile act.[74] The enclave was overrun by Serb Bosnian forces on 11 July 1995. NATO aircraft stationed in Italy, which included Dutch fighter aircraft that might have repelled the attack, were not called into action. It has remained unclear whether this was due to inaction on the part mainly of the United Nations command or of the Dutch government. One Dutch soldier was killed when the town was taken, and the Dutch contingent was allowed to leave the enclave without further losses.[75] During the first two weeks of July, the Serbs expelled 23,000 Bosnian Muslim women and children and captured and executed several thousand Muslim male civilians.[76] The degree to which the Dutch government and the Dutch forces share indirect responsibility for this war crime has been the subject of public debate in the Netherlands ever since. The government managed to survive a number of parliamentary debates, among other reasons because a parliamentary majority shared responsibility, because it had in the past always given its support to the government's policy in regard to the former Yugoslavia. At the request of parliament, the government approached the United Nations Secretariat and some members of the Security Council to conduct a thorough study of the matter. This request was, however, turned down.[77] Thereupon, the government requested the National Institute for War Documentation in Amsterdam (RIOD), which has a reputation for its specialized knowledge on the role of the Netherlands in the Second World War, to undertake a major study of the issue. This action on the part of the government was widely interpreted as a move to take the issue out of the political debate.[78]

The Srebrenica operation was a disaster because of the massacre of thousands of unarmed Muslim civilians, who, though residents of a UNproclaimed "safe area," did not receive the necessary protection from the UN troops. For the Dutch it was a truly traumatic experience,[79] as it ran counter to cherished Dutch views in favour of contributing to UN peacekeeping operations and undertaking activities on behalf of human rights and humanitarian law. Many questions have so far remained unanswered:

- Could and should the Dutch battalion have tried to resist the Serbian onslaught, at the risk of major losses among Dutch soldiers?
- If it was impossible to defend the enclave, could and should the Dutch soldiers have done more to prevent the massacre of the Muslims?
- Why was the Dutch unit only lightly armed, which included the dismantling of the 25 mm cannons on its armed personnel carriers and their replacement by machine guns?[80]
- What truth is there in newspaper reports that the Dutch military displayed considerably more sympathy for the supposedly well-disciplined Bosnian Serbs than for the Muslim civilian population, whom they were meant to protect?
- Why was no NATO air support given to the Dutch at the time of the Serbian onslaught?[81]
- Why were the Dutch soldiers not immediately debriefed on their return to the Netherlands, but sent on leave first?[82]
- Who should ultimately be held responsible: the United Nations or the Dutch government?

It remains to be seen whether the study by the Amsterdam institute will provide answers to these and many other sensitive questions. At the time of writing this chapter, the study is still under way.

In a more positive vein, also relating to Yugoslavia, since 1993 the Netherlands has hosted the International Criminal Tribunal for the former Yugoslavia in The Hague. In addition to making available courtroom and other facilities to the Tribunal, the Netherlands supplies detention facilities for the accused. This involved considerable costs to the Dutch taxpayer.[83] The position of Registrar of the Tribunal is held by a Dutch citizen.[84] Whatever one may think of the achievements of the Tribunal so far,[85] the Netherlands government considers it of great importance to make The Hague, which also houses the International Court of Justice and the Permanent Court of Arbitration, and will house the soon to be established Permanent International Criminal Court, into what former UN Secretary-General Boutros Boutros-Ghali once called the "international legal capital of the world."

## *The European Union*

The original treaties that form the basis of the European Community (nowadays the European Union) did not contain specific references to human rights. Gradually, the main European organs, the Council of Ministers, the European Commission, and the European Parliament, began to pay greater attention to the subject. This resulted in a number of declarations[86] and in the provisions of a Common Foreign and Security Policy of the Treaty on European Union (the "Maastricht Treaty"), which entered into force in 1993. Its objectives include explicitly "to develop and consolidate democracy and the rule of law, and respect for human rights and fundamental freedoms." Most of this Common Foreign and Security Policy is still in a preparatory stage. For the time being, foreign policy-making remains more a matter of intergovernmental co-operation than of real common European policy.[87]

At meetings of international organizations and at international conferences, EU member states meet on a regular basis to consult with each other and exchange information. At meetings of the United Nations Commission on Human Rights, joint statements are delivered by the government that holds the presidency of the European Council of Ministers and on occasion the EU members may jointly sponsor draft resolutions. In 1997, the Netherlands, on behalf of the European Union, co-sponsored draft resolutions on Iran, Iraq, Burma, Zaire, East Timor, Nigeria, and the rights of the child.[88] Also in 1997, the European Commission addressed the session of the UN Commission on Human Rights for the first time. Commissioner Hans van den Broek, himself a former Dutch Foreign Minister, spoke about various aspects of the Union's human rights activities. These included its support for international and regional initiatives (international tribunals, human rights observation missions), positive measures to promote human rights in developing countries, election assistance, and conflict prevention and limitation.[89]

On occasion, however, such efforts may fail, as the Netherlands found to its regret in the case of its attempt to introduce a joint resolution on China during the 1997 session of the Commission on Human Rights. The Netherlands, as President of the Council of Ministers of the European Union, proposed to introduce a resolution on behalf of the EU criticizing China's record in human rights. Such a resolution had been proposed – and not acted upon by the Commission – by the EU during previous sessions.[90] This time, however, France, later joined by Germany, Italy, Spain, and Greece, refused to support this initiative.[91] It was left to EU member Denmark to introduce the resolution on its own behalf. As in previous years, China managed to block consideration of the resolution by having a "no action" proposal adopted. The lack of agreement among the European partners was widely assumed to be connected to a planned visit by French President Jacques Chirac to China, during which he was to conclude a profitable contract for the European Airbus company. Denmark and the Netherlands were strongly criticized by China for what it considered as involvement in its domestic affairs. China cancelled a number of visits by Danish and Dutch ministers and threatened to suspend trade relations.

## *Organization for Security and Cooperation in Europe*

The Netherlands played a leading role in the adoption of supervision mechanisms with regard to the "human dimension" in the 1989 Vienna follow-up meeting of the Conference on Security and Cooperation in Europe (CSCE; now the OSCE). The Dutch proposal for a High Commissioner on National Minorities was adopted by the summit meeting of the CSCE participating states in Helsinki in July 1992. A Dutchman was the first – and up till now the only – person to be appointed to that position: former Foreign Minister Max van der Stoel. He conducts most of his activities beyond the glare of publicity, laying emphasis on an approach of quiet diplomacy. As an instrument of conflict prevention he must call for early warnings and, if necessary, for early action, whenever the position of national minorities might lead to tensions. This presents him with a dual task: he must try to contain the tensions that fall within his mandate and he must warn the OSCE when the tensions could escalate to a level that he can no longer contain with the tools at his disposal.[92] Mr. van der Stoel's role has been widely appreciated and he is reputed to have helped to contain a number of potential conflicts. His success is hard to estimate, however; it lies in the *non*-occurrence of events that would have taken place had he not acted. The number of states in which he has been involved is to say the least impressive. Among these were: Albania, Croatia, Estonia, Macedonia, Hungary, Kazakhstan, Kyrgyzstan, Latvia, Lithuania, Moldova, Romania, Slovakia, and Ukraine.[93] The establishment of his office has probably been the most successful Dutch initiative within OSCE.

## *The Council of Europe*

The Council of Europe has built up a reputation of harbouring the most effective regional instrument of human rights supervision: the European Convention for the Protection of Human Rights and Fundamental Freedoms. The findings of its main organs, the European Court of Human Rights and the European Commission of Human Rights,[94] are generally respected by the States Parties. In recent years, the number of states that are party to the Convention has greatly increased through the accession of the former members of the communist bloc in Eastern Europe. Admission to membership of the Council of Europe used to be seen as a seal of approval by the European states that the new member had met certain minimum criteria of democratic government and observance of human rights. This seems nowadays to be no longer true. Experts have questioned whether such newly admitted member states as Croatia, Romania, Ukraine, and the Russian Federation have actually met these minimum requirements. The Netherlands, together with Greece, was at first opposed to Romania's membership, but in the end sided with the majority. After that, the admission of the other states mentioned was politically more or less a foregone conclusion. Many of these states see membership of the Council of Europe as an approach toward membership of the European Union – which may be legal nonsense, but is politically sound reasoning. With the accession of these new members, the nature of the Council and its organs may change drastically, moving away from the strict application of the human rights rules of the European Convention.

The Netherlands government has said that it will continue to support the human rights activities of the Council and try to prevent duplications with the European Union and the Organization for Security and Cooperation in Europe. It will continue to bring about the best possible effectiveness of the supervisory mechanisms.[95]

In 1996, 12,143 cases were lodged with the European Commission on Human Rights. At the moment, 140 cases against the Netherlands are being dealt with by the European Commission. Annually, about five such cases reach the European Court.[96]

## VI. Bilateral policy

In a parliamentary debate in June 1997, the Dutch Minister of Foreign Affairs, Hans van Mierlo, made the point that, in the field of human rights, multilateral policy had a greater chance of success than bilateral policy:

> Although the government does not tend to let the bilateral policy disappear altogether, it remains a fact that a powerful state can achieve more bilaterally than a less powerful state. It should not be forgotten that the Netherlands is a member of the EU [European Union], a forum that gives more and more emphasis to the field of human rights.[97]

### *Turkey*

One case in which the tension between considerations of human rights and other foreign policy considerations was at issue has been relations with NATO ally Turkey. For many years, Turkey has been criticized for its violations of fundamental human rights, for example through the practice of torture occurring in places of detention. The Western states have on the whole been rather reluctant to express public criticism of Turkey. A state complaint, which was lodged under the rules of the European Convention on Human Rights by Denmark, Norway, Sweden, France, and the Netherlands in 1982, ended in 1985 with a friendly settlement. In this settlement, Turkey committed itself to submit three reports on the measures it had taken to ensure the prohibition of torture practices. Critics felt at the time that the Turkish government had made little or no commitment to improve the human rights situation and was let off far too easily.[98] Recent efforts by non-governmental organizations to revive the state complaint have so far come to naught.[99] Although human rights violations in Turkey have continued, especially with regard to the Kurdish population, it seems obvious that security interests have prevailed over human rights considerations.

## *Human rights and development assistance*

In its bilateral policy, the Netherlands has found it especially hard to combine the two policy objectives of the promotion and protection of human rights on the one hand, and the giving of financial support to poor countries in the form of development assistance on the other.[100] Other countries, such as Norway, struggle with the same problem.[101] Should aid be continued in the face of gross and systematic human rights violations? Should it be used as an instrument on behalf of the promotion of human rights? The Minister for Development Cooperation, Jan Pronk, mentioned in a parliamentary debate the following examples of such policy: to certain countries, such as Syria, Burma, Zaire, and Kazakhstan, no development assistance was given because of the human rights situation in those countries; in respect of other countries, such as Chile, Mauretania, Sri Lanka, Mali, Sudan, Niger, and the Gambia, development assistance was suspended because of the human rights situation; because of the improvement in the human rights situation, aid to Cambodia,[102] Haiti, Malawi, Chile, and Guatemala was resumed.[103]

## *Relations with Indonesia*

The problem of the linkage between human rights and development assistance has manifested itself especially in the relationship of the Netherlands with two former colonies, Indonesia and Surinam.[104] The suppression by the Indonesian army of a *coup d'état* of left-wing officers on 30 September 1965 led to a period of gross violations of human rights. Between 1965 and 1968 more than 1 million people were killed.[105] Arrests took place on a massive scale. According to official statistics,

750,000 people were arrested in this period. These huge numbers of political prisoners were not put on any kind of trial, or only after a long time. Many were detained in camps and tortured, which often led to their death. Hygiene and nutrition in the camps were grossly deficient. The survivors were only gradually released, often after many years of detention. After their release, these "ex-Tapols" remained subject to all sorts of restrictions.[106]

At the time, the question was raised in the Netherlands whether and to what extent development aid should be used to put pressure on the Indonesian authorities to get the political prisoners released. The international position of the Netherlands was strengthened when it became chairman of an international donor consortium for Indonesia, the Inter-Governmental Group on Indonesia (IGGI), established in 1967. Non-governmental human rights organizations repeatedly requested that the human rights situation in Indonesia be put on the IGGI agenda, but this was rejected by the Netherlands and the other IGGI members. The human rights situation in Indonesia deteriorated further in the early 1970s, when death squads wantonly killed opponents of the Suharto regime. In 1975, Indonesia invaded and incorporated the former Portuguese colony of East Timor, suppressing the East Timorese independence movement. The Indonesian army also acted mercilessly against separatist movements in Aceh and Irian Jaya.

What should the Netherlands do in these circumstances? Economic and business relations with Indonesia had improved after 1966. Almost 10 per cent of Dutch development aid went to Indonesia. Trade with Indonesia rose from 450 million guilders in 1966 to more than 1,500 million guilders in 1984. Cultural relations showed a growing improvement. In 1970, President Suharto paid an official visit to the Netherlands, which was returned by Queen Juliana in 1971.

On the other hand, non-governmental organizations urged the Dutch government to do something about the deteriorating human rights situation in Indonesia. Also, within the Dutch Labour Party and the smaller Radical Party (Politieke Partij Radicalen), both of which formed part of the governing coalition, voices were heard in favour of cutting or suspending development aid to Indonesia to express Dutch concern about the human rights situation. In 1975, Minister Pronk did indeed cut development aid to Indonesia, claiming that Indonesia's need for aid had decreased. He announced that he would shortly review the entire development aid programme for Indonesia in a policy review paper. The government fell before Pronk's policy review paper was issued, but its contents were widely leaked. He concluded that he would not discontinue development aid to Indonesia because the Indonesian government, under international pressure, had announced that it would do something about the problem of the political prisoners. He did argue in favour of the dissolution of IGGI and its replacement by a development consortium of the World Bank, which would not be chaired by the Netherlands.[107] The latter recommendation was not taken up by the successor government, in which the Labour Party was not represented. The development aid programme for Indonesia was continued without changes.

The human rights situation in Indonesia received renewed international attention in 1985 when four former bodyguards of President Sukarno, who had been detained because of their involvement in the 1965 military coup, were executed. Many people felt that it was against basic humanitarian principles to execute them after so many years of detention. Other aspects of the human rights situation in Indonesia caused international concern as well. Between 1982 and 1984, a number of "mysterious murders" took place, which President Suharto, in his autobiography published in 1989, later said had occurred on official orders. There were reports of human rights violations by the security forces in Irian Jaya, Aceh, and East Timor. On East Timor, matters came to a head when the Indonesian military opened fire on a funeral procession in the East Timorese capital of Dili, killing an estimated 100 people.[108] Since then, both intergovernmental and non-governmental organizations have reported on continued human rights violations in East Timor.

In the Netherlands, Mr. Pronk had returned as Minister for Development Cooperation in 1989. He reacted to the execution of another four former bodyguards of President Sukarno by withdrawing 27 million guilders of additional aid for Indonesia. This announcement was of little *financial* importance, but it was generally seen as a cause for renewed tension between the Netherlands and Indonesia. The announcement that Indonesia was planning to execute another six former bodyguards – later denied by the Indonesian authorities – led to *démarches* by the President of the Council of Ministers of the European Communities as well as by the governments of the Netherlands and other European countries. Pronk discussed the matter during his visit to Indonesia in April 1990 and in informal meetings at the IGGI meeting in June 1990. Pronk was perhaps encouraged by his alleged "success" when the bodyguards were in fact not executed.[109] He publicly expressed his aversion to the human rights situation in Indonesia.

A first preliminary investigation of the Dili affair by a national Indonesian commission was widely seen as inadequate. In the Dutch parliament and the press critical questions were raised. The Netherlands government reacted by suspending another 27 million guilders of aid for 1992. At first, the Netherlands did not stand alone in this. Two other donor countries, Denmark and Canada, announced that they would stop their aid programmes for Indonesia. However, no consultations about this took place among the three countries. Portugal, the former colonial ruler over East Timor, led the efforts to arrive at an international condemnation of the Dili massacre. Also the European Communities suspended its aid programme and in the European Parliament the establishment of an arms embargo was being urged.[110] A second investigation took place, this time by the military, which by Indonesian standards was very critical: the military response to the demonstration in Dili was described as excessive and not in line with instructions. President Suharto reacted by firing two generals and by having a number of lower-ranking officers prosecuted.

In these circumstances, the Netherlands government announced in January 1992 its willingness to resume its aid programme for Indonesia. It stated that it assumed that the Indonesian–Portuguese negotiations about the future of East Timor, which were to take place under the supervision of the Secretary-General of the United Nations, would lead to a satisfactory solution. But it added that, should these negotiations not lead to satisfactory results, *it would discuss possible consequences with its European partners*. This threat caused Indonesia to postpone negotiations about the distribution of the new Dutch development money and to start a diplomatic offensive in order to prevent other donor countries from associating themselves with the Dutch approach. The Indonesian Minister of Foreign Affairs, Ali Alatas, visited a number of foreign capitals and succeeded in receiving the support he requested. On 13 February 1992, President Suharto, on the occasion of accepting the credentials of the new Dutch ambassador, spoke of Dutch "colonial" behaviour, as had become apparent from the continued Dutch interference in the domestic affairs of Indonesia. The establishment of a link between human rights and economic aid he termed "typically Western." At the same time, Mr. Pronk made preparations for his annual visit to Indonesia, which this time was to include Aceh, where human rights violations by the Indonesian army were allegedly still taking place. He was clearly not prepared for the announcement by the Indonesian government on 25 March 1992 that henceforth it did not want to receive Dutch aid any more and that it had asked the Netherlands to discontinue its chairmanship of IGGI. By way of explanation, Indonesia referred to the "reckless use of development aid as an instrument of intimidation or as a tool to threaten Indonesia."[111]

## *Double standards?*

Non-governmental criticism of the Netherlands attitude towards Indonesia did not diminish when, in December 1982, the Netherlands government unilaterally suspended its development aid to Surinam, another former Dutch colony, where 15 known opponents of the military regime had been killed in cold blood.[112] The then Minister for Development Cooperation, Mrs. Schoo, informed parliament that the bilateral treaty[113] had been suspended, because circumstances had changed so much that the continued supply of development aid could not be demanded of the Netherlands.

From the beginning, it was alleged by critics of the government that the suspension of aid to Surinam, when this was initially not done in the case of Indonesia, reflected a policy of double standards. The Netherlands government has, however, steadfastly denied that such was the case. It emphasized the unique, treaty-bound character of the development relationship with Surinam. Aid to Surinam not only was very extensive, but also formed the lion's share of total international aid to that country. A further important consideration for suspending aid was the seriousness of the human rights violations in a country that had always had a tradition of an absence of violence in politics. The December 1982 assassinations destroyed in one blow the core of the political opposition in Surinam.

Apart from these factors mentioned by the government, there were undoubtedly other political considerations as well. Surinam is a relatively small, powerless country, and the Netherlands is one of the few foreign states that has shown some real interest in its fate. The case of Indonesia is entirely different. That country is large and potentially powerful, located in a geographically important strategic position. For Dutch business interests Indonesia is far more important than Surinam.[114] Annual Dutch aid to Indonesia was small in comparison to the size of its population and represented only a small proportion of total international aid given to Indonesia.

To a certain extent the Netherlands government has definitely applied double standards with reference to Surinam and Indonesia. It claimed at the time that the assassinations in Surinam had changed the situation so drastically that continuation of the aid effort was impossible. It also pointed out that, according to its policy principles adopted earlier, development aid should never be used to support repressive regimes or lead to complicity in gross violations of human rights. The government did not say, however, that it had suspended the treaty with Surinam *in order to* improve the human rights situation in that country. It mentioned other means that it had used for that purpose, including the circulation of a memorandum at the 1983 session of the UN Commission on Human Rights in Geneva. In Surinam, however, the suspension of aid was seen as a sanction in reaction to the violation of human rights. It certainly did not contribute to the credibility of Dutch human rights policy, especially as in both cases the same kinds of violations of human rights (summary and arbitrary executions, disappearances, torture, arbitrary arrests) were at stake.

The Dutch argument that the situation in Surinam had changed so much that, according to the international law principle "*rebus sic stantibus*," it was not obliged to continue its aid programme has been questioned.[115] For instance, the Advisory Committee on Human Rights and Foreign Policy has pointed out that the picture offered by Surinam before the events of 8 December 1982 was one of a continuing deterioration in the human rights situation: "The December murders should thus not be seen as an isolated incident, but as a climax in a chain of events."[116]

No doubt, the Netherlands government exposed itself to criticism by suspending aid to Surinam while at the time not doing so in the case of Indonesia. It "solved" this dilemma by denying the similarity of the two cases. This did not of course silence its domestic critics. One may wonder, however, whether the government had any viable alternative. It could have avoided the accusation of applying double standards either by suspending aid to Indonesia, which at that time it did not want to do, or by continuing aid to Surinam, which was domestically not acceptable.[117] Theoretically, there was a third possibility: to admit that it was indeed applying double standards, which in the circumstances would have been the most sensible thing to do. It is not likely, however, that this third possibility was ever seriously considered. Governments prefer to present their policies as consistent and coherent. Applying double standards has no place in such a presentation.

The Advisory Committee on Human Rights and Foreign Policy has called development aid to Surinam a "classic example of a dilemma," stemming from the 1979 policy paper *Human Rights in Foreign Policy*. On the one hand, the Netherlands did not want to use development aid or its suspension as a reward or sanction for human rights performance (policy conclusion no. 35). On the other hand, it did not want its development aid to contribute to the continuation of repression (policy conclusion no. 38).[118] Nevertheless, the Dutch measure was widely interpreted as a form of sanction. The dilemma received extra emphasis because of the obvious comparison with the situation in Indonesia.

The Netherlands government had to face strong domestic political pressure at times. Human rights organizations have repeatedly pointed to the deficiencies in the human rights situation in Indonesia. This criticism was led by the non-governmental Indonesia Committee, which has exerted constant pressure on the Dutch government. In addition, within the Dutch Labour Party – which at times formed part of the governing coalition – and the smaller political parties of the left, continued reference was made to Dutch commitments to human rights and the consequences thereof for its relations with Indonesia. On the other hand, the Netherlands had clear economic interests that demanded extension of trade relations with Indonesia and an improved climate for investments. These interests were not served by explicit criticism of Indonesian government policies, in the realm of human rights or elsewhere.

The various Dutch governmental agencies did not always see eye to eye. The Ministry of Foreign Affairs was traditionally strongly engaged in the promotion of human rights, while at the same time pursuing a policy of combating poverty as a main aim of development policy. The Ministry of Economic Affairs was mainly interested in restoring mutual trade relations. The Ministry of Education and Sciences stressed cultural relations, while the Ministry of Justice wanted to be involved in the elaboration and extension of the Indonesian legal system, which is mainly based on the old Dutch system.

## VII. Conclusions

On the whole, the Netherlands government has given strong support to internationally recognized human rights, especially in the field of civil and political rights. Although it has repeatedly claimed that economic, social, and cultural rights should hold a position of equality with civil and political rights, this has been less the case in actual policy decisions. For example, the Netherlands – like most other governments – has so far refused to support the idea of an optional protocol to the International Covenant on Economic, Social, and Cultural Rights on a right to complaint for individuals.[119] In its support for human rights, the Netherlands government has on the whole preferred individual over collective rights.

Is there going to be a future for Dutch human rights policy? That remains to be seen. The member states of the European Union have lost some of their former ability to carry out a policy of their own. For instance, in the field of international commercial policy the European organs hold exclusive authority. This means that the member states cannot independently impose economic sanctions. Also the extension of common external powers has limited the possibilities of the member states to carry out a foreign policy of their own. This does not mean, however, that a joint European foreign policy already exists. The Maastricht Treaty on European Union (1992) states that there is a Common Foreign and Security Policy that explicitly includes human rights. The recent Treaty of Amsterdam has reaffirmed that position. Whether this will indeed lead to such a common foreign policy is still very much a matter of speculation. So far, this common foreign policy has been more a matter of pious sermons than of concrete actions.[120] The failure on the part of the member states to sponsor a joint resolution on China at the 1997 session of the UN Commission on Human Rights serves as an illustration of the failure to reach a common position on an issue of human rights. It seems fair to assume that, at least in the near future, there will be room for the Netherlands to conduct a human rights policy of its own. One of the more "positive" consequences of the China incident was that the Dutch Foreign Minister, Hans van Mierlo, who had been the target of domestic criticism before for his alleged lack of initiative in the area of human rights, from now on was regarded at home as an active figure in the struggle for human rights in China. His third follow-up memorandum on human rights and foreign policy, which was shortly afterward debated in parliament, consequently met with little comment or criticism. With regard to human rights violations in Turkey, the Netherlands has in recent years been as cautious as most other Western governments.

In Dutch political life, human rights – and development assistance policy – remain an almost sacred subject. The least the government must do – like many other governments – is to pay lip-service to the issue. Members of parliament, the press, and informed public opinion want more than that, however. The government is expected to take initiatives on a world-wide scale to show its commitment to human rights. However, there are also countervailing tendencies to put more emphasis on national (economic) interests. In the original report that resulted from the major review of foreign policy, more attention was paid to such interests than to human rights. Within the Ministry of Foreign Affairs, a thematic directorate for "conflict, humanitarian assistance and human rights" was to be created, which was to combine perspectives of foreign policy, development cooperation, and military considerations.[121] The protests, especially from human rights NGOs, with which these proposals were received forced the government to revise them. What resulted was the creation of a thematic directorate "Human Rights, Good Governance and Democratization," whose aim is "to promote a strong and consistent bilateral and multilateral policy in the field of human rights, good governance and democratization."[122] This directorate comprises 21 people, which makes it – at least quantitatively – one of the stronger sections within the ministry. A separate directorate now deals with Crisis Management and Humanitarian Assistance. The incident does not necessarily prove that more attention will be paid to human rights – that depends in the end on the political leadership given by the Foreign Minister. But it does show that the activities of the minister in the field of human rights, including the organization of his department, are closely watched by the human rights community, which continues to possess a considerable amount of political leverage. The amount of attention that is paid to issues of human rights does not tell us much about what policy decisions will be taken.

Foreign policy in general and human rights policy in particular generate policy dilemmas that are not easy to resolve.[123] An illustration is the conflict that can arise between human rights policy and development assistance policy, as occurred in the relations of the Netherlands with its two former colonies, Indonesia and Surinam. Its policy toward both countries has not been very successful. Indonesia showed its disdain for Dutch human rights considerations by unilaterally breaking off the development aid relationship. In the case of Surinam, the Netherlands seems to have influenced the domestic political situation only marginally – if at all.[124] If there was a case of applying double standards, as has widely been suggested, this has not helped the credibility of Dutch policies. However, in the case of foreign policy, some degree of double standards is not always avoidable. It may be true that Dutch policy-makers lacked a degree of subtlety and refinement in dealing with Indonesia, but that was mainly a matter of political style, not of content. The content of human rights policy towards Indonesia was fully in accordance with the principles and objectives set out in the 1979 policy memorandum.

In the case of Srebrenica, Dutch foreign policy-makers[125] were, for the first time since the failed reaction to the Indonesian independence movement in the late 1940s, directly confronted with gross human rights violations. It is difficult to say whether the civilian and military leaders, the officers, and the enlisted men could or should have done more. What may be learnt from the experience is that, before becoming engaged in such an operation, one should weigh the political and military risks one is going to face even more carefully. It seems to be certain that the Dutch military in the field were singularly unprepared for what eventually happened. With the benefit of hindsight one can say that it might have been wiser or smarter not to participate in UNPROFOR in the first place. However, for a country that prides itself on international engagement and its role in the promotion and protection of human rights, what is smarter is not necessarily the most noble policy. The experience in Srebrenica created a collective trauma that will not easily be overcome.

Has the human rights policy of the Netherlands lived up to the admiring description by Jan Egeland, quoted at the beginning of this chapter? It may be that Egeland was already exaggerating a bit when he wrote his article in 1984. The Netherlands is not a holy country and the dilemmas it faces are not easier to resolve than those of other countries. It may be true that the Netherlands government pays somewhat more attention to the views of an enlightened public opinion, which does not mean that it always acts according to the wishes of that public opinion. As has been shown in this chapter, the record has been one of successes and failures. Therefore, rather than subscribing to Egeland's glowing account, it seems to be more correct to describe the Netherlands human rights policy as one of trials and errors. Both should be seen as part of a learning experience.

## Acknowledgements

I want to express my thanks to Ineke Boerefijn, Monique Castermans, Fred Grünfeld, and Tiemo Oostenbrink for their comments and to Mignon Senders for her comments and research assistance.

## Notes

1. Jan Egeland, "Focus on Human Rights – Ineffective Big States, Potent Small States," *Journal of Peace Research* 21/3 (1984), 210.
2. By now a classic description is J. J. C. Voorhoeve, *Peace, Profits and Principles: A Study of Dutch Foreign Policy* (The Hague: Martinus Nijhoff, 1979).
3. The Netherlands has 15 million inhabitants in a territory of 16,000 sq. miles.
4. See Peter R. Baehr, "The Netherlands and the United Nations: The Future Lies in the Past," in Chadwick F. Alger, Gene M. Lyons, and John E. Trent, eds., *The United Nations System: The Policies of Member States* (Tokyo: United Nations University Press, 1995), 271–328.
5. See Bas de Gaay Fortman, "De Vredespolitiek van de Radicalen" [The Peace Politics of the Radicals], *Internationale Spectator* 27/4 (February 1973), 109–113.
6. For a number of relevant case-studies see P. P. Everts, ed., *Controversies at Home: Domestic Factors in the Foreign Policy of the Netherlands* (Dordrecht: Martinus Nijhoff, 1985). A summary is contained in Peter R. Baehr and Fred Grünfeld, "Mensenrechten en Buitenlands Beleid: Goedkope Solidariteit" [Human Rights and Foreign Policy: Inexpensive Solidarity], *Intermediair* 21/4 (1 November 1985), 53–59.
7. See Peter R. Baehr, "Problems of Aid Conditionality: The Netherlands and Indonesia," *Third World Quarterly* 18/2 (June 1997), 363–376.
8. Voorhoeve, *Peace, Profits and Principles*, op. cit., 281.
9. Ibid., 49 ff.
10. Ministry of Foreign Affairs of the Netherlands, *Human Rights and Foreign Policy*, Memorandum presented to the Lower House of the States General of the Kingdom of the Netherlands on 3 May 1979 by the Minister for Foreign Affairs and the Minister for Development Cooperation. *Second Chamber of the States General, 1978–1979*, 15 571, nos. 1–2. References are to the official English version of that document; hereafter cited as *Human Rights and Foreign Policy*. Since then, the Foreign Minister has sent three follow-up memoranda to parliament, which basically confirmed the outlines of the 1979 paper: *Tweede Kamer der Staten-Generaal, 1986–1987*, 19 700, no. 125; *Tweede Kamer der Staten-Generaal, 1990–1991*, 21 800, no. 91; *Tweede Kamer der Staten-Generaal, 1996–1997*, 25 300, no. 1. Of these memoranda no official English translations are available.
11. In a meeting with the Parliamentary Committee for Foreign Affairs, 5 June 1997, *Tweede Kamer der Staten-Generaal, 1996–1997*, 25 300, no. 3, p. 11. During that meeting, the Minister for Development Cooperation, Jan Pronk, made the same point (ibid., p. 16);

12. *Human Rights and Foreign Policy*, op. cit., 10.
13. Ibid.
14. Ibid., 96.
15. Ibid., 134, conclusion no. 14.
16. Ibid., 71.
17. Ibid., 12.
18. Advisory Committee on Human Rights and Foreign Policy, *Collective Rights*, Advisory Report No. 19 (The Hague: Ministry of Foreign Affairs, May 1995).
19. Letter from the Foreign Minister to the Chairman of the Advisory Committee on Human Rights and Foreign Policy, 5 March 1996 (translated from the original Dutch). The Minister reconfirmed his position in a second letter, dated 19 November 1996.
20. *Human Rights and Foreign Policy*, op. cit., 10.
21. In its 1997 memorandum, the government reaffirmed that "there are only few collective rights which cannot better be defined as individual rights." Only the right of self-determination was mentioned as "perhaps" an exception to this rule. *Voortgangsnotitie Rechten van de Mens in het Buitenlands Beleid* [Progress Report on Human Rights in Foreign Policy], *Tweede Kamer der Staten-Generaal, 1996–1997*, 25 300, no. 1, 9 April 1997, p. 3 (translated from the original Dutch).
22. *Human Rights and Foreign Policy*, op. cit., 13.
23. Ibid., 11.
24. Ibid., 139, conclusion no. 39.
25. Ibid., 138, conclusion no. 35.
26. Ibid., 138, conclusion no. 34.
27. *A World of Difference: A New Framework for Development Cooperation in the 1990s, Tweede Kamer der Staten-Generaal, 1990–1991*, 21 813, nos. 1–2; hereafter cited as *A World of Difference*. Though written by Mr. Pronk, it reflects official governmental policies.
28. This paragraph is partly based on a study by Oda van Cranenburgh, "Development Cooperation and Human Rights: Linkage Politics in the Netherlands," in Peter R. Baehr, Hilde Hey, Jacqueline Smith, and Theresa Swinehart, eds., *Human Rights in Developing Countries: Yearbook 1995* (The Hague: Kluwer Law International, 1995), 29–55.
29. *A World of Difference*, op. cit., 61.
30. Ibid., 61.
31. Ibid., 171.
32. Ibid., 211.
33. *A World in Dispute* (The Hague: Ministry of Foreign Affairs, 1993).
34. Ibid., 26.
35. *Human Rights and Foreign Policy*, op. cit., 135, conclusion no. 20.
36. Ibid., 133, conclusion no. 14.
37. Ibid., 136, conclusion no. 24.
38. Ibid., 135, conclusion no. 19.
39. Ibid., 135, conclusion no. 21.
40. Ibid., 134, conclusion no. 14.
41. Ibid., 133, conclusion no. 13.
42. Ibid., 134, conclusion no. 14.
43. Ibid., 134, conclusion no. 17.
44. Ibid., 134, conclusion no. 18.
45. Ibid., 134, conclusion no. 17.
46. Ibid., 134, conclusion no. 15.
47. Ibid., 134, conclusion no. 14.

48. Ibid., 134, conclusion no. 19.
49. Ibid., 135, conclusion no. 20.
50. *Voortgangsnotitie Rechten van de Mens in het Buitenlands Beleid*, op. cit., 7 (translated from the original Dutch). It is not clear whether or not the reference to the "tracks" is the same as earlier statements that human rights are "a central element" of Dutch foreign policy.
51. J. Herman Burgers, "Dutch Nongovernmental Organizations and Foreign Policy in the Field of Human Rights," in P. J. van Krieken & C. O. Pannenborg, eds., *Liber Akkerman: In- and Outlaws in War* (Apeldoorn/Antwerpen: MAKLU, 1992), 161: "The bulk of the protesters opposed the American warfare in Vietnam because they thought it inflicted unjustifiable suffering on the Vietnamese people and not because they wanted to side with the East in the East–West conflict."
52. Commission Justitia et Pax, Dutch Refugee Council, YWCA Netherlands, Working Group Human Rights of the Netherlands Council of Churches, League for Human Rights, the Netherlands Organization for International Development Cooperation, Women's Consultation Group for Development Policy, and the Committee for International Cooperation and Sustainable Development.
53. C. Flinterman and Y. S. Klerk, "The Advisory Committee on Human Rights and Foreign Policy in the Netherlands," *Netherlands Quarterly of Human Rights* 11/3 (1993), 283–292.
54. Almost all of these reports have been translated into English and can be obtained from the Secretary of the Committee at the Ministry of Foreign Affairs. The following reports were issued:
    1. "On an Equal Footing: Foreign Affairs and Human Rights" (1984)
    2. "Support for Human Rights: Suriname and Human Rights" (1984)
    3. "Crossing Borders: The Right to Leave a Country and the Right to Return" (1986)
    4. "Freedom of Information" (1986)
    5. "Development Co-operation and Human Rights" (1987)
    6. "Threatened Women and Refugee Status" (1987)
    7. "Human Rights Conventions under UN Supervision" (1988)
    8. "Towards a Semi-permanent European Commission of Human Rights" (1989)
    9. "The International Mechanism for Supervising Observance of the European Convention on Human Rights and Fundamental Freedoms" (1990)
    10. "Harmonisation of Asylum Law in Western Europe" (1990)
    11. "Democracy and Human Rights in Eastern Europe" (1990)
    12. "Human Rights and International Economic Relations" (1991)
    13. "The Human Dimension of CSCE" (1991)
    14. "The Traffic in Persons" (1992)
    15. "The Use of Force for Humanitarian Purposes" (1992)
    16. "Indigenous Peoples" (1993)
    17. "The 1993 World Conference on Human Rights" (1993)
    18. "Economic, Social and Cultural Human Rights" (1994)
    19. "Collective Rights" (1995)
    20. "The Role of the Sub-Commission on Prevention of Discrimination and Protection of Minorities" (1996)
    21. "The European Union and Human Rights" (1996)
    22. "UN Supervision of Human Rights" (1996)
    23. "National Minorities, with particular reference to Central- and Eastern Europe" (1996)
55. Currently, the cabinet is made up of members of the Labour Party, the Liberal Party, and D66.

56. Christian Democratic Appeal, *Samen Leven Doe Je Niet Alleen* [You Do Not Live Together on Your Own], Draft Election Programme 1998–2002, 40.
57. Labour Party, *Een Wereld te Winnen* [To Gain a World], Draft Election Programme 1998–2002, 58.
58. People's Party for Freedom and Democracy, *Investeren in de Toekomst* [Investing in the Future], Draft Electoral Programme 1998–2002, 53.
59. D66, *Bewogen in Beweging* [Moved in Movement], Draft Election Programme 1998–2002, 52.
60. This arrangement lasted until 1996, when, as the result of a major review of foreign affairs, a separate division for Human Rights, Democracy, and Good Governance was created within the ministry.
61. This view has been reaffirmed by his successor as Foreign Minister, Hans van Mierlo. See *Tweede Kamer der Staten-Generaal, 1996–1997*, 25 300, no. 4, p. 5.
62. Foreign Minister Hans van Mierlo was in addition the political leader of one of the three political parties that made up the government coalition. This made his political position almost unassailable.
63. Researchers from the Netherlands Research School on Human Rights are now engaged in studying whether or not this decrease in attention is also true of the ministry itself and, if so, why.
64. Attention should also be paid to the media, which act both as a channel of communication and as a political factor in their own right.
65. Parts of this and the following paragraphs have been taken from: Peter R. Baehr and Monique C. Castermans-Holleman, "The Promotion of Human Rights – The Netherlands at the UN," in Peter R. Baehr and Monique C. Castermans-Holleman, eds., *The Netherlands and the United Nations: Selected Issues* (The Hague: T. M. C. Asser Institute, 1990), 29–30.
66. UNGA Resolution 37/194.
67. For a detailed presentation of this case-study, see Peter R. Baehr, "The General Assembly: Negotiating the Convention on Torture," in David P. Forsythe, ed., *The United Nations in the World Political Economy: Essays in Honor of Leon Gordenker* (London: Macmillan, 1989), 36–53. See also J. Herman Burgers, "An Arduous Delivery: The United Nations Convention against Torture (1984)," in Johan Kaufmann, ed., *Effective Negotiation: Case Studies in Conference Diplomacy* (Dordrecht: Kluwer, 1989), 45–52. It then took the Netherlands four years before it finally ratified the Convention. The Netherlands had not yet ratified the Convention when it entered into force in 1987, precluding it from being a candidate for membership of the Committee against Torture, which supervises observance of the Convention. This delay was partly caused by Dutch legal tradition, which calls for a meticulous search of needed changes in domestic legislation before a treaty is ratified. In other countries, a treaty may be ratified at an earlier stage, while the process of studying domestic legislation is still in progress.
68. This was recalled by the Commission in 1995 in a resolution in which it appealed to states to enact legislation and to take measures aimed at exemption from military service on the basis of genuinely held conscientious objection to armed service (Resolution 1995/83). See also *Report of the Secretary-General Prepared Pursuant to Commission Resolution 1995/83*, E/CN.4/1997/99, 16 January 1997.
69. He served in that position until 1993, when he was appointed Minister of Foreign Affairs. Nigel Rodley, a British subject and former legal adviser to Amnesty International, succeeded him as UN Rapporteur on Torture.
70. Advisory Report no. 20 (The Hague: Ministry of Foreign Affairs, January 1996).
71. Advisory Report no. 22 (The Hague: Ministry of Foreign Affairs, October 1996).

72. "Human Rights Questions: Human Rights Situations and Reports of Special Rapporteurs and Special Representatives," UNGA A/52/64, 29 January 1997.
73. In this paper, no fine distinction is made between violations of human rights law and humanitarian law. For the victims of extra-judicial executions, torture, abduction, rape, and arbitrary detention, such as have happened in the former Yugoslavia and elsewhere, it does not make much difference whether such abuses occur in a situation that is legally defined as a state of war or non-war.
74. UN Security Council Resolution 819, 16 April 1993.
75. The operation was at first perceived in the Netherlands as having been quite successful. See Leon Wecke, "Het Jaar van de Nasleep: De Val van Srebrenica" [The Year of Aftermath: The Fall of Srebrenica], *Jaarboek Vrede en Veiligheid* (Nijmegen: Studiecentrum voor Vredesvraagstukken, 1996), 136. The Dutch soldiers were received in Zagreb, Croatia, in a festive ceremony attended by a number of Dutch dignitaries, including Crown Prince Willem Alexander, Prime Minister Wim Kok, and Minister of Defence Joris Voorhoeve: "A party, complete with a forty-two-piece brass band playing Glenn Miller songs, cases of beer and drunken Dutch soldiers dancing in a chorus line, was thrown that afternoon" (David Rohde, *A Safe Area: Srebrenica: Europe's Worst Massacre Since the Second World War*, London: Pocket Books, 1997, 325). The authorities only later realized that this grand reception was quite out of proportion to what had happened.
76. Jan Willem Honig and Norbert Both, *Srebrenica: Record of a War Crime* (Harmondsworth, Middx: Penguin Books, 1996). According to official UN figures, 7,079 men were listed as missing. See also Frank Westerman and Bart Rijs, *Srebrenica: Het Zwartste Scenario* [Srebrenica: The Blackest Scenario] (Amsterdam/Antwerp: Uitgeverij Atlas, 1997).
77. Letter from the Minister of Foreign Affairs to the Parliamentary Committees of Foreign Affairs and Defence, 24 June 1996; letter from the Ministers of Foreign Affairs and of Defence to the Second Chamber of parliament, 6 September 1996: "The government was forced to conclude that such an investigation was seen as most unusual and lacking sufficient support.... Therefore, the government has decided not to put a formal request to the Secretary-General" (translated from the original Dutch). In a letter dated 28 October 1996, the Foreign Minister elaborated this point as follows: "It must be concluded that our conversation partners [in New York] showed a certain amount of embarrassment about the Dutch probes. On the one hand, they did not want to offend the Netherlands, while on the other hand, they did not consider the investigation desired by the Netherlands as opportune at this juncture of the Bosnian problem. It is against this background that one should view the official reaction by the UN Secretary-General, when he stated that a possible request by the Netherlands to the UN to start an independent investigation would be without precedent and raise many preliminary questions. Only when clarity had been reached about these questions, could he determine how and under whose responsibility such an investigation could be executed" (*Tweede Kamer der Staten-Generaal, 1996–1997*, 25 069, no. 2, 28 October 1996, translated from the original Dutch). For the parliamentary debate about this letter, see *Tweede Kamer der Staten-Generaal, 1996–1997*, 25 069, no. 6, 13 November 1996.
78. "RIOD-onderzoek naar Srebrenica kan jaren duren" [RIOD Research on Srebrenica May Take Years], *De Volkskrant* (Amsterdam), 31 October 1996.
79. Though perhaps less so than in the case of Canada, Belgium, and Italy, whose soldiers serving with the United Nations peacekeeping force in Somalia were themselves alleged to have taken part in cruel, inhuman, or degrading behaviour toward Somalian civilians.

80. According to Honig and Both, the heavier weapons were considered "too heavy and too aggressive" (Honig and Both, *Srebrenica*, op. cit., 125).
81. Studies published so far tend to put a great deal of blame on the commander of UNPROFOR, French general Bernard Janvier, who refused to give the necessary orders. Rohde (*A Safe Area*, op. cit., 368) calls Janvier "more responsible than any other individual for the fall of Srebrenica."
82. A systematic debriefing took place later. On the basis of the debriefing, a report was published by the Ministry of Defence: *Rapport Gebaseerd op de Debriefing Srebrenica* [Report Based on Debriefing Srebrenica], Assen, 4 October 1995. Rohde (*A Safe Area*, op. cit., 327–328) calls this debriefing report "an exercise in obfuscation."
83. In addition to its obligatory assessment of 495,000 guilders (about US$250,000), the Dutch government spends an annual amount of about 5.8 million guilders (US$2.9 million) on security, telephone costs, etc. (information supplied by the Permanent Mission of the Netherlands to the United Nations in New York).
84. From 1993 to 1995, Professor Theo van Boven; since 1995, Mrs. Dorothee de Sampayo Garrido-Nijgh.
85. See David P. Forsythe, "International Criminal Courts: A Political View," *Netherlands Quarterly of Human Rights* 15/1 (March 1997), 5–19.
86. Joint Declaration on Fundamental Rights by the European Parliament, Council and Commission of 5 April 1977, [1977] OJ C 103/1; Declaration on Human Rights of the Ministers of Foreign Affairs meeting in the framework of European Political Cooperation and Council, 21 July 1986, Bull. EC 7/8–1986, 2.4.4; Declaration on Human Rights of the Luxembourg European Council (28 and 29 June 1991), in C. Duparc, *The European Community and Human Rights* (Luxembourg: Office for official publications of the European Communities, 1993), 48–51.
87. The Treaty of Amsterdam, which was concluded in June 1997 and which has not yet entered into force, basically leaves this situation unchanged. The European Council of Ministers may take decisions by unanimity "on common strategies to be implemented by the Union in areas where the Member States have important interests in common."
88. M. C. Castermans-Holleman, "De 53e Zitting van de VN Commissie voor de Rechten van de Mens" [The 53rd Session of the UN Commission on Human Rights], *NJCM Bulletin* 22/5 (1997), 668.
89. Johannes van der Klaauw, "European Union," *Netherlands Quarterly of Human Rights* 15/2 (June 1997), 210.
90. See also Ann Kent, "China and the International Human Rights Regime: A Case Study of Multilateral Monitoring, 1989–1994," *Human Rights Quarterly* 17/1 (February 1995), 1–47
91. However, the Dutch Foreign Minister, Hans van Mierlo, addressing the Commission on Human Rights on behalf of the European Union on 13 March 1997, had castigated China for keeping a well-known human rights defender, Wei Jingsheng, imprisoned. On 8 April 1997, the Dutch delegate, Peter van Wulfften Palthe, again speaking on behalf of the European Union, criticized China for its "system of re-education through labour and the excessive use of the death penalty." He continued as follows: "The continued and increased prosecution of those with dissenting views is a worrying development, as well as the number of people detained arbitrarily or detained simply because of their views. We are also concerned about human rights in Tibet. We call upon the government of China to cease all activities that threaten the distinct cultural, ethnic and religious identity of Tibetans. We also remain concerned about prison conditions in China. Notably, we deplore the lack of medical care and the use of forced labour." I have been assured by the Dutch Ministry of Foreign Affairs that this speech had received the prior approval of all members of the EU. Apparently, the political

issue was the possible adoption of a resolution, not so much a speech that was equally critical of China's human rights record.

92. Max van der Stoel, "De Rol van de Hoge Commissaris inzake Nationale Minderheden [The Role of the High Commissioner on National Minorities], *Internationale Spectator* 48/3 (March 1994), 102.
93. See Rob Zaagman and Joanne Thorburn, *The Role of the High Commissioner on National Minorities in OSCE Conflict Prevention: An Introduction* (The Hague: Foundation on Inter-Ethnic Relations, June 1997).
94. These two organs were merged when the 11th Protocol entered into force in 1998. See Yvonne Klerk, "Protocol No. 11 to the European Convention for Human Rights: A Drastic Revision of the Supervisory Mechanism under the ECHR," *Netherlands Quarterly of Human Rights* 14/1 (March 1996), 35–46.
95. *Voortgangsnotitie Rechten van de Mens in het Buitenlands Beleid*, 29–31.
96. Ibid., 30.
97. *Tweede Kamer der Staten-Generaal, 1996–1997*, 25 300, no. 3, 5 June 1997, p. 12.
98. See Leo Zwaak, "A Friendly Settlement in the European Inter-State Complaints Against Turkey," *SIM Newsletter* 13 (February 1986), 44–48. This critical view was confirmed in December 1992, when the European Committee for the Prevention of Torture issued a rare public report, which concluded that the practice of torture and other forms of severe ill-treatment of persons in police custody still remained widespread in Turkey. See European Committee for the Prevention of Torture and Inhuman or Degrading Treatment or Punishment, *Public Statement on Turkey*, adopted on 15 December 1992. The Committee reiterated its criticism of Turkish practices in another public report, issued in December 1996: *Public Statement on Turkey*, CPT/Inf(96)34, 6 December 1996. Turkey was one of five countries selected by Amnesty International for special attention in its submission to the 1997 session of the UN Commission on Human Rights: *1997 UN Commission on Human Rights – 50 Years Old*, AI INDEX: IOR 41/01/97, January 1997.
99. During a parliamentary debate, the Dutch Minister of Foreign Affairs, Hans van Mierlo, said that the states' complaints procedure under the European Convention on Human Rights was only seldom used because of the political nature of such complaints. The minister also said that Turkey was repeatedly addressed in the Council of Europe for its violations of human rights and that therefore less attention was given to it in other international gatherings. "It must be stated that the states' complaint has not met with the expectations of its designers, which could be a reason to think about other, better forms" (*Tweede Kamer der Staten-Generaal, 1996–1997*, 25 300, no. 3, 5 June 1997, pp. 15–16; translated from the original Dutch).
100. This paragraph contains material that was published before in Peter R. Baehr, "Problems of Aid Conditionality: The Netherlands and Indonesia," *Third World Quarterly*, 18/2 (June 1997), 363–376.
101. For a comparative case-study, see Peter R. Baehr, Hilde Selbervik, and Arne Tostensen, "Responses to Human Rights Criticism: Kenya–Norway and Indonesia–the Netherlands," in Baehr, Hey, Smith, and Swinehart, eds., *Human Rights in Developing Countries: Yearbook 1995*, op. cit., 57–87.
102. The statement was made before the murderous *coup d'état* of Prime Minister Hun Sen in July 1997.
103. *Tweede Kamer der Staten-Generaal, 1996–1997*, 25 300, no. 3, 5 June 1997, p. 17.
104. For an account of similar problems in the relationship between the Netherlands and Vietnam, see Duco Hellema, "Nederland en de Wederopbouw van Vietnam" [The Netherlands and the Reconstruction of Vietnam], *Internationale Spectator* 47/7–8 (July/August 1993), 426–434.

105. Peer Baneke, *Nederland en de Indonesische Gevangenen* [The Netherlands and the Indonesian Prisoners] (Amsterdam: Wiardi Beckman Stichting, 1983), 9.
106. As late as August 1995, on the occasion of the celebration of the fiftieth anniversary of Indonesian independence, three prominent political prisoners were released, including former deputy prime minister Subandrio, who had been under arrest for 30 years.
107. Draft policy review paper on Indonesia, as quoted by Mr. Pronk himself in Baneke, *Nederland en de Indonesische Gevangenen*, op. cit., 100.
108. See Hans Goderbauer, "Indonesia and East Timor," in Bård Anders Andreassen and Theresa Swinehart, eds., *Human Rights in Developing Countries Yearbook 1993* (Oslo: Nordic Human Rights Publications, 1993), 137. For a comparative analysis of Canadian and Dutch reaction see David Gillies, *Between Principle and Practice: Human Rights in North–South Relations* (Montreal: McGill-Queen's University Press, 1996), 174-198.
109. Nico G. Schulte Nordholt, "Aid and Conditionality: The Case of Dutch–Indonesian Relationships," in Olav Stokke, ed., *Aid and Political Conditionality* (London: Frank Cass, 1995), 141.
110. Katarina Tomasevski, *Development Aid and Human Rights Revisited* (London: Pinter, 1993), 113. The United States stopped its aid programme to Indonesia in June 1992. But Tomasevski comments: "Indonesia did not lose much aid – at the donor meeting in July 1992 USD 4. 94 billion was approved, more than the previous year, and even slightly more than the World Bank had recommended." See also Andrew MacIntyre, "Indonesia in 1992: Coming to Terms with the Outside World," *Asian Survey* 2 (February 1993), 204–211.
111. Press release by the Indonesian government, 25 March 1992.
112. See Nederlands Juristen Comité voor de Rechten van de Mens, "De Gebeurtenissen in Paramaribo, Suriname, 8–13 December 1982: de Gewelddadige Dood van 14 Surinamers en 1 Nederlander" [The Events in Paramaribo, Suriname, 8–13 December 1982: The Violent Death of 14 Surinamese and 1 Dutchman], 14 February 1983; "De Recente Gebeurtenissen in Suriname: Verslag van een Mondeling Overleg" [The Recent Events in Suriname: Report of an Oral Consultation], *Tweede Kamer der Staten-Generaal, 1982–1983*, 17723, no. 1.; Inter-American Commission on Human Rights, *Report on the Situation of Human Rights in Suriname,* OAS/Ser.L/II.61 Doc. 6, Rev. 1, 5 October 1983; SIM, "Suriname," in Manfred Nowak and Theresa Swinehart, eds., *Human Rights in Developing Countries Yearbook 1989* (Kehl: N. P. Engel, 1989), 352–375; Marcel Zwamborn, "Suriname," in Bård-Anders Andreassen and Theresa Swinehart, eds., *Human Rights in Developing Countries Yearbook 1991* (Oslo: Scandinavian University Press, 1992), 286–314; Caroline Ort, "Suriname," in Baehr, Hey, Smith, and Swinehart, eds., *Human Rights in Developing Countries Yearbook 1995*, op. cit., 367–401.
113. Development cooperation between Surinam and the Netherlands formed part of a bilateral treaty concluded in 1975, according to which the Netherlands was obligated to provide 3,500 million guilders over a period of 10–15 years to Surinam to carry out a long-term development programme.
114. That was made evident when in August 1995 no fewer than 50 high-ranking representatives of Dutch business firms – the largest delegation of its kind – visited Indonesia in the wake of Queen Beatrix's official visit.
115. See Dionne Bosma, "The Dutch–Suriname Treaty on Development Assistance: A Correct Appeal to Fundamental Change of Circumstances?" *Leiden Journal of International Law* 3/2 (October 1990), 201–220.
116. Advisory Committee on Human Rights and Foreign Policy, *Aid for Human Rights: Suriname and Human Rights*, Advisory Report No. 2 (The Hague: Ministry of Foreign Affairs, 1984), 13 (translation from the original Dutch).

117. The Advisory Committee on Human Rights and Foreign Policy has called the suspension of aid to Surinam "politically unavoidable" (*Aid for Human Rights*, op. cit., 22).
118. Ibid., 20.
119. This idea was proposed by the UN Committee on Economic, Social and Cultural Rights and received support from the Dutch Advisory Committee on Human Rights and Foreign Policy: *Economic, Social and Cultural Human Rights*, Advisory Report no. 18 (The Hague, 1994), 15–16.
120. The European Parliament has adopted a resolution in which it expressed its disappointment at the lack of progress in the development of a common foreign policy. Sending delegates to places of crisis was not considered sufficient. The EU ignores situations where agreements on human rights and democratization are being violated. The member states were asked to give their unconditional support to the Common Foreign and Security Policy of the Union, as stipulated in the Maastricht Treaty (Resolution A4-0193/97).
121. *De Herijking van het Buitenlands Beleid* [Review of Foreign Policy] (The Hague: Ministry of Foreign Affairs, September 1995), 41.
122. *Formatieplan Ministerie van Buitenlandse Zaken* [Job Formation Plan Ministry of Foreign Affairs] (The Hague: Ministry of Foreign Affairs, 1996), 59.
123. See Philip P. Everts, ed., *Dilemma's in de Buitenlandse Politiek van Nederland* [Dilemmas in the Foreign Policy of the Netherlands] (Leiden: DSWO Press, 1996).
124. The man who is widely regarded as the mastermind behind the 1982 assassinations, Colonel Desi Bouterse, currently holds the position of senior adviser to the government of Surinam, and is reputedly the real political leader of the country. Because of his alleged involvement in the international trade in drugs, the Netherlands government asked Interpol in early August 1997 to circulate an international call for his arrest. This helped to further freeze the relations between the two countries.
125. It remains a matter of surprise that it was the Minister of Defence, rather than the Minister of Foreign Affairs, who was the main butt of public criticism on the issue of Srebrenica.

# 4

# British foreign policy and human rights: From low to high politics

*Sally Morphet*

## I. Introduction

British foreign policy on human rights has been driven primarily by three factors: Britain's own national development; its perceived national interests; and international discourse and action on human rights. Understanding Britain's national development helps to explain why there is no general consensus on human rights within Britain and how this has affected the main political parties. In general there are both differences and similarities between British human rights foreign policy and that of its main partners – certain continental Europeans and the United States. British governments have normally concentrated on the promotion and protection of civil and political rights plus occasionally a few economic and social rights (e.g. the right to education).[1] Arms sales and aid policy in the 1990s are discussed in the section on bilateral policy.

The chapter begins by looking at the historical development of Britain's interest in human rights both domestically and internationally before it joined the European Economic Community (EEC, now the European Union) in 1973 and became a founding member of the Conference on Security and Cooperation in Europe (CSCE, now OSCE) in 1975. It goes on to discuss the presentation of British foreign policy in this area in three Foreign Policy Documents of 1978, 1991, and 1996 following British ratification of the International Covenants on Civil and Political Rights (ICCPR) and Economic, Social, and Cultural Rights (ICESCR) in

1976, and the new directions introduced by the incoming Labour government in 1997 and the means through which it operates. It then explores the major domestic factors influencing British human rights foreign policy and goes on to delineate British multilateral and bilateral human rights policy (on both a global and a regional level).

In many ways the analysis bears out the contention that foreign policy may be most usefully considered not in terms of the legal and constitutional framework of sovereignty and statehood, of law-making and war-making, but rather as the product of a complex interplay of international, transnational, and domestic influences.[2] But, as will also be seen, law (both national and international) and respect for law remain central to the development of human rights foreign policy in Britain[3] for all political parties. This is why the main emphasis in this chapter is given to the rights from the Universal Declaration that were put into legally binding form in the ICCPR and the ICESCR and the similar rights in the European Convention on Human Rights and its concomitant Social Charter.

## II. The historical context

In terms of human rights Britain has been particularly influenced by its distinctive history and its concern for precedent as well as by its general Western and conservative orientation on human rights questions.

### *The basic history*

The English Bill of Rights of 1689 is usually regarded as the first major document of modern constitutional history. Lauterpacht argues that, although it was the work of Churchmen and of the rich Whig gentry who perpetuated their hold on the country to the exclusion of the masses of the people by submitting the Crown to the supremacy of Parliament and by enthroning the right of resistance as part of a fundamental constitutional document, it accomplished the greatest thing done by the English nation.[4] It contained such civil rights as equality before the law, trial by jury, and the prohibition of inhuman treatment and of excessive bail or fines.[5] (Freedom from arbitrary arrest had already been secured by the Habeas Corpus Acts of 1640 and 1679.) Political rights proclaimed included the prohibition of the levying of money without the consent of Parliament, and provision for the free election of Members of Parliament, for frequent sessions, and for immunity of the proceedings of Parliament. However the Bill was not designed to "establish a comprehensive set of rights for the people as a whole" and tended to reinforce "existing inequalities and discriminations" by, for example, giving special rights to Protestants, "who alone were allowed to bear arms."[6]

Freedom of the press was established by the decision not to renew the Licensing Act in 1695, and the beginning of religious freedom was established by the Toleration Act of 1689. Independence of the judiciary was established by the Act of Settlement (1700).

This British tradition stemmed from constitutional charters of liberty (in particular the Magna Carta), a strong legal framework, and the ideas of men like Locke who considered that sovereignty pertained to the people as a whole and that the individual conveyed to society as a whole the right to exercise certain functions best exercised collectively.[7] This tradition was one of the principal factors behind the major eighteenth-century declarations on rights in the United States (the 1776 Virginia Bill of Rights and the Declaration of Independence) and France (the Declarations of 1789 and of 1793, which included references to economic and social rights).[8]

These latter influenced a number of European and Latin American constitutions in the nineteenth century. By contrast, the rights that came to the fore in Britain and the United States at the same time were those concerned with political participation, a transformation linked to democratization.[9] Solutions to the problems posed by the industrial revolution were often couched in terms of economic and social rights. Trade unions were legalized in Britain progressively from 1871. The International Labour Organization (ILO; now a UN specialized agency) was set up by the Treaty of Versailles in 1919, though it was not controlled by the League of Nations.

These developments had been enriched by a long-standing tradition of Western thinking going back to the Greeks, followed by Stoic conceptions of natural law and the emergence of Christianity with its assumption that Christians must distinguish between service to God and the State; to the affirmation of the existence of a natural higher law in the Middle Ages and its tradition of charters of liberties, rights, and franchises; and to Vitoria, who in the sixteenth century argued that primitive peoples were entitled to the protection of law. These ideas were put into a modern international context with the Peace of Westphalia (1648), which contained provisions about the rights of religious groups and ushered in the system of equal sovereign states with the ending of the Thirty Years War and the claims of superiority of the Holy Roman Empire. Grotius had already maintained (1625) that standards of justice applicable to individuals were valid in relation to states and originated the idea of humanitarian intervention for the protection of individual rights. Ideas on self-determination for states began to be expressed during the nineteenth century with the setting up of states such as Greece and the unification of Germany and Italy. They were given an even greater prominence by President Wilson after the First World War and were behind the institution of mandates by the League of Nations.

### *The 1940s to the 1960s*

The carnage of the Second World War propelled human rights ideas forward, giving rise to the making of the UN Charter (1945), the Universal Declaration (1948), and the two succeeding major Covenants – the ICCPR and the ICESCR – which put the rights in the Human Rights Declaration into binding legal instruments. Britain played a major part in this standard-setting and in the making of similar regional instruments – the European Convention on Human Rights (ECHR) of 1953, which set up a Court of Human Rights, and its accompanying Social Charter (1965).

One major British interest that then needed to be protected was its colonial inheritance. Both its major political parties considered in the 1940s that colonial rule was not an oppressive relationship, but rather a partnership between Britain and its dependent territories.[10] This concern influenced British policy towards the right of individual petition and self-determination. The government feared that individual petition might be used as a weapon of political agitation in the Cold War and that it might subvert the respect of dependent peoples for the established imperial authorities.[11] They therefore made sure that individual petition was added to the first Protocol of the ICCPR (which Britain has never ratified) and not to the ICCPR itself or to the draft ECHR.[12] The government also tried, unsuccessfully, to ensure that the article on self-determination was not added to the draft Covenants by the United Nations' third world constituency. By the early 1960s, however, decolonization had made the issue less urgent and the political implications of the articles on self-determination seemed less important.[13] Britain accepted the right of petition for individuals in Britain under the ECHR as early as 1966,[14] and for individuals in its Crown Dependencies and dependent territories in 1967. It signed both the Covenants in 1968.

By the 1960s human rights were given more publicity as international outrage over the South African government's apartheid policies grew in the United Nations (particularly after the admission of 16 Black African states in 1960) and in the Commonwealth – fanned by non-governmental organizations (NGOs) such as the British-based Anti-Apartheid Movement founded in 1959.[15] The British government voted for the preparation of a UN Convention against Racial Discrimination in 1963,[16] and in 1965 passed the first British Race Relations Act and voted for the ensuing

Convention. In 1966 it decided "that Articles 55 and 56 of the Charter impose on member Governments of the United Nations a positive obligation to pursue a policy designed to promote respect for and observance of human rights and to co-operate within the United Nations to that end ... The South African government's policy over apartheid is a clear breach of obligation according to this interpretation." This generous interpretation of Articles 55 and 56 enabled the British government both to avoid using Article 2.7 (on intervention in the domestic jurisdiction of a state) and to express concern more appropriately over human rights breaches in other states. The British government went on to ratify the Racial Discrimination Convention in 1969 and presented its first report to the monitoring Committee in 1971.

## III. Basic elements of British human rights foreign policy

There is much continuity between aspects of British human rights policies in the 1970s and subsequently. Britain was influenced by its new membership of the European Economic Community, which it joined in 1973, and its participation in the 1973–1975 diplomatic meeting that launched the on-going Conference on Security and Cooperation in Europe. Overall the main thrust of its policy moved from concern with colonial issues and standard-setting to the problems raised by the implementation of human rights legal standards at both international and regional level, and the continuing debate on the place of human rights in foreign policy following British ratification of both the ICCPR and the ICESCR in 1976 – the year they came into force. In 1977, a Foreign and Commonwealth Office (FCO) minister, Evan Luard, began a detailed examination of British human rights policy. This, in a new departure in 1978, was given a partial public airing in a Foreign Policy Document on *British Policy towards the United Nations*.[17] This document and two subsequent Foreign Policy Documents of 1991 and 1996 (both called *Human Rights in Foreign Policy*) issued after the end of the Cold War, described below, remain some of the most useful sources for British government thinking about human rights and foreign policy over this period. They have been built on by the new Labour government since May 1997.

### *The Foreign Policy Documents – 1978, 1991, 1996*

The 1978 Foreign Policy Document included a 13-page British paper on "Human Rights and Foreign Policy," which tried to answer a number of questions on a range of human rights foreign policy issues. What steps can be taken in relation to other countries where glaring violations of human rights occur? This looked at 14 categories of possible actions that could be taken, as well as the United Kingdom's legal and political standing to raise human rights with foreign governments; policy considerations; possible aid adjustments; arms exports; and trade sanctions. Should the government attempt a consistent application of rules or treat each country on an ad hoc basis? The important answer was that Britain should have a consistent posture on human rights throughout the world; the government should undertake an annual consideration of the performance of each country and the implications for British policy towards it; posts should include regular reports on this area; submissions and briefings to ministers on, for instance, arms and aid should refer to human rights issues. Should the government concentrate particularly on the worst offenders of all? The FCO should consider this but should avoid the appearance of a vendetta. It should work with the EEC, the United States, and Commonwealth partners.

On the UN side it asked: What action can Britain take to improve the effectiveness of the UN Commission on Human Rights in dealing with such questions? The government should try to improve the effectiveness of the Commission in conjunction with other Western countries. What other actions are open to the government to improve the United Nations' performance in this field? It should continue to press for a High Commissioner for Human Rights and find ways of improving the United Nations' performance on human rights by pressing the British General Assembly initiative of 1974 on alternative ways of improving the enjoyment of human rights in the UN system.

On other possibilities it noted, could the government expand the activities of other organs? It should explore the possibility of establishing regional commissions with Britain's EC partners, beginning in Africa. Are there particular human rights issues and abuses that the government should press particularly hard to discuss? The British priority should remain violations against the integrity of the person. Britain should recognize the third world emphasis on economic rights but should not allow this as an excuse for the violation of basic human rights.

What can the government do to support the non-official organizations, such as the International Commission for Jurists, Amnesty International, and so on? It should continue to support them without infringing their independence. What more can or should Britain do in public statements to demonstrate its concern on such matters? The government should continue making statements in appropriate venues, including the House of Commons. What steps should it take to consult and cooperate with other governments, especially its EEC partners and the United States, in any or all of these actions? Britain should continue to work with the

EEC, the United States and other NATO allies, the Commonwealth and like-minded nations including non-Western countries with excellent human rights records.

The 1978 Foreign Policy Document went on to give details of British bilateral human rights policy in the context of aid, arms exports, and trade. On aid it revealed that ministers had privately urged Indonesian leaders to release detainees, and that at a recent meeting of the Inter-Governmental Group on Indonesia (an international aid donors' consortium) the leader of the British delegation had pointed out that the early release of detainees would make it easier to defend its aid to Indonesia. It noted that the government had decided not to offer aid to the mining equipment sector in Bolivia or to enter into new aid commitments to Ethiopia. In two cases (both under the previous Conservative government) Britain had phased out its aid entirely following serious human rights violations: Uganda in November 1972 and Chile[18] in March 1974 (except for a small educational technical cooperation programme). Britain had also used its influence in the EEC on Uganda and Equatorial Guinea. On arms exports it stated that there had been embargoes on arms sales to South Africa since 1964 and to Chile since 1974. Exports of arms and military equipment were subject to license by officials at the Department of Trade after consulting the Ministry of Defence, the FCO, and, sometimes, ministers. More problems occurred in the context of trade, where the only example was the special case of Rhodesia. Using trade as a means of putting pressure created problems: the mechanics were difficult; markets could also simply be handed to British competitors; retaliation against British investments or exports could also be expected.

The pamphlet also supported the use of the confidential ECOSOC 1503 procedure (examining complaints against countries sent to the UN Secretary-General by individuals and NGOs) by the UN Human Rights Commission. It noted that Britain had used it to pursue the cases of both Uganda and Chile.

The Labour government felt comfortable with the US Carter administration,[19] which had both written the first comprehensive Country Reports on Human Rights Practices, and, in October 1977, signed both Covenants. In the section on human rights at the United Nations in the Foreign Policy Document, the government welcomed the increased attention being devoted to human rights and its agencies and shared the US appreciation of regional human rights bodies. It considered that measures to expand UN human rights activities should be based on existing machinery and systems. It thought that the ECOSOC 1503 procedure was the most effective way of investigating human rights abuses in the UN machinery, that the Human Rights Commission should concentrate on the effective implementation of international instruments on human rights, and that Britain should continue to press for a High Commissioner on Human Rights.

This initiative was not repeated until January 1991, when detailed guidelines summarizing British policy and practice on human rights as they had evolved in recent years were published in a further Foreign Policy Document.[20] They reflected not so much a change of policy as a recognition on the part of ministers and officials, at home and abroad, that there is a need for greater emphasis on the human rights dimension of UK foreign policy. As its introduction pointed out, "developments in Eastern Europe have demonstrated both the corrosive effect that a prolonged record of human rights abuses can have on the stability of a regime and that a consistent Western policy of support for human rights can over time lend powerful impetus to forces working for political pluralism and the rule of law."

The 1991 Foreign Policy Document went on to discuss universal human rights standards; the government's standing to raise human rights; ways in which the government raises human rights (bilateral action, joint action with the EU, and multilateral action in the context of the United Nations, the Commonwealth, the Council of Europe, and the CSCE – details are given in the sections on multilateral and bilateral policy); aid; defence sales; responding to public and parliamentary concerns; raising human rights with other governments; responding to questions about Britain's own human rights performance, as well as the responsibilities of posts abroad and departments within the FCO. A further Foreign Policy Document on *Human Rights in Foreign Policy* was issued in 1996.[21] This, as in 1991, noted that it reflected a recognition on the part of ministers and officials that there was a need for greater emphasis on the human rights dimension of British foreign policy. It stated that Britain and other UN members had a legal obligation under the UN Charter to promote and protect human rights.

### *The new Labour government and human rights, 1997*

On 12 May 1997 the new Labour Foreign Secretary issued a Mission Statement for the FCO whose aim was to promote the national interests of the United Kingdom and to contribute to a strong world community. Four benefits were sought: security; prosperity; quality of life; and mutual respect. For mutual respect it noted: "We shall work through international forums and bilateral relationships to spread the values of human rights, civil liberties and democracy which we demand for ourselves." He opened the press conference launching the Statement by stating: "the Labour Government will put human rights at the heart of our foreign policy and will publish an annual report on our work in promoting human rights abroad." The government also announced that it would incorporate the ECHR into British domestic law.[22]

In early July 1997, a major review of British policy towards international human rights instruments was announced, including the question of accession to Protocols to the ECHR and the ICCPR and the acceptance of the right of individual petition under other human rights treaties. The government would also consider whether any of Britain's reservations to human rights treaties could be withdrawn. Britain would work to strengthen the UN Register of Conventional Arms. This was followed by a major speech[23] by the Foreign Secretary on 17 July in which he discussed six core civil and political rights from the Universal Declaration that he considered Britain had a duty to demand for those who did not yet enjoy them. He noted that the World Bank had recently concluded that the economies with faster growth were those where political equality has produced the fairest shares of income, and that the separate Department for International Development would soon publish a White Paper setting out policies for tackling global poverty and promoting sustainable development.

He then set 12 policies to put into effect the British human rights commitment, including: giving support to measures within the international community to condemn regimes that grotesquely violate human rights; supporting sanctions applied by the international community; refusing arms equipment to problematic regimes; ensuring trade measures did not undermine human rights (e.g. in the context of child labour); supporting measures at multilateral conferences and in bilateral contacts that criticize abuses of human rights; calling for observance of universal standards; supporting a permanent International Criminal Court and providing more resources for international criminal tribunals; ensuring that the UK Military Assistance Training Scheme better supports UK human rights objectives; giving stronger support to the media under threat from authoritarian regimes; publishing an annual report on the government's activities; and ensuring that Britain's own record can be respected.

### *Means*

The Foreign and Commonwealth Office (FCO), formed in 1968,[24] takes the lead on questions of human rights and foreign policy, though certain legal issues may be discussed with the Lord Chancellor's Department and the Home Office. Human rights foreign policy is, of course, ultimately set by ministers in the context of British legal obligations under the human rights instruments to which Britain is a party. The Human Rights Policy Department (formerly part of the United Nations Department) within the FCO deals with human rights issues on a regional level and throughout the UN system. This was set up as a Human Rights Policy Unit in 1992 and became a Department (HRPD) two years later. Like other FCO departments, it is advised by a Legal Adviser and has access to researchers.

Members of HRPD and diplomats from New York and Geneva discuss human rights questions at the UN Human Rights Commission (in the spring); the resolutions adopted there are then discussed in the United Nations' Economic and Social Council (in the summer), and subsequently discussed in the Third Committee of the UN General Assembly. HRPD also takes the lead for Britain at major conferences on human rights issues (e.g. Vienna in 1993). It provides briefing and advice to ministers and organizes the submission of the British reports to the different monitoring committees, which usually include major contributions from appropriate domestic departments. Britain now reports to six such committees.[25] HRPD officials also cover major meetings of EU members on human rights and liaise closely on human rights matters with the department that covers the Council of Europe (CoE) at Strasbourg (FCO Legal Advisers are closely involved, particularly with proceedings under the ECHR in which they act as agent for the government) and the OSCE. The ILO, which deals *inter alia* with trade union human rights matters, is covered by British diplomats at Geneva (as well as the Department for Education and Employment, which send officials to its annual meetings). UNESCO, which also deals with certain human rights questions, is (when Britain is a member) handled by diplomats from the British Embassy in Paris under the aegis of the Department for International Development.

Human rights matters at a country level are reported on from posts, who send reports to appropriate FCO geographical departments, to the HRPD, and to the OSCE/CoE Department. Civil servants in these and previous departments have worked closely with certain NGOs since the mid-1970s (see below). FCO researchers and others maintain close contacts with academics.

## IV. Domestic factors

British citizens and their governments, both Labour and Conservative, have been highly influenced by their evolutionary inheritance, which can be contrasted with the comprehensive codes dear to many continental Europeans. As one recent book dealing with civil and political rights notes, "Citizens of the United Kingdom believe that they are among the freest people in the world, a belief going back to the ancient resistance of Anglo-Saxons to the 'Norman yoke' and the Magna Carta ... Yet the British tradition of ancient 'constitutional rights' is a double-edged legacy. This tradition conflates ideas of 'strong' government and public order with civil liberties, and the first two are usually paramount in the minds of the country's rulers."[26] It has also meant that "the revolutionary ideas of collective enforcement and the right of individual petition to independent outside bodies ... have undoubtedly proved unwelcome to British governments."[27]

Another contemporary author notes the "philosophical gulf" between the British and their fellow Europeans. She argues that British cases in which the European Court of Human Rights has found a violation are most often "cases involving people in the custody of the state or who have turned to it for help," and she suggests that these cases "stem from a failure to recognize that what are at issue are *rights*. In so far as the constitutional system in the United Kingdom regards the interests as privileges, which need to be earned or which are residual and vulnerable to legislative or executive removal, it denies their character as rights."

She suggests that the incorporation of the ECHR will not provide a solution to the failure to recognize that what are at issue are rights. "What is needed is a change of attitude on the part not only of the institutions of government but also of the public at large. They need to learn to think in terms of rights: the incorporation of the Convention could play an educational role."[28]

Another laments "the absence of a charter of fundamental rights" to provide "a framework for individual identity and action when the elements of identity provided by custom and manners no longer suffice."[29]

## *Political parties*

The intellectual inheritance noted above has affected both main political parties and meant that rights language comes more naturally to Labour supporters than to Conservatives. As will already be apparent, most of the initiatives on human rights since the Second World War have been taken by Labour rather than Conservative governments, though they have subsequently been accepted by Conservative governments.[30]

Certain differences between the parties are illustrated by their 1997 election manifestos. The Conservative manifesto did not mention human rights except to state in the section on Parliament that a new Bill of Rights would risk transferring power away from Parliament to legal courts – undermining the democratic supremacy of Parliament as representative of the people. The Liberal Democrats *inter alia* called for the incorporation of the ECHR into British law, for the setting up of a Human Rights Commission to strengthen protection of individual rights, and for the promotion of an enforceable framework of international law, human rights, and the environment. Labour called for the incorporation of the ECHR into British law, stated it would make the protection and promotion of human rights a central part of British foreign policy, and indicated it would work for a permanent international criminal court to investigate genocide, war crimes, and crimes against humanity.

### *Parliament*

Parliamentary interest in human rights questions has become greater over the years as the subject has gained in political importance. A cross-party Parliamentary Human Rights Group was formed in 1976. And a colloquium sponsored by British and United States NGOs on "Human Rights in United States and United Kingdom Foreign Policy" was held in the Palace of Westminster in November 1978.[31] Until 1997 the House of Commons had never focused on human rights overall. The House of Lords examined the question of human rights, democracy, and development in the context of the Council of Europe in 1992.[32] Questions of human rights, of course, also came up in, for instance, the House of Lords' examination of relations between Britain and China in 1994. The Parliamentary Foreign Affairs Committee decided, in 1997, to conduct an inquiry on foreign policy and human rights. The report, which came out in December 1998, covered international obligations, policy objectives, and policy implementation.[33] It attempted to assess the implementation and effects of government policies against the initial policy commitments made by the Foreign Secretary in July 1997 and made 47 specific conclusions and recommendations. The government's reply of March 1999 welcomed the endorsement of the positive changes that had been made and set out further detailed observations on the conclusions and recommendations.[34]

### *Non-governmental organizations*

Domestic pressure groups (now often acting transnationally) have played a role in the making of human rights foreign policy since the 1940s. Pressure from pro-European groups appears to have been particularly effective in the early 1950s.[35] Other well-known pressure groups often date back to the 1960s (e.g. Amnesty International founded in 1961). The first parliamentary question that referred to these new pressure groups was asked in 1966.[36] British governments have been working closely with a number of these groups in the human rights arena since the Labour government of the late 1970s first began to meet with them and discuss aspects of human rights. Many are extremely involved with aspects of the United Nations and the committees monitoring the major human rights instruments.[37] NGO representatives often meet Foreign Office officials;

for example, there is an annual meeting between the leader of the Human Rights delegation to the Human Rights Commission a few weeks before its Geneva session begins. Important human rights NGOs active in British politics (not all of which are headquartered in Britain) include Amnesty International, the Anti-Slavery Society, Article 19, Human Rights Watch, Interrights, International Alert, the International Commission of Jurists, the Minority Rights Group, Rights and Humanity, the Charities Aid Foundation, Penal Reform International, British Refugee Council, the Jubilee Campaign, the Commonwealth Human Rights Initiative, Index on Censorship, and the National Alliance of Women's Organizations.

NGO representatives have, on occasion, served as members of British delegations to major conferences with a major human rights aspect (e.g. the 1995 Women's conference at Beijing) and have been involved with the drafting of major conventions (e.g. the Convention on the Rights of the Child).[38] They also play a big part in hearings of the main committees monitoring British reports. In July 1995 the UN Human Rights Committee reported that the evidence from "a wide range" of organizations committed to human rights and democracy during its hearings on the UK human rights record "not only greatly assisted the Committee, but [was] also a tribute to the democratic nature of UK society" (CCPR/C/798/Add.55, para. 3).[39]

### *The media*

The British media do not give a consistent picture of the human rights activities of the British government. Governmental reports to the major monitoring committees are usually not covered, and media reporting of British government activity on human rights questions is exceptionally patchy. However, on some issues which resonate emotionally, such as apartheid, certain media campaigns have had a major influence on public opinion.

## V. Multilateral policy (regional and international)

It is important to emphasize the fact that British governments' policy towards human rights questions, both past and present, has also been influenced by international factors and the international context (or climate of opinion) in which it operates. I share the analysis put forward by Martha Finnemore in which she suggests that states are more socially responsive entities than is recognized by traditional international relations theory. State policies and structures are influenced by intersubjective systemic factors, specifically by norms promulgated within the international system.[40] Since the late 1970s when, it can be argued, human rights started to become part of high politics (through British ratification of the human rights covenants in 1976 and the major speech by the Foreign Secretary in 1977), Britain has worked with regional and a variety of multilateral partners to put the major norms into practice.

## Britain and regional organizations

### The Council of Europe

The parties to the 1948 regional Brussels Treaty (including Britain), which reaffirmed "their faith in fundamental human rights ... and in the other ideals proclaimed in the Charter of the United Nations,"[41] agreed, in London in May 1949, to establish the Council of Europe. After a series of complex negotiations at official and cabinet level (and pressure from pro-European NGOs), the government signed the ECHR (negotiated through the Council) in November 1950 and ratified it in February 1951. This outcome transpired despite the Lord Chancellor's view "that we were not prepared to encourage our European friends to jeopardize our whole system of law, which we have laboriously built up over centuries, in favour of some half-baked scheme to be administered by some unknown court."[42] The ECHR was subsequently complemented by the European Social Charter, dealing with 19 economic and social rights similar to those in the draft ICESCR. This was opened for signature in 1961, ratified by Britain in 1962 (14 years before it ratified the ICESCR), and came into force in 1965. Britain signed the revised, updated Social Charter in November 1997.

The European Court of Human Rights was inaugurated in January 1959 and, as has already been noted, the British government allowed petitions from individuals from Britain in 1966 and from its Crown Dependencies and dependent territories in 1967. It also played a major part at the first Council of Europe Ministerial Conference on Human Rights in March 1985 just after it had ratified the Eighth Protocol to the ECHR designed to reduce delays in the institutions. (In 1987 ministers decided to "Strasbourg proof" all British legislation, i.e. ensure that it could not be subject to a case in the European Court of Human Rights.)[43] Britain also ratified the European Convention for the Prevention of Torture and Inhuman or Degrading Treatment or Punishment in 1988.

The revival of nationalism in post–Cold War Europe soon led to concern about minority questions in Eastern Europe. In February 1995 the British government signed the Council of Europe Framework Convention for the protection of national minorities. The government also raised concerns about the future constitution and functioning of the machinery of enforcement for the ECHR in 1996. The Lord Chancellor visited Strasbourg to discuss the question with the President of the European Court in November. He said that he considered that it was important that when Protocol 11 of the Convention was implemented and the Commission and Court were combined, its procedures should be such as not only to facilitate the work of the Court but also to be demonstrably fair to all parties. The British government then opened discussion on the selection of judges, court procedure, and the application of the doctrine of margin of appreciation – which it saw as important for the continuing support of the member states.[44] In 1997 the incoming Labour government announced that the ECHR would finally be incorporated into British law.

*The European Union*

Since Britain finally joined the EC (now the EU) on 1 January 1973 it has worked primarily with its EU colleagues in the United Nations and, of course, in the EU itself on human rights matters. It was also in the Chair in July 1986 when EC foreign ministers made their first major overall Declaration on human rights (the 1957 Treaty of Rome had made no specific reference to human rights). Ministers reaffirmed that respect for human rights was one of the cornerstones of European cooperation. They noted that "the promotion of economic, social and cultural rights as well as of civil and political rights is of paramount importance for the full realization of human dignity and for the attainment of the legitimate aspirations of every individual."[45] EC divisions on the right to development were, however, noticeable in the vote on the Declaration in the General Assembly in December 1986. Denmark, Germany, and the United Kingdom abstained; the other EC members voted in favour. Britain finally accepted the right to development in 1993 at the Vienna Conference.

The 1991 Foreign Policy Document[46] on *Human Rights in Foreign Policy* noted that the EC partners had taken action on human rights through Declarations both general (e.g. on Sudan in March and November 1989) and specific (e.g. on the murder of six Jesuit priests in El Salvador in November 1989), and *démarches* (around 70 in 1989 in all regions of the world) by the Presidency, the Troika or all ambassadors of the EC Twelve resident in a capital. These were usually confidential, though officials were able to refer to them in correspondence with MPs, NGOs, etc. On a multilateral level the EC states had taken joint and separate action at relevant UN and CSCE meetings. In a limited number of cases, concern among the EC states at human rights abuses had led to decisions on common action. These usually took the form of coordinated diplomatic measures, for example against Burma, China, and Noriega's Panama, but could extend to actual measures taken by the Council (e.g. the decision to rescind Romania's benefits under the Generalized System of Preferences before Ceauşescu's fall in 1989 and the Council decision in April 1989 to suspend negotiations on an EC/Romanian agreement). In 1998 the EU, now with 15 members, took the common position that it would not support a resolution in the UN Human Rights Commission condemning China's human rights policies. The previous year, EU members had been badly divided on that same issue.

The 1991 Foreign Policy Document went on to explain that action by EC states often followed from recommendations made by Heads of Mission in joint reports on human rights. Such reports were usually commissioned by the Twelve's regional working groups or when agreement on the need for a report was reached. Guidelines for the preparation of these reports were drawn up in 1987 by the EC Working Group on Human Rights.

The subsequent 1996 Foreign Policy Document referred to the further comprehensive EU Declaration on Human Rights adopted in June 1991 and stated that to develop and consolidate democracy and the rule of law and respect for human rights and fundamental freedoms was also one of the declared objectives of Common Foreign and Security Policy. It also noted that joint action by the EU often carried greater weight than bilateral action. It stated that the European Union had made around 85 statements in 1995 besides taking coordinated diplomatic action against Burma and Nigeria and issuing confidential *démarches*.

### *The Organization for Security and Cooperation in Europe*

Five of the 10 Principles Guiding Relations between Participating States in the final Helsinki Act (August 1975) of the Conference on Security and Cooperation in Europe are to be found in the 1970 UN Friendly Relations Declaration, which was the fruit of a study of certain Charter principles, including the principle of equal rights and self-determination of peoples "with a view to their progressive development and codification, so as to secure their more effective application." The negotiators were also able to use language already agreed in the two main human rights Covenants. This explains why it was relatively easy to add a further Principle VII on respect for human rights and fundamental freedoms, including freedom of thought, conscience, and belief, to the Act. The Helsinki Final Act also had similar participants (the third world being represented by its European non-aligned members – Yugoslavia, Cyprus, and Malta); it provided useful agreed language including on aspects of human rights; and it showed that negotiation on these kinds of issues could be brought to fruition.[47]

The achievements of the Conference, outlined in a House of Commons debate by a Labour FCO minister in February 1976, were: the establishment of a code of conduct between European states; the creation of confidence-building military measures; and the fact that the CSCE had "stipulated a number of ways in which the rights of individuals – the right to free movement, the right to be reunited with their families, and the right to receive information – should be safeguarded."[48] This change from low politics towards high politics was highlighted in a speech given by the new Labour Foreign Secretary, David Owen, in March 1977. In it he discussed the usefulness of the Helsinki Final Act, saying that it had already begun to be an inspiration and a point of reference for those who wanted to see their societies evolve peacefully and constitutionally in a more open direction. He went on to affirm that the Charter, the Universal Declaration, the Covenants, and the Final Act "demonstrate beyond any shadow of doubt that abuses of human rights, wherever they may occur, are the legitimate subject of international concern. The dignity of man stands on values which transcend national frontiers. And in the democracies of the West it is inevitable and right that foreign policy should not only reflect the values of society, but that those who conduct foreign affairs should respond positively to the weight of public opinion and concern. In Britain we will take our stand on human rights in every corner of the globe ... We will apply the same standards and judgments to Communist countries as we do to Chile, Uganda and South Africa."[49]

The incoming Conservative government in 1979 continued to play a similar role on the question of human rights and foreign policy to its Labour predecessor, though it did not give the issue such a high profile and it shifted the emphasis, even more, to East–West relations by underlining the human rights dimension of the CSCE process. In December 1980 the British minister at the CSCE Madrid review conference suggested that the meeting should first consider matters in which the framework of conduct had not been fully respected; and secondly insist on better implementation of the seventh principle on respect for human rights and fundamental freedoms – particularly freedom of thought, religion, information, and movement.[50]

The Vienna CSCE Follow-up Meeting ended in January 1989 with agreement on a new and continuous monitoring mechanism on human rights within the CSCE process – the Conference on the Human Dimension (CHD) mechanism. This provided four separate ways of raising with any other CSCE state specific human rights cases and situations within that state's territory. The mechanism has been invoked on a number of occasions by Britain nationally as well as jointly by the Twelve. CHD meetings assess among other things the functioning of this mechanism, and also offer a forum for reviewing other CSCE member states' overall implementation of their human rights commitments.

## *Britain and global international organizations*

### *The United Nations*

Britain, as one of the main Allied victors at the end of the Second World War, was able to ensure that the language in its memorandum setting out proposals for the proposed new UN Organization's purposes and principles (including human rights) was incorporated with little change into Article 1 of the UN Charter. These proposals were designed to appeal to smaller powers because they would in theory prevent the Great Powers from acting like tyrants.[51] The ensuing UN Human Rights Commission's Drafting Committee agreed in June 1947 that the articles in a British draft could be submitted as a basis for a draft convention with the addition of articles on torture, the right to a legal personality, and asylum.[52] This draft bill, agreed by a Cabinet Office committee, covered only civil and political rights, and did not include provision for either individual appeal or enforcement mechanisms. Economic and social rights (e.g. the right to work and to social security) were mentioned in a further draft General Assembly resolution, but it was noted that they could not by their nature be defined in the form of legal obligations for states. Britain voted for the Universal Declaration of Human Rights on 10 December 1948 even though it included references to economic, social, and cultural rights, which were not in its draft bill.

Britain continued to take a prominent role in putting the rights set out in the 1948 Universal Declaration into legal form. It also continued to accept, though not enthusiastically, economic, social, and cultural rights. The Human Rights Commission submitted draft texts of the articles on economic, social, and cultural rights to the Economic and Social Council (ECOSOC) and the General Assembly in 1954. Between 1956 and 1958 these draft articles were approved in the General Assembly with little major amendment. These negotiations undoubtedly had an effect on the negotiations then going on to complement the ECHR with a European Social Charter.

The two Covenants on civil and political and economic, social, and cultural rights were signed by Britain in 1968. This "implied an expectation that the United Kingdom would ratify the Covenants in due course. It was also consistent with the United Kingdom's view that its internal law and practice must be carefully assessed and, if necessary, amended before undertaking international obligations."[53] The Labour Foreign Secretary, in his speech to the General Assembly in September 1976, called on all states to join Britain in ratifying the Covenants and to give full support to its monitoring committee. "Our task is to create a world in which all men can live in peace, prosperity and freedom, guaranteed by the rule of law."[54]

The Conservative government continued to press human rights considerations in a number of forums and supported the appointment of a Rapporteur in Afghanistan at the Human Rights Commission in early 1984.[55] It ratified the Convention on the Elimination of Discrimination against Women in 1986 and the Convention against Torture in 1988. On the United Nations, it noted in the 1991 Foreign Policy Document that UN mechanisms are inevitably cumbersome and slow but the cumulative effect of the criticism at the United Nations can bring considerable pressure on governments. It also ratified the Convention on the Rights of the Child in December 1991 (it had come into force in 1990).[56]

A Foreign Office minister, as is normally the case, addressed the UN Human Rights Commission in February 1995. He pointed out that a year ago they were celebrating both the outcome of the 1993 Vienna World Conference on human rights and the creation of a High Commissioner for Human Rights. At the conference the British government had accepted both the right to development (as it had not in 1986) and also that "all human rights are universal, indivisible, and interdependent and interrelated." He hoped that the Commission would discuss the vital relationship between democracy, development, and human rights. He suggested that the Commission needed to pay close attention to economic, social, and cultural rights, as well as to civil and political rights and to look in particular at how governments implement them.[57]

After the Labour government came into office in May 1997 it ended the ban on free association, which had been applied to the civil servants at the Government Communications Headquarters against ILO standards.

### *The Commonwealth*

The 1971 Declaration of Commonwealth Principles at the Heads of Government meeting at Singapore noted, *inter alia*: "We believe in the liberty of the individual, in equal rights for all citizens regardless of race, colour, creed or political belief, and in their inalienable right to participate by means of free and democratic political processes in framing the society in which they live." This was reaffirmed at the 1981 Commonwealth Heads of Government meeting. Participants were urged to accede to the relevant global and regional instruments. The Heads of Government also endorsed in principle the recommendation of a Commonwealth Working Party on Human Rights concerning the establishment of a special unit in the Secretariat for the promotion of human rights within the Commonwealth. This was eventually set up in 1985.[58]

Within the Commonwealth, Britain was working after the end of the Cold War to strengthen the Commonwealth role in promoting human rights, notably by assisting the development of legal and administrative infrastructures, by increasing understanding of the major international human rights instruments, and by encouraging ratification of these instruments by Commonwealth countries.[59] In 1991 the Commonwealth Heads of Government issued a Declaration at Harare stressing the need to protect and promote democracy, the rule of law, just and honest government, and the independence of the judiciary; fundamental human rights including equal rights and opportunities for all citizens regardless of race, colour, creed, or political belief; equality for women so that they can exercise their full and equal rights; provision of universal access to education; and continuing action to bring about an end to apartheid and the establishment of a free, democratic, non-racial, and prosperous South Africa.[60]

### *The G7*

It is important to note that the Group of 7 industrialized nations (now a Group of 8 including Russia), of which Britain is a member, also uses human rights language. At Houston in July 1990 the governments stated: "We welcome unreservedly the spread of multiparty democracy, the practice of free elections, the freedom of expression and assembly, the increased respect for human rights, the rule of law, and the increasing recognition of the principles of the open and competitive economy. These events proclaim loudly man's inalienable rights: when people are free to choose, they choose freedom."[61]

## VI. Bilateral policy

### *Before the end of the Cold War*

Many British bilateral actions on human rights questions were, and continue to be, enacted behind the scenes. A number on aid (relating to Bolivia, Chile, Ethiopia, Indonesia, and Uganda), arms exports (Chile and South Africa), and trade (Rhodesia) were noted in the 1978 Foreign Policy Document (for more detail see section III). Since then, more and more attention has been given to human rights in the House of Commons. In the 1980–1981 session there were six subject entries, two of which were devoted to specific countries (Pakistan and Syria). In the

1988–1989 session there were 74 such entries, 51 of which were devoted to specific countries.

The Foreign Secretary gave an account of the December 1984 guidelines for arms exports to Iran and Iraq in October 1985.[62] Britain would continue not to supply any lethal equipment but, subject to this, it should attempt to fulfil existing contracts. In March 1986 the House was told that the government had not provided any new aid to the governments of Vietnam or Afghanistan since 1979 because of human rights violations and related issues.[63]

The British government's response to the violent suppression of peaceful demonstrations in Tiananmen Square was announced in the House of Commons on 6 June 1989. The Foreign Secretary stated that all Members of Parliament shared the worldwide sense of horror and would join in the international condemnation of the slaughter of innocent people. They condemned "merciless treatment of peaceful demonstrators, and deeply deplored the use of force to suppress the democratic aspirations of the Chinese people." The government looked to the Chinese to fulfil their obligations to Hong Kong in the 1984 joint declaration. There could be no question of continuing normal business with the Chinese authorities. The government had decided that all scheduled ministerial exchanges between Britain and China would be suspended; the proposed visit of the Prince and Princess of Wales to China in November would not take place so long as those responsible for the atrocities remained in control of the Chinese government; all high-level contacts with China would be suspended; and all arms sales to China would be banned.[64]

## *After the end of the Cold War*

Since the 1990s, British bilateral policy towards human rights issues has been mainly confined to questions of arms sales and certain aspects of aid policy. Other bilateral action is often carried out in conjunction with other regional or multilateral action. In 1991 these included attendance at trials (e.g. in Iran) and supporting training courses (in Honduras for public security forces) and seminars (e.g. in the Cameroons). The 1996 Foreign Policy Document mentioned instances of confidential representations up to and including the prime ministerial level; public statements; curtailment of aid; enquiry about individual cases of concern to the British public or Parliament; attending trials; sending observers to elections; looking for opportunities to support local human rights work; arranging sponsored visits of human rights related workers; and maintaining contacts with and supporting local human rights organizations.

One major exception was the question of the former head of state of

Chile, General Pinochet. His extradition was sought by Spain to face trial for various crimes against humanity allegedly committed while he was head of state. Two provisional warrants for his arrest were issued by magistrates under the 1989 Extradition Act. These were quashed by the Divisional Courts but the quashing of the second warrant was stayed to enable an appeal to the House of Lords on the question of the proper interpretation of the immunity enjoyed by a former head of state from arrest and extradition proceedings in the United Kingdom in respect of acts committed while he was head of state. Amnesty International was granted leave to intervene in the proceedings. On 25 November 1998 the House of Lords allowed the appeal by a majority of three to two and the second warrant was restored. The Home Secretary subsequently gave authority to proceed. However, this second order was set aside on 15 January 1999 on the ground that one of the Lords giving the judgment had links with Amnesty International, which could give the appearance of possible bias.[65] The House of Lords decided on 24 March that a former head of state had no immunity from extradition from the United Kingdom to a third country for acts of torture committed in his own country while he was head of state and after the date that the Torture Convention came into legal force in all three countries. At the time of writing the matter had been referred back to the Home Secretary.

The 1991 and 1996 Foreign Policy Documents have practically identical statements on policy regarding British arms exports. They "require an export licence and every proposed sale of defence or internal security equipment is subject to strict vetting procedures," which take into account *inter alia* the human rights situation in the country concerned. They did not sanction the export from the United Kingdom of any defence or internal security equipment likely to be used for internal repression.

Under the Labour government, in 1997 Britain announced the introduction of new criteria for considering applications for the export of conventional arms. This was to give effect to its manifesto commitment not to export arms to regimes that might use them for internal repression or international aggression. Under the new criteria there was a ban on the export of equipment, such as electro-shock batons, where there is clear evidence it has been used for torture.

Both Foreign Policy Documents of the 1990s noted that aid and development assistance could be used to promote good government, including accountability and respect for human rights, as an end in itself and as a basis of economic and human development. There was an explicit linkage between economic and political reform and human rights. In 1990, the House of Commons was told that British development aid to Burma and project aid to Somalia had been stopped on the grounds of human rights abuses while project aid to the Sudan was being run down and programme aid promised to Sri Lanka had been postponed.[66] In 1991 the British government bilaterally curtailed aid to Malawi, Nigeria, and the Gambia.

The Department for International Development issued a White Paper in November 1997 entitled "Eliminating World Poverty: A Challenge for the 21st Century."[67] This discussed the question under four headings: the challenge of development; building partnerships; consistency of policies, including giving particular attention to human rights, transparent and accountable government, and core labour standards – building on the government's ethical approach to international relations; and building support for development. Although it mentions human rights and development, it does not attempt to promote any synthesis of human rights ideas with those dealing with sustainable international development.

## VII. Conclusion

What are the main factors that have shaped British human rights foreign policy since the Second World War? This chapter suggests that they can be found in three separate areas: Britain's interests; the way it has influenced and been influenced by the developing international debate and action on this subject; and the way it works domestically, including the legacy of its historical development.

Over the period in question British governments have acted in the light of both fixed and changing interests in the context of a long-standing involvement with many corners of the globe. The process of decolonization meant that British governments became progressively less concerned about the problem of self-determination in their dependent territories in the late 1950s as more became independent. They also found it easier to accept the references to national self-determination that had been added to both Covenants and were, despite these, finally able to sign both in 1968, and eventually ratify both in 1976. They also found it possible to allow the right of individual petition to the European Human Rights Commission and the compulsory jurisdiction of the European Court of Human Rights to British citizens in 1966 and to citizens of its Crown Dependencies (e.g. Jersey) and its dependent territories as early as September 1967.[68]

The enduring interests continue to be Britain's range of global concerns (many of which can be seen in the way it acts as a permanent member of the Security Council); its relationship with continental Europe, both West and East; its relationship with the United States; and the Commonwealth (though the weight given to it has changed both up and down over the years). The interrelationship between these was recognized in the 1950 House of Commons debate on the proposed Council of Europe after the government had signed the Convention on 4 November. The FO minister then stated: "The policy of this government, and the peculiar function of the United Kingdom, is to reconcile purely European interests with the wider interests and connections upon which European survival is dependent." The Foreign Secretary sounded a note of caution at the end of the debate when he noted that human rights issues had got tangled up with Britain's colonial troubles and its overseas territories.[69]

On a regional level, British governments have supported and become more involved with the Council of Europe and the European Convention on Human Rights. Their regional European interests have been strengthened since the 1970s through membership of the EU and their involvement in the OSCE process. Human rights considerations have progressively become more centre stage in both these European organizations.

British concern with the United States can be seen in their work with President Roosevelt during the Second World War and subsequently. They sought to ensure that two Covenants were drafted, in order to make it easier for the United States eventually to ratify the ICCPR, and to co-operate on human rights matters with the Carter administration in the late 1970s. On the Commonwealth, as with other institutions, human rights have slowly been pushed more centre stage.

Britain has also influenced and been influenced by the way the world has developed internationally. British governmental concern for order and justice in the world overall can be seen in its contribution to the making of the UN Charter; the submission of a draft International Bill of Human Rights to the United Nations in 1947; its determination to develop international law, including appropriate global human rights instruments (e.g. the Covenants; the Committee for the Elimination of Racial Discrimination; and, most recently, the Convention on the Rights of the Child); its changing attitude to self-determination; and its generally constructive attitude to decolonization as well as its changed views on the question of domestic intervention in the affairs of states. It is also noticeable in the elaboration of Charter principles, and in the respect and co-operation Britain has given to the treaty monitoring bodies.

Finally British governments' attitudes to the human rights debate have been affected by government's historical development and the way it works domestically. Both non-governmental organizations and the media have affected its thinking. And the beginning of its racial legislation owed much to the developments at the United Nations.

Labour governments have tended to take more initiatives in the field of human rights and foreign policy. But, as Evan Luard pointed out in 1980, some double standards remained in effect, both from the government itself and in the context of public opinion. He maintained that the Labour government's close economic involvement in South Africa had constrained it to be cautious over sanctions. Its economic and strategic interests had also prevailed in the context of Iran and of Argentina. He also noted the effect of British need for oil on criticism of the Gulf states and Saudi Arabia. He went on to state: "British governments have not hesitated to express their condemnation of the policies of, for example, the Soviet Union, Uganda, Chile and South Africa, because public opinion at home demanded it. They have spoken out less strongly about the policies of Equatorial Guinea, the Central African Republic, Uruguay, Cuba and Ethiopia because British public opinion and even British human rights organizations have not expressed themselves as strongly on that subject, not because it is thought important not to prejudice relations with those states."[70]

These sorts of issues remain a challenge to the Labour government now in office.

## Notes

The opinions expressed in this chapter are the author's own and should not be taken as an expression of official governmental policy.

1. Which right falls into which category (civil, cultural, economic, political, and social) is a complex matter. Many can be looked at in more than one way. See Sally Morphet, *The Balance between Civil and Political Rights and Economic and Social Rights: Origins of the Human Rights Declaration and Covenants and Subsequent Developments*, Foreign Policy Document No. 127, December 1978, 2–4.
2. Robert Boardman and A. J. R. Groom, eds., *The Management of Britain's External Relations* (London: Macmillan, 1973), 2–3.
3. In September 1949, the Foreign Secretary, Mr. Bevin, in an address to the General Assembly noted that the United Nations and its debates were "gradually helping to develop in the minds and hearts of the people a greater understanding of the importance of international law, of the rule of law, of the moral acceptance of law, the necessity for the adoption of a high standard of moral values in the enforcement of that law, and the necessity ... for the universal adoption of the optional clauses and the willing acceptance of decisions, even if they may not be quite to our liking."
4. H. Lauterpacht, *International Law and Human Rights* (London: Stevens, 1950), 127–133.
5. A. H. Robertson, *Human Rights in the World* (New York: St. Martin's, 1982), 6–8.
6. Francesca Klug, Keir Starmier, and Stuart Weir, *The Three Pillars of Liberty, Political Rights and Freedoms in the United Kingdom* (London: Routledge, 1996), 4.
7. J. F. Green, *The United Nations and Human Rights* (Washington, DC: Brookings, 1956), 14.
8. B. Mirkine-Guetzevitch, "L'ONU et la Doctrine Moderne des Droits de L'Homme," *Revue Générale de Droit International Public* (1951), 50–51, and C. J. Friedrich, "Rights, Liberties and Freedoms: A Reappraisal," *American Political Science Review* (1963), 843.
9. Friedrich, "Rights, Liberties and Freedoms," op. cit., 842.

10. John Sankey, "Decolonisation and the UN," in Erik Jensen and Thomas Fisher, eds., *The United Kingdom – The United Nations* (London: Macmillan, 1990), 97–8.
11. Geoffrey Marston, "The United Kingdom's Part in the Preparation of the European Convention on Human Rights," *International and Comparative Law Quarterly* 42 (October 1993), 825. Independence for India, Pakistan, Burma, and Ceylon in 1947–48 did not immediately mean the end of Empire. No other imperial territory came to independence until the Anglo-Egyptian Sudan, Malaya, and Ghana in 1956–57; thereafter the pace of decolonization steadily increased.
12. Ibid., 820.
13. Sally Morphet, "Article 1 of the Human Rights Covenants: Its Development and Current Significance," in Dilys Hill, ed., *Human Rights and Foreign Policy Principles and Practice* (London: Macmillan, 1989), 78.
14. K. R. Simmonds, "The United Kingdom and the European Convention on Human Rights," *International and Comparative Law Quarterly* 15 (April 1966), 539–541. See also Treaty Series No. 8 (1966), Cmnd. 2894.
15. For a detailed history of its activities, see "The Anti-Apartheid Movement and Racism in Southern Africa," by Abdul S. Minty in Peter Willetts, ed., *Pressure Groups in the Global System* (London: Frances Pinter, 1982), 28–45.
16. For detail see Natan Lerner, *The U.N. Convention on the Elimination of all Forms of Racial Discrimination* (Leiden: Sijthoff & Noordhoff, 1980). A further useful general book is Michael Banton, *International Action against Racial Discrimination* (Oxford: Clarendon Press, 1996).
17. *British Policy towards the United Nations*, Foreign Policy Document No. 26 (London: HMSO, 1978).
18. Ben Whitaker, the British expert who served on the UN Sub-Commission on Minorities, notes that a watershed occurred in the discussion of individual countries in the United Nations in 1973 when the Soviet Union, because of its concern at the coup against President Allende, "dropped their objections and allowed a debate on human rights violations specifically in Chile." This precedent was used to allow debates on other countries. See "Constructive Criticism: The United Nations and Human Rights," in Jensen and Fisher, eds., *The United Kingdom – The United Nations*, op. cit., 151.
19. Sally Morphet, "Economic, Social and Cultural Rights: The Development of Governments' Views 1941–88," in Ralph Bedard and Dilys Hill, eds., *Economic, Social and Cultural Rights: Progress and Achievement* (London: Macmillan, 1992), 84–5.
20. *Human Rights in Foreign Policy*, Foreign Policy Document No. 215 (Human Rights Unit, Foreign and Commonwealth Office, January 1991).
21. *Human Rights in Foreign Policy*, Foreign Policy Document No. 268 (Foreign and Commonwealth Office, July 1996).
22. For discussion of options for a United Kingdom Human Rights Commission, see Sarah Spencer and Ian Bynoe, *A Human Rights Commission for the United Kingdom – Some Options, EHRLR Issue 2* (London: Sweet & Maxwell, 1997).
23. *Survey of Current Affairs* 27/8 (August 1997) (London: Foreign and Commonwealth Office), 296–300.
24. *The Merger of the Foreign Office and the Commonwealth Office* (London: HMSO, 1968).
25. These are the Human Rights Committee (the ICCPR); the Economic, Social and Cultural Rights Committee (the ICESCR); the Committee on the Elimination of Racial Discrimination (CERD); the Committee on the Elimination of Discrimination against Women (CEDAW); the Convention against Torture (CAT); and the Convention on the Rights of the Child (CRC).
26. Klug, Starmier, and Weir, *The Three Pillars*, op. cit., 3–4.
27. Ibid., 7.

28. Francoise Hampson, "The United Kingdom before the European Court of Human Rights," *Yearbook of European Law* (1989), 173.
29. L. A. Siedentop, "Viewpoint: The Strange Life of Liberal England," *Times Literary Supplement*, 16 August 1985, p. 900.
30. Early in the Second World War (1939–1945) a coalition government came into office (1940–1945). It was succeeded by the following governments: Conservative, May–July 1945; Labour, July 1945 – October 1951; Conservative, October 1951 – October 1964; Labour, October 1964 – June 1970; Conservative, June 1970 – March 1974; Labour, March 1974 – May 1979; Conservative, May 1979 – May 1997; Labour, May 1997– .
31. Shirley Stewart, ed., *Human Rights in United States & United Kingdom Foreign Policy: A Colloquium* (New York: American Association for the International Commission of Jurists, 1979).
32. *Human Rights Re-Examined*, House of Lords Session 1992–93, Select Committee on the European Communities (London: HMSO, June 1992).
33. *Foreign Policy and Human Rights, Volume 1*, House of Commons Session 1998–9, Foreign Affairs Committee (London: Stationery Office, December 1998).
34. *First Report of the Foreign Affairs Committee Session 1998–9. Foreign Policy and Human Rights: Response of the Secretary of State for Foreign and Commonwealth Affairs*, Cm. 4299 (London: Stationery Office, 23 March 1999).
35. Marston, "The United Kingdom's Part," op. cit., 800–802.
36. *Hansard*, House of Commons, written answer, cols. 166–7, 14 February 1966.
37. See, for instance, Helena Cook, "Amnesty International at the United Nations," in Peter Willetts, ed., *"The Conscience of the World": The Influence of Non-Governmental Organisations in the U.N. System* (London: C. Hurst, 1996).
38. See Michael Longford, "NGOs and the Rights of the Child," in Peter Willetts, ed., *"The Conscience of the World,"* op. cit.
39. Klug, Starmier, and Weir, *The Three Pillars*, op. cit., 3.
40. Martha Finnemore, "International Organizations as Teachers of Norms: The United Nations Educational, Scientific, and Cultural Organization and Science Policy," *International Organization* 47/4 (Autumn 1993), 593.
41. Marston, "The United Kingdom's Part," op. cit., 800.
42. Ibid., 813.
43. *Survey of Current Affairs*, 15/4 (April 1985) (London: Central Office of Information), 104–106.
44. *Survey of Current Affairs* 26/12 (December 1996) (London: Foreign & Commonwealth Office), 462–463.
45. *Human Rights in Foreign Policy*, Foreign Policy Document No. 215, op. cit., Annex E.
46. Ibid., 16–18.
47. See also Ian Sinclair, "The Significance of the Friendly Relations Declaration," in Vaughan Lowe and Colin Warbrick, eds., *The United Nations and the Principles of International Law* (London: Routledge, 1994), 29.
48. *Selected Documents Relating to Problems of Security and Cooperation in Europe 1954–77*, Miscellaneous No. 17, Cmnd. 6932 (London: HMSO, 1977), 306.
49. Ibid., 331–40.
50. *Survey of Current Affairs* 11/1 (January 1981) (London: Central Office of Information), 12.
51. Lord Gladwyn, "Founding the United Nations: Principles and Objects," in Jensen and Fisher, eds., *The United Kingdom – The United Nations*, op. cit., p. 37.
52. *UN Yearbook 1946–47* (New York: UN Department of Public Information), 525–526.
53. Dominic McGoldrick and Nigel Parker, "The United Kingdom Perspective on the International Covenant on Civil and Political Rights," in David Harris and Sarah Joseph,

eds., *The International Covenant on Civil and Political Rights and United Kingdom Law* (Oxford: Clarendon Press, 1995), 70.
54. See *Survey of Current Affairs* 6/10 (October 1976) (London: Central Office of Information), 383.
55. *Survey of Current Affairs* 15/1 (January 1985) (London: Central Office of Information), 15.
56. See Longford, "NGOs and the Rights of the Child," op. cit.
57. *Survey of Current Affairs* 25/2 (February 1995) (London: Foreign & Commonwealth Office), 34–35.
58. *Survey of Current Affairs* 15/11 (November 1985) (London: Central Office of Information), 341.
59. *Human Rights in Foreign Policy*, Foreign Policy Document No. 215, 7.
60. *Survey of Current Affairs* 21/11 (November 1991) (London: Foreign & Commonwealth Office), 403.
61. http: //sung7.univ-lyon2.fr/toronto/90intro.htm.
62. *Hansard, House of Commons*, written answer 450, 29 October 1985.
63. *Hansard, House of Commons*, written answer 122, 18 March 1986.
64. *Survey of Current Affairs* 19/6 (June 1989) (London: Central Office of Information), 233.
65. *New Law Journal Practitioner*, 22 January 1999, 88.
66. *Hansard, House of Commons*, written answer 31, 19 November 1990.
67. *Eliminating World Poverty: A Challenge for the 21st Century*, Cm. 3789, November 1997.
68. The right of individual petition remains for all the Crown and dependent territories with the exception of the British Virgin Islands, for which it was stopped in January 1981, and the Cayman Islands, for which it was stopped in January 1986. See also *Hansard, House of Commons*, written answer 29, 14 February 1995.
69. *Hansard, House of Commons*, cols. 1397–1398 and col. 1502, 13 November 1950.
70. Evan Luard, "Human Rights and Foreign Policy," *International Affairs* (Autumn 1980), 587. See also Evan Luard, *Human Rights and Foreign Policy* (pamphlet published on behalf of the British United Nations Association by the Pergamon Press, 1981).

# 5

# Japan's foreign policy towards human rights: Uncertain changes

*Yozo Yokota and Chiyuki Aoi*

Japan's foreign policy towards human rights was almost non-existent until the 1980s. Japan avoided taking political risks in its external relations as a matter of general principle, as exemplified by its single-minded pursuit of economic self-interest. Human rights, being seen by Tokyo as highly political and greatly complicating foreign relations, were not allowed to interfere with central concerns such as the economy – and national security. This posture resulted in contradictions with its pro-Western diplomatic allies in multilateral forums. Such a passive stance in human rights diplomacy is, however, gradually giving way – albeit slowly – to a more active one that gives some importance to human rights. This shift is still uncertain. It ranges from support for the abstract principles of universal human rights, and thus opposition to special Asian values, to a new foreign aid policy that sometimes includes considerations of democratization and human rights in the recipient countries.

## I. Introduction

In Japan, as in other nations, there is a contemporary effort to associate national history with human rights. One can read that: "[E]ven before the opening of doors to the world, under the Tokugawa Shogunate, there were rules and customs in Japan related to human rights and humanitarian concerns."[1] These norms, however, sought to teach rulers principles of good governance, as in: "one should treat one's subjects and subordinates with benevolence and mercy," based on Confucianism, Buddhism, and traditional Japanese mores including Bushido. These norms were not based on the concept of human rights as we understand them today. Such norms reflected not entitlement of persons but wise guidelines for rulers. They were thus very different from the concept of human rights found in the writings of Western political philosophers such as Jean-Jacques Rousseau, Montesquieu, and John Locke, or in such Western historical documents as the English Magna Carta of 1215, the Petition of Right of 1628, the Bill of Rights of 1689, the Virginia Declaration of Rights of 1776, or the French Declaration of the Rights of Man and of the Citizen of 1789.

It is therefore correct for Professors Kentaro Serita and Pierre-Marie Dupuy to begin the analysis of Japanese practice in the field of human rights by reference to the human rights provisions of the Meiji Constitution of 1889.[2] Indeed, the Meiji Constitution provided for some basic freedoms and rights, understood as human rights in the Western sense of the term, such as the freedom of residence and movement (Art. 22), the principle of no arrest, detention, interrogation, or punishment except under the law (Art. 23), the right to a fair trial (Art. 24), the right to property (Art. 27), the freedom of religion (Art. 28), the freedoms of expression, print, assembly, and association (Art. 29), and the right to petition (Art. 30).

However, those rights and freedoms were subjected to the prerogative of the Emperor in the event of war or national emergency (Art. 31). Furthermore, many of those rights and freedoms were ensured only within the scope of the law. In other words, such rights and freedoms could be restricted by legislation passed by the Diet. In 1925, the infamous Maintenance of Public Order Act (*Chian-iji Ho*) was promulgated, and under this act serious human rights violations were committed by special police and other governmental officials.[3]

The Meiji Constitution's provisions for freedoms and rights had another serious limitation. Such freedoms and rights were granted only to Japanese subjects. Accordingly, foreigners in Japanese territories or non-Japanese residents in territories under Japanese military occupation did not *ipso facto* enjoy the constitutional rights and freedoms. Consequently, many Koreans, Chinese, Filipinos, etc., suffered from serious human rights violations committed by Japanese military and civilian officials under their rule without the protection of constitutional provisions.

The situation drastically changed after Japan's defeat in the Second World War. Under the occupation administration by the General Headquarters of the Allied Forces headed by General Douglas MacArthur, a new Constitution was enacted. It did not abolish the imperial system itself but took away from the Emperor practically all of the political powers and prerogatives he used to enjoy under the old Meiji Constitution. Article 1 of the new Constitution stipulates that "[T]he Emperor shall be the symbol of the State and of the unity of the people, deriving his position from the will of the people with whom resides sovereign power." Article 3 further provides that "[T]he advice and approval of the Cabinet shall be required for all acts of the Emperor in matters of state, and the Cabinet shall be responsible therefor." In other words, the new Constitution clearly provides that Japan would henceforth be a democratic state where the real source of power lies in the people rather than the Emperor.

Based on this democratic principle, the new Constitution contains many provisions for the protection of human rights and fundamental freedoms. Article 11 provides in general terms that "[T]he people shall not be prevented from enjoying any of the fundamental human rights. These fundamental human rights guaranteed to the people by this Constitution shall be conferred upon the people of this and future generations as eternal and inviolate rights." Professor Nobuyoshi Ashibe, a contemporary authority on the Japanese Constitution, writes that the expression "inviolate rights" contained in this provision means: "contrary to the rights and freedoms provided in the Meiji Constitution which could be restricted by law, these fundamental human rights cannot be violated by any State powers including not only the Government but also the Diet."[4]

There are two more articles in the new Constitution related to human rights that are of a more general nature. Article 13 provides: "All of the people shall be respected as individuals. Their right to life, liberty, and the pursuit of happiness shall, to the extent that it does not interfere with the public welfare, be the supreme consideration in legislation and in other governmental affairs." Paragraph 1 of Article 14 further provides: "All of the people are equal under the law and there shall be no discrimination in political, economic or social relations because of race, creed, sex, social status or family origin."

On the basis of the general provisions referred to above, the new Constitution contains many detailed provisions for the protection of human rights, which can be classified for convenience into three categories under the headings: (a) basic freedoms; (b) civil and political rights; and (c) economic, social, and cultural rights.

First, the new Constitution guarantees to the people such basic freedoms as: freedom of thought and conscience (Art. 19), freedom of religion (Art. 20), freedom of assembly and association as well as of speech, press, and all other forms of expression (Art. 21), freedom to choose and change one's residence and to choose one's occupation (Art. 22, para. 1), freedom of all persons to move to a foreign country (Art. 22, para. 2), and academic freedom (Art. 23).

Secondly, the Constitution also ensures many civil and political rights, which are much more detailed and comprehensive than those of the Meiji Constitution. For example, the right of peaceful petition (Art. 16), the right to sue for redress from the state in the event one has suffered damage through an illegal act of any public official (Art. 17), the right not to be held in bondage (Art. 18), the right to life or liberty, including the principle of no criminal penalty except according to procedure established by law (Art. 31), the right of access to the courts (Art. 32), the right not to be apprehended except upon warrant issued by a competent judicial officer (Art. 33), the right of all persons to be secure in their homes, papers, and effects against entries, searches, and seizures (Art. 35), the right not to be subjected to "torture" or "cruel punishments" (Art. 36), the right (of the accused in criminal cases) to a speedy and public trial by an impartial tribunal and to the assistance of competent counsel (Art. 37, paras. 1 and 3), the right not to be compelled to testify against oneself (Art. 37, para. 1), and the right not to be held criminally liable for an act that was lawful at the time it was committed and not to be placed in double jeopardy (Art. 39).

Thirdly, the new Constitution further provides for a number of basic human rights that could be broadly characterized as economic, social, and cultural rights. This category of rights was not found in the old Meiji Constitution. Article 25, paragraph 1, of the new Constitution, for example, stipulates that: "[A]ll people shall have the right to maintain the minimum standards of wholesome and cultured living." Article 26, paragraph 1, provides that: "[A]ll people shall have the right to receive an equal education correspondent to their ability." Furthermore, Article 27 provides for "the right to work," while Article 28 provides for "the right of workers to organize and to bargain and act collectively." Finally, Article 29 sets forth the "right to own or to hold property and the right to just compensation in case private property is taken for public use."

As shown above, the provisions for fundamental human rights in the new Constitution of Japan are much more detailed and comprehensive than those of the old Meiji Constitution. They are also without restriction by the Emperor's prerogatives, by the government's powers, or by legislation. As human rights advocates, activists, and specialists now point out, however, legal provisions of human rights are one thing but the actual protection of human rights is another.[5] Particularly when it comes to human rights consideration in Japanese foreign relations, the government's stance was more passive than active even after the Second World War until the mid-1980s. The Constitution's many detailed provisions for fundamental freedoms and human rights did not directly impact foreign policy to any appreciable extent.

## II. Domestic factors

### *The traditional situation*

As with any other state, Japan's foreign policy can be considered as an outgrowth of its domestic political and social dynamics, interacting with the international environment.

One important domestic determinant of the Japanese approach to human rights abroad is the legacy of its behaviour in the 1930s and 1940s. After 1945, Japan, unlike some of its Western counterparts, did not feel itself to be in a position to promote international human rights standards. This was mostly owing to the recognition of its own serious and systematic violations of human rights committed before and during the Second World War, particularly in neighbouring Asian countries. Japan thus felt itself to be in a position to learn, rather than preach, about human rights, which it acknowledged as an imported concept from the West. Such reserve fitted well with an emerging preference for quiet diplomacy and a low-profile and non-confrontational approach, or equi-distance stance, to international relations in general. Thus Japan's "lessons of history" fitted with its emerging national style in foreign policy. Both history and diplomatic style led to a desire to avoid the subject of human rights in the international arena.

Other important factors also supported this orientation. For much of the time between renewed independence (1952) and the 1980s, Japan was ruled by the Liberal Democratic Party (LDP), which reflected primarily business interests and emphasized a foreign policy of economic self-interest. The destruction caused by the Second World War naturally led to a central emphasis on economic growth and recovery. This emphasis was generally endorsed by the United States, first Japan's occupier and then its principal security and trading partner.

These LDP conservative governments built up a strong bureaucratic system that was itself devoted to traditional concerns in foreign policy such as economic interest and national security (traditionally understood). It should be stressed that dependence on bureaucracy in foreign policy-making and its implementation was particularly notable in the field of foreign economic aid, the single most visible foreign policy area for Japan. In Official Development Aid (ODA) policy, 19 agencies including the Ministry of Foreign Affairs (MOFA), the Ministry of Finance (MOF), and the Ministry of Construction hold their own ODA budget.[6] In particular, with regard to highly technical multilateral economic assistance, the Ministry of Finance has traditionally exercised the strongest authority over aid policy. MOF and other economic bureaucracies, particularly the

Ministry of International Trade and Industry (MITI), have never considered human rights as within their routine competence.

For its part, MOFA lacked a unit specialized in human rights issues until 1984, when the Human Rights and Refugee Division was created in what was then the United Nations Policy Bureau. The creation of this division was clearly an important improvement, particularly given that only a few officers had been assigned to human rights issues prior to its creation. With its initial size of 10 persons, however, it was difficult for such a small division to do much more than just meet various human rights reporting obligations under various treaties, and deal with a growing number of Indo-Chinese refugees in the 1980s, and other related issues.[7]

Economic ministries such as MOF, MITI, and the Economic Planning Agency, strengthened relative to politics as well as other bureaucracies during the period of rapid growth in the 1960s, became influential in determining multilateral and bilateral foreign aid, but their authority and mandate do not touch upon human rights aspects. Thus Japan's bureaucracy lacked a structure suited to the formulation of foreign policies that were sensitive to human rights and other political elements. The Civil Liberties Bureau of the Ministry of Justice is responsible for domestic human rights issues, but foreign relations do not fall under its responsibility.

Finally, the mass public supported the élite's orientation toward a conservative and low-key foreign policy that emphasized economic self-interest under the protection of the US security umbrella. There was widespread public deference to a conservative and élitist democracy. Interest groups that demanded a different orientation, i.e. more emphasis on human rights, were weak or mostly lacking in influence.

During this period domestic human rights issues were indeed debated. But, ironically, this domestic debate served to reinforce passivity on human rights abroad. Because the domestic debates revealed ideological differences and great complexity, conservative governments found added reason to remain mostly silent on international human rights. Domestic debates covered such subjects as *dowa* issues (group of persons historically considered to belong to a lower caste, thus subject to serious discrimination), labour rights, the treatment of Koreans residing in Japan, and indigenous Ainu people. Less politicized human rights issues – freedom of expression, religion, and the press, children's rights, women's rights, and rights of the mentally handicapped – remained strictly domestic issues. Parts of the all-powerful bureaucracy that focused on domestic issues might take up such questions, but the Foreign Ministry and other related offices were indifferent.

However, some of these human rights issues that were debated in

Japan began to be raised in various UN forums, usually triggered by a number of non-governmental organizations, which often put the government in a defensive position. For example, the International Labour Organization took up the issue of labour rights in national corporations in Japan during the late 1950s to 1960s at the request of the labour unions (*Sohyo*). ILO investigations, although leading to some progressive changes in Japan, certainly did not encourage conservative governments to take a leadership position on other human rights issues at the United Nations.

## III. Indications of change?

Since the mid-1980s, Japan's institutions have become more prepared to deal with human rights concerns more systematically – at least relative to the past. Japan's more active participation in international human rights forums contributed to this change. The size of the Human Rights and Refugee Division was expanded to more than 20 by the 1990s.[8] The Foreign Policy Bureau was created in 1993, supervising the United Nations Policy Division, the Human Rights and Refugee Division, and other divisions. A more integrated foreign policy resulted, with more attention to human rights.

In the early 1990s, some signs of change in the conservative political alignment also emerged. Most notably, the shift in the political power alignment in the "reformist" era of 1993–1994 and the historic liberal–conservative coalition era of 1994–1996 gave a momentum to addressing issues that had not been dealt with under conservative one-party rule,[9] including war reparation issues. In general, the historical consensus on foreign policy preferences among the conservative political forces, the bureaucracy, business, and the public became disrupted during these eras. The LDP's ties with the bureaucracy were weakened, and the public, discontented with a number of corruption incidents involving public officials, had less confidence in the bureaucracy.[10]

One notable example reflecting this changed political environment was the public attention given to the issue known as "comfort women," and the subsequent actions taken by the conservative–liberal coalition government on this issue. Following the Miyazawa LDP government's initiative on starting an investigation – a measure considered to be extremely open by the standard of preceding conservative governments – plans to deal with this issue gradually materialized under the coalition government.[11] The final compensation plan itself can best be perceived as a result of inter-party negotiation within the coalition government, indicating increased policy inputs from the former opposition parties and the changed role of the bureaucracy.[12] The decision-making process also involved independent experts and non-governmental organizations, encouraging the government often behind the scenes to make a timely decision and implement the plan. Such a political process was quite different from traditional foreign policy-making, which was heavily influenced by the bureaucracy and business. This was also a case where non-governmental organizations in the area of human rights were more active and influential in their demands on the government. Given the rapid changes in Japanese politics that brought the LDP back to power, however, one cannot make any firm conclusions about the political foundation of Japanese foreign policy-making, particularly in the area of human rights diplomacy.

Another case of important change may be in the area of foreign economic policy. The Ministry of Finance and the Ministry of Foreign Affairs seem to be cooperating more closely and giving more attention to human rights. This tentative evaluation stems from the adoption of the 1992 ODA Charter (as explained below), with its provisions on human rights and democracy, and from the expansion of Japan's aid to former Soviet Union republics and Eastern Europe, where transitions to market democracies have required new thinking at MOF and MOFA. One study suggests that Japanese involvement in the politicized East European development encouraged closer coordination between these ministries.[13] Yet these collaborations appear at best ad hoc and selective. Thus, national domestic factors in Japanese foreign policy-making exhibit some sporadic changes in selected issue areas, necessitated by the changed domestic and international environment. There are both continuities and changes.

## IV. Multilateral policy

### *Status of the International Bill of Rights*

Japan did not become fully part of the international human rights regime until the very end of the 1970s. This was yet another reason for Japan's mostly passive stance concerning the advancement of international human rights up until that time. Japan ratified the two basic Covenants on Civil and Political Rights and on Economic, Social, and Cultural Rights in 1979, preceded by two treaties in the 1950s – namely, the Convention on the Political Rights of Women (1955) and the Convention for the Suppression of the Traffic in Persons and of the Exploitation of the Prostitution of Others (1958). In the early 1980s Japan started to participate in various UN human rights mechanisms. Japan was elected by the

Economic and Social Council (ECOSOC) to the UN Commission on Human Rights for the first time in 1982, and two individual Japanese experts participated in the UN Sub-Commission on Prevention of Discrimination and Protection of Minorities for the first time in 1984. In that same year, in order to coordinate activities related to human rights, the Ministry of Foreign Affairs established the Human Rights and Refugee Division (noted above). Subsequently, Japan ratified a range of human rights treaties: the Convention Relating to the Status of Refugees (1981); the Convention on the Elimination of All Forms of Discrimination against Women (1985); the Convention on the Rights of the Child (1994); and the International Convention on the Elimination of All Forms of Racial Discrimination (1995).

As of 1998 Japan had not ratified the First Optional Protocol to the Covenant on Civil and Political Rights, based on the view that its provisions are not compatible with the principles of the separation of power and judicial independence.[14] Japan also is not a party to Article 41 of the Covenant on Civil and Political Rights. Although Japan has registered no formal reservations with regard to the Covenant on Civil and Political Rights, it has put a de facto reservation on its Article 22(2) on the labour rights of public employees, as well as the related Article 8(2) of the Covenant on Economic, Social, and Cultural Rights.[15] It has put the following reservations on the Covenant on Economic, Social, and Cultural Rights: Article 7(d), in particular the right to remuneration for public holidays, based on the domestic law that leaves the matter to each corporation and labour union; Article 8, para. 1(d), the right to strike of the police and armed forces, which is understood by the Japanese government to include fire-fighters and state administrators; and Article 13, para. 2(b) and (c), the government's duty to introduce free education progressively in higher education.

The gap between the provisions of the International Bill of Rights and the Japanese domestic legal system and social practice in some issue areas has been suggested as an explanation for the delay in Japan's ratifying some international human rights conventions. Domestic controversy has been acute on such issues as nationality law, labour rights for public workers, the death penalty, women's rights, minority rights, the rights of elders, and the rights of the handicapped.[16] However, in contrast to the case of the United States, where resistance is strong against accepting meaningful international modifications of its national law, Japan has had relatively few public controversies over adhering to international human rights instruments once the policy has been decided by the government.

Joining the international legal regime on human rights has had some positive effects on some areas of the Japanese legal system over the long run. For example, in 1985 Japan's nationality law, which had denied nationality to children born in Japan to Japanese mothers but non-Japanese fathers, was changed in accordance with international standards so as not to discriminate on grounds of gender. The Covenants and other human rights conventions, particularly the Convention on the Elimination of All Forms of Discrimination against Women, have served as a basis from which to reassess family law and other domestic laws and practices concerning women's rights, though improvements are still called for by various civil groups.[17] One notable event in the domestic application of these international instruments was the case in which the Sapporo District Court of Japan recognized the indigenous character of the Ainu people, reflecting the debate on the rights of indigenous people at the United Nations.

Japan's earlier position concerning the drafting of the two central Covenants, as expressed in debates in the General Assembly, is noteworthy. Tokyo tended to see itself as a developing economy and thus adopted some positions that were usually associated with the global South. On other issues Tokyo sought a middle ground between Western states and developing countries, in particular, neighbouring Asian states.[18] In the 1950s, for example, Japan participated in the debates concerning the draft Covenant on Economic, Social, and Cultural Rights. Tokyo emphasized its commitment to improving living standards and the need for international cooperation to achieve it.[19] At the adoption of the Covenant on Civil and Political Rights and the First Optional Protocol during the twenty-first session of the General Assembly, Japan generally sided with the non-aligned nations. It argued against the proposed mandatory arbitration system, based on the view that such a system might be suited to advanced states but was difficult to accept for the majority of states with different domestic circumstances.[20] Japan then abstained in the vote on the First Optional Protocol, on the basis that individual petitions would be an inappropriate system that would be difficult to administer, likely to be politically abused, and unlikely to be adopted.[21]

As Japan joined other UN human rights forums, its activities in human rights standard-setting accordingly diversified to include a wider range of issues. Normally taking a pro-Western stance, Japan in principle endorsed both International Covenants in the UN forums – as we have seen. Until the 1980s, however, Japan's position on human rights was rather equivocal. Tokyo observed the politicization of human rights issues during the Cold War, and especially the differing interpretations by the Western states and the developing and socialist countries. The differences were pronounced concerning group rights versus individual rights, and universality versus cultural relativism and particularism. Japan's commitment to the international human rights principles and standards was nevertheless strengthened in the 1990s. Japan became more outspoken in its assertion that international human rights standards are universally applicable to all states, regardless of their social, cultural, or economic particularities.

In official statements on the occasion of the World Conference on Human Rights in Vienna held in June 1993, Tokyo supported the universality and indivisibility of human rights, carefully distancing itself from those Asian states championing "Asian values." Japan also claimed that human rights should not be sacrificed to development, and reaffirmed the role of Official Development Assistance (ODA) in promoting the human rights of individuals.[22] Likewise in the Asia Regional Preparatory Meeting for the World Conference on Human Rights, held in Bangkok in March 1993, Japan defended the universality and indivisibility of human rights. It contested the sections of the Bangkok Declaration that opposed linking aid to human rights. The Japanese delegation stated: "Japan firmly believes that human rights are universal values common to all mankind, and that the international community should remain committed to the principles set forth in the Universal Declaration of Human Rights ... It is the duty of all States, whatever their cultural tradition, whatever their political or economic system, to protect and promote these values."[23]

Thus, in so far as abstract principles are concerned, Japan's commitment to international human rights standards became clearer in the 1990s, and its endorsements of international human rights norms became more explicit.

### *Regional developments*

There is no regional intergovernmental organization for human rights in Asia, unlike most other regions of the world. There has been a consistent tendency in the Asian region to detach human rights dialogues from political and economic processes, especially within the Association of South East Asian Nations (ASEAN). State sovereignty is a particularly sensitive issue in Asia. Most Asian governments have argued that there is a necessity to accommodate multiple types of political systems within the region's diplomatic and security frameworks. The complexity of the region's colonial experiences, ethnic compositions, and institutional history on which authorities are founded further adds to the sensitivity of the issue of sovereignty.[24]

Furthermore, relative economic success in the region – until the economic crisis in 1998 – contributed to the growing assertiveness of some policy-makers. They claim that human rights are Western concepts and are not to be accommodated within "Asian ways" of promoting and maintaining domestic stability, peace, and economic prosperity.[25] Most

Asian leaders have been extremely sensitive about what they regard as Western attempts to influence their domestic affairs. Thus they have long opposed linking trade or aid with human rights.

In this context the 1993 Bangkok Declaration on Human Rights can be seen as yet another manifestation of such Asian leaders' dislike of the so-called human rights diplomacy as practised by the Western nations. In the conference held in preparation for the Vienna World Conference on Human Rights, Asian leaders emphasized that human rights implementation should also consider countries' socio-economic and cultural backgrounds. China specifically argued that development should be given priority over civil and political rights in certain circumstances.[26]

Japan's main foreign policy interest in the region has traditionally been economic and, even though Japan has recently sought to assume some political role in the region, it has not been so active yet in promoting human rights. Its approach to human rights violations in the region has been pragmatic and country specific.[27]

Three interrelated factors account for this pragmatism, in addition to the general sensitivity over sovereignty in the region. The first factor is the security concern. Japan has long considered it important to keep China politically stable and economically "modernizing." Hence, it has been hesitant to apply conditionality to its aid based upon China's human rights record. It believes that an isolated China is highly destabilizing given the territorial disputes surrounding China, and given the unstable political situation in the Korean peninsula and in Indo-China. In addition, it understands China as a polity that is not susceptible to outside pressures, thus negative human rights diplomacy – sanctions and other punitive inducements – would be counter-productive. Other countries, such as Indonesia, are both important exporters of natural resources vital to Japan's national security and economy as well as important markets for its investment and goods, as Japan reduces its dependence on the US market. These economic factors are closely linked to Japan's security concerns.

The second factor behind Japan's pragmatic approach to human rights in Asia is its identity as a mediator between East and West.[28] From the mid-1950s, Japan sought to identify closely with Asian countries as well as to cooperate with the free democratic nations as the foundation of its foreign policy.[29] Further, it is seeking a more active role in Asia through multilateral political and economic forums such as the Asian Development Bank, the ASEAN Regional Forum, and the Asia-Pacific Economic Cooperation network. Such a dual role, however, has been difficult to play in human rights diplomacy. Japan has often found itself in the awkward position of having to balance Asian and Western preferences. One such example was the Tiananmen Square incident, where Japan's intermediary efforts evoked considerable suspicion and criticism among the Western nations.[30] More recently, at the Bangkok meeting preceding the World Conference on Human Rights, Japan, having supported the universality of human rights, was subject to considerable criticism by some Asian representatives including China.[31]

The third element behind the Japanese reluctance to play Western-style human rights diplomacy in Asia is its colonial and military history, as we noted earlier. Owing to its historical relations with its Asian neighbours, Japan has not been in a position to speak strongly for human rights. Even though Japan has vigorously pursued its goal of establishing friendly relations and a leadership role in Asia, its true intentions have often been viewed with suspicion by its neighbours.

In sum, unlike Europe, Asia is far from building a common framework for dealing with human rights issues within the region. Japan has been reluctant to assume leadership for human rights largely owing to economic and security considerations, a desire to mediate between Western and Asian states, and its historical record. True, in recent years, Tokyo has exercised leadership in conflict-resolution and peace-building activities in Cambodia, in peace-making in the Korean peninsula, and in actions against nuclear testing in China. But, with the exception of Cambodia, where considerable attention to human rights was involved, Japan's leadership was shown mainly in the areas of security and development.

At the time of the admission of Myanmar (Burma) to ASEAN, a major event concerning ASEAN, Japan quietly observed the event, signalling its approval of the ASEAN argument for constructive engagement, in contrast with some Western governments which were more critical of Myanmar's admission. With regard to the coup in Cambodia in July 1997, when the then Second Prime Minister, Hun Sen, expelled the First Prime Minister, in violation of the Paris Peace Agreement and the prior election results, Japan also took a position largely in line with the ASEAN approach to Cambodia. Unlike some Western states, Japan did not officially freeze its Official Development Aid to Cambodia, though much of its implementation in effect ceased after the event. Japan also supported the ASEAN decision to postpone Cambodia's entry to ASEAN and continued dialogues with the Cambodian government, expressing its view that peace in that country was indispensable and that human rights must be respected.[32] Japan then provided both financial contributions and personnel to supervise the general election held in 1998.

In this regard, it is noteworthy that the Japanese government has supported the idea of establishing a regional human rights mechanism. In the UN General Assembly as well as in the UN Commission on Human Rights, it has sponsored resolutions that state that any region without regional arrangements for human rights protection should promote discussions towards establishing one.[33] Since 1995 the Japanese government has also held an international symposium for human rights experts from the region, with a view to promoting further discussions concerning the possibility for a regional mechanism for human rights in the Asia and Pacific region. Such an effort may be seen as Tokyo's cautious but increasingly active stance in the field of human rights.

### *International financial institutions*

Multilateral economic aid through the World Bank, the International Monetary Fund (IMF), and regional development banks has been an important element in Japan's foreign policy. In addition to bilateral aid, multilateral aid has served to advance Japan's interests, such as increasing its multilateral influence, developing Asian markets, promoting favourable relations with recipient countries, and reducing a large monetary surplus that had attracted considerable international criticism. The importance Japan attaches to multilateral development agencies has increased in the post–Cold War era,[34] and is likely to remain high in the near future – even though Japan decided to reduce its contribution to multilateral agencies by some 10 per cent in 1998 as a result of economic difficulties.

Japan has practically been silent on issues related to human rights in international financial institutions. Under the banner of "*Seikei Bunri*," meaning the separation of economic issues from political considerations, a slogan that has dominated Japanese foreign economic policy since the 1960s, Tokyo has been rather careful not to be seen as pursuing political objectives through multilateral financial institutions. Japan likewise tends to oppose any political conditionality argument in multilateral financial institutions designed to induce recipient governments to curb human rights violations, especially pertaining to ASEAN states.[35] This tendency corresponded to the basic thinking in Japan – until the adoption of the 1992 ODA Charter – that political and human rights conditionalities in development aid were inappropriate in light of the principle of non-intervention in the internal affairs of recipient states. This tendency can also partly be attributed to the fact that the economic ministries, which have considered human rights issues as outside their competence or concern, hold direct responsibility for matters related to development banks. Further, the complexity of the development assistance process in Tokyo, involving close to 20 ministries and agencies, adds to the difficulty of achieving the coordination required for the integration of human rights with development aid.

The Asian Development Bank (ADB) is the only notable multilateral financial institution initiated and shaped by Japan, albeit under the general US tolerance particular to the era around the time the Bank was created and developed.[36] Since the establishment of the ADB in 1966, Japan has been one of the two largest shareholders of the Bank, co-equal with the United States.[37] All ADB presidents have been Japanese, mostly seconded from the Ministry of Finance. Since the mid-1980s, as Japan became particularly keen to increase its influence in the Bank to suit its general diplomatic agenda,[38] its financial presence became stronger in the Bank. In 1996, Japan's contribution to the Asian Development Fund (ADF), a soft-loan arm of the Bank, stood at US$9,351.70 million out of total contributed resources of US$18,203.26 million. The US contribution was only US$2,287.91 million.[39] Japan's contribution to the Technical Assistance Special Fund in 1996 amounted to about 56 per cent of the total supplied.[40] Between 1988 and 1996, Japan contributed US$633.9 million to the Special Fund.[41] Thus Japan's potential leverage in ADB is great, should it choose to link human rights conditions to such financial contributions.

In line with most international financial institutions, however, the ADB has followed strictly "non-political" objectives, with particular emphasis on developing infrastructure and industries in the region. The ADB has been particularly reluctant to link human rights with its operational objectives in any way. This reluctance can partly be attributed to the sensitivity of the Bank's shareholders, which include Asian states that particularly disfavour human rights diplomacy. Furthermore, the nature of Japanese leadership in the Bank can also be considered as a factor behind such reluctance to link aid to human rights in the Asian context. As noted, human rights did not receive much attention in Japanese foreign economic policy until 1992 when the ODA Charter was adopted. Even after 1992, Japan's interest in the ADB's policies and operations remained primarily economic and strategic. As Woo-Cumings points out, Tokyo's rationale for creating and supporting the Bank was primarily to augment the market in Asia for Japanese capital and goods.[42] Japan remained committed to trying to achieve a vertical integration of Asian markets.

The Bank's lending patterns suggest that they reflect Japanese preferences. Indonesia, one of the main recipients of Japanese bilateral aid, has also been a main recipient of the Bank's multilateral loans. Indonesia received the highest percentage of Ordinary Capital Resources (OCR) loans among all recipient countries between 1978 and 1992, receiving more than 30 per cent of total OCR loans between 1983 and 1992.[43] China has also consistently been a major recipient since it joined the Bank in 1986, receiving 12.3 per cent of total OCR loans in the 1988–1992 period and 31.5 per cent in the 1993–1996 period.[44] Smaller but growing countries in South-East Asia such as Thailand, Vietnam, and the Philippines received approximately 6 per cent of total loans in 1996, which coincided with Tokyo's interest in the South-East region.[45]

Some point out that such lending patterns at times conflicted with socio-economic rights in certain poorer countries in the region. The Bank, however, has put more emphasis on poverty reduction and social infrastructure since the 1980s and, more recently, on governance issues to increase transparency in economic management. But, like the World Bank, the ADB continues to resist overt and explicit linkage to human rights. As at the World Bank, governance issues are understood mostly in accounting terms like transparency, not in terms of democracy and civil rights.

The general reluctance in the ADB to implement political conditionality based upon human rights records can be overcome in the case of exceptionally severe human rights violations, under the pressure of some key shareholders such as the United States. One such case was China, where after the Tiananmen Square incident in 1989 Japan followed the United States and other Western donors in suspending ADB loans to China. World Bank loans were also frozen after the event. In general, however, Japan played an intermediary role between China and major Western donors in the post-Tiananmen ADB process. This was consistent with Japan's intermediary role in getting China to join the ADB in 1986.[46] After Tiananmen, having supported an early partial freeze on ADB loans to China, Japan then successfully lobbied in November 1990 for an approval of a US$50 million agricultural loan and a US$480,000 technical assistance (TA) grant to China.[47] In April 1991, at the ADB Board of Directors' meeting, Japan pressed for a full resumption of loans to China.[48] These actions inside the ADB coincided with Japanese actions outside the Bank. The ADB, nevertheless, was not the only agency to resume loans to China. The World Bank also decided partially to resume loans to China in February 1990, a move that indicated waning US interest in continued sanctions against China through multilateral banks as well as through private transactions.[49]

After the 1997 coup in Cambodia by Second Prime Minister Hun Sen, the processing of ADB loans and TA grants was suspended, although the implementation of existing loans and TA projects continued. No explanation was given by the Bank about its position in response to the coup. Given the complexity of the problems this coup entailed, there was a general lack of consensus on what measures could realistically and legitimately be taken among the ADB shareholders.

Since the 1990s Japan's traditional development philosophy has been in some disarray, mainly because of the new thinking about development stemming from the East European situation. There had been a tendency among the economic ministries in Tokyo to argue that there is an Asian model of development, which favours political stability and an active and large governmental role, and that this model is more suitable to developing countries. Preference for this Asian or non-Western model of development persisted in the Japanese economic bureaucracy, despite rhetoric from other parts of the state rejecting Asian values and endorsing universal human rights. Japan's continuing support for this model can be compared to Western liberal models of development integrating liberalization, democratization, and other human rights simultaneously.

As Japan started to provide economic aid to Eastern Europe, where democratization was an official objective of the transition from communism that was supposedly as important as the introduction of a market economy, it found itself supporting both development models – the liberal one in Eastern Europe and the illiberal one in the non-Western world. This was not necessarily irrational, but it was not fully consistent with the new rhetoric, as at Vienna in 1993, in favour of universal human rights.

In 1990, for example, then Prime Minister Toshiaki Kaifu visited Europe and agreed that Japan would provide economic assistance to Eastern Europe aiming at democratization and privatization.[50] He also agreed to support the European Bank for Reconstruction and Development (EBRD). The EBRD is the only development bank that includes advancing democracy and human rights in its mandate. The Bank does take democracy and human rights into account in its loan making, and Japan has been supporting these policies, holding a share of 8.5 per cent, second to that of the United States and the same as that of Germany, France, and England.[51]

Japan's support for the EBRD can be understood as compatible with its policy to collaborate with the Western states. Japan's involvement in the EBRD is also quite limited compared with that of ADB, where Japan holds a predominant status and influence in management. However, these developments in the context of Eastern Europe are adding another dimension to Japanese multilateral aid policy, even though opinions are not at all uniform among policy-makers about the compatibility of such developments with the older approach.

### *United Nations*

Since it joined the United Nations in 1957, Japan has attached particular importance to the organization, placing it in the centre of its foreign policy concerns together with cooperation with Western states.[52] Tokyo has considered it imperative to cooperate with other states in the United Nations to endorse the purposes of the organization, including human rights, partly as a means to heighten its international status, which suffered greatly under the legacy of Tokyo's policies in the 1930s and 1940s. As already noted, Japan's policy towards human rights at the United Nations became more active from the early to mid-1980s when the government and private experts became members of various UN human rights bodies. Against the background of membership in the General Assembly, Japan's participation in the Human Rights Commission from 1982, and its nationals' involvement in the Sub-Commission on Prevention of Discrimination and Protection of Minorities from 1984, enabled Japanese, whether as instructed governmental representatives or as uninstructed individual experts, to take part in the regular UN forums concerning human rights, thus diversifying its activities in the field of human rights. As is true for other states, most uninstructed Japanese experts, although not state officials, are drawn from a social network that broadly includes state officials, and they normally stay in close contact with state officials. Japan was also sometimes elected to the UN Security Council, which increasingly dealt with human rights issues after the Cold war. In addition, after the ratification by Japan of the two Covenants in 1979, Japanese nationals began to be elected to the Human Rights Committee that monitors the International Covenant on Civil and Political Rights.

Even though, as we shall see, Japan tends to be clearly cautious in openly practising human rights diplomacy in bilateral relations, in the UN forums it has maintained in essence a liberal position on human rights very similar to that of other Western-style democracies. This tendency became clearer as the 1990s progressed, partially reflecting Tokyo's greater interest in a more active multilateral diplomacy. This activism, in turn, was said to be linked to Japan's interest in securing a permanent seat on the UN Security Council.

In grave humanitarian crises in the post–Cold War period, such as in the former Yugoslavia, Rwanda, Somalia, Zaire (Democratic Republic of the Congo), and elsewhere, Japan was in general supportive of all UN Security Council resolutions and decisions, providing large financial contributions to UN peacekeeping and humanitarian activities. It has also supported the establishment of international tribunals for the former Yugoslavia and Rwanda. It voted in favour of the draft statute for a standing international criminal court, linked to the United Nations, at a diplomatic conference in Rome in July 1998. Even though it has not made special efforts to increase the small budget allocated for the Office of the UN High Commissioner for Human Rights, a budget amounting to merely 1 per cent of the total UN budget, it has contributed special resources for its technical assistance and handling of information. Japan has made major contributions to the UN Office of the High Commissioner for Refugees, where a Japanese national, Sadako Ogata, heads the agency centrally involved in many human rights and humanitarian issues. Yet, within this broader framework of liberal multilateral diplomacy, Japan reserves some degree of flexibility in its approach towards certain individual countries, as exemplified by its attitude to China – and more recently to Myanmar.

Since the Tiananmen incident, Japan has joined other Western states in the UN Commission on Human Rights to sponsor draft resolutions critical of China's human rights record. The draft resolutions, initiated by the United States and European states such as Denmark and the Netherlands, nevertheless were never adopted owing to Chinese blocking actions supported by much of the global South. The attempt to pass a critical resolution gradually lost impetus even among Western states after 1995, however, mainly owing to shifts in the policies of the larger European states to favour access to the Chinese market. Japan was among the defectors in 1997, together with France, Germany, Greece, Italy, and Spain, and did not co-sponsor the draft resolution on China, even though it voted against the Chinese blocking, or no-action, motion.[53] The loss of Western cohesion on the issue was one factor that encouraged Japan to prioritize the improvement of its bilateral relations with China, which had deteriorated in 1996–1997 over events that heightened Japan's security concerns in East Asia.[54]

With regard to Myanmar, both the Commission on Human Rights and the Third Committee of the General Assembly expressed concern over its human rights situation. It was an uncontested fact that the State Law and Order Restoration Council (SLORC) government had ignored the 1990 general election results and repressed political opponents. In the Commission on Human Rights, Japan has not co-sponsored the resolution on the situation of human rights in Myanmar, adopted every year without a vote, even though it has welcomed its adoption and endorsed it.[55] Likewise, Japan has endorsed, without becoming a co-sponsor, the Third Committee's consensus resolution on the situation on human rights in Myanmar.[56] Yet, in 1990 and in 1991 Tokyo attempted to mediate the positions of the Western sponsors and Myanmar in the Third Committee.[57] When Sweden introduced a draft resolution in 1990 in the Third Committee, demanding that the Burmese military government hold new elections and release political prisoners,[58] Japan proposed that the Committee refrain from taking action that year in view of the forthcoming completion of the report by the UN Independent Expert on Myanmar, appointed by the Commission on Human Rights. The reasoning given by the Japanese government was to avoid prejudging the consideration of that report, or any decision it might lead to.[59] In the following year, Sweden introduced a new text again addressing the continuing repression of the political opposition. Japan then proposed to soften the language of the resolution and, with Sweden's concession, the resolution was adopted without a vote.[60]

Thus in UN meetings in New York and Geneva Japan usually adopted a position in favour of human rights, but occasionally tried to mediate between Western states and the targets of critical resolutions in Asia. Even more important was Japan's leadership for human rights in Cambodia, where it led a second-generation or complex peacekeeping mission.[61] This major field operation, between 1992 and 1996, was headed by a Japanese and largely funded by Tokyo. It sought to organize and supervise national free and fair elections for the first time in Cambodian history, as well as to carry out human rights education and to reform the police and military establishments so as to make them more sensitive to human rights. This is not the place for a detailed analysis of the activities of the UN Transitional Authority in Cambodia (UNTAC). Suffice it to say that its long-term record of success was mixed, particularly given the unwillingness of some of the major Cambodian political leaders and movements to live up to human rights provisions in the related agreements. Nevertheless, Japan was certainly a major player, perhaps the most important state, in trying to create and consolidate democracy with human rights in Cambodia. Likewise Japan was quite active, including the supplying of military personnel, in a UN effort to bring a liberal democratic peace to Mozambique.[62] These extensive activities, which in Cambodia included the placing of Japanese military personnel on the Asian mainland for the first time since the days of Japan's misguided policies during the 1930s and 1940s, were generally regarded to be linked to Japan's quest for a permanent place on the Security Council.

## V. Bilateral policy

### *Linkage to trade/aid*

It was in the middle of the 1970s that some aid agencies such as the World Bank began to question the wisdom of extending financial assistance to countries that were under authoritarian rule and characterized by corruption. They were pushed into this new orientation by certain Western states such as the Netherlands and the Scandinavians. They focused on countries such as Chile under Pinochet and the Philippines under Marcos, and on some African states. For Japan, however, which was becoming one of the leading donor countries, this policy of linking foreign aid to the human rights record of a recipient country was not yet a reality. This is confirmed by the fact that annual reports of the Japanese government on foreign aid in the 1970s made no reference to the human rights situations of the recipient countries. As noted above, the main concerns of the Japanese aid agencies at that time were economy and security.

Again as noted earlier, in the 1980s Japan began to pay more attention to the human rights record and to the condition of the human environment when extending assistance to a developing country. The issue became acute for Japan, as we have noted, when the Burmese/Myanmar military took power in 1988, and also when the Chinese authorities used violence at Tiananmen in 1989. There were strong pressures within and outside of Japan, both public and private, to criticize such repressive acts by the military and to stop extending foreign aid to these governments. In the wake of these events, the Japanese government adopted the Official Development Assistance Charter in June 1992, in which the government regulates how military spending, human rights, and democratization relate to ODA.[63] The core of the ODA Charter reads as follows:

> Taking into account comprehensively each recipient country's requests, its socio-economic conditions, and Japan's bilateral relations with the recipient country, Japan's ODA will be provided in accordance with the principles of the United Nations Charter (especially sovereign equality and non-intervention in domestic matters), as well as the following four principles:
> 1. Environmental conservation and development should be pursued in tandem.
> 2. Any use of ODA for military purposes or for aggravation of international conflicts should be avoided.
> 3. Full attention should be paid to trends in recipient countries' military expenditures, their development and production of mass destruction weapons and missiles, their export and import of arms, etc., so as to maintain and strengthen international peace and stability and from the viewpoint that developing countries should place appropriate priorities in the allocation of their resources on their own economic and social development.
> 4. Full attention should be paid to efforts for promoting democratization and introduction of a market-oriented economy, and the situation regarding the securing of basic human rights and freedoms in the recipient country.

Although the ODA Charter is clearly a step forward in the direction of placing human rights as a central goal of the Japanese government's foreign policy, it is by no means an ideal document from the viewpoint of human rights. First of all, the human rights element is included as the fourth principle instead of the first or second. Certainly there is no wording to suggest that the consideration of human rights in the recipient country is the *sine qua non* of Japanese ODA. As long as "[f]ull attention" is paid to "the situation regarding the securing of basic human rights and freedoms in the recipient country," the aid may continue. Even more troubling, the application of the four principles is subjected to the maintenance of Japan's bilateral relations with the recipient country and the principle of "non-intervention in domestic matters." The wording of the Charter suggests a certain reserve on the part of the Japanese government in addressing human rights abroad. According to one observer, in "implementing these principles, however, Japan makes it a rule to closely observe trends in the specific situation in which each country is placed since the security environment surrounding each country and its cultural and social conditions vary. When there are problems in the eyes of the international community and the Japanese people, Japan will first confirm the case by checking with the country involved and, if necessary, express its concern. If the situation is not improved, Japan will review its aid policy toward that country."[64] The policy toward Myanmar/Burma and China illustrates this sort of flexibility. Tokyo's willingness to act on human rights is heavily conditioned by other considerations, not least of which is pressure to act from the West.

As a general background factor behind this cautious flexibility, the importance Japan attaches to the development of the Asian region in general must be pointed out. In Tokyo's bilateral ODA, Asia has long been considered as the most important area given the economic and strategic importance of the region. In the late 1960s, 90 per cent of Japan's bilateral ODA went to the Asian region, with about 70 per cent concentrating on East Asia. As the recipients of Japanese ODA diversified to include Africa and the Middle East after the 1970s, the figures went down to between 40 and 50 per cent.[65] In the 1990s, Japan still provided around 55 per cent of its bilateral ODA to the Asian region, whereas Africa received 12.6 per cent, Latin America 10.8 per cent, the Middle East 6.8 per cent, Europe 1.5 per cent, and Oceania 1.5 per cent (1995 figures).[66]

China has been one of the largest recipients of Japanese bilateral ODA. Since Japan normalized its diplomatic relations with China in 1972, Japan has sought to develop economic, cultural, and political ties with the country. In his 1979 visit, Prime Minister Masayoshi Ohira agreed that the first loan of ¥330.9 billion would be provided in 1979–1983, to build up its economic infrastructure. A second loan followed in 1984–1989 totalling ¥470 billion, again including transportation, energy, communication, and other infrastructures. On his visit to Beijing in August 1988, Prime Minister Noboru Takeshita announced that Japan was prepared to provide a third loan of ¥810 billion in 1990–1995.[67] Between 1982 and 1986, authoritarian and undemocratic China was the largest recipient of Japanese bilateral ODA, and between 1987 and 1990 it was the second largest.[68] After dropping to become the fourth-largest recipient of bilateral aid in 1991 (largely owing to the Tiananmen incident), by 1995 China was again the largest recipient of bilateral ODA – with technical cooperation in the amount of US$304.75 million (8.8 per cent of all technical cooperation) and ODA loans of US$992.28 million

(24.07 per cent).[69] Grant aid however was reduced in 1995, following China's much criticized nuclear tests, from ¥7.79 billion in 1994 to ¥480 million (US$83.2 million) in 1995.[70]

The Tiananmen incident on 4 June 1989 illustrated that, under pressure from Western states, grave human rights violations in an aid recipient country can affect Japan's aid policy, despite the strategic importance of the country.[71] After the incident, though with a delay, Japan followed Western countries on 20 June in freezing new economic assistance to China. It stopped processing new grants and loans, while promising to implement already agreed, on-going projects. Diplomatically, albeit in milder language and with a slower reaction, many of the Japanese policies in the months following the event did not differ much in substance from those of the Western states.[72] Japan joined other members of the Paris Summit of G7 states in issuing a communiqué expressing concern over the incident and approving the punitive measures taken by individual countries. The Japanese Ministry of Foreign Affairs did try to restrict the return of Japanese business to China, a process already under way only one month after the incident, by issuing a special request to three major Japanese business associations on 22 June that asked each corporation to decide "with prudence" whether to allow its employees to return to or visit China. The Ministry of International Trade and Industry postponed the establishment of a business association for investment in China, which had been planned for 7 June, and lowered China's credit rating to reflect the higher risks associated with commerce and trade.[73]

Tiananmen, however, affected Japanese aid to China only briefly, and Tokyo had already moved to normalize its relations with Beijing one year later. Even during the Paris Summit, Japan was trying to persuade other Western states not to pressure China into diplomatic isolation, referring to the importance of China in maintaining security in the region, which led to the adoption of a joint communiqué short of imposing new joint sanctions, while encouraging China to do its utmost to avoid international isolation.[74] In August 1989, in the area of technical cooperation, Japan began to resume some volunteer missions as well as emergency disaster relief. In September, restrictions on travel to China were lifted. In December, an agreement was reached concerning the continuation of existing grant programmes.[75] In early 1990, LDP leaders, in particular former Prime Minister Takeshita, and Japanese government officials started to discuss a partial resumption of the third yen loan to China.[76] This move was in a way stimulated by events in the United States, including the approval by President Bush of the sale of three communication satellites to China in December 1989, as well as his decision earlier in the year to renew China's most-favoured-nation status for another year. The World Bank also decided to ease the freeze of its loans in

February 1990. At the Houston Summit of G7 states in July 1990, Japan officially announced its decision partially to resume its loan programme to China. In late 1990, Japan provided a loan of ¥120 billion, and in 1991, ¥120 billion.[77] Further, on 18 December, a five-year trade agreement was signed, promising China US$8 billion in technology, plant, and construction equipment in exchange for oil and coal.[78]

Thus, after a brief halt in bilateral aid, Japan's aid programme to China returned more or less to normal. The resumption of ODA reflected, most of all, Japan's traditional concern for China's importance for the security and prosperity of the region, and, indeed, for world security. It was understood by the Japanese government that the isolation of China was a serious matter, and suspension of Japan's ODA, the largest in the world, was more destabilizing to China than sanctions imposed by other countries.[79] There was also profound business interest in China, even though some business leaders, such as Takashi Ishiwara of *Keizai Doyu Kai* (Japan Association of Corporate Executives), were vocal advocates of Japan acting closely with other Western states.[80]

Overall, the Tiananmen incident again illustrated the difficult balance Japan maintained between its role as a Western partner and that as an Eastern state. Although economic assistance was halted in line with the policy of other Western states, Japan, from security concerns, refrained from taking an overly critical stance verbally, and also from continuing with the cancellation of its ODA to China for any length of time. Concerns about avoiding criticism and isolation from other Western states had to be balanced against the danger of isolating China. In addition, as Prime Minister Uno himself remarked on 7 June, it was widely recognized that past Japanese involvement in China made it inappropriate for Japan to take sides. He observed as well that Japan's relations with China could not be understood in the same way as US relations with China were.[81] There was thus persistent support for the principle of non-interference within the Japanese government and direct reference to human rights was often avoided, even though there was constant mention of humanitarian concerns.[82]

In 1995, in protest against the nuclear tests that China had carried out, the Japanese government applied the principles of the ODA Charter, thereby withholding its grant aid – except for humanitarian and grass-roots assistance. Despite this action, Japan was still the largest bilateral aid donor to China, providing more than US$1.38 billion in 1995.[83]

As for Myanmar, the Japanese government has applied a policy of constructive engagement, as exemplified by its actions in the UN forums noted above. However, in terms of bilateral aid, Japan's action has been more consistent than in the case of China.

Until the end of the 1980s, the Japanese government considered

Myanmar (then Burma) to be an important recipient of Japanese bilateral ODA, together with ASEAN states, for economic and strategic reasons.[84] After Myanmar was classified as a least developed country (LDC) in December 1987, Japanese grants to Myanmar increased to about ¥10 billion in 1988. Loans to Myanmar started in 1969 with a yen loan of ¥10.8 billion and increased in 1976 to ¥20 billion, and in 1982 to about ¥40 billion.[85] Dependence of Myanmar on trade with Japan was the highest in the region, with its imports from Japan amounting to over 40 per cent of its total in 1987. Japan was the largest aid donor to Myanmar, providing more than 71.5 per cent of all aid the country received in 1987 and 80 per cent in 1988.

However, in September 1988, Japanese ODA to Myanmar in effect had to be halted,[86] owing to the *coup d'état* and lack of normal relations with the new military government. The Ministry of Foreign Affairs communicated to the new government that Japan would be unable to resume economic assistance until the political situation calmed down and efforts were made to reform the economy.[87] As a result, total bilateral ODA dropped from US$260 million in 1988 to US$71 million in 1989, US$61 million in 1990, and US$85 million in 1991, while grant aid also dropped from about ¥10 billion in previous years to ¥3.7 billion in 1988, no grant aid in 1989, ¥3.5 billion for debt relief in 1990, and ¥5.0 billion for debt relief in 1991.[88] The freeze on new aid continues at the time of writing. Nevertheless, Japanese aid to Myanmar remains by far the largest among the countries of the Development Assistance Committee (DAC). In 1994, Japan provided US$133.8 million of the total US$142.8 million the country received as ODA from DAC countries.[89] Moreover, the Japanese government split from the Western position in order to recognize the SLORC government in February 1989 and started partially to resume assistance to on-going projects as well as emergency humanitarian relief, including food and disaster relief. The Japanese government maintains that it has continued dialogues with the Myanmar government in order to encourage it to release political prisoners. In response to the release of the democratic leader Aung San Suu Kyi from house arrest in July 1995, the Japanese government decided to implement suspended on-going projects and those based upon the assessment of basic human needs. In October 1995, it decided to provide grant aid for the expansion of the Institute of Nursing in Myanmar. However, as the situation deteriorated again in 1996, no new commitments of foreign assistance have been made.[90]

Indonesia, Peru, and Thailand were cases that exhibited less flexibility in Japanese aid policy. Indonesia has been one of the largest recipients of Japanese bilateral aid, second only to China. In 1987–1990, it was the largest recipient. In 1995, it was the second largest, receiving about

US$892 million.[91] In November 1991, the Indonesian military harshly suppressed a generally peaceful demonstration in East Timor, which resulted in more than 100 deaths. This incident did not lead to a halt in Japanese aid to Indonesia, however, despite pledges by the opposition party, based upon the judgement that diplomatic pressures from Japan and the international community had led to a calming of the situation and that the Indonesian government had taken measures to investigate, punish those responsible, and prevent the occurrence of similar events.[92] In this case, Japan officially took no stance with regard to the conditionality of aid linked to the human rights performance of a recipient country. Similarly, events in Peru in April 1992, when President Fujimori resorted to emergency measures to dissolve parliament, or in Thailand in May 1992 did not lead Japan to reconsider its aid policy to these countries, on the basis that they were heading back to normalcy under effective international pressures.[93]

As regards North Korea, Japan has provided emergency relief, based purely upon humanitarian concerns, despite persistent problems in the normalization process. In 1997, Japan provided US$27 million in response to the UN appeal and SFr 11 million in response to the International Federation of Red Cross appeal. However, North Korea's firing of a missile over Japanese territory in September 1998 forced Japan to halt these transactions.

The spirit of the ODA Charter has been most closely followed in the context of Eastern Europe. In 1990 Prime Minister Toshiaki Kaifu promised to provide a US$150 million loan through the IMF to Poland, technical cooperation of US$50 million, a five-year loan of US$500 million from the Export-Import Bank, and export credits to Poland and Hungary.[94] Japan has expanded its aid to other East European countries where democratization is a key issue, even though the sums remain small in comparison with key Asian aid recipients. As regards African countries, Japan has suspended aid to Nigeria, the Sudan, and the Gambia, on the grounds of serious human rights violations, and reduced aid to Kenya and Malawi.[95]

Such examples signify an inconsistent application of the 1992 ODA Charter, which would suggest uneven political support for the text itself. Although the ODA Charter is certainly a cornerstone of Japanese aid philosophy, inconsistency in its application as well as ambiguity in its content remain issues to be addressed in the future.

## VI. Conclusion

This paper has attempted to demonstrate the change that has occurred in Japan's foreign policy on human rights. Because of various historical, domestic, and international factors, Japan did not have a clear-cut foreign policy on human rights from the mid-1950s to the mid-1980s. But from the 1980s a changing international environment and, to a lesser degree, changing domestic politics moved Japan to pay more attention to human rights in other countries. Japan presents an interesting case of a non-Western state with a different political and foreign policy tradition gradually moving to accommodate increasingly salient human rights issues.

As part of the Western coalition of liberal democratic states, Japan has been under informal and formal pressure to act with them in order to advance human rights in world politics. This has been especially so given the importance of the Japanese economy and associated foreign assistance programme. At times, and within certain limits, Japan has responded positively to these Western pressures for action on human rights abroad. Tokyo spoke out for universal human rights when some of its authoritarian neighbours were pushing "Asian values." It applied some economic pressure on both Myanmar and China in the name of human rights. It supported a transition to market democracies in Eastern Europe. It made a major commitment to a liberal democratic state in Cambodia, and a minor commitment to a liberal democratic order in other failed states such as Mozambique. That Japan had other interests in some of these situations, such as securing a permanent seat on the UN Security Council, does not detract from the reality of its support for democracy and civil rights in several situations.

At the same time, apart perhaps from Cambodia, it is difficult to chart a bold policy of Japanese leadership in the field of international human rights. Frequently its support for human rights has been tinged with caution and reservation. Often it has tried to play an intermediary or mediating role between those Western states willing to press for progress on the human rights front and the targeted Asian states. Japan has frequently combined its interest in human rights with other interests, particularly economics and security. Thus its interruption of business with China was brief after the events of Tiananmen Square, and Tokyo has also been less willing than certain Western states to apply major and consistent sanctions against Myanmar. For the most part, its policies on trade and aid have not been seriously influenced by human rights considerations.

Although Japan has been under international pressure at times to play a more active role on human rights, the nature of domestic politics in Japan is a restraining factor. Public demand for more attention to human rights abroad is relatively weak, especially as demonstrated by the lack of interest among Japanese human rights NGOs and media in human rights situations in other countries. Pressures from the Diet are also weak, and the strong Japanese bureaucracy is still dominated by economic and security interests – although there has been some slight change toward incorporating greater concerns for human rights in agencies interested in

UN and refugee affairs. Still, in relation to many of the Western liberal democracies, Japanese political culture is more deferential than demanding on the issue of human rights in foreign policy.

There has indeed been change in Japanese foreign policy regarding human rights in the past 50 years, but the future direction and strength of that change remain uncertain on the eve of the twenty-first century.

## Notes

1. International Symposium in Commemoration of the Centennial of the Japanese Association of International Law, *Japan and International Law: Past, Present and Future*, Kyoto International Conference Hall, 13–14 September 1997, p. 189.
2. Kentaro Serita, "Japan's Adoption and Implementation of Human Rights in Law and Practice," in *Japan and International Law: Past, Present and Future,* op. cit., 191 and Pierre-Marie Dupuy, "Western Views of Japanese Practice in the Field of Human Rights and Humanitarian Law," in ibid., 212.
3. The very first case of the application of this act was against a student movement in Kyoto called "the Kyoto Gakuren Incident." Serita, "Japan's Adoption," op. cit., 192.
4. Nobuyoshi Ashibe, *Kenpogaku* [Constitution], vol. II (General Theory of Human Rights) (Tokyo: Yuhikaku Publishing Company, 1997), 62.
5. See, for instance, Amnesty International, "Japan's Human Rights Record Must Be Challenged," News Release, 26 October 1998 (London, Amnesty International, International Secretariat); "JAPAN: Japan Complacent over Human Rights – Government Must Implement UN Human Rights Committee's Recommendations," News Release, 9 November 1998 (London, Amnesty International, International Secretariat).
6. Yozo Yokota, "Kironi tatsu Nihon no Seihu Kaihatsu Enjo" [Japan's ODA in Transition], *Kokusai Mondai* 451 (October 1997), 18.
7. John Peek, "Japan, the United Nations, and Human Rights," *Asian Survey* 32/3 (March 1992), 218–219.
8. Ibid.
9. The LDP lost popularity over a series of scandals involving high-ranking LDP officials at the end of the 1980s. The LDP lost in the general election in 1993 against a coalition of the New Frontier Party, the Social Democratic Party (SDPJ, former Socialist Party), and the Clean Government Party. The reformist government soon gave way in 1994 to the historic coalition of the LDP and the Social Democratic Party, in addition to the Sakigake New Party.
10. Ahn notes the increased difficulty in party–bureaucracy coordination during this era. C. S. Ahn, "Government–Party Coordination in Japan's Foreign Policy-Making: The Issue of Permanent Membership in the UNSC," *Asian Survey* 37/4 (April 1997), 368–382.
11. In the 1990s, movements demanding apologies and compensation from the Japanese government became strong, particularly in Korea. Following this, in December 1991, then LDP Prime Minister Kiichi Miyazawa started the investigation of six ministries that might have kept relevant documents to reveal whether or not the then Japanese government was involved in the matter. Official documents provided by the Asia Women's Fund.
12. See further Kozo Igarashi, *Kantei no Rasen Kaidan* (Tokyo: Gyosei, 1997).
13. Dennis T. Yasutomo, *The New Multilateralism in Japan's Foreign Policy* (New York, St. Martin's Press, 1995), 146.

14. Among scholars, however, there is a strong view that, by ratifying the First Optional Protocol to the Civil and Political Rights Covenant, Japan will not violate the relevant constitutional law provisions.
15. See, for example, Shigeki Miyazaki, ed., *Kokusai Jinken Kiyaku* (Tokyo: Nihon Hyoron Sha, 1996), 5.
16. John Peek, "Japan and the International Bill of Rights," *Journal of Northeast Asian Studies* 10/3 (Fall 1991), 3–15.
17. Ibid., 10; Miyazaki, *Kokusai Jinken Kiyaku*, op. cit., 240.
18. Seiichiro Takagi, "Japan's Policy towards China after Tiananmen," in James T. H. Tang, ed., *Human Rights and International Relations in the Asia Pacific* (London: Pinter, 1995), 98–99.
19. See Gaimusho [Ministry of Foreign Affairs of Japan], *Waga Gaiko no Kinkyo, 1957* (Tokyo), 123–124.
20. Gaimusho, *Waga Gaiko no Kinkyo, 1967*, 86–89.
21. Ibid.
22. Statement by Nobuo Matsunaga, Envoy of the Government of Japan and Representative of Japan to the World Conference on Human Rights, Vienna, 18 June 1993.
23. Statement by Seiichiro Otsuka, Minister, Embassy of Japan in Thailand and Representative of Japan to the Regional Meeting for Asia of the World Conference on Human Rights, Bangkok, 30 March 1993.
24. For the complexity of human rights issues in Asia, see Susumu Yamakage, "Tonan Ajia ni okeru Jinken mondai no Tayosei" [The Diversity of Human Rights Problems in South-east Asia], in Akio Watanabe, ed., *Asia no Jinken* [Human Rights in Asia], Kokusai Mondai Kenkyu-jo (Tokyo: Japan Institute for International Affairs, 1997).
25. The most vocal advocates of Asian approaches to maintaining domestic peace, stability, and prosperity are political leaders and members of the élite such as Lee Kwan Yew of Singapore and Mohamed Mahathir of Malaysia.
26. Joseph Chan, "The Asian Challenge to Universal Human Rights: A Philosophical Appraisal," in Tang, *Human Rights*, op. cit.
27. Yasuhiro Ueki, "Japan's New Diplomacy: Sources of Passivism and Activism," in Gerald Curtis, ed., *Japan's Foreign Policy after the Cold War: Coping with Change* (New York: M. E. Sharpe, 1993). See also Ogata's earlier account of Japan's pragmatism – Sadako Ogata, *Kokuren karano Shiten* [A View from the United Nations] (Tokyo: Asahi Evening News, 1980), chap. 4.
28. Ueki, "Japan's New Diplomacy," op. cit.; David Arase, "Japanese Policy toward Democracy and Human Rights in Asia," *Asian Survey* 33/10 (October 1993), 935–952, esp. 943–945.
29. Gaimusho, *Waga Gaiko no Kinkyo, 1958* (Tokyo), 5. Ueki, "Japan's New Diplomacy," op. cit., 350.
30. See, for example, Arase, "Japanese Policy," op. cit., and K. V. Kesavan, "Japan and the Tiananmen Square Incident," *Asian Survey* 30/7 (July 1990), 669–681.
31. Takagi, "Japan's Policy toward China," op. cit., 108.
32. Press conference by the press secretary, 11 July 1997 and 15 July 1997.
33. GA 49/189; E/CN.4/1997/34.
34. The *Diplomatic Bluebook 1995* (Ministry of Foreign Affairs of Japan, Tokyo) states Japan's interest in multilateral cooperation. The possibility of growing importance being attached to multilateralism is suggested by Curtis, *Japan's Foreign Policy*, op. cit.
35. Dennis T. Yasutomo, "The Politicization of Japan's 'Post-Cold War' Multilateral Diplomacy," in Curtis, *Japan's Foreign Policy*, op. cit., 329; Susumu Amanohara, "The US and Japan at the World Bank," in Peter Gourevitch, Takashi Inoguchi, and Courtney Purrington, eds., *United States–Japan Relations and International Institutions after the Cold War* (San Diego: University of California, San Diego, 1995).

36. For the Japanese leadership in the Bank, see for example Ming Wan, "Japan and the Asian Development Bank," *Pacific Affairs* 68/4 (1995), 509–528; Yasutomo, "The Politicization," op. cit. Concerning the US as well as Japanese interest in establishing the Bank, see Meredith Woo-Cumings, "The Asian Development Bank and the Politics of Development in East Asia," in Gourevitch, Inoguchi, and Purrington, *United States–Japan Relations*, op. cit.
37. Both Japan and the United States donate 16.054 per cent of the total subscribed capital, and are entitled to 13.2 per cent of the total voting. Asian Development Bank, *Annual Report, 1996* (Manila).
38. Yasutomo, "The Politicization," op. cit.
39. Asian Development Bank, *Annual Report, 1996*, 302.
40. Ibid., 303.
41. Ibid., 304.
42. Woo-Cumings, "The Asian Development Bank," op. cit.
43. Asian Development Bank, *Annual Report, 1996*, 268–269.
44. Ibid.
45. Ibid.
46. Yasutomo, "The Policization," op. cit., 328–329.
47. Ibid.
48. Ibid.
49. Kesavan, "Japan and the Tiananmen Square Incident," op. cit., 675.
50. Juichi Inada, "Nihon no Enjo Gaiko" [Japan's Aid Diplomacy], in Atsushi Kusano and Tetsuya Umemoto, eds., *Nihon Gaiko no Bunseki* [An Analysis of Japanese Diplomacy] (Tokyo: University of Tokyo Press, 1995), 158.
51. Ibid.
52. Gaimusho, *Waga Gaiko no Kinkyo, 1958* (Tokyo), 5–7.
53. United Nations, *Report of the Commission on Human Rights on its Fifty-Third Session*, E/CN.4/1997/150, 30 March 1997.
54. In 1998 a draft resolution was not submitted to the Commission, indicating a substantive change in US policy, given the earlier indication that European states would not sponsor another China resolution. China also made sure that certain concessions on rights issues, including its promise to sign the Covenant on Civil and Political Rights, were announced with the right timing.
55. See the explanation given by the Japanese government, for example, E/CN.4/1995/SR.62.
56. Japan's statements in A/C.3/51/SR.54, A/C.3/48/SR.53, and A/C.3/47/SR.59.
57. For a critical view of this policy, see Arase, "Japanese Policy," op. cit., 946.
58. A/C.3/45/L.58.
59. See the Japanese delegate's statement on 29 November 1990, A/C.3/45/SR.57.
60. A/C.3/46/SR.56, 29 November 1991 meeting.
61. See, for instance, Ministry of Foreign Affairs of Japan, "Japanese Participation in UN Peace-keeping Operation," *Foreign Policies: UN Peace-keeping Operations* (Tokyo: MOFA, January 1997).
62. Ibid.
63. Study Group for Cross-Cultural Communication, *Japanese Viewpoints* (Tokyo: Japan Times, 1995), 74.
64. Ibid.
65. See Gaimusho, *Waga Kunino Seifu Kaihatsu Enjo, 1990* [Japan's ODA, 1990] (Tokyo), 86.
66. Ministry of Foreign Affairs, *Japan's Official Development Assistance Annual Report 1996* (Tokyo), 89.

67. *Waga Kunino Seifu Kaihatsu Enjo, 1990*, 88.
68. Ibid., 86.
69. Ibid., 93, Chart 36.
70. Ibid., 41.
71. See also Inada, "Nihon no Enjo Gaiko," op. cit., 161.
72. Akihiko Tanaka, "ATiananmen igo no Chugoku wo Meguru Kokusai Kankyo" [International Environment for China after Tiananmen], *Kokusai Mondai*, no. 358 (January 1990), 36.
73. Ibid.
74. Kesavan, "Japan and the Tiananmen Square Incident," op. cit., 674.
75. *Waga Kunino Seifu Kaihatsu Enjo, 1990*, 89.
76. Kesavan, "Japan and the Tiananmen Square Incident," op. cit., p. 676.
77. Inada, "Nihon no Enjo Gaiko," op. cit., p. 161.
78. Arase, "Japanese Policy," op. cit., 944.
79. Takagi, "Japan's Policy," op. cit., 102.
80. Tanaka, "ATiananmen," op. cit., 35; Takagi, "Japan's Policy," op. cit., 101.
81. In his remark in the Diet session on 7 June; Tanaka, "ATiananmen," op. cit., 35.
82. Takagi, "Japan's Policy," op. cit., 101.
83. *Japan's ODA 1996*, 93; Gaimusho, *Gaiko Seisho: Waga Gaiko no Kinkyo 1997* (Tokyo), vol. 2, 22.
84. *Waga Kunino Seifu Kaihatsu Enjo, 1989*, 118.
85. Ibid.
86. *Waga Kunino Seifu Kaihatsu Enjo, 1991*, 131.
87. Inada, "Nihon no Enjo Gaiko," op. cit., 156.
88. *Waga Kunino Seifu Kaihatsu Enjo, 1993*, 133.
89. *Japan's ODA 1996*, 278.
90. Ibid., 41.
91. Ibid., 93.
92. *Waga Kunino Seifu Kaihatsu Enjo, 1992*, 33.
93. Ibid.
94. Inada, "Nihon no Enjo Gaiko," op. cit., 158.
95. *Japan's ODA 1996*, 41.

# Part II

# Some other states

# 6

# Russian foreign policy and human rights: Conflicted culture and uncertain policy

*Sergei V. Chugrov*

Two political myths concerning human rights in Russia are widely aired in the West. According to one of them, Russia historically followed the lead of the West towards liberalism, and only the 1917 Bolshevik revolution resulted in mass repressions and the negation of all human rights in the Soviet Union. The other myth stipulates that Russia has never developed the conditions for human rights and is hardly able to develop them now. Both arguments appear to be wrong. For centuries, Russia was torn by two cultural traditions. One of them, the Westernizing one, considers rights of the individual to be its cornerstone. The other, Slavophile, one accepts authoritarian government and severe restrictions on human rights, while seeing the source of the country's further development in its own particular traditions. The Westernizing tradition embraces universal rights, while the Slavophile tradition emphasizes cultural relativism and national particularism.

The first tendency pushes Russia towards the West, while the second one results in Russia pursuing a policy of self-isolation. The Westernizing tradition has always been weaker than the Slavophile one. This does not mean, however, that the seeds of liberal freedoms were eradicated from the national political culture; they were always there and remain so today. Rather, they are emerging from their suppression.

## I. Historical introduction

For about three centuries, up to 1480, the Muscovite principality was under the domination of Tatars. Some students of the Russian mentality see in this experience the sources of Russia's traditional adherence to non-freedom and its antipathy to human rights issues – as well as of Moscow's intrinsically aggressive attitude towards neighbouring principalities and countries. Russian authoritarianism was perhaps personified by Ivan the Terrible. Later, Peter the Great, while visiting one of the British battleships, wanted to watch a traditional corporal punishment in the fleet (whipping with a seven-tailed jack-o'-seven) and could not understand why the captain opposed his wish, there being no sailors who deserved to be punished. In Russia this circumstance might not have been viewed as an obstacle.[1] (On the other hand, Petrine Russia may serve as an eloquent example of the controversial Westernization of the country).

Russia turned out to be one of the countries most hostile to the French Revolution. The traditional Russian ideal society was a religious community that had no need to defend human rights because Love and Good took the place of rights. In this model, ideals and not law were supposed to be a guideline. In reality, there was a mixture of legal and religious rules, resulting in an unstructured complex network of relations between individuals and the state. This sort of collectivism paralysed much individual responsibility. In the real life, ethical norms are often in conflict with the law. In the extreme form, under Love, slavery is a happiness. Russia's strong peasant community (*mir*) emerged as a complex phenomenon with many elements of a parochial isolated community based on the idea of sacrificing individual rights for the sake of collectivist values. This imperative has turned out to be disastrous for Russia, leading to bloodshed and martyrs.[2] Even many Russian intellectuals of the nineteenth century demonstrated their rejection of law and put ethical norms in place of law. Thus the Russian legal tradition is weak.

Nevertheless, it is easy to see a counter-tendency. Catherine the Great, inspired by her contacts with French Enlightenment figures, initiated elections to a Legislative Commission in 1767 to consider the problems of rights. After 1861, Tsar Alexander II initiated a discussion about reforming the state's legal system in order to give rights to the representatives of new estates. It was Russia's initiative that led to the first world conference in The Hague on international law in 1899 to discuss humanitarian issues. Peter Stolypin, Russia's then controversial prime minister, forcibly moved peasants to Siberia, but nonetheless paid special attention to the problem of formal human rights and moved the country closer to European standards.

The fear of excessive liberties facilitated the acceptance of a totalitarian style of government after 1917. The very first steps of the Soviet leadership in 1917–1918 provide us with evidence of the new élite's low opinion of human beings and lack of respect for law. In the 1920s and 1930s, so-called "revolutionary expediency" was the clear excuse for unbridled violations of human rights. Therefore, the new Soviet Russia became isolated from the outer world. The division of the world into "bourgeois democracies" and "people's democracies" explains many conflicts with the outer world, including the 1956 invasion of Hungary and the 1968 invasion of Czechoslovakia. As a counter-example, after Stalin's death, the Khrushchev "thaw" opened a period of exchanges with the West, thus undermining Soviet isolation. Some see every crack in isolation as at least a long-term and indirect step forward in the promotion of human rights. (The opposite is certainly true: any promotion of human rights is a heavy blow to self-isolation).

The improvement in East–West relations in the early 1970s, known as détente, stemmed from the military parity achieved by the Soviet Union with the United States. But détente was quickly followed by a Western foreign policy line emphasizing human rights issues, which forced them to the front of Russian domestic policies. The human rights issue was important, though not always the key issue, in East–West relations. Soviet dissidents contributed to the launching of the Helsinki process. The signing of the Helsinki Agreement on 1 August 1975 was an event of special, albeit ambiguous, importance. On the one hand, Helsinki diplomacy served as a source of the "new thinking." On the other hand, provisions on human rights in the Agreement were a source of constant irritation to the Brezhnev leadership.

It has been said that: "It is only continuing and unremitting pressure by the U.S. and the West on human rights that led to improvements in individual situations and the possibility of long-term systemic change."[3] I find this argument one-dimensional and therefore not totally convincing. Of course, pressure from the United States and other Western states was a powerful driving force. However, all we know about the Gorbachev period testifies that it was a bilateral process because Gorbachev saw more clearly than any of his predecessors the links between domestic and foreign policy and appreciated that, as long as the Soviet Union persecuted dissidents, Soviet relations with the West would be based on mistrust.[4]

Implementation of at least some human rights was a cornerstone of Gorbachev's new thinking.[5] Yet even after the attempted coup against this new thinking by hard-line communists, he still saw a preferred role for his communist party.[6] In May 1991, the notorious decree of 17 February 1967 on repealing the Soviet citizenship of émigrés to Israel was abolished.[7] In foreign policy Gorbachev rejected the existence of any one correct model of socialism in the spring of 1987.

In summary, Russia has faced great difficulty in coming to terms with human rights in its own culture, hence the lack of coherence in Russia's foreign policy on rights – and its vacillations between East and West. The Russian intellectual tradition is plagued by a paradox: the longing for Russia's modernization, which includes human rights, is matched in intensity only by the fear of it.[8] The central thesis of this chapter is that the complicated national attitude to human rights explains many of the zigzags of Russian foreign policy.

## II. Domestic factors

After the honeymoon of Gorbachev's perestroika and the first year of the Yeltsin–Gaidar liberal reforms, especially with the exacerbation of economic hardships, the wave of enthusiasm concerning liberal values began to fade in the new Russia. A drift towards relative isolation from the West became more visible. As for domestic sources of the shift, two major factors – cultural and institutional – were at work. Many Western experts consider the strengthening of national institutions devoted to the development of human rights to be the best prevention against grave violations.[9] Russia's case shows that the political culture is of major importance. Russian society remains a distinctive hybrid system: it endorses widely recognized liberal rights, while at the same time it is constantly looking back to its traditions of authoritarian rule.[10]

### *Political culture*

The start of reform resulted in a substitution of civil-political for socio-economic rights. Under communism, the general population, lacking political freedoms, nevertheless benefited from social welfare. This welfare system, although sometimes a disaster, with hours in line at a doctor's office, by and large guaranteed minimal standards of socio-economic rights.[11] The reform era brought in political freedoms but has also almost demolished the old system of social guarantees. This replacement of socio-economic by civil-political rights was immensely painful for the general population, especially in the provinces. From the standpoint of an average Russian, freedom of speech led to pornography and the propaganda of violence, and freedom of conscience threatened to turn into the importation of pathological sects. Thus those who lost out during the reform period view liberal values mostly as involving moral decay, excessive luxury, and, above all, the "Mafiaization of Russia." These deviations, being generally attributed to Western values, result in lingering doubts concerning civil-political rights. Devoid of socio-economic rights, the general population is not in a position to benefit from the new political freedoms. One can also see the widespread rejection of universal human rights norms, which are considered by many to be uniquely Western ones. One can also understand the strong pressure upon the Kremlin to assume generally anti-Western policies, and thus save Russia from degeneration under the Western-dominated international system. Even some politicians of the new generation stress the vital necessity for Russia not to align only with the West but to search out its own path.

A major cleavage appears to have emerged between the notions of "liberal rights" and "order." In the nostalgic public view, the former have become a synonym for disorder. As a result, many people appear to believe that the government should control people speaking out against it and foster appropriate social attitudes and values. Paradoxically, most advocates of civil responsibility – a group one would expect to be particularly likely to support human rights – express concern at the excess of political freedom and free speech, as well as a belief that the government should take more of a role in guiding society.[12]

What are the transmission belts of these anti-Western attitudes to decision-making in foreign policy? Some interest groups and non-governmental organizations (NGOs) try to pressure the Russian government into pursuing more anti-Western policies, making use of negative and sometimes distorted perceptions of the human rights issue by the general public. A part of the Russian establishment, discouraged by military cuts, stands to gain from the exacerbation of international tensions. Vested interests of the military and the law enforcement organizations make some of them hostile to respecting human rights. As for foreign policy decision-making, a 1993 survey of 113 representatives of the Russian foreign policy élite showed that 52 per cent adhered to Western-type democratic principles while 45 per cent considered themselves to be advocates of Russia's distinctive way of development.[13]

Conflicting views persist regarding human rights versus centuries-old political traditions. The part of society that has been accustomed to perceiving itself within a system of ideological categories feels the need for a unifying, central idea. If the concept of human rights does not succeed in establishing firm roots, especially in a situation of instability and impatience, the concept of national particularism will triumph. A lack of respect for human rights leads to nostalgic protest, xenophobia, and anti-Western diplomacy.

### *Institutions*

From an institutional point of view, by and large Russia has already brought its legal system into line with international standards. Some articles of the 1993 Russian Constitution concerning human rights (i.e. Articles 15(4), 16, 18, and 42) declare the priority of international law over national legislation and the right of any citizen to address the European Court of Human Rights (once the European Convention on Human Rights had been ratified by the State Duma).[14] By a presidential decree[15] the Commission on Human Rights was formed. The Russian parliament adopted a federal law for an Ombudsman. However, the leftist majority in the State Duma did its best to replace the prominent human rights activist Sergei Kovalyov because of his stance on Chechnya.[16] The confrontation between the executive and legislative branches of power remains one of the main domestic factors hampering a clear line on human rights.

*Major domestic problems*

The impact of traditions and conflicting institutions makes the human rights situation in Russia an object of criticism from international organizations, Western governments, and NGOs. The issue of capital punishment is a salient focus. In new penal legislation, adopted in the Soviet Union under Gorbachev on 15 December 1988, capital punishment remained an exceptional measure until its abolition as a sanction for high treason and other most grave crimes.[17] Since then, the problem has been monitored by world public opinion, international organizations, and even committees of the US Congress.[18] After the demise of the Soviet Union, responding to world public opinion, Russia declared its intention to abolish capital sentences. A year-long moratorium was to be implemented, but the State Duma has not confirmed this. Yeltsin declared a moratorium by decree, and starting from the beginning of 1997 death sentences have not been carried out.[19] Society is split on the problem, as elsewhere, and prospects for the adoption by the leftist Duma of legislation urging that the current moratorium on the death penalty be made permanent are vague.[20]

The struggle connected with the law on freedom of conscience and religious organizations is a pointed example of the power of domestic traditions and of the weakness of pressure from foreign human rights groups. According to its opponents, the 1997 law curbs the activities of all but four religions – the Russian Orthodox Church, Judaism, Buddhism, and Islam – which are regarded as "traditional" to Russia. This contradicts the 1981 Declaration on the Elimination of All Forms of Intolerance and of Discrimination Based on Religion or Belief. The "newer religious groups" and denominations (among them are Catholics, Baptists, Adventists, etc.) deplore the serious infringement of their rights – being forbidden to open bank accounts, convene religious meetings in public, or hold property for 15 years. The President was under direct pressure from the US Senate, which voted in July 1997 (by 94 to 4) to cut American aid to Russia by US$195 million if the bill became law. Thus, US legislators backed human rights militants and religious groups to urge Yeltsin to veto the bill. Pope John Paul II also conveyed his deep concern over the bill, which he believed discriminates against Catholics in Russia.

On the other side, the Orthodox Church threw its weight behind the bill, openly saying that it needed the law to protect Russia from the depredations of Western missionaries and to prevent the further spiritual and moral destabilization of the country.[21] The law has also mobilized a strong anti-Western consensus in the Federal Assembly, where both houses passed it with overwhelming majorities.

President Yeltsin at first vetoed the bill in the summer of 1997, but eventually, in October, signed it after the Duma introduced some amendments. Signing the bill was not only a symptom of a lack of respect for the rights of religious minorities but also a new barrier between Russia and the West.[22] In fact, it was a manifestation of the crucial impact of domestic factors in human rights issues.

Among other serious domestic problems are high-profile murders involving journalists, financial tycoons, and other prominent figures. In November 1998, the country was shocked by the assassination of a prominent liberal Duma deputy and human rights activist, Galina Starovoitova.

Human rights organizations around the world challenged the legal judgment against the St. Petersburg environmentalist Alexander Nikitin as being politically motivated. This former naval officer was detained in St. Petersburg in February 1996 on suspicion of revealing state secrets to a Norwegian environmental foundation, Bellona. Nikitin and Bellona have demonstrated that all of the information they published was from open sources. However, he was kept in jail for a long time.

Another source of concern for the West is the lack of independence of the judiciary, which prevents it from acting as an effective counterweight to the other branches of government. Judges in Russia traditionally remain subject to some influence from the executive, the military, and the security forces, especially in high-profile or political cases.[23]

Thus, as we can clearly see, the emergence of modern institutions such as ombudsmen and human rights commissions is a necessary but not a sufficient condition for Russia's real adherence to human rights norms. Unfortunately, Russian institutions reflect an underlying conflicted political culture, and therefore their record is far from being in full conformity with international rights standards. Constitutional declarations do not change behaviour overnight.[24]

## III. Multilateral policy

### *International Bill of Rights*

From the very beginning of the Cold War, the Soviet Union demonstrated a very controversial approach towards human rights issues. It abstained on the Universal Declaration of Human Rights in the UN General Assembly on 10 December 1948, stressing that some of its articles "ignored the sovereign rights of some democratic governments."[25] Then Soviet diplomats worked hard to shape the two basic Covenants to the USSR's own views. Moscow formally adhered to both of the Covenants;[26] but, like the later US policy, it did not accept the Optional Protocol to the Civil-Political Covenant, which permitted individual complaints about violations, and it argued that only national authorities, not international agencies, were competent to pass judgement on the implementation of the standards. Russia's voting for pacts dealing with liberal values was quite formal and legalistic, since virtually all international rights documents of the period stemmed from compromise between East and West. This resulted in general language whose essence depended on subsequent interpretation.[27]

After the ending of the Cold War, according to the official view, the initial contribution of the Russian Federation catalysed UN activities on a number of human rights issues. Russia made the protection of human rights, including the rights of national minorities, a priority of its foreign policy, especially in the territory of the former Soviet Union.[28] The new Russia professes to emphasize especially civil and political rights both at home and abroad.[29]

### *Policy patterns*

One can outline three different periods in Russian foreign policy and human rights since 1991. From late 1991 to mid-1993 Russia appeared simply to defer to the West in regard to human rights issues. Russian delegations in UN institutions followed the lead of the West and voted with the US delegation on the bulk of major issues. Russia was one of the most energetic actors in creating new human rights infrastructures. For example, it worked extensively on the Vienna Declaration and Programme of Action, which was adopted by the World Conference on Human Rights in June 1993. Also, being interested in more focused international support for Russian-speaking minorities in the former Soviet republics, Russia insisted on transforming the Conference on Security and Cooperation in Europe into the more efficient Organization for Security and Cooperation in Europe (OSCE).

In mid-1993, important shifts in Russia's foreign policy occurred. Moscow's proposed sale of cryogenic rockets to India may be regarded as a watershed in its relations with the West. Washington not only rejected Russia's requests to share military and space technology markets, but exerted obvious pressure in order to cancel Russia's deal with Delhi. Even ardent supporters of the Russian alliance with the West were shocked and raised their voices in favour of Russia's pursuing its distinct national interests. After nationalists emerged victorious at the December 1993 general elections, they pressed the government to back Belgrade in the violent struggles in the former Yugoslavia. Russian foreign policy seemed torn between pleasing the West and protecting the Serbs. Later on, Moscow gave diplomatic support to the Bosnian Serbs against the Croats, the Muslims, and the West, openly challenging the United States. The period of euphoria over cooperation with the West was over. Officially sticking to its line towards independent decision-making devoid of double standards,[30] Moscow has become more cautious about adopting new human rights documents – in part because they make it more difficult to implement previous obligations.[31]

Since 1995–96, notwithstanding formal condemnation of authoritarian regimes, Russia's practical policies towards them have become more pragmatic and flexible. Moscow demonstrates the legacy of its conflicted political culture and its mixed record of cooperation with the United Nations and its mechanisms. On the one hand, Russia usually sides with other Western countries on general issues, such as the role of the United Nations in the promotion of democratization, respect for the principles of national sovereignty, etc.[32] For instance, after the United Nations proclaimed 1998 to be the year of Human Rights, Russia was one of the first countries to form a national committee for the celebration of the anniversary of the declaration.[33] Russia has consistently abided by the UN Security Council's resolutions concerning arms embargoes on its traditional allies Iraq, Libya, and the former Yugoslavia at different stages of UN-sanctioned operations. On the other hand, since 1995, Russia has preferred to express an independent opinion in matters concerning specific issues. For example, having voted at the Security Council for prolonging the UN field mission in Eastern Slavonia, Russia also emphasized the necessity to protect the rights of Serbian displaced persons. Concerning applications filed by the Republic of Bosnia and Hercegovina in the Registry of the International Court of Justice in 1993, instituting proceedings against the Federal Republic of Yugoslavia "for violating the Genocide Convention," the Russian judge took the side of Yugoslavia. Judge Tarassov's dissenting opinion was joined by ad hoc Judge Kreca, who was appointed by, and represented the interests of, Belgrade.[34]

Moscow continued to criticize what it considered the West's excessive blaming of Serbia and the Bosnian Serbs for following the policy of ethnic cleansing. In early 1994, when the United Nations called for the use of force against the Serbs, Russian top analysts even advised that the State Duma would abstain from ratifying the START-2 treaty in the event the bombing went ahead.[35] Moscow's efforts to keep a high profile in foreign policy notwithstanding, in post-Dayton Bosnia Russia has been routinely ignored by the United States and NATO. As a result, Russia has secured only the right to complain, not to decide.[36] Russia does its best to make UN resolutions less confrontational.[37] At the 1997 session of the UN Human Rights Commission (UNHRC), Russia joined the consensus regarding the former Yugoslavia. But it made a special statement on the motives of voting, pointing to the necessity of restoring Yugoslav membership in the United Nations, the OSCE, and other international organizations. On these issues Russia constantly resists the anti-Serb line of the Western countries.

In its relations with Iraq, Moscow traditionally tries to appease the West. After the General Assembly and UNHRC adopted resolutions expressing strong condemnation of the massive violations of human rights of the gravest nature in Iraq,[38] the Russian Foreign Ministry tried to get the United Nations to lift the oil embargo against Baghdad. When the UN Security Council relaxed the embargo in 1996 so that Iraq could purchase food and medicine, it turned out that there had already been multiple contracts to provide these supplies, but none with Russian companies. The consequences were also painful for Russian oil companies, which, during the full embargo, had taken Iraq's place in certain markets, thanks to the similarity in the chemical composition of Russian and Iraqi oil. Russia was forced to leave these markets when Iraq was allowed to sell some oil once again. The UN Security Council having decided to extend the oil-for-goods deal in September 1997, Russia abstained, putting forward a specious excuse.[39]

Russia's support for Libya is limited and conditional. For example, on 10 July 1997, at the Security Council's review meeting on Libyan sanctions, Russia insisted on sending a representative of the Secretary-General to Libya to compile a report on the humanitarian implications of the sanctions regime for the general population of Libya.

Collective human rights such as the problem of self-determination of peoples had been the focal point of Moscow's foreign policy during the Cold War, especially the rights of the Palestinian people and the Middle East peace process. Russia generally tends to vote in favour of support for the rights of the Palestinians. However, since normalization of relations with Israel, Russia has become far more sensitive about the wording of related resolutions.[40] When the General Assembly approved a resolution on the rights of Palestinians in December 1995, by 145 to 2, Russia was among the 9 countries that abstained (only the United States and Israel voted against it).[41] At the 53rd session of the UN Human Rights Commission in 1997, Russia supported a resolution condemning human rights violations in southern Lebanon and in the Bekaa valley region (the United States voted against it and one delegation abstained). Russia also voted for a General Assembly resolution submitted by the European Union (EU) on Israeli settlements in occupied Arab territory (the United States voted against and two delegations abstained). These were not the only examples of the cleavage with the United States on human rights violations in the Middle East. For the first time, at the 1997 UNHRC session, Russia was not among the co-authors of the so-called positive resolution on the Middle East peace process, because the US delegation, its major sponsor, refused to mention in the text the role of multilateral mechanisms and the importance of sticking to the achieved Palestine–Israeli agreements.

When a UN body takes up human rights abuses in Cuba, Russia quite often sides with the United States on procedural matters, such as, for instance, extending the mandate of the Special Rapporteur on the situation of human rights in Cuba at the Human Rights Commission or the Economic and Social Council session.[42] Russia also aligns with the United States on some generalized matters, such as bringing the observance of human rights and fundamental freedoms in Cuba into conformity with international law and international human rights instruments.[43] Russia was among the states that abstained, however, when the 1997 UNHRC session, by a vote of 19 to 10, with 22 abstentions, adopted the more detailed and critical US-sponsored resolution on the situation of human rights in Cuba.

Russia's voting record concerning human rights in China is rather contradictory. For example, at the 51st session of the UNHRC held in Geneva in 1995, the Russian delegation first voted procedurally for taking up the matter, but then voted against the Western-sponsored resolution condemning human rights violations in China.[44] At the 1997 UNHRC session, Russia abstained in procedural voting on whether or not to adopt any resolution concerning human rights violations in China. This position was obviously dictated by a new rapprochement between Russia and China and reflects Russia's pragmatic stance. The situation will tend to reproduce itself until real changes take place in China.

More generally, Russia's voting record at the 53rd session of the UNHRC in Geneva, 10–18 April 1997, may serve as a clear example of Russia's attempts to shape an independent policy on international human rights issues. Russia's official position was based on a presumption that the human rights issues should bring nations closer together rather than dividing them. In Russia's view, a constructive dialogue between nations should draw on human rights as a universal principle and transform them into a cornerstone of security and stability.

On Russia's initiative, the UNHRC for the first time labelled the repealing of citizenship as a violation of basic human rights (the co-authors of the resolution were Mexico, Peru, Nicaragua, Colombia, Portugal, and Belarus). Russia's initiative condemning the barbaric practices of taking hostages turned into a consensus resolution that won support of multiple co-sponsors. Russia backed resolutions on human rights abuses in Iraq, Iran, the Sudan, Burundi, Zaire, Nigeria, Rwanda, Equatorial Guinea, and Myanmar. Russian diplomats stress that Russia's stance is far from blacklisting these countries but is a sort of invitation to a positive dialogue with international organizations.

One of the characteristic traits of Russia's foreign policy is consistent support for the idea of the inseparability of democracy, development, and human rights. Therefore, Russia was one of the most active co-authors of the resolution on the right to development.

There was an intense struggle regarding an Italian draft resolution on the abolition of capital punishment. The United States and a group of Asian countries bitterly criticized the resolution, emphasizing the right of sovereign countries to establish measures of responsibility. The resolution was adopted by 27 (including Russia and the EU) to 11 (including the United States, Japan, and China), with 14 abstentions (including Great Britain, Cuba, and India).[45]

Since the 1993 Vienna Declaration, ongoing political dialogue with the Council of Europe (CoE) has been a priority for Moscow. Judging by official statements, Russia's foreign policy entrepreneurs needed membership in the Council in order to protect the rights of Russians in the "near abroad."[46] Actually, an even more important rationale was to have a say in European affairs. Russia's joining the CoE has been one of the most controversial decisions in the history of the organization. Vladimir Zhirinovsky, leader of the mis-named Liberal Democratic Party of Russia, challenged the Parliamentary Assembly of the Council of Europe (PACE) deputies in his mocking manner: "If you want to invite Russia, you should know that you invite Russia as a state and not citizen Kovalyov who dislikes something. He is as sick as thousands of Europeans who suffer from different diseases."[47] In its Opinion no. 193 on the Russian request for membership in the Council of Europe, adopted in January 1996, note was taken of the Russian Federation's intention to settle international as well as internal disputes by peaceful means, as well as of the commitment strictly to respect the provisions of international humanitarian law, including in cases of armed conflict on its territory.[48]

Russia has become more cooperative with Amnesty International in matters of application of the Convention against Torture, illegal imprisonment and psychiatric confinement for political reasons, death sentences, introduction of a civilian alternative to military service, restrictions on religious activities, and the situation in Chechnya.[49]

The International Red Cross took part in efforts to protect and assist people in order to soften the consequences of the conflict in Chechnya. In spite of the special status accorded it concerning the implementation of international humanitarian law by the Geneva Conventions of 1949 and Protocols of 1977, six Red Cross workers were killed in late 1996. After the incident, the remaining members of the Red Cross had to quit Chechnya since neither the Russian troops nor the Chechen authorities would provide them with guarantees respecting provisions of international humanitarian law.

### *Regional developments*

Human rights groups have compiled a number of accounts of serious abuses during the Chechen conflict. Human Rights Watch reported that the Russian military "failed adequately to investigate, let alone prosecute, the most glaring combat-related violations of humanitarian law." Separatist forces also violated international humanitarian law by taking and executing hostages and using prisoners as human shields. The Glasnost Fund established an international intergovernmental tribunal on crimes against humanity and war crimes in Chechnya, which plans to conduct investigations and forward its findings to the Council of Europe and the European Court of Human Rights.[50]

Moscow's use of force in Chechnya, which showed no concern either about human lives or about the reaction of public opinion inside or outside Russia, became a test for Western human rights policies. The reaction of the Western countries and international organizations surprised the Russian leadership, being far more tolerant than Moscow had expected. The West and international organizations condemned Russia for excessive violence and human rights violations. However, no country and no organization mentioned any sanctions or proposed exerting pressure on Russia, considering the Chechen conflict to be Russia's internal affair or not an issue at all.[51] This was interpreted in Moscow as a *carte blanche* for such kinds of military operations not only in Chechnya but in the vast space of the former Soviet Union.

After the Budapest summit of the OSCE held in November 1994, Moscow clearly saw that it would not be possible to keep the West from an expansion of NATO eastwards. In exchange for dropping attempts to prevent it, Moscow welcomed the idea of dividing zones of responsibility in Europe along the borders between the Central European states and the former Soviet Union, with the exception of the Baltics, which were supposed to belong to the Western zone. This drift toward a more "Great Power" stance and the ferocity of the military operation in Chechnya were interconnected symptoms of the old imperial habit. The West chose the lesser of the evils as a way forward, as noted above, but to the detriment of the human rights issue.[52]

After NATO's official decision to expand eastward, the West was stunned by the broad consensus in Russia against it. If we ignore security considerations, we can see the psychological explanation for this nationwide anti-NATO consensus. Russian liberal intellectuals had an acute feeling of having been betrayed by the West. It was a sort of psychological trauma for advocates of rapprochement with the West, who were shocked by the lack of Western respect for Russia's sensitivities. In any case, the Russian leadership concluded that Western states are rarely guided by ethical norms in foreign policy. Thus Russian national interests were increasingly emphasized in foreign policy during NATO's post-enlargement period.

### *International financial institutions*

International financial institutions (IFIs) are in the limelight of political discussions in Russia. Two major questions arise: Would the West significantly increase its credits to Russia if Moscow more carefully observed human rights? If the IFIs increased their aid to Russia, would Moscow be more active in human rights observance?

The main international financial organizations appear to be preoccupied more with economic reform – i.e. Russia's budgetary indicators such as inflation rates, currency reserves, etc. – than with the observance of human rights. The International Monetary Fund (IMF) and the World Bank consistently support the Russian government's tight fiscal and monetary policy to bring down inflation in spite of the fact that many workers are not paid for months. The head of the IMF's Second European Department, Yusuke Horiguchi, has repeatedly emphasized the necessity for the Russian government to exert pressure upon huge corporate debtors to cope with the problem of arrears. The head of the IMF, Michel Camdessue, while visiting Russia, stressed that the "situation when pensioners do not receive their pensions is really shocking."[53] Also, the World Bank earmarked up to US$2 billion for urgent social problems, such as helping the government pay wage and pension arrears.[54]

But, in general, the IFIs have not let human rights issues affect loans to Russia. The major constraints for Western assistance to Russia lie not so much in the sphere of human rights but in the economic sphere. If relations were blocked by poor human rights observance in Russia, the West would have no incentive to give the large amounts of assistance and credits that it is currently giving. Given the fact that the West is already giving substantial loans, there is no effective leverage on Russia's human rights policy. Moreover, in Russia, with the exception of a very narrow circle, the effect of Western assistance is generally viewed as destructive for Russia's economy, stimulating corruption and criminality, as well as ruining defence, the social system, science, culture, etc.[55] The mass media are sometimes extremely outspoken in their criticism of Western assistance. For example, the *Nezavisimaya Gazeta* (Independent Newspaper), which is usually viewed as a pro-reform daily, blames the IFIs for distortion of the economy, immense losses, etc. as well as political manipulations.

The fact that the interests of the IMF and the World Bank are alien to Russia's interests derives not only from the poor results from reforming the national economy in conformity with their standards. Missions of these organizations are represented in all countries of the former Soviet Union. It is not by mere chance that centrifugal trends keep growing every year to the detriment of the countries' economic and political interests, first of all at the expense of Russia's interests.[56]

The linking of IFI activity and human rights would only increase criticism in these circles.[57] It is the Open Society Institute (George Soros Foundation) that is clearly linking its grants to human rights, supporting scholars and journalists involved in research or the reporting of human rights issues. It is noteworthy that Russian humanitarian or human rights centres are totally financed by foreign financial and charitable organizations.[58]

## IV. Bilateral

Russia's major human rights concerns in foreign policy are focused on the former Soviet Union zone. In spite of the existence of the Commonwealth of Independent States (CIS), there is still no viable mechanism for solving these problems on a multilateral basis. The breakup of the Soviet Union left about 25 million ethnic Russians and Russian speakers beyond the new Russian borders. The years since then have shown that Moscow remains deeply embroiled in the affairs of all the former Soviet republics. Indeed, most of those in the Russian state today view the former republics as neither part of their state nor wholly foreign. Western scholars tend to exaggerate Russia's imperial ambitions. As Bruce Porter and Carol Saivetz put it:

The CIS is, moreover, only one of several tools Russia has employed to exert its influence in the former Soviet sphere. Its efforts to retain a measure of hegemony have included economic pressures, such as manipulation of Russian oil and natural gas deliveries; diplomatic support of Russians living in the Near Abroad; fiscal inducements, such as debt relief and currency management; and outright military blackmail, such as threats to keep troops stationed in the Baltic states or the refusal in late 1993 to assist the government of Georgia against twin uprising unless it agreed to enter the CIS.[59]

The source of Russia's diplomatic activities in the "near abroad" is that Moscow in many respects appears to be extremely sensitive towards developments in the former republics.[60] Acknowledging Russia's legitimate interests in the region, Western foreign policy decision makers hesitate to recognize what in any other context would be called a protection racket: encouraging separatist movements under the guise of defending embattled Russian minorities, and then intervening as a peacemaker when the conflicts between the separatists and the successor regimes get out of hand.[61] A draft national security White Paper in 1996 listed among the most serious problems for Russia in the "near abroad" kin ethnic contradictions, deterioration of the economy, and loss of consumer markets, as well as violations of the human rights and freedoms of the Russian-speaking population.[62] Violations of minorities' rights within the "near abroad" would endanger Russia's key interests. Therefore the highest priority for Russian foreign policy is the relationship with a number of ex-Soviet republics, above all Ukraine, Belarus, and Kazakhstan.[63]

### *Ukraine*

The rights of the Russian minority in Ukraine have been a target for Moscow's diplomatic activities since 1992, especially in the Crimea. Ethnic Russians there have made enormous efforts to try to get the peninsula to become a part of the Russian Federation, with Sevastopol as a stronghold of this movement. However, with the signing of the "big treaty" with Kiev, Moscow has failed to achieve its main goal. The Crimea remains a part of the independent Ukrainian state, and the problem of the Russian minority remains unsolved.

The Crimea became part of Russia in 1783 after the Russian victory over the Turkish Ottoman armies. Over the next century and a half numerous people, mainly Russians, settled in the Crimea. In 1954, it was transferred to Ukraine by the then Soviet leader, Nikita Khruschev, to commemorate the 300th anniversary of Russia's merger with Ukraine as a propaganda symbol of the friendship of the two republics.

The forced deportation of the Crimean Tatars under Stalin fundamentally changed the ethnic balance of the Crimea. Ethnic Russians were brought in to fill their place. The Tatars were allowed to return to the Crimea only at the beginning of the 1970s. Up to 100,000 Tatars subsequently sought to move to the Crimea, only to be prevented from resettling by bureaucratic resistance, police harassment, and brutality.

According to the 1989 census, the ethnic composition of Crimea is as follows: Russians 67 per cent, Ukrainians 25.6 per cent (almost half of whom are Russian speakers), Crimean Tatars 1.6 per cent, other nationalities 6 per cent. Despite substantial regional and some ethnic diversity in the Crimean political situation, the peninsula was very stable till 1992. In May 1992 the Russian parliament passed a resolution declaring the 1954 transfer of the Crimea illegal. In July 1993 the Supreme Soviet of the Russian Federation issued a declaration asserting control over Sevastopol as a Russian town. Ukraine appealed to the UN Security Council, which confirmed that these decisions were illegal because they contradicted Ukrainian–Russian treaties and the aims and principles of the United Nations.

At the same time, the passage of a law on language led to a drive for separatism in the Crimea. The Crimean Republic demanded its reunification with Russia under the guise of separate membership of the Commonwealth of Independent States. The turmoil in the Crimea demonstrated the anger of the peninsula's population towards the economic situation and Kiev's policies.

The internal situation has also been complicated by the return of the Crimean Tatars creating additional social problems. Many Crimean Tatars see the only solution to their socio-economic and cultural problems in the creation of a single ethnic Tatar state. Thus, Russia's foreign policy faces a series of challenges vis-à-vis Ukraine. The major challenge is that the open backing of the Russian diaspora might push Ukraine further in the direction of the West and NATO. This scenario is considered to be a nightmare by the Russian foreign policy élite.

### *Belarus*

President Alexander Lukashenko, showing little tolerance for dissent and having adopted a dictatorial style of government, has turned Moscow's relationship with the republic into a legal puzzle. Russian human rights groups accuse Lukashenko of total disregard for the democratically elected parliament, which was disbanded in 1996, and of strongly repressing any opposition to his regime. In January 1997, the Council of Europe excluded Belarus from candidature for membership. Russia insists on the restoration of the Belorussian membership.

The major concern for Russian diplomacy has become Lukashenko's repressing the press.[64] In June 1997, he made the authorities withdraw accreditation for Pavel Sheremet, the Minsk bureau chief of Russian Public Television (ORT), accusing him of insulting and tendentious reporting. Within a week, the journalist and his TV crew were arrested and charged with illegally crossing the Belorussian–Lithuanian border while filming a report on Belarus's poorly guarded frontiers. Yeltsin bitterly criticized the president of Belarus, threatening to revise the Statute on the Union between the two countries. This may be the strongest and most sincere of Russia's condemnations of human rights violations in a neighbouring state.[65]

Russia's painful foreign policy dilemma is whether to strengthen cooperation with Belarus or to break with Lukashenko, who has amassed a notorious human rights record. On the one hand, Belarus is the first real candidate for integration. On the other hand, implementation of the document on the forming of the union with Belarus, signed in April 1997, could mean Russia's losing status in the Council of Europe and losing face in the world community – because the observance of human rights in the newly emerging Centaurs cannot be guaranteed.[66] Again we see a pointed example of the Russian difficulty in meshing attitudes towards human rights with other policy goals.

### *Kazakhstan*

In 1997, ethnic Kazakhs accounted for only 51 per cent of Kazakhstan's population, and only about a third in its northern regions. The Russian population is estimated at about 6.2 million. Yet many Russians say they feel uncomfortable, notably because of an increase in broadcasting in Kazakh and because their children have to study the Kazakh language at school. Hard-line nationalists in Moscow are trying to blackmail the Kazakh authorities with the threat of encouraging the secession of its northern and eastern regions in order to prevent Muslim, Western, or Chinese expansionism in the region.[67] Diplomats are doing their best to prevent further aggravation of the situation.

### *The Baltics*

Russia's most active diplomatic intervention for human rights reasons occurs in the Baltic countries (Estonia, Latvia, and, to a lesser extent, Lithuania), after their winning independence in 1991.[68] The core of the problem is that the plight of the Russian-speaking minorities and Russia's concerns with the shift of the Baltic states away from its sphere of influence towards the West are closely intertwined. It is clear that Russia points to violations of human rights in the Baltics while keeping silent on much worse situations in the Central Asian newly independent countries, such as Tajikistan and Uzbekistan, whose governments demonstrate political loyalty to Moscow. Russia is certainly sincerely preoccupied with the human rights situation in the Baltics. At the same time, it makes use of the human rights issues in purely political terms to try to prevent the Baltic states aligning with the West.

Many ethnic Russians, Ukrainians, Belorussians, and Jews have failed to get citizenship in the Baltic states. Unfortunately, there is little love for them among the indigenous citizens, who remember the "Soviet liberation" in 1944 as the start of mass repressions and irritating Russification.[69] The situation in Estonia is, perhaps, the most extreme example of the status of Russian speakers in the region.

Since 1991, Estonia has certainly made considerable progress towards the fulfilment of its obligations and commitments in regard to the rights of Russians living in its territory. In particular, Estonia has ratified the European Convention on Human Rights. However, some problematic areas concerning Estonia's obligations under the European Convention remain. Estonia entered into two commitments before accession to the Council of Europe: to base its policy regarding the protection of historic minorities on principles laid down in the Council's recommendation and an additional protocol on the rights of national minorities to the ECHR, and to treat the "non-historic" Russian-speaking minority fairly. There are no huge problems concerning "historic" Russians (those who settled before the Soviet invasion in the Second World War). As for the treatment of the "non-historic" Russian-speaking minority, who settled during Soviet rule, not all problems are being dealt with in a satisfactory manner. Over 400,000 of Estonia's population are Russians.[70] According to the official Russian point of view, they are subject to special hardships, owing to restrictions imposed on them that are more severe than those on members of majority groups. As we shall see, in reality this large group is devoid of principal rights.

According to the new Law on Citizenship adopted by the Estonian parliament in January 1995, a person who wishes to obtain Estonian citizenship cannot apply until he or she has passed two extremely difficult tests: a general language test and a test on the Estonian constitution and citizenship law.[71] The Estonian authorities are thus in practice pursuing a policy of discrimination with respect to the ethnic Russians and the Russian language, which is the second language spoken after Estonian.[72]

Moscow has repeatedly issued diplomatic statements on minority rights since late 1991. On 1 October 1991, the Russian State Council declared that the Russian leadership was responsible for all Russians living in the former Soviet republics. In February 1992, then Foreign Minister Andrei Kozyrev made it clear in a speech at a UN conference on human rights that Russia regarded this issue as a very high priority in its foreign policy.

However, Russia has rather limited resources to influence the human rights situation in Estonia and Latvia. The use of force is ruled out, so Russia has only diplomatic and economic instruments at its disposal as a last resort to prevent discrimination against Russians there. According to then Foreign Minister Primakov, Moscow could slap economic sanctions on states accused of mistreating their Russian minorities. Russia has already linked agreement on an accord defining the border between the two countries to an improvement in the plight of Estonia's Russian-speaking population. Moscow's offer of security guarantees to the Baltic states, made in early November 1997, was unanimously declined by all three countries. Moscow is likely to develop less abrasive relations with the Baltic states at all levels. However, desperate to keep NATO out of the region, Moscow is likely steadily to increase political pressure on the Baltic states in order to defend ethnic Russians and to pursue its political interests there.

### *Refugees*

Russia became a party to international refugee treaties when in 1993 it ratified the 1951 Geneva Convention and the 1967 Protocol to it. Moscow takes an active part in discussions and in drafting resolutions on refugees and displaced persons. For example, Russia put forward a proposal to the UN General Assembly for a conference to identify regional solutions as supported by the international community, which was held in Geneva on 30–31 May 1996.[73] However, because of various pressures and over-complicated formalities (often taking about three months to establish refugee status) inside the Federation, Russia finds it hard to protect the rights of refugees and displaced persons efficiently. According to a report by the Human Rights Commission advising the President of the Russian Federation, the number of asylum seekers in Russia from non-CIS countries comes to around 500,000, of whom some 46,000 have been registered by the UN High Commissioner for Refugees. The Federal Migration Service had given refugee status to only 70 of them by January 1997. In the fall of 1997, the Office of the High Commissioner asked the Moscow authorities to facilitate formalities for about 15,000 refugees. This came after the office of the UN Centre for Refugees in Moscow had been attacked and occupied by indignant Africans.[74]

The position of CIS refugees and internal forced migrants is even more complicated, in spite of the fact that in September 1993 Russia, Azerbaijan, Armenia, Belarus, Kazakhstan, Kyrgyzstan, Tajikistan, Turkmenistan, and Uzbekistan concluded an agreement on assistance to refugees and forced migrants. The main obstacle seriously undermining the safeguards that legislation affords to refugees is the *propiska* (residence permit) system. In July 1997, Russia's Constitutional Court ruled that regional governments cannot charge for the right to live on their territory. However, the *propiska* system, which the USSR introduced in 1932, is still widely used in the CIS countries. It was formally abolished in Russia by Yeltsin in June 1993 and replaced by a system of "notifying" the authorities of the place of residence. The authorities concerned say they are merely protecting the rights of the local community from influxes of new arrivals who allegedly threaten economic stability (particularly wage levels), cause an increase in crime, place too much strain on the infrastructure, etc. According to the Civic Assistance Committee, a Moscow-based human rights group, 30 provincial governments around Russia (including Krasnodar and Stavropol provinces, Voronezh and Leningrad regions, and the city of St. Petersburg) continue to restrict freedom of residence. The tenacity with which many regions stick to the *propiska* system suggests that Russia is not ready for the right to freedom of movement that is enshrined in Article 75 of the Constitution.[75]

If they are prevented from registering, new arrivals, who are mostly refugees, are often unable to get access to public schools for their children. It should be recalled that the International Bill of Rights provides that everyone has a right to education, and the International Covenant on Economic, Social, and Cultural Rights also reiterates that primary education shall be compulsory, even for children of illegal immigrants.[76] Under Article 12 of the 1966 Covenant on Civil and Political Rights, everyone lawfully within the territory of a state has the right to liberty of movement and freedom to choose his residence, and that right can be restricted only in the cases specified in that article.[77] The Constitutional Court was under the pressure of regional international law as well since Russia joined the Council of Europe and was strictly obliged to stick to its treaty norms.

About 9 million people have moved within the Commonwealth of Independent States (CIS) since 1989, most of them involuntarily. This plight has had various causes: violations of minority rights; economic, social, and ecological problems; armed conflicts; virulent nationalism; insecurity, etc. The number of people displaced by armed conflicts alone in the CIS is over 3.5 million. Major conflicts are concentrated in the southern regions. One of Russia's most important foreign policy goals is to play a leading role in mediating such conflicts in order to avoid further unwanted migration.

For example, about 30,000 Ossets (100,000 according to the Ossetian authorities) have moved from South Ossetia (Georgia) to North Ossetia (Russian Federation). However, under Russian pressure, regional politicians agreed in 1996 on the need to address the refugee problem.

Russia is playing a key role in the Georgian dispute with its Abkhazia region, whose leaders keep insisting on equal status with Georgia within a federation or confederation. Abkhaz sources claim that as many as 320,000, the majority of the 525,000-strong population registered in the 1989 census, now live in Abkhazia. Over 100,000 people, including ethnic Russians, have left Abkhazia and gone to Russia. For Russia, the case of Abkhazia is not so much the problem of Russian refugees as a litmus test for its foreign policy in regard to human rights violations. Georgia hopes that Russia will bring its influence to bear for Georgia's unity. Russia is trying to expedite the return to their homes of ethnic Georgians who fled from the region during hostilities. Moscow cannot openly support the Abkhaz move to secede from Georgia for fear of the precedent this could set for the many other multi-ethnic republics of the former Soviet Union.[78] However, it engaged in active diplomacy on the question. Under Russian pressure, the UN Security Council adopted a resolution on 21 July 1992 approving a Russian peacekeeping mission in Abkhazia. According to media reports, Russian representative Yuli Vorontsov said that otherwise Russia would oppose US involvement in Haiti.[79] During the G7/G8 meeting in Denver in 1997, Yeltsin called for an enhanced UN role in the settlement of conflicts, including the Abkhazian war.[80]

In the Tajik war, some 700,000 people were displaced, and the country has actually lost its Russian-speaking population.[81] In June 1997, Tajikistan and its Islamic opposition signed a peace accord, with Russia's active diplomatic mediation.

Some 100,000 people were displaced by the conflict in the Trans-Dniester area. The Russian speakers left Moldova because of a threat of "Romanization" of the mostly Russian population of the region, notably the introduction of the Moldovan (Romanian) language as the official language in this Russian-speaking area. The situation in the Trans-Dniester region is basically frozen. It is still uncertain whether a political compromise can be reached because the separatists aim at preserving the de facto independence of Trans-Dniester, whereas Moldova is resolutely against recognizing the region as enjoying statehood. Russia favours a special status for Trans-Dniester within Moldova, but not full independence for the region.[82]

In both its legislation and its practice, Russia sometimes fails to apply a number of basic human rights recognized by international law. One of them is the prohibition on forced return based on Article 33(1) of the Refugee Convention.[83] There is also a general prohibition deriving from Article 3 of the European Convention on Human Rights, prohibiting the expulsion of anyone who is in serious danger of being subjected to torture or to inhuman or degrading treatment or punishment. Similarly the Convention against Torture and Other Cruel, Inhuman or Degrading Treatment or Punishment (1984) prohibits the return, expulsion, or extradition of any person to a third state when there is serious reason to believe that he or she risks being subjected to torture there. For example, there have been cases of the dangerous extradition of human rights activists to Uzbekistan; the Russian authorities have also turned a blind eye to the activities of the Uzbek secret services in Russian cities which target refugees from that state.

It is clear that United Nations assistance programmes for the hundreds of thousands of persons displaced as a result of ethnic conflicts in the "near abroad" are far from adequate. In August 1994 Yeltsin signed a decree on the major directions of state policy of the Russian Federation regarding compatriots living abroad. This proclaims that stopping new flights of refugees is one of the highest priorities of Moscow's foreign policy towards the "near abroad." Russian attempts to promote the idea of dual citizenship and also Russian as a second state language in the former Soviet republics cause many accusations about Moscow's imperial ambitions to re-establish control over the post-Soviet space and represent a constant headache for the Kremlin.[84]

## V. Conclusions

After the Cold War, Russia made a breakthrough in expanding its formal acceptance of the international law of human rights. The long-term potential of this breakthrough cannot be overestimated. Nevertheless, Russia's attitude towards specific human rights issues remains controversial. The authoritarian tradition remains strong, frequently overshadowing liberal trends in its foreign policy. Therefore, Russian foreign policy on human rights is marked by uncertainty, competition over values, and lack of predictability.

Another major factor in Russia's ambivalent behaviour in international relations is that it has not yet formulated its foreign policy doctrine and the place of human rights in it. Formally, Russian authorities are generally supportive of international law and human rights policies. In practice, foreign policy institutions are highly selective about endorsement and action (for example, in the former Yugoslavia).

Russia is being pressured by the West to take rights seriously in Iraq or Serbia. The open linkage of financial assistance to Russia with observance of human rights is an instrument with limited efficiency. In some rare cases it may work, but more often it appears to be counter-productive. However, the very existence of Western models and assistance may help support the development of a political culture more conducive to Russia's more consistent implementation of human rights standards. Human rights education is especially needed in Russia, a country without a strong tradition of respect for liberal and legal values.

One cannot say that Russia's foreign policy is generally opposed to human rights. In fact, Russian political entrepreneurs clearly understand that a drastic change of political course and a rupture with the West would result in Russia's isolation. Therefore, Moscow does support some human rights issues and is cautiously trying to find a niche for them in the new system of international relations.

During the early 1990s in the sphere of foreign politics, the Soviet Union/Russia demonstrated unlimited readiness to cooperate with the West. Moreover, this often involved real sacrifice. The most spectacular example was the Soviet consent to German unification with no political conditions and with a hasty withdrawal of Soviet troops from Eastern Europe. Former Minister of Foreign Affairs Kozyrev made serious unilateral concessions to the United States and the West. In return he counted strongly on Western support on issues of importance to Moscow. Russia's cooperativeness cannot be explained simply by Western pressure and its victory in the Cold War. Much can be explained by the euphoria of that time and Russia's alleged joining the system of Western political and social values – including human rights. In a sense, Moscow offered sacrifices as a token of a common future. However, Russia would also like to make money, pursue a high-profile policy, and be recognized as more than a loser in the Cold War or a poor cousin of the United States. The West has lacked imagination in dealing with Russia, and the window of opportunity has almost closed.

An analysis of the key international factors – security issues and failures in international assistance to Russia – shows that they are not the main sources of the anti-Western shift in Russian foreign policy. The West could recognize Russian sensitivity to its loss of superpower status and understand that Russia's second-class treatment threatens Western interests and human rights in Russia. Unfortunately, Russia is losing its initial incentive concerning human rights issues in foreign policy.

One cannot change political culture overnight. Continuation of the conflicted political culture has yet to resolve itself in favour of strong and clear support for liberal rights in Russia – at home or abroad.

## Notes

1. V. Fyodorov, "K istorii telesnykh nakazanii v Rossii" [On the History of Corporal Punishment in Russia], in *Problemy rossiiskogo zakonodatelstva* [The Problems of Russian Law, Collection] (Vladivostok: Far East University Press, 1997), 133–138.

2. Boris Paramonov, "On Love and Sin," Russian Questions, Radio Liberty, 15 July 1997.
3. Mikhail Tsipkin, "Soviet Human Rights under Gorbachev," *The Backgrounder*, The Heritage Foundation, 10 February 1987, pp. 1–2.
4. Archie Brown, *The Gorbachev Factor* (Oxford: Oxford University Press, 1996).
5. Nadine Marie, *Le Droit retrouvé? Essai sur les droits de l'homme en URSS* (Paris: Presses Universitaires de France, 1989), 175, 185; B. Gross, P. Juliver, E. Lukasheva, and V. Kartashkin, eds., *Prava cheloveka nakanune 21 veka* [Human Rights on the Eve of the 21st Century] (Moscow: Progress, Kultura, 1994), 151.
6. *Amnesty International Report, 1990* (London: Amnesty International Publications, 1991), 244.
7. *Vedomosti Syezda Narodnykh Deputatov i Verkhovnogo Sovieta SSSR* [Documents of the Congress of People's Deputies and the Supreme Soviet of the USSR], no. 24 (1994), 688.
8. Elena Chernyaeva, "The Search for the 'Russian Idea'," *Transitions* 4/1 (June 1997), 45.
9. *HCHR News*, 1/2 (December 1995), 4.
10. Sergei Chugrov, "Russian Political Culture: Prospects for Democracy," in Mark Salter, ed., *After the Revolutions: Democracy in East Central Europe* (Uppsala: Life and Peace Institute, 1966), 35–36.
11. Interview with Professor Nadine Marie, Paris, May 1997.
12. V. Lapkin and V. Pantin, "Russkii poryadok" [Russian Order], *Polis*, no. 3 (1997), 80–81.
13. Survey results cited in Sergei Chugrov, "Ideological Stereotypes and Foreign Policy Consciousness," *Mirovaya Ekonomika i Mezhdunarodnye Otnosheniya* [The World Economy and International Relations], no. 2 (1993), 38–48 (in Russian).
14. For details see A. N. Talalaev, "Sootnosheniye mezhdunarodnogo prava i vnutrigosudarstvennogo prava i konstitutsii Rossiiskoi Federatsii" [Balance between International Law and Domestic Law and the Constitution of the Russian Federation], *Moskovskii zhurnal mezhdunarodnogo prava* [Moscow Journal of International Law], no. 4 (1994), 3–4.
15. Presidential Decree no. 1798, 1 November 1993.
16. In 1990–1994, Sergei Kovalyov headed Russia's delegation to the Commission on Human Rights in Geneva; in 1990, he was elected chairman of the Human Rights Committee in the Supreme Soviet of Russia; in January 1994 he was elected Ombudsman and in March 1995 was replaced by the State Duma; in January 1996, Kovalyov resigned from the post of chairman of the Presidential Human Rights Commission in protest at Yeltsin's human rights record. Nikolai Troitsky, "Beznadyozhnoye delo zashchitnika Kovalyova" [Helpless Cause of Defender Kovalyov], *Itogi*, no. 12 (30 July 1996), 28–29.
17. Marie, *Le Droit retrouvé?*, op. cit., 193.
18. UN Statement by the representative of the Russian Federation at the 51st Session of the UN Commission on Human Rights. Agenda item 10: Question of the human rights of all persons subjected to any form of detention or imprisonment, in particular: torture and other cruel, inhuman or degrading treatment or punishment (Geneva, 17 February 1995); Report submitted to the Committee on Foreign Relations, US Senate, and Committee on Foreign Affairs, US House of Representatives, by the Department of State in accordance with sections 116(d) and 502(b) of the Foreign Assistance Act of 1961, as amended. Translations into Russian are published in *Prava cheloveka v Rossii – Mezhdunarodnye izmereniye. Sbornik dokumentov* [Human Rights in Russia – International Dimension. Collection of Documents] (Moscow: Prava cheloveka, 1995), 309–344.
19. Lev Razgon, "Prisons Mirror on Russia's Present Moral State," *Moscow Times*, 23 July 1997, p. 9; *Segodnya*, 22 July 1997, p. 5.

20. S. Ya. Uletsky, "Primeneniye smertnoi kazni i ispolzovaniye sily pri krainei neobkhodimosti" [Death Penalties and the Use of Force in Contingency Situations], in *Problemy rossiiskogo gosudarstvennogo stoitelstva i zakonodatelstva* [Problems of Russian State-Building and Legislature] (Vladivostok: Far East University Press, 1994), 115.
21. Maxim Shevchenko and Sergei Startsev, "Novyi zakon o svobode sovesti i veroispovedanii stanovitsya predmetom politicheskogo torga" [New Law on Freedom of Conscience and Religious Associations Becomes a Political Bargaining Chip], *Nezavisimaya Gazeta*, 19 July 1997, p. 1.
22. Deacon Alexander Bulekov, "Tserkov v zakone" [Church in Law], *Moskovskii Komsomolets*, 3 July 1997, p. 2; Simon Saradzhyan, "Orthodox, Catholic Churches Collide," *Moscow Tribune*, 18 July 1997, p. 2.
23. *Country Reports on Human Rights Practices for 1996*, Report Submitted to the Committee on Foreign Relations, US Senate, and the Committee on International Relations, US House of Representatives, by the Department of State, 105th Congress, 1st Session, Joint Committee Print, February 1997, pp. 1082–1103.
24. Vladimir Kartashkin, "Chelovek – vysshaya tsennost" [Human Being as a Highest Priority], *Nezavisimaya Gazeta*, 9 July 1997, p. 1.
25. Peter Meyer, "The International Bill: A Brief History," in Paul Williams, ed., *The International Bill of Rights* (Glen Ellen: Entwhistle Books, 1981), xxx–xxxi.
26. Edward Lawson, ed., *Encyclopedia of Human Rights* (New York: Taylor & Francis, 1991), 1842–1843.
27. S. V. Sirotkin, "Novoe rossiiskoye zakonodatelstvo i Evropeiskaya Konventsiya o zashchite prav cheloveka..." [New Russian Laws and the European Human Rights Convention], *Moskovskii zhurnal mezhdunarodnogo prava* [Moscow Journal of International Law], no. 4 (1994), 28–34.
28. State Committee of the Russian Federation on Statistics, Ministry of Foreign Affairs of the Russian Federation, *Rossiya i OON: K 50-letiyu obrazovaniya OON* [Russia and United Nations: 50 Years of the UN Founding. Facts and Figures] (Moscow, 1995), 30.
29. *Vedomosti Syezda Narodnykh Deputatov i Verkhovnogo Sovieta RSFSR* [Collection of Documents of the Congresses of People's Deputies and the Supreme Soviet of the RSFSR], no. 52 (1991), 1865.
30. Vladimir Petrovsky, "Mezhdunarodnoye pravo i novaya OON" [International Law and the New UN], Report to the UN Commission on International Law, 12 July 1994, *Moskovskii zhurnal mezhdunarodnogo prava* [Moscow Journal of International Law], no. 4 (1994), 31.
31. V. V. Gavrilov, "Voprosy sovershenstvovaniya normotvorcheskoi deyatelnosti OON v oblasti prav cheloveka" [Problems of Promotion of UN Legislative Activities Concerning Human Rights], in *Problemy rossiiskogo zakonodatelstva*, op. cit., 121.
32. Strengthening the Role of the United Nations in Enhancing the Effectiveness of the Principle of Periodic and Genuine Elections and the Promotion of Democratization, General Assembly Resolution 50/185, 22 December 1995, meeting 99; Respect for the Principles of National Sovereignty and Non-interference in the Internal Affairs of States in their Electoral Processes, General Assembly Resolution 50/172, 22 December 1995, meeting 99.
33. Alexei Kiva, "Ombudsmeny i derzhmordy. Pravozashchitnaya deyatelnost: mirovoi opyt i rossiiskii put" [Ombudsmen and Ruthless Cops. Human Rights: World Experience and the Russian Path], *Vechernaia Moskva*, 30 June 1997, p. 3.
34. Report of the International Court of Justice, 1 August 1995–31 July 1996, General Assembly, Official Records, Fifty-first Session, Supplement No. 4 (A/51/4) (New York: United Nations, 1996), 16–23.

35. Stan Markotich, "Former Communist States Respond to NATO Ultimatum," *RFE/RL Research Report* 3/8 (25 February 1994), 10.
36. Michael Mihalka, "Cauldron of the Emerging Security Order," *Transition*, 12 January 1996, p. 42; Konstanty Gebert, "In Investigating Human Rights Abuses, Reporting Is Not Enough," *Transition*, 26 January 1996, pp. 40–44.
37. Situation of Human Rights in the Republic of Bosnia and Hercegovina, the Republic of Croatia and the Federal Republic of Yugoslavia (Serbia and Montenegro), General Assembly Resolution 50/193, 11 March 1995.
38. Situation of Human Rights in Iraq, General Assembly Resolution 49/203, 23 December 1994; General Assembly Resolution 50/191, 6 March 1996; HRC Resolution 1991/74, 6 March 1991.
39. Vladimir Abarinov, "Gazprom diplomacy," *Moscow Times*, 24 October 1997, p. 3.
40. Report of the Special Committee to Investigate Israeli Practices Affecting the Human Rights of the Palestinian People and Other Arabs of the Occupied Territories, General Assembly Resolution 50/29, 5 February 1996.
41. The Right of the Palestinian People to Self-determination, General Assembly Resolution 50/140, 21 December 1995.
42. Economic and Social Council Decision 1995/277, 25 July 1995.
43. Situation of Human Rights in Cuba, General Assembly Resolution 50/198, 22 December 1995.
44. "Zametki o 51-i sessii Komissii OON po pravam cheloveka" [Notes on the 51st Session of the UN Human Rights Commission], *Pravozashchitnik* [Human Rights Defender], no. 2 (April–June 1995), 7.
45. "Osnovnye itogi 53 sessii Komissii OON po pravam cheloveka" [Major Results of the 53rd Session of the UN Human Rights Commission], *Diplomaticheskii vestnik* [Diplomatic Monitor], no. 8 (1997), 49–53.
46. *Dumskii vestnik* [The State Duma Monitor], no. 1 (1996), 163.
47. "Vystupleniye V. V. Zhirinovskogo" [V. V. Zhirinovsky's Speech], *Pravo Sovieta Evropy i Rossiya* [Legislation of the Council of Europe and Russia, Collection of Documents and Materials] (Krasnodar: Sovetskaya Kuban, 1996), 76.
48. Parliamentary Assembly of the Council of Europe (PACE), Resolution no. 1086 (1996) on developments of the Russian Federation in relation to the situation in Chechnya, in Council of Europe Parliamentary Assembly 1996 Ordinary Session (Second Part), *Texts Adopted by the Assembly, 1996 Ordinary Session (Second Part), 22–26 April 1996* (Strasbourg, 1996), 1–3.
49. "Human Rights Defenders Said to Be under Pressure in Regions," *OMRI Daily Digest* 1/9, part II, 11 April 1997.
50. *Country Reports on Human Rights Practices for 1996*, op. cit., 1091.
51. *Yearbook of the United Nations 1995*, vol. 49 (The Hague: Martinus Nijhoff, 1996), 819–820.
52. Sergei Chugrov, "NATO Expansion and the Chechen Link," *The Parliamentary Brief* (London, March/April 1995), 3–5. Vadim Ilyin, "Prodolzhayutsya poiski vinovnikov voiny" [In Search of Instigators of the War], *Nezavisimaya Gazeta*, 24 June 1997, p. 3.
53. Elena Stepanova, "Missionery vozvrashchayutsya v Moskvu" [Missions Return to Moscow], *Segodnya*, 22 July 1977, p. 6; Johnathan Lynn, "IMF Likely to Find Stabler Economy," *Moscow Times*, 23 July 1977, p. 11.
54. *OMRI Daily Digest*, 12 April 1997, part I.
55. Alexei Arbatov, "Vneshnepoliticheskii konsensus v Rossii" [Foreign Policy Consensus in Russia], *Nezavisimaya Gazeta*, 14 March 1997, p. 5.
56. Vladimir Sanko, "Rezultat konsultatsii zapadnykh ekspertov" [The Results of Consultations of Western Experts], *Nezavisimaya Gazeta*, 24 June 1997, p. 4.

57. Sergei Chugrov, "Domestic Sources of Russian Foreign Policy towards Japan in the 1990s," *Harvard Journal of World Affairs* 4/1 (1995), 67–68.
58. Zoya Svetlova, "V poiskakh grazhdanskogo obshchestva" [In Search of Civil Society], *Russkaya mysl* [La pensée russe] (Paris), no. 4171, 1–7 May 1997, p. 8.
59. Bruce D. Porter and Carol R. Saivetz, "The Once and Future Empire: Russia and the 'Near Abroad'," *Washington Quarterly* 17/3 (1994), 75–76.
60. Nikolai Kosolapov, "International Conflicts in Post-Soviet Space: Problems of Definition and Typology," Report at the Academic Council of IMEMO, March 1996, preprint, p. 20.
61. Charles King, "Eurasian Letter: Moldova with a Russian Face," *Foreign Policy*, no. 97 (Winter 1994–95), 107.
62. "National Security Policy of the Russian Federation (1996–2000)," draft project, Russian Scientific Foundation, Federation of Peace and Accord, Moscow, April 1996, pp. 29, 37.
63. Alexei Arbatov, "Russian Foreign Policy Thinking in Transition," in Vladimir Baranovsky, ed., *Russia and Europe: The Emerging Security Agenda* (Oxford: Oxford University Press, 1997), 144.
64. "Lukashenko Calls for Law and Order," *Moscow Tribune*, 15 July 1997, p. 6.
65. Maxim Yusin, "Lukashenko predpochyol obshchatsya s Yeltsinym cherez svoyu press-sluzhbu" [Lukashenko Has Preferred to Communicate with Yeltsin with the Help of His Press Service], *Izvestia*, 1 August 1977, p. 2; Olga Ulevich, "Ya obyasnyuss Yeltsinym..." [I Will Settle It with Yeltsin...], *Komslomolskaya Pravda*, 2 August 1997, pp. 1–2; "Lukashenko Locks up 14 More Journalists," *Moscow Times*, 1 August 1997, pp. 1–2.
66. Leonid Velekhov, "Plata za souz" [Payment for the Union], *Itogi*, no. 17 (29 April 1997), 30–31.
67. Arbatov, "Russian Foreign Policy Thinking in Transition," op. cit., 152.
68. M. V. Puchkova, "O probleme prav malochislennykh narodov i natsionalnykh grupp" [The Problem of Rights of Small Peoples and National Groups], *Prava cheloveka: Vremya trudnykh resheniy* [Human Rights: Time of Difficult Decisions] (Moscow: Institut gosudarstva i prava, 1991), 137.
69. Alexander A. Sergounin, "In Search for a New Strategy in the Baltic\Nordic Area," in Baranovsky, *Russia and Europe*, op. cit., 341; Sebastian Smith, "Estonia Grapples with Soviet Monuments," *Moscow Times*, 6 June 1997, p. 7.
70. A. A. Trynkov, "Rossiya – Estoniya: novoye nachalo?" [Russia – Estonia: The New Start?], in *Novaya Evraziya: otnosheniya Rossii so stranami blizhnego zarubezhya* [New Eurasia: Russia's Relations with the Near Abroad Countries] (Moscow: Russian Institute of Strategic Analysis, 1995, no. 3), 141.
71. PACE, *Report on the Honoring of Obligations and Commitments by Estonia* (Rapporteur: Mr. Rudolf Bindig, Germany, Socialist Group), 20 December 1996, Doc. 7715, pp. 1–26.
72. PACE, *Motion for a Resolution on Human Rights and the Situation of the Russian National Minority in Estonia, Presented by Mr. Glotov and Others,* 2 October 1996, Doc. 7671, pp. 1–2; *Reply from the Committee of Ministers to Written Question No. 368, by Mr. van der Maelen on the Rights of the Russian Minority in Estonia*, 29 October 1996, Doc. 7689, pp. 1–2.
73. PACE, *Report on Refugees, Asylum Seekers and Displaced Persons in the Commonwealth of Independent States (CIS)*, 15 May 1997, Doc. 7829, p. 11.
74. Denis Kudryashov, "Dyadya Tom predpochitaet khizhinu v Moskve" [Uncle Tom Prefers a Hut in Moscow], *Moskva: Argumenty i fakty* [Moscow: Arguments and Facts], no. 44 (October 1997), 1.

75. PACE, *Report on Refugees*, op. cit., 16; Alla Alova, "Propiska – veshch dorogaya i nezakonnaya" [Residence Permits Are Expensive and Illegal], *Obshchaya gazeta*, no. 28 (17–23 July 1997), 3; Bronwyn McLaren, "Court Deals a Blow to Hated 'Propiskas'," "Let Citizens Move Freely about Russia," *Moscow Times*, 10 July 1997, pp. 1–2, 8.
76. Nirmala Chandrahasan, "The Effects of Refugee Law on Families," in Kathleen E. Mahoney and Paul Mahoney, eds., *Human Rights in the Twenty-First Century: A Global Challenge* (Dordrecht: Martinus Nijhoff, 1993), 653.
77. Article 12 reads: "1. Everyone lawfully within the territory of a State shall, within that territory, have the right to liberty of movement and freedom to choose his residence. 2. Everyone shall be free to leave any country, including his own. 3. The above-mentioned rights shall not be subject to any restrictions except those which are provided by law, are necessary to protect national security, public order (*ordre publique*), public health or morals or the rights and freedoms of others, and are consistent with other rights recognized in the present Convention." Similarly, Article 2 of Protocol No. 4 to the European Convention on Human Rights provides that everyone lawfully within the territory of a state has the right to liberty of movement and freedom to choose his residence. PACE, *Report on Refugees*, op. cit., 12–13.
78. "Russia: Georgian Dilemma," *Oxford Analytica Daily Brief*, 25 October 1993.
79. M. M. Zelinsky and V. G. Mityaev, "Gruzino–abkhazskii konflikt i rol Rossii v ego uregulirovanii" [Georgia–Abkhazia Conflict and Russia's Role in Its Settlement], in *Novaya Evraziya*, op. cit., 35.
80. Elizaveta Kharket, "Gosduma prinyala zayavleniye po KMS" [The State Duma Has Adopted a Statement on the Peace-Keeping Forces], *Nezavisimaya Gazeta*, 24 June 1997, p. 3.
81. V. G. Mityaev and R. A. Shilova, "Polozheniye russkoazychnogo naseleniya v gosudarstvakh Srednei Azii" [The Russian-Speaking Population in Middle Asia], in *Novaya Evraziya*, op. cit., 77.
82. Vladimir Baranovsky, "Russia: Conflicts and Its Security Environment," *SIPRI Yearbook 1997*, 117–118; for the text of the Agreement see *Diplomaticheskiy Vestnik*, no. 21–22 (November 1994), 47–51.
83. "No Contracting State shall expel or return ('refouler') a refugee in any manner whatsoever to the frontiers of territories where his life or freedom would be threatened on account of his race, religion, nationality, membership of a particular social group or political opinion."
84. Mityaev and Shilova, "Polozheniye russkoazychnogo naseleniya v gosudarstvakh Srednei Azii," op. cit.

7

# India's human rights diplomacy: Crisis and transformation

*Sanjoy Banerjee*

## I. Introduction

In the first decades after independence, India became an international advocate of human rights. Opposing European colonialism and apartheid, and later Israeli actions against Palestinians, it was a leader among non-aligned nations in a quest to end the state-enforced social inequality that had characterized the world order in the preceding centuries. India engaged in assertive diplomacy, criticizing states well beyond the reach of its limited material power. It twice intervened militarily outside its borders, invoking human rights: opposing the government in East Pakistan in 1971 and aligning with the government in Sri Lanka in 1987. Before the end of the Cold War, external human rights pressure on India was low, in spite of events that might easily have occasioned such pressure. For example, there were anti-Sikh riots in Delhi after the assassination of Indira Gandhi in 1984, with the clear involvement of politicians in the ruling Congress Party, yet India faced little criticism about this from other states.

India's foreign policy environment changed abruptly in 1991. The disappearance of the USSR was accompanied by a multifaceted domestic crisis in India. The USSR had been India's primary arms supplier and its rivalry with the West had created the possibility of non-alignment for post-colonial states. India went from being a non-aligned country with room for manoeuvre in a bipolar world to being a vulnerable state in a unipolar world. The US performance in the Gulf War demonstrated its overwhelming military supremacy, and the continuing deadly sanctions on Iraq after the war were a powerful demonstration of unipolar discipline.

The period after 1989 witnessed a profound transformation in India's human rights diplomacy, which switched from an assertive to a defensive mode. The new world order brought in its train an invigorated but highly inconsistent international human rights regime dominated by Western states and by influential non-governmental organizations (NGOs) rooted entirely or mainly in the West. India and other developing countries struggled to preserve their sovereignty in the face of the changed regime. The early 1990s saw the peak of secessionist insurgencies in the history of independent India, and police and security forces committed human rights violations while combating insurgents. The government faced the dilemma that punishing members of the security forces severely or openly was expected to harm their collective morale. India entered a severe economic crisis in the early 1990s, which also brought home an awareness of how far India had fallen behind its Asian neighbours in economic development. The conjunction of international and domestic circumstances led the Indian government to the conclusion that the diplomatic activism of the past was no longer wise and India needed to put its own house in order before giving advice to others.

Although retreating from assertive diplomacy, India became aggressive in the preservation of its sovereignty, in both substance and appearance. Sovereignty was understood as a necessary condition of democracy. The structural changes in India during the 1990s did serve to reconstruct internal unity sufficiently to preserve effective sovereignty. Delhi mounted an energetic diplomatic campaign to rebut some of the accusations and to persuade several sections of the international community that it had no deliberate campaign to violate human rights, and that the excesses of its forces were being mitigated through administrative discipline. In the defensive mode, India's domestic policies and politics became more directly linked to its diplomatic posture. As the Indian polity stabilized, human rights violations began to decline and India began to enjoy a modicum of success in its campaign of defensive human rights diplomacy.

India's human rights diplomacy in all periods has been based on a moral consensus of fluctuating strength within the polity. Through most of the post-independence period the vast majority of people and parties have agreed on certain broad values, in particular upon the desirability of democracy within India[1] and opposition to colonialism and racism abroad. The point of Indian human rights diplomacy has been to promote, at least rhetorically, selected values in that moral consensus, and to prevent foreign initiatives in India that would undermine its sovereignty and the effective supremacy of those values. In the early 1990s the strength of the moral consensus in the Indian polity reached a nadir. Centrally, the value of secularism came under effective assault as Hindu nationalists broadened their popular support using anti-Muslim appeals and as secessionist movements grew. This contraction of the moral consensus diminished the credibility, even in the domestic scene, of assertive human rights diplomacy. As the 1990s progressed, a moral and constitutional consensus was restored. The challenge to secularism was politically marginalized by the tide of lower-caste political mobilization and upper-caste acquiescence, and by the moderation of Hindu nationalism. A period of political leadership free from charisma enabled the judiciary and other non-political institutions to establish unprecedented programmes of action against various forms of illegality and corruption, with wide popular acclaim. The restored moral consensus strengthened domestic confidence in India's institutions and in its defensive human rights diplomacy.

There have been limits to the moral consensus, even within the state apparatus. The inability of the political leadership to discipline the security forces reflects the limitations in its own credibility. All major political parties have agreed that the security forces should respect human rights in their operations. Yet widespread corruption as well as divisive politics has diminished the capacity of political leaders convincingly to represent a national moral consensus in commanding the security forces. The result is an enfeebled administration that must rely exclusively on bureaucratic means and face a stringent tradeoff between morale and discipline in the forces. This condition in turn generated a stream of human rights violations, especially in the first half of the 1990s, and forced Indian human rights diplomacy on to the defensive.

## *Indian foreign policy on human rights*

A state's human rights diplomacy may be assertive or defensive. Assertive diplomacy will use a variety of means to influence global human rights practices, agreements, and institutions. It will accuse other states of violating human rights and pursue those accusations in international institutions or in its direct relations with the accused and other states. Assertive human rights diplomacy often entails the implication that the assertive state has superior knowledge and practice of human rights compared with accused states. In recent decades, the United States and other Western states have conducted assertive human rights diplomacy with such broad claims implicit or explicit. Pakistan, in spite of many domestic and international problems, has conducted assertive human rights diplomacy against India regarding Kashmir. Defensive human rights diplomacy opposes other states' assertive diplomacy. It usually proclaims state sovereignty and the adequacy of the state's human rights performance under existing local conditions and global agreements. It denies the legitimacy of intrusions by international human rights institutions and foreign NGOs. Defensive diplomacy criticizes other states primarily to question their standing to conduct assertive diplomacy. China's human rights diplomacy, especially after the Tiananmen Square incident in 1989, has been defensive. The United States has pursued defensive diplomacy regarding Israel's actions in its occupied territories.

Defensive human rights diplomacy may be the defence of democracy and sovereignty against imperialist or aggressive stratagems disguised as human rights concern. Or it may be the use of the state's power and international institutions of sovereignty to protect a programme of human rights violations. Assertive human rights diplomacy, similarly, can range from being what it claims to be to being imperialism or aggression in disguise. One must independently judge the truth of the claims of the instances of human rights diplomacy.

In the Indian case, the post–Cold War period has witnessed very little in the way of assertive human rights diplomacy. Indian rhetoric about human rights violations in Pakistan has been more muted than that of Western human rights organizations. During the Cold War, India had criticized actions resulting in civilian deaths in the course of Western interventions in the third world. Indian rhetoric about civilian deaths during the 1991 Gulf War and deaths due to the embargo on Iraq was quite muted couching its concerns as humanitarian, not invoking human rights. Both the government and non-governmental observers in India displayed limited sympathy for Western governmental, media, and NGO criticisms of other states. Most Indian observers did not consider Western criticism of India to be balanced, and concluded that Western criticism of many other developing states was equally unbalanced. In addition to disengaging from Western assertive diplomacy against other states, Delhi was not eager to strengthen the institutions of international human rights, expecting them to retain structures of adjudication disproportionately influenced by the West.

India and China arrived at an understanding to undertake joint defensive diplomacy on human rights, each remaining silent about the other's human rights violations. In the aftermath of the Tiananmen Square incident in June 1989, statements from Delhi avoided the suggestion that the Chinese government had violated human rights. That period was one of improving India–China relations. There was a series of meetings between Indian and Chinese officials in subsequent months, and Indian official statements avoided any comment on the incident.[2] China in turn came to India's aid at a crucial vote on a Pakistani resolution about Kashmir in 1994 at the UN Human Rights Commission.

Indian human rights diplomacy in the post–Cold War period has been primarily defensive. It has consisted of rebutting charges against India in international forums, making common cause with some developing countries, using its economic reforms to seek favour with wealthy nations, and, to a degree, getting better at fighting insurgencies without killing civilians. Although the Indian political establishment considered many specific human rights accusations by Western sources to be politically biased, its members were deeply embarrassed by them, and acknowledged that Indian security forces were committing real human rights violations. The several facets of the predominant Indian attitude on these matters were well summarized by Atal Behari Vajpayee, a leader of the Hindu nationalist Bharatiya Janata Party (BJP), after he led an Indian delegation that successfully blocked Pakistani assertive diplomacy at the UN Human Rights Commission in Geneva in 1994: "For a great nation like us, there was a certain humiliation involved in having to go around begging for votes on a human rights issue. Let us now use this reprieve to clean up our act in Kashmir or there will be a Geneva every few months."[3]

India has faced numerous armed challenges from groups that are extremely small in relation to the whole of the country. Active militants in Punjab never numbered more than about 10,000. In Kashmir, militants have never exceeded 12,000, while the Indian security forces have numbered over 400,000. Secessionist insurgents have pinned their hopes in part on the prospects of support from other states. Pakistan has supplied these groups with arms and training, and in Kashmir has sent Pakistani, Afghan, and other nationals in to fight with local insurgents. However, Pakistan is widely recognized by militant groups as being an insufficiently powerful ally. A long-term goal has been to gain US and Western support. It is significant that when Indira Gandhi's Sikh bodyguards assassinated her in 1984, a group of pro-separatist Sikh immigrants in New York danced in front of the Indian UN mission waving American flags. Pro-separatist Sikh and Kashmiri immigrant groups in the United States have energetically lobbied members of Congress. Accusations of human rights violations have been at the heart of the lobbying rhetoric. Groups aligned with the insurgent movements have played a key role in generating human rights accusations against the Indian state. These accusations are part of the global political strategy of the insurgents. They understand the West to dominate the international adjudication of human rights accusations. Their hope has been to mobilize the centres of world power in their favour to the extent they can in an otherwise unequal struggle.

The Indian state and much of society have viewed Western and Islamic accusations of human rights violations in the context of the international strategies of the militant organizations and Pakistan. Indians, inside and outside the government, have viewed international organizations, human rights NGOs, and foreign governments less as sincere adjudicators of human rights accusations than as objects of political struggle and as politically motivated actors.

Although India's economic globalization and liberalization were undertaken for mainly economic reasons, the benefits in terms of defensive human rights diplomacy were well recognized. Further, throughout the 1990s there was a sustained government effort to reduce the number of actual human rights violations, especially in Kashmir, again mainly for domestic reasons, but with its international reputation being in second place among the expected benefits.

India's efforts to improve the international reputation of its domestic human rights performance did enjoy some success. The US State Department's annual human rights report in 1996, although critical of India on many issues, said of civilian deaths in Kashmir:

> Civilian deaths caused by security forces diminished for the third consecutive year in Kashmir. The explanation appears to lie in press scrutiny and public outcry over abuses in previous years, increased training of military and paramilitary forces in humanitarian law, and greater sensitivity of commanders to rule of law issues. The improvement has taken the form of increased discipline and care in avoiding collateral civilian injuries and deaths (i.e., deaths in crossfire).[4]

## *The international context of Indian human rights diplomacy*

James Ron observes that in the period 1982–1994 the frequency of use of the phrase "human rights" increased six-fold in Reuters World Service news reports, seven-fold in British Broadcasting Corporation reports, eleven-fold in the Xinhua General Overseas News Service, and four-fold in stories in the Current Digest of the Soviet Press.[5] This clearly reflects its increasing frequency of use in overall international and national discourses as well as a growing sensitivity of the international media to the phrase. All this does not necessarily mean that states, weak or powerful, are more willing now to make sacrifices to avoid violating the unconditional prohibitions of the doctrine of human rights in their conduct at home and abroad. Nor does it mean that the international discourse on human rights is gaining in honesty and consistency.

The adoption of the Universal Declaration of Human Rights without a negative vote by the United Nations General Assembly in 1948 brought into being a qualitatively new international regime of human rights.[6] It is useful to define the term "international regime" broadly. The regime as a whole includes a complex of formal international agreements and institutions, a culture of diplomatic practice, as well as a global array of NGOs advocating human rights. The reason for calling these various elements a single international regime is that they closely affect each other. In particular, the NGOs can promote a climate of opinion that influences diplomacy on certain issues, as well as the functioning of international human rights institutions. For example, Human Rights Watch regularly testifies before the US Congress.

The ending of the Cold War, in transforming international politics as a whole, suddenly transformed the politics of the international human rights regime. During the Cold War the regime had elaborately defined norms and standards but weak enforcement.[7] After 1989 it became a regime with elaborate norms and stronger yet selective enforcement, and with asymmetrical informal roles for different states and NGOs within the emerging monitoring and enforcement mechanisms. The international human rights regime is a political structure, and its participants have unequal power and conflicting objectives.

India's human rights diplomacy in the post–Cold War era has been both constrained and enabled by the politics of the international regime on human rights. The impact of the regime has been multifaceted. There is a widespread perception in India that the international institutions, diplomacy, and rhetoric of human rights are biased according to the larger inequalities of power and wealth in the world. Indeed, many Indian observers have expressed the suspicion that Western governmental and non-governmental human rights accusations against India are part of a strategy of Western power maintenance. At the same time, most Indian observers perceive the institutions and practices of the regime at least partially as reflecting values that India holds and cannot ignore in its domestic or foreign actions. All actors, state and non-state, who have impinged on Indian human rights diplomacy have also perceived a formal and informal regime of human rights in the world and have acted on that basis.

An assessment of the performance of the post–Cold War international human rights regime must acknowledge some major failures and some successes. At present, the regime is best judged not only by its limited ability to prevent or stop human rights violations, but also by the consistency and even-handedness with which it criticizes and punishes them. It is clear that many genuine human rights violations have been criticized and sanctioned by states and international human rights institutions in the post–Cold War era. Violations in the former Yugoslavia, Haiti, and Rwanda are such cases. In Haiti, the United States took action in 1994 with the support of the UN Security Council to remove a regime that was violating human rights from power. Yet there have also been massive failures of the international human rights regime since the end of the Cold War.

The UN sanctions against Iraq after the Iraqi invasion of Kuwait in

1990 have caused the largest number of civilian deaths of any coercive programme in the 1990s and constitute a massive human rights violation. The sanctions prevented the purchase of food and medicines by Iraq, until they were relaxed slightly in 1997. Deteriorating nutritional and health conditions in the nation of 17 million have led to sharply higher death rates. The mortality rate for children under 5 in Iraq has risen six-fold since 1989/90.[8] Two scientists from the United Nations' Food and Agriculture Organization estimated in 1995 that 567,000 children had died as a result of the sanctions.[9] Adult deaths owing to the sanctions also number in the hundreds of thousands. The sanctions against Iraq have been the most effective and indiscriminate of the post-colonial period. The UN sanctions resolution against Serbia and Montenegro in 1992 was worded similarly to the resolutions against Iraq, but those sanctions were expected to be and were far less effective.[10] Thus the sanctions against Serbia did not have a comparable human impact. The sanctions against Iraq did not merely prevent weapons or industrial imports. Initially the sanctions explicitly prohibited imports of food and medicine, and later just prohibited exports, achieving similar results.[11] The United Nations Security Council is the legal agent of the sanctions, but the United States, and to an extent the United Kingdom, are the principal political agents. The United States used its political power to maintain the sanctions even as other states have sought to loosen them. The United States viewed the sanctions as a lever to force the Iraqi people to overthrow Saddam Hussein. President Bush said to the United Nations General Assembly in September 1991 that the sanctions should remain in place until Saddam Hussein was out of power.[12]

The principal moral debate about the sanctions against Iraq has been not about the number of deaths in Iraq, but over responsibility for them. The United States has advanced the argument that the Iraqi government is responsible for the deaths because, had it agreed to the conditions set by the United Nations, or had Saddam Hussein left office, the sanctions would have been eased or lifted. The logic of human rights, as advocated by the United States itself, is that certain actions are forbidden regardless of the behaviour of others. The US position is tantamount to asserting that there are no unconditional human rights constraints on economic sanctions.

The international community has had very little to say about the human rights implications of the sanctions against Iraq. The Security Council votes on sanctions have usually been unanimous, with no state prepared to challenge US power. India joined the rest of the international community in its diplomatic silence on the human rights aspects of the sanctions, voicing only "humanitarian" concerns about the impact on the Iraqi people. The gap between proclaimed values and performance has been even greater for leading Western human rights organizations. Amnesty International's 1995 annual report, for example, has only two sentences on the topic of the sanctions against Iraq, neither of which suggests that there are any human rights constraints on the imposition of economic sanctions.[13] Human Rights Watch has been equally silent on the issue. Physicians for Human Rights issued a strong and detailed criticism of the sanctions on Iraq in 1991, but fell silent afterwards.[14] The absence of human rights pressure on the United States on this issue has been all the more tragic because the interests the United States pursued through the sanctions in their severe form were of secondary priority. Over the years it became clear that the sanctions were not effective in forcing a popular rebellion in Iraq, yet the United States felt no need to take further action to that end. More carefully focused sanctions could have prevented the rearmament of Iraq while sparing the lives of over 1 million people.

The case of the sanctions against Iraq reveals a power structure and a resulting bias in the international human rights regime in the post–Cold War era. Because the sanctions were promoted by the dominant power of the era – the United States – other states chose to maintain a discreet silence. Western human rights organizations have largely excluded the topic of civilian deaths in Iraq resulting from sanctions from their reports. The regime has instead focused on accusing weaker states. Biases in the international human rights regime were keenly recognized within India, and its credibility suffered accordingly.

## II. Historical origins

Human rights concerns were central to the Indian independence movement. Above all, the movement abhorred the systematic racial discrimination the British empire embodied. The independence movement also promoted social reform within India. Of greatest concern was the elimination of caste discrimination and avoidance of religious bigotry. The adoption of the Constitution in 1951 gave a legal basis to the quest for social reform. Universal suffrage was implemented in India at a time when European imperial states continued to disenfranchise their colonized peoples and the United States disenfranchised most African-Americans.

Indian human rights judgements have been based on a set of traditions and concerns rooted in Indian history. The independence movement, and the leadership of Mahatma Gandhi, recovered from the long philosophical and religious debate of Indian history a political ideology that transcended the opposition of a modern West and a traditional India that the British empire had circulated.

Mahatma Gandhi received his professional training as a lawyer in London. He returned to India from South Africa as one who believed in the ideals of civil liberty in the rhetoric of the British empire. The 1919 massacre in Amritsar of unarmed and peaceful Indian demonstrators by troops of the colonial army was a turning point in Gandhi's attitude toward the British. The light punishment of General Dyer, the British commander on the scene, and the indifference of the British public convinced Gandhi and many Indians that the British rhetoric about the ideals of civil liberty was insincere.

In Gandhi's conception, freedom was indivisible. Freedom from colonialism was morally inseparable from the elimination of untouchability and other "social evils." At the 1926 meeting of the Indian National Congress, Gandhi debated with a party colleague about the link between self-rule and untouchability. Srinivasa Aiyengar said: "Neither foreign nor domestic critics are right when they assert that untouchability is a formidable obstacle for Swaraj (self-rule). We cannot wait for Swaraj till it is removed anymore than we can wait till caste is abolished."[15] Gandhi responded that, although the existence of untouchability was not a valid excuse for Britain to resist the move toward independence,

> Real organic Swaraj is a different question. That freedom which is associated in the popular mind with the term Swaraj is no doubt unattainable without not only the removal of untouchability and the promotion of heart unity between different sections but also without removing many other social evils which can easily be named. That inward growth which must never stop we have come to understand by the comprehensive term Swaraj.[16]

In 1928, in an impassioned argument against untouchability, Gandhi compressed his understanding of freedom into a metaphor: "No man takes another into a pit without descending into it himself and sinning in the bargain."[17]

The Gandhian conception of Swaraj was different in its logic from the Western conception of human rights over the course of its evolution since the seventeenth century. It was based on prevailing Indian assumptions about the nature of persons. Conceptions such as "heart unity" and "inward growth" were more rooted in the Indian philosophical tradition. The Gandhian prescriptions were directed at society and not the state. As Donnelly correctly notes, what is distinctive about the Western conception of human rights is that is formulated as rights against the state.[18] Western liberal ideas arose as a philosophy for the regulation of bureaucratic states in the metropoles and colonies of empires. Comparable state development or state-focused discourse outside the West was precluded until the late colonial and post-colonial period because bureaucratic states developed in the West during the colonial era. Gandhi's conception of organic Swaraj, not divisible between the national and interpersonal levels, stands in sharp contrast to imperialist and racist ideas and practices prominent within Western liberalism around 1926. The Gandhian discourse of Swaraj was the leading edge of a profound transformation of social thought over the course of the independence movement and, more effectively than Nehruvian socialist rhetoric, provided the ideological underpinning of a democratic state in a society with deep inegalitarian traditions.

India's moral reasoning about international human rights is guided by a model of political evil that has been profoundly shaped by two experiences and by the prevalent constructions of those experiences in Indian political discourse. The two experiences are the British Indian empire of 1757–1947 and the separation of Pakistan at the end of the colonial period.[19]

British colonialism transformed India from one of the world's wealthiest societies to one of the poorest, entailing a series of massive unprecedented famines. The first major famine of the British period was in colonial Bengal in the early 1770s, in which 30–40 per cent of the population of Bengal died.[20] It was the first major famine in Bengal in 150 years.[21] In the nineteenth century, there were at least 20 million famine deaths in the British Indian empire. The last major famine in India was in 1942–1943, again in Bengal, and it cost 2–3 million lives. British actions during this famine, such as refusing to allow food shipments into Bengal from other parts of India, continuing wartime food procurement from Bengal, and destroying parts of the food transportation system ostensibly to deny its use to would-be Japanese invaders, clearly exacerbated the famine.[22]

The British empire also exacerbated, by deliberate action or by precluding or delaying corrective action, a host of social evils. There was a resurgence of *sati* (widow immolation) mainly in and around Calcutta in the 1790s after centuries of relative infrequency throughout India.[23] The British empire initially gave *sati* legal sanction and did not ban it until 1829. The British presided over an intensification of caste discrimination during the first century of their empire. C. A. Bayly writes: "hierarchy and Brahmin interpretation of Hindu society which was theoretical rather than actual over much of India as late as 1750 was firmly ensconsed a century later."[24] The British colonial authorities, under the leadership of Warren Hastings, began to enforce the Laws of Manu, a severely hierarchical ancient code, in 1794. The British also took other steps in this period to give legal sanction to caste hierarchy. Finally, there is a record stretching back to the mid-nineteenth century of high-level British statements about the advantage to the empire of Hindu–Muslim disunity, and a record of actions to match.[25] The colonial experience, a combination of immiseration, political manipulation, and racism, deeply shaped the Indian understanding of political evil in the twentieth century.

The rhetoric of the Pakistan movement and the violent partition was the second experience that shaped the Indian understanding of political evil. The conflict between the Indian National Congress and the Muslim League in the decades before independence in 1947, and then between India and Pakistan, was between an ideology of unity in diversity and one of Muslim nationalism. The Indian conception of secularism took form in opposition to the ideology of the Pakistan movement in the decade before independence. The Congress spoke of Hindus and Muslims as having a common Indian identity, common obligations and social bonds, and equal rights. The League spoke of Hindus and Muslims as two separate nations with no valued social bonds. For the League, the morality linking the two states was to be international in form; their obligation was to recognize their separation and for each nation to treat the other fairly and to respect minority rights. On the subcontinent, tens of millions of Hindus and Muslims lived in areas where they were intermixed. When partition came, millions found themselves on the "wrong" side. The process of separation just prior to independence turned violent and cost half a million lives. The Indian secular view has been that there is a contradiction between proclaiming a religious basis for nationhood and equal rights for religious minorities. A person officially defined as of a secondary religion could not be consistently treated with equality by the state.

The newly independent state became a strong voice in world affairs for human rights concerns generated by the model of political evil described above. India was a prominent and consistent supporter of independence movements in the remaining colonies. It denounced the atrocities of European imperialists in their colonial wars. India was the first state to denounce apartheid in South Africa as a violation of human rights. India's criticism of Zionism was based on analogies to the Indian experience of both colonialism and religious nationalism. India also criticized the bombing campaign by the United States in the Vietnam War for causing civilian casualties. India's major military intervention in the name of human rights was in the war in 1971 to aid the secession of Bangladesh after the Pakistani Army had killed, by conservative estimates, 1 million civilians there and 10 million refugees had walked to India.

The focus on eliminating colonialism and neocolonialism and on opposing religious nationalism made independent India less sensitive to the new structures of human rights violations that emerged in the twentieth century. Dictatorial states where oppression was not based on ethnic inequality did not fit the Indian model of evil. Indians were relatively uncritical of human rights violations in and by the Soviet bloc. One reason was that the Soviet bloc buttressed India's political autonomy by serving as a counterweight to Western power, but another was the misfit between the bloc's mode of human rights violations and the Indian model of political evil.

## III. Domestic factors

India's human rights diplomacy after 1989 has been profoundly shaped by structural transformation that has taken place within India in this period. There was an unprecedented crisis with economic, political, and social facets in 1991 and a new order afterwards. The year 1990 ended with the collapse of a coalition government of anti-Congress parties that had included both the BJP and secular parties. India nearly ran out of foreign exchange in the first half of 1991. Economic growth in the year ending in March 1992 was 1 per cent, after 15 years of growth averaging 5 per cent. In May, Rajiv Gandhi was assassinated, ending the dynastic leadership of the Nehru family. At that point it became difficult to envision effective national leadership on the basis of historical experience.

The secular ethos that had governed Indian politics since independence was gravely weakened in 1991. The BJP and its allies had chosen to claim that a sixteenth-century mosque in the Hindu holy city of Ayodhya in Uttar Pradesh was built on an important temple, although archaeological evidence strongly suggests otherwise. This campaign triggered a wave of Hindu–Muslim violence in many parts of India. The polarization between Hindus and Muslims worked to the advantage of the BJP. India's communal crisis peaked in the period December 1992 to March 1993. In December, a mob assembled by BJP leaders destroyed the Babri Mosque in Ayodhya, with the acquiescence of the BJP state government in Uttar Pradesh. That triggered a wave of Hindu–Muslim violence. The central government dismissed all four BJP state governments on the day after the mosque demolition. The presence of such moral contradiction and uncertainty within the Indian polity further disabled it from conducting assertive human rights diplomacy. Instead, India had to defend itself against human rights criticism from Muslim and Western sources.

The early 1990s witnessed the greatest level of separatist insurgency of any period since independence, attracting the support of up to 5 per cent of the Indian population. An insurgency in Punjab, seeking an independent Sikh state to be called Khalistan, peaked in 1991. The Kashmir insurgency, which began in late 1989, gained momentum in 1991. There was also a significant insurgency in Assam, in the north-east. Although the insurgents had little chance of seceding, the combination of terrorist actions against local minorities loyal to India and strong support for insurgents from a majority or large minority of their co-ethnics created conditions ripe for human rights violations by ill-disciplined security forces.

The 1990s also witnessed some important social trends with human rights implications. The 1991 census recorded an Indian literacy rate of 52 per cent, far below that in East and South-East Asian countries that had had levels close to India's decades earlier, but above the majority point for the first time. The women's literacy rate was only 39 per cent. In the 1990s a large literacy movement by the government and NGOs made over 66 million people literate, about two-thirds of them women. By 1997, the Indian literacy rate had reached 60 per cent.[26] The 1991 census also recorded a decline in the ratio of women to men since 1981, down to 927 to 1000. This reflected profound discrimination against girls and women within families and within society. Income distribution in India remained one of the more egalitarian in the world, with the richest fifth of households earning 4.7 times the income of the poorest fifth.[27]

The conjuncture of the early 1990s precluded assertive human rights diplomacy and made India vulnerable to human rights criticisms in a variety of ways. The deterioration in the sex ratio as well as continuing dowry murders, sex-selection abortions, and other discriminatory practices against females drew national and global attention to the severity of discrimination against girls and women in India. There was also an upsurge in actions by the security forces and mobs that violated human rights. In the politics of the period, the erosion of the moral consensus, especially on the question of secularism, made coherent moral judgement by the polity difficult and undermined both assertive and defensive human rights diplomacy. There was also a political polarization of society that led dissatisfied minorities, and their kin living abroad, to appeal to Western states and human rights organizations for support. And finally, India's heightened economic weakness reduced the cost of accusatory human rights diplomacy toward India.

The Indian state reacted to the crisis of 1991 primarily by a series of reforms, some planned from above, others initiated by middle levels of the state. The period also witnessed the renegotiation of a moral consensus through the workings of the democratic system. Economic liberalization brought an end to the foreign exchange crisis within a few months. The crisis and the reforms intensified poverty in the first year, but that was reversed in later years. After the reforms began, economic growth accelerated, averaging 7 per cent per annum during the three years before March 1997. One effect of the reforms was that India became a far more attractive investment destination and export market than it was before, though still far behind its neighbours in East and

South-East Asia. The economic attraction of India proved to be a lever by which it could limit Western human rights accusations and defend its sovereignty.

Politics were also profoundly restructured in the 1990s, leading to new patterns of empowerment and participation. That restructuring has enabled a restoration of moral consensus on basic political questions. The break in the rule of the Nehru–Gandhi dynasty in 1991 brought in its train four critical trends with implications for human rights and human rights diplomacy.

The first important trend is a substantial growth in parties based on middle and lower castes, leading to the empowerment of these castes in relation to the upper castes. Previously, most leaders of established parties, especially in northern states, came from the upper castes, and they sought support from the rest of society. In the 1990s, parties led by middle and lower castes scored crucial victories. The most critical instance was the 1993 state elections in Uttar Pradesh, the largest state. The BJP, in the aftermath of the demolition of the sixteenth-century mosque in Ayodhya, was riding a wave of militant Hindu nationalism in the state, but in 1993 it was defeated by a coalition of middle- and lower-caste parties. Subsequently, the BJP gave support during two brief periods to governments in Uttar Pradesh of the Bahujan Samaj Party (BSP), led and supported mainly by Dalits (ex-untouchables). The BSP used its brief stints in power in Uttar Pradesh to make substantial and lasting changes in the state administrative personnel, land reforms, and the development of villages with large Dalit populations. The empowerment of the lower castes has substantially reduced the social inequalities among castes.

The second trend is that militant Hindu nationalism, which had surged in the late 1980s and peaked with the destruction of the mosque in Ayodhya in 1992, has subsided. The defeat of the BJP in the Uttar Pradesh state elections in 1993 marked the turning point. Since then, the BJP and other Hindu nationalists have moderated their stance toward Muslims. They have ceased their emotional campaigns relating to contested places of worship and otherwise toned down their rhetoric in relation to Muslims. Popular support for the BJP has increased since 1993, but within the framework of its moderation. This has greatly reduced the scale of Hindu–Muslim violence. It has also restored a broad moral consensus among parties, and has thus strengthened defensive human rights diplomacy. An example of this effect is that it was the moderate BJP leader Vajpayee who headed the successful Indian delegation at the UN Human Rights Commission meeting in 1994, at the invitation of the rival Congress government.

The third important trend is that the non-political institutions have gained strength in relation to politicians and parties. This trend began with the aggressive approach taken by the Chief Election Commissioner T. N. Seshan from 1994 in enforcing election laws. He succeeded in reducing the scale of illegal spending by candidates and reducing other election abuses. That was followed by stronger action by the judiciary against political corruption. The enhanced independence and credibility of the Election Commission played a key role in giving some international credibility to the elections held in Kashmir in 1996.

The National Human Rights Commission was established in 1993 as a quasi-judicial body to investigate human rights violations. It was widely reported that this action was taken in response to international human rights criticism of India. Foreign governments and NGOs have responded positively to the establishment of the commission.[28] Although the commission has acted vigorously within its capabilities, it is fundamentally a supplement to the established legal system.

The fourth trend is the abatement of the Kashmir insurgency. The single most important issue in Indian defensive human rights diplomacy has been the insurgency and counter-insurgency in Kashmir that began in 1989. The Kashmir insurgency grew steadily until it began to lose popular support in the mid-1990s. India sent in 400,000 troops and the insurgents failed to deliver a quick victory. Pakistan's credibility as a power that could and would give adequate aid to the insurgency waned. The attraction of joining Pakistan declined as conditions deteriorated there. Pakistan's favouritism toward the pro-Pakistan insurgency over the pro-independence insurgency was unpopular. As the number of Kashmiri volunteers waned, Pakistan began to send Afghan and Pakistani militants into Kashmir.[29] They proved unpopular among Kashmiri Muslims. By the mid-1990s, Indian security forces succeeded in pushing the militants out of most urban areas in Kashmir, and this reduced the number of instances of troops killing civilians. In the Kashmir state election of September 1996, voter turnout was 55 per cent even though leading separatist politicians campaigned door-to-door calling for an election boycott.[30] Several previous election attempts announced by the Indian government had to be aborted owing to popular hostility and the insurgency. The successful holding of elections reflects a changed political balance in Kashmir. Moreover, voter turnout in the September 1996 elections can be taken as an accurate reflection of public sentiment in Kashmir. There were reports by Indian and Western journalists in Kashmir that in the July 1996 national elections voters were forced to the polls in Kashmir. There were few such allegations in the Indian or Western media about the September 1996 state elections in Kashmir. In the case of the July elections, no reporter in Kashmir claimed actually to have witnessed any voter being led to polls at gunpoint; rather, several journalists reported such claims by some people. There is some evidence of more subtle pressure to vote by security forces in the July 1996 elections. However, there were no reports of the security forces taking action against any of the majority of Kashmiris who did not vote in those elections. In both elections the voting lines were long and voters had to wait for hours. Kashmiri Muslims have a long record of public demonstrations, they had safety in numbers on voting days, and there was a large international media presence during voting. Given these conditions, it stands to reason that, had a significant proportion of voters been coerced, there would have been large protest demonstrations on voting days. There were not.

The stabilization after the early 1990s restored a moral consensus in the polity. The moderation of the BJP and the mobilization of the lower castes resurrected Indian secularism. The embracing of economic liberalization by the United Front government established a broad agreement about the need for a capitalist developmentalist state, although that consensus remains far from mature. Rival political parties agree on the need to fight corruption actively and to let the non-political state institutions function far more autonomously than before. There is a continuing consensus on the need to avoid "a second partition" of India through the secession of any region. This consensus set the agenda for India's defensive human rights diplomacy.

Yet this restored consensus carries its own contradictions. Although the mobilization of the lower castes has deepened democratic participation and increased equality in the public sphere, caste and other divisions in society continue. Relations between different castes and religions, and between political parties rooted in these groupings, remain filled with mistrust and manoeuvring. Marriages across traditional lines remain rare. In these circumstances, the moral consensus is restricted.

## IV. Multilateral policies

### *Diplomacy in international institutions*

India's human rights objectives within international institutions can be understood from some aspects of its rhetoric in those forums. Indian delegates to the UN General Assembly and UN Human Rights Commission have repeated certain themes during the 1990s. They have maintained that, in spite of differences in civilizations and culture, universal norms of human rights are desirable. Salman Khurshid, then Minister of State for External Affairs, said in 1996 to the Human Rights Commission that newly independent countries were among the first to give unconditional approval to the Universal Declaration of Human Rights because of their expectation that the comity of nations was finally proceeding to realize a common vision of a world based on the sovereign equality of nations, where the same rights would be recognized and the same liberties defended in all parts of the world, despite differences of language, tradition, culture, and civilization. Khurshid added that "the course of human history has been marked by the search in different civilizations for ways of expressing and protecting the human dignity of every individual."[31] India did not intend to assert that cultural differences form the basis of different human rights across countries.

Indian delegates have consistently criticized Western diplomacy in international human rights institutions in the 1990s. Salman Khurshid continued in the speech cited above:

> Today, we are concerned that the spirit of consensus and cooperation that had marked the adoption of the Vienna Declaration [of the World Conference on Human Rights of the UN General Assembly in 1993] is being steadily eroded through the politicization of the human rights agenda (and) the selective targeting of certain countries. Attempts to make human rights issues a matter of North–South or bilateral confrontation are an anti-thesis to what we had agreed a few short years ago. The politics of power in order to establish dominance and legally suspect theories of the right of intervention on humanitarian grounds unfortunately appear to have become popular with some countries.

Here Khurshid expressed perceptions central to India's defensive human rights diplomacy. Opposition to the unfair and intrusive use of the international human rights regime by Western countries has been conceived as a key Indian objective.

Indian delegates have proclaimed that intolerance and terrorism are both violations of human rights and have urged international human rights institutions to tackle the problem in a manner more sensitive to Indian concerns. For example, M. A. Baby, a Member of Parliament, criticized the responses of developed countries to terrorism in a speech in 1997 to the UN General Assembly:

> We are however, dismayed, that despite a growing international consensus against the menace of terrorism and in favour of the need for collective action to combat it, not enough is being done to counter it. There is justifiable outrage against terrorist incidents when they occur closer to home. But when it happens elsewhere, even in other democracies in the developing world, the victims become pawns in a larger game of neutrality and causes, hostages of indifference, or an unwillingness to comprehend the occurrence of the same phenomena elsewhere.[32]

Baby expressed India's frustration that militancy directed at India did not evoke a similar response from Western countries as militancy directed at them, and sought more intense expressions of outrage in such circumstances.

Indian delegates have emphasized the right to development as an important right and have criticized its neglect by human rights institutions. M. A. Baby, in the speech cited above, alluding to colonialism and the need to rectify its damage, said that "developing countries see the right to development as the broadest conception of human rights, one that incorporates the notions of history and telos, of the deprivations of time past, redress in the present, and the promise of the future." Baby lamented the marginalization of the right to development: "while the ICCPR [International Covenant on Civil and Political Rights] and the ICESCR [International Covenant on Economic, Social, and Cultural Rights], and even their Optional Protocols, are seen as comprising an international bill of rights, the Declaration on the Right to Development is not." He proceeds to argue that "the right to development, like the ICCPR and the ICESCR, derives from concepts and values inherent in the Universal Declaration of Human Rights." The critical point in the right to development is that it would restrict the rights of developed countries to impose economic sanctions on developing countries, restrict protectionism in developed countries, and impose other requirements on developed countries in furtherance of perceived development interests.

Indian human rights diplomacy in international institutions served its overall defensive posture. The examples of rhetoric quoted above reveal a presumption of Western dominance of those institutions. Indian diplomatic rhetoric took the form of appeals to the West and signals to non-Western countries to join India in a countervailing coalition. Indian delegates repeatedly expressed concerns that the overall functioning of international institutions was excessively directed by Western countries and inadequately sensitive to Indian priorities. India sought to insert its concerns into the dialogue of those institutions, and to prevent them from intruding on its own sovereignty.

### *India's defensive human rights diplomacy on Kashmir*

United Nations bodies have emerged as critical arenas of Indian defensive human rights diplomacy. This is the result of a Pakistani policy to pursue its claim on Kashmir, especially in the context of the insurgency there, in multilateral forums, where Pakistan's size disadvantage might be overcome. India has mounted defences and built international coalitions to block Pakistani initiatives.

India and Pakistan have struggled over Kashmir since their independence in 1947. Pakistanis have referred to the Kashmir dispute as the "unfinished business of the Partition." Because the British Indian empire was partitioned along religious lines in 1947, and Kashmir has a Muslim majority, Pakistanis reason that it should be part of Pakistan. Indians have rejected the theory that Hindus and Muslims form two separate nations, and thus deny that Kashmir's religious composition is a basis for allocating it to Pakistan. Indians argue that Kashmir has been ruled from Delhi for millennia and, further, that its inclusion in India is an important symbol of Indian secularism. For Indian Muslims, who are approximately as numerous as their co-religionists in Pakistan, India's possession of Kashmir is especially important since they more than anyone wish to avoid creating the impression that India is exclusively Hindu. Further, the accession to India by the Hindu king of Kashmir in 1947 following the armed attack on Kashmir by raiders from Pakistan is the legal basis of India's claim to the territory.

The Indo-Pakistani struggle over Kashmir has been conducted by various means, ranging from open warfare, to irregular warfare, to global diplomacy. The most crucial episode in the diplomatic struggle over Kashmir since 1989 was the meeting of the United Nations Human Rights Commission in 1994 in Geneva. Pakistan had planned to introduce a resolution critical of the Indian human rights record in Kashmir. The stakes for both sides were modest but significant. A diplomatic victory for Pakistan would likely have raised the morale and credibility of Muslim militants in Kashmir. It was clear that all but a handful of states intended to abstain on the resolution. However, the votes of some Muslim countries appeared likely to tip the scales in favour of Pakistan. India's delegation was headed by Atal Behari Vajpayee from the Hindu nationalist Bharatiya Janata Party, Salman Khurshid, a cabinet minister with responsibility for foreign affairs, and Farooq Abdallah, who had been and later became again chief minister of Kashmir. The delegation symbolized the unity between Hindus and Muslims in India over the Kashmir issue.

Indian diplomacy in the months preceding the 1994 UN Human Rights Commission meeting had worked on several tracks. A European Union delegation of ambassadors had been invited to visit Kashmir and speak with secessionists as well as Indian loyalists and government personnel. This helped to seal the European abstention. Moreover, economic liberalization had increased European economic interest in India. Iran had been a focus of Indian diplomacy as well. Narasimha Rao had visited Iran in the previous year and had offered to aid it in the area of defence-related technologies while challenging its fundamentalist ideology.[33] For Iran, Pakistan's quest for Western and US support against India undermined its own anti-American goals. Further, India had supported China in the United Nations in the face of Western criticism of China's human rights record. All these moves reaped rewards for India in Geneva. Iran and China, traditionally two crucial allies of Pakistan, pressured it to withdraw its resolution altogether. The failure of Pakistan in Geneva demoralized separatist militants in Kashmir.[34]

The Organization of the Islamic Conference has regularly issued statements critical of the Indian human rights record on Kashmir. Indian diplomacy toward this organization as a whole has not been successful. It has been more successful in regard to most Muslim states. No other Muslim state has taken a vocal and consistent stand endorsing the Pakistani position on Indian human rights violations in Kashmir. Saudi Arabia is relatively sympathetic to the Pakistani position, but is muted in its public diplomacy on the issue. India has consistently sought to build ties with Muslim counties. The main commonality has been secularism and third world solidarity. This has been a key in building ties with Egypt, Malaysia, and Indonesia. In the case of Shia Iran, secularism as such has not been a factor, but the Sunni–Shia split and concern about third world solidarity have motivated Iran to view the Indian position sympathetically.

One issue where India has undertaken some assertive diplomacy is in the condemnation of international terrorism. The 1994 Human Rights Commission meeting did pass a resolution condemning international terrorism, with leadership coming from India. Accusing Pakistan of sponsoring terrorism in Kashmir and other regions in India, the Indian government has sought to isolate Pakistan on the issue of international terrorism.

## *Debates about human rights conditions in India*

Several groups participate in the global debate about human rights conditions in India: the Indian political establishment, constitutionalist NGOs, private media, and some opposition parties; unarmed and armed separatists; Western governments, NGOs, and media; South Asian immigrant groups; Pakistani government, parties, and NGOs; and Islamic countries. An example of this debate is in a publication by Asia Watch and Physicians for Human Rights that makes detailed claims about human rights violations by Indian security forces and separatist militants in Kashmir.[35] In an appendix, a press release by the Indian embassy in Washington rebuts some of the factual claims and challenges the validity of the report's ways of gathering and assessing evidence.

The international debate about human rights in India entails disagreement on the extent of violations by security forces. Indian governmental and non-governmental observers contend that a large number of specific accusations, including some endorsed by Western NGOs, are false propaganda. Secondary debates on this point revolve around the validity of evidence and the reliability of witnesses. Another debate involves the question of responsibility for the actions of soldiers. The Indian government has held that, when security personnel kill unarmed persons contrary to their orders, the sanction of dismissal is sufficient to absolve the state of responsibility for the crime. Only in the second half of the 1990s have criminal prosecutions against security personnel for human rights violations been pursued. Amnesty International and Asia Watch have argued that a far more severe punishment than dismissal is required.

Most of the specific accusations of killing against Indian forces in publications by Western human rights organizations are by people claiming to be witnesses.[36] The Indian government and media have held that there is a campaign among separatist organizations to plant disinformation by inducing people to make false claims. In some cases the evidence is incontrovertible, such as when the person making allegations has torture symptoms, or when large incidents are described consistently by many people and reported in the news media. But in allegations of extrajudicial killings, the evidence that the militant in question was arrested and did not die in battle is sometimes questionable. In the context of rebutting rape allegations endorsed by Asia Watch, the Indian embassy in the United States wrote:

> Asia Watch's tendency to accept allegations as genuine is inexplicable considering that the report itself recognizes fear of militants among the population. It states that "most Kashmiris are reluctant to discuss abuses by militants out of fear of reprisal. It is the same fear and element of coercion which forces innocent civilians to make false allegations against security forces."[37]

The Indian government has also challenged a number of generalizations and analyses of motivations made by Asia Watch about conditions in Kashmir.

The reports by Asia Watch and Amnesty International are vulnerable to criticism on several points, but nonetheless present a picture of human rights violations in Kashmir, Punjab, as well as other parts of India that is broadly consistent with information from other sources, notably the Indian news media. Indeed, what is distinctive about these reports is not the information they present. Rather such reports compile partially authenticated claims about human rights violations in India and present them to the international media. The reports have been the occasion of considerable embarrassment to the Indian government and concerned sections of society. Criticisms by NGOs and other international criticism of India's human rights record have been a spur to some corrective action, such as improved discipline among armed forces in Kashmir and the establishment of the National Human Rights Commission.

## V. Bilateral policy

Three important bilateral relationships in India's human rights diplomacy since 1989 are with the United States, Sri Lanka, and Pakistan. India has refrained from human rights criticism of the United States for either international or domestic actions since 1989, in line with its shift to a defensive posture. Instead India has sought to moderate US human rights criticism of India. The post–Cold War era has been one of unprecedented US criticism of India on human rights grounds. Although the level and intensity of US criticism against India were a fraction of those against China and some other states, Indian sensitivity to that criticism was high.

The United States began to criticize Indian counter-insurgency methods in Punjab and Kashmir. It also criticized India for child labour, dowry murders, and other abuses. In the case of Kashmir, the Clinton administration revived the formulation that Kashmir was a disputed territory. A series of American statements in late 1993 and early 1994 were perceived by Kashmiri separatists as indications that the United States was growing more sympathetic to their cause.[38] These statements raised fears in India that the resolve of the militants would be strengthened by them. In the case of Punjab, several resolutions in the US Congress, which came close to passing, condemned India for alleged human rights violations there. These were pressed at the behest of persons in the American Sikh community who had made significant campaign contributions to US Congressmen. American newspapers harshly criticized India's human rights record. US news media accounts of Indian human rights issues in the 1990s were sharply negative and paralleled those of Western human rights organizations.[39]

The US Congress and administration, like some other developed countries, pressed criticism of India for child labour. Child labour is far from being eliminated in some of these developed countries, including the United States and Britain, in spite of their wealth. The United States has been especially concerned about child labour in export industries, such as carpets, even though these account for a small fraction of overall child labour in India. The majority of child labour in India is in agriculture. The United States and other wealthy nations have taken steps to reduce imports of carpets produced by child bonded labour, without adequate provisions for alternative sustenance for the children. Government programmes and NGOs within India that rescue children from bonded labour educate and feed the children afterwards. Rescue efforts that neglect to support the children afterwards have frequently failed, with the children returning to bonded labour. India has opposed the inclusion of clauses in the General Agreement on Tariffs and Trade that ban trade in goods produced by child labour on the grounds that these would do little actually to reduce the problem and would harm the exports of developing countries. The only realistic remedy for child labour is the universalization of primary education. Expenditure on primary education in India has increased sharply in the 1990s, and a national programme of free lunches for some schoolchildren began in 1995. Yet India will take several years to attain universal primary education even if the current growth rate of expenditure is maintained.

There have been some trends limiting US accusatory diplomacy against India. India's policies of economic globalization have played a key role. Indiana Republican Congressman Dan Burton, who is on the right wing of his party, introduced a bill every year from 1993 to cut US aid to India on the grounds of human rights violations in Punjab. In 1995, his bill lost by only 19 votes, whereas by 1997 the margin of defeat had broadened to 260 votes, mainly owing to pro-India lobbying by US corporations.[40] Indian immigrants in the United States have also courted allies in the US Congress. There are significant pro- and anti-India groups in the US Congress, cutting across party lines, which fight regular skirmishes of letters to colleagues.[41] Finally, the growing power of China has made the United States more conscious of the need to court other Asian states to balance China's power, and this has also limited America's critique of India's human rights record.

In 1987, the Indian Peace Keeping Force (IPKF) was sent to Sri Lanka as part of the Indo-Sri Lankan accord. The original intention was for the force to disarm the Liberation Tigers of Tamil Eelam (LTTE) in order to enable political reforms on the island to proceed. India itself had originally aided the LTTE in reaction to anti-Tamil action and sentiments promoted by the Sri Lankan state.[42] The Tigers chose not to disarm and instead to fight, and the IPKF fought an unsuccessful three-year war against them. Several aspects of Indian human rights diplomacy became entangled with this intervention. Throughout India opposed the division of Sri Lanka on religious lines, seeking to enhance the credibility of its domestic ideology of secularism and unity in diversity. Over the years, India shifted its assessment of the main threat to its ideology in Sri Lanka. Prior to 1987, India had accused the Sri Lankan government of human rights violations against its Tamil minority. After the intervention, the focus of Indian accusations shifted to the LTTE itself. The IPKF was also accused of committing some human rights violations, and India prosecuted some soldiers and defended itself internationally against charges it considered exaggerated. After the withdrawal of the IPKF in 1990, the Indian focus on Sri Lanka abated for a year, until it was suddenly reactivated in 1991 by the assassination of Rajiv Gandhi by an LTTE team. However, Indian human rights diplomacy toward Sri Lanka remained muted. The Sri Lankan state disciplined its armed forces more effectively and massacres of Tamils ended, while the LTTE continued a campaign of attacks against civilians. Indian diplomatic sympathy has remained with the government, and it regarded LTTE violations in Sri Lanka as crimes under the jurisdiction of the Sri Lankan government.

Indian human rights diplomacy toward Pakistan is highly revealing of the new overall posture. Pakistan has maintained an aggressive posture of accusatory diplomacy toward India with regard to Kashmir, and briefly over the Ayodhya issue. India has accused Pakistan of supporting terrorism in Kashmir and other parts of India, and has held it responsible for human rights violations committed in terrorist actions in Kashmir and elsewhere. Yet India has been muted in its criticism of human rights violations committed by Pakistani security forces within Pakistan. The 1990s have been the most violent decade in Pakistan since 1971. Although the Indian government has made a few critical statements, it has not engaged in a diplomatic campaign of criticism. This approach reflects the commitment to defensive diplomacy, as well as a desire to keep international human rights institutions disengaged from South Asia.

The course of the struggle over Kashmir has been decisively influenced by domestic trends in both India and Pakistan. During the 1990s, events have conspired to shift the balance of power and influence regarding Kashmir in favour of India. In the summer of 1990, Pakistan appeared to many, especially in Kashmir, to represent the future. The USSR was in decline and its intervention in Afghanistan had been defeated by the steadfastness of the US–Pakistani alliance. Pakistan had kept a more open economy than India since independence and had just instituted a fresh round of market reforms. Its Islamic political orientation appeared more authentic and coherent than the confusion of inconsistent secularism, violent separatism, and communal antagonism prevalent in India. And Pakistan was riding the wave of Islamist sentiment throughout the Middle East and Central Asia. In Kashmir, the examples of the Afghan mujaheddin and the Palestinian intifada gave new credibility to Islamist sentiment and an insurgency favouring accession to Pakistan gained a foothold, alongside a pro-independence insurgency.[43] It is clear that Pakistan gave large-scale material support to both these insurgencies, although aid to the pro-independence insurgency was later cut off.

As the 1990s progressed, India's economic and political recovery coincided with a multifaceted crisis in Pakistan. The end of overt military dictatorship upon the death of General Zia ul-Haq in 1988 gave way to an electoral system without civilian supremacy, what an earlier military dictator of Pakistan had called "guided democracy." Pakistani presidents, supported by the military, dismissed three elected governments before their terms ran out. Unelected caretaker governments then carried out far-reaching reforms. Further, the military kept a tight rein on the nuclear weapons establishment, Kashmir policy, and the military budget. Spending over 6 per cent of its GNP on the military, Pakistan could not keep its budget and trade deficits in check. Its economy has stagnated and it has been forced to borrow from the IMF with severe conditions. Pakistan also came to be listed by the World Bank as one of the most corrupt states in the world, and corruption was cited as the main cause in each of its three government dismissals. Pakistan's two main Great Power allies, the United States and China, began to distance themselves from Pakistan's stand on Kashmir, especially after 1996. In 1997, the Pakistani Muslim League won elections by a landslide and amended the constitution to ban presidential intervention. It has begun to reduce military spending and to initiate talks with India. Yet the ideological disagreement between Muslim-nationalist Pakistan and secular, Hindu-majority India remains large, and that makes the Kashmir issue difficult to solve. The swing of the balance of influence in India's favour has created a modicum of stability in Kashmir, and has led third states to move to a position on the issue more to India's liking than Pakistan's. This in turn has facilitated India's defensive human rights diplomacy regarding Kashmir.

## VI. Conclusion

The period since 1989 has witnessed a broad transformation of Indian human rights diplomacy. It has moved from an accusatory approach to a defensive one. This transformation has been caused by both global and national trends. At the global level, the emergence of unipolarity led to a changed international regime of human rights. There was a much stronger emphasis on the violations committed by governments of developing countries against their citizens, deliberately or through negligence. Civilian deaths caused by the international actions of Great Powers were ignored.

At the national level, India has gone through a profound multifaceted transformation during the 1990s that has affected its human rights diplomacy in a variety of ways. The economic crisis at the start of the decade was accompanied by crises in its political leadership structure, national unity, and Hindu–Muslim relations. As the decade progressed, India resolved most of its immediate crises and emerged with new structures that replaced the older collapsed ones. The new stronger structure led to an improvement in the domestic human rights performance, in tandem with a decline in violent challenges to the state. There was also a moderation of Hindu nationalism, as the simplistic violent techniques of the early 1990s led to critical electoral defeats. Peace was restored in Punjab. India's human rights and overall security performance in Kashmir improved. The improved situation led to a more successful defensive diplomacy in multilateral institutions and bilateral relations. Yet the road back to assertive human rights diplomacy will be a long one for India.

## Notes

1. Some parties and factions did reject key features of the Indian Constitution. Among communists, there have been parties rejecting the parliamentary path and favouring armed revolution. Some Hindu nationalist and communalist groups have openly rejected the equal rights of Muslims. Secessionist and minority communalist groups have been present. Open support of caste discrimination by political parties has been rare, although tacit support has been more common. Nonetheless, before 1991 parties openly opposing central features of the Indian Constitution did not command more than 20 per cent of popular votes or informal support.
2. Indian Ministry of External Affairs, *Foreign Affairs Record*, vol. 35, 1989.
3. *India Today*, 31 March 1994, p. 26.
4. US Department of State, "India Country Report on Human Rights Practices for 1996" (www.state.gov/www/global/human_rights/1996_hrp_report/india.html). Last visited on 16 February 1998.
5. James Ron, "Varying Methods of State Violence," *International Organization* 51/2 (1997), 280–281.
6. David P. Forsythe, *Human Rights and World Politics* (Lincoln and London: University of Nebraska Press, 1989), 11; and Jack Donnelly, "International Human Rights: A Regime Analysis," *International Organization* 40/3 (1986), 599–642.
7. Donnelly, "International Human Rights," op. cit., 602–603.
8. World Health Organization, "The Health Conditions of the Population in Iraq since the Gulf Crisis," WHO/EHA/96.1 (www.who.ch/programmes/eha/countryr/gulfrep.htm). Last visited on 16 February 1998.
9. Sarah Zaidi and May C. Smith Fawzi, "Health of Baghdad's Children," *The Lancet* 346 (2 December 1995), 1485.
10. *New York Times*, 31 May 1992, p. 8.
11. World Health Organization, "The Health Conditions of the Population in Iraq," op. cit. A detailed chronology and criticism of the sanctions are contained in Geoff Simons, *The Scourging of Iraq: Sanctions, Law, and Natural Justice* (New York: St. Martin's Press, 1996), 33–104.
12. *Guardian*, 29 September 1991.
13. Amnesty International, *Amnesty International Report 1995* (New York: Amnesty International, 1995), 166.
14. Physicians for Human Rights (gopher://gopher.igc.apc.org:5000/00/int/phr/war/6). Last visited on 16 February 1998.
15. Dennis G. Dalton, *Indian Idea of Freedom: Political Thought of Swami Vivekananda, Aurobindo Ghosh, Mahatma Gandhi and Rabindranath Tagore* (Gurgaon, Haryana: Academic Press, 1982), 168.
16. Ibid., 169.
17. Ibid., 167.
18. Jack Donnelly, "Human Rights and Human Dignity: An Analytic Critique of Non-Western Conceptions of Human Rights," *American Political Science Review* (1982), 76.
19. The most salient construction of the colonial experience is in Jawaharlal Nehru's *Discovery of India* (Garden City, NY: Anchor Books, 1960).
20. Dharma Kumar and Meghnad Desai, *The Cambridge Economic History of India, Volume 2: c.1757–c.1970* (Cambridge: Cambridge University Press, 1982), 528; Ashis Nandy, *At the Edge of Psychology* (Delhi: Oxford University Press, 1980), 4.
21. Nandy, *At the Edge of Psychology*, op. cit., 4.
22. Paul R. Greenough, *Prosperity and Misery in Modern Bengal* (New York: Oxford University Press, 1982), 97–98.

23. Nandy, *At the Edge of Psychology*, op. cit., 3.
24. C. A. Bayly, *Indian Society and the Making of the British Empire* (Cambridge: Cambridge University Press, 1987), 158.
25. Bipin Chandra, *Communalism in Modern India* (New Delhi: Vikas, 1984), 242–245.
26. *Deccan Herald*, 4 February 1998 (www.deccanherald.com). Last visited on 4 February 1998.
27. United Nations Development Programme, *Human Development Report 1996* (New York: Oxford University Press, 1996), 171. In comparison, the figure for China was 6.5, the United States 8.9, and Norway 5.9 (ibid., 170, 198).
28. For example, qualified praise was given by Amnesty International to the commission in its 1995 annual report, *Amnesty International Report 1995*, op. cit., 157.
29. Sumit Ganguly, *The Crisis in Kashmir: Portents of War, Hopes for Peace* (Cambridge: Cambridge University Press, 1997), 169–171.
30. *India Today*, 30 September 1996, p. 26.
31. Address by Mr. Salman Khurshid, Minister of State for External Affairs and Leader of the Indian Delegation, 52nd Session of the Commission on Human Rights, 20 March 1996. Permanent Mission of India to the United Nations Office, Geneva.
32. Statement by Mr. M. A. Baby, Member of the Indian Parliament, on agenda item 112 (b to e): Human Rights Questions, at the Third Committee of the 52nd Session of the General Assembly, 19 November 1997, New York. Permanent Mission of India to the United Nations.
33. *India Today*, 31 March 1994, p. 30.
34. Ibid., 36.
35. Asia Watch and Physicians for Human Rights, *The Human Rights Crisis in Kashmir: A Pattern of Impunity* (New York: Human Rights Watch, 1993).
36. Asia Watch does assert that it follows a procedure, whenever possible, that would indeed have a high probability of accurate findings from witness claims. Ibid., 12.
37. Ibid., 205.
38. *India Today*, 15 March 1997, p. 37.
39. Some examples of critical US newspaper coverage are: "India's Shallow Democracy," *New York Times*, 29 January 1995, p. 14; "US Proves Once Again That It's Business, Not Human Rights, That Matters," *Boston Globe*, 23 January 1995, p. 11; "India's Dirty Little War," *New York Times*, 6 September 1994, p. 18; "Valley of Blood and Tears," *Los Angeles Times*, 4 September 1993, p. B7; "2 Reports Find Wide Abuses by India in Kashmir," *New York Times*, 8 November 1992, p. 21; and "Radicals Hearten Many in Kashmir," *New York Times*, 21 December 1989, p. 11. There was a much smaller volume of coverage sympathetic to India's human rights performance in the mainstream US media, such as the editorial "Why India's Unity Matters," *New York Times*, 20 June 1991, p. 22.
40. Swaminathan S. Anklesaria Aiyar, "US Corporations, Our New Foreign Policy Allies," *Times of India* (www.timesofindia.com), 7 September 1997. Last visited on 7 September 1997. A parallel interpretation was put forward by a critic of India's human rights record. See also Patricia Gossman, "The US Proves Once Again That It's Business and Not Human Rights That Matters," *Boston Globe*, 23 January 1995, p. 11.
41. *Dawn*, 31 July 1997 (dawn.com).
42. David Little, *Sri Lanka: The Invention of Enmity* (Washington, DC: United States Institute of Peace Press, 1994).
43. Ganguly, *The Crisis in Kashmir*, op. cit., 41–42.

# 8

# Iran and human rights

*Zachary Karabell*

## I. Historical introduction

At the height of the Cold War, Iran allied itself with the Western bloc. The Shah of Iran, Muhammed Reza Pahlavi, owed his throne in no small measure to the assistance of the US Central Intelligence Agency and the British Secret Service, which in 1953 had helped him organize a coup against the nationalist leader Muhammad Mossadegh.[1]

The Shah saw himself as the heir to a thousands-year-old tradition of Persian monarchy. He desperately wanted Iran to become a modern, industrial state, with an educated populace, but he resisted the notion that Iran should democratize.[2] Over the years, various American administrations pressured him to open up the political system, allow for political opposition and elections, and loosen the laws of land ownership. The Shah periodically made gestures in that direction but refused to make more substantive changes, claiming the West failed to appreciate the challenges of Iranian society. If ever the pressure became too great, the Shah would subtly remind Western diplomats that any changes that might result in upheaval could jeopardize the stability of Iran and thereby undermine Western influence in the "Northern Tier."

In the late 1970s, however, the Shah faced internal challenges brought on by rapid urbanization and inflation. His response was often to crack down on opposition, using the security service SAVAK as one of his primary tools of repression. SAVAK had an unsavoury reputation, and United Nations human rights forums called attention to SAVAK's tendency to resort to torture, detention without stated cause, and other violations of international human rights norms.

When US President Jimmy Carter placed at least the rhetoric of human rights at the centre of his administration's foreign policy, Iran came under intense and unfavourable scrutiny. Even before Carter, the 1973 Foreign Assistance Act forbade US aid to any government that "practiced the internment or imprisonment of that country's citizens for political purposes." The Shah, who was by this time ill with cancer, reacted to the new American focus on human rights with a series of reforms, decrees, and gestures. He did allow opposition parties greater latitude, and he apparently closed some of the more notorious SAVAK detention centres.[3]

In 1979, the Shah of Iran was overthrown. Within two years, forces loyal to the Ayatollah Ruhollah Khomeini came to dominate the post-Shah revolutionary government. The initial opposition to the Shah was a loose coalition of Marxist guerrillas, radical students, disaffected and underemployed technocrats, affluent merchants, liberal intelligentsia, and Shiite clerics. But it was the clerics, and Khomeini in particular, who commanded the loyalty of the urban masses. With support from the bazaari merchants and with the income from the many mosque foundations, the clerics were able to mobilize people and resources more effectively than other revolutionary factions. The radical clerics also were not shy about using force, and they were ruthless in eliminating opponents.

The resulting Iranian revolution was hostile not just to the old regime but to its international supporters. As the United States was the primary ally of and patron to the Shah, it received the brunt of the revolution's animus. Iran's international human rights policy is intimately entwined with its relations with the United States. Over time, anti-Americanism became institutionalized by the revolutionary regime, with regular gatherings organized by the clerical authorities that included ritual and repeated denunciations of the United States as the "Great Satan."

The United States, for its part, demonized Iran as the "godfather" of international terrorism. Under the successive administrations of Ronald Reagan, George Bush, and Bill Clinton, Iran was singled out as a "rogue state" and treated as an international pariah.

Throughout the 1980s and 1990s, the United States government consistently labelled Iran a "terrorist state." US intelligence agencies saw a direct link between Tehran and Lebanon's Hezbollah faction, which was responsible for multiple kidnappings of US citizens in the 1980s. Iran was also implicated in the bombing of American soldiers in Khobar, Saudi Arabia, in 1996. Dozens of Iranian dissidents living abroad in exile have been assassinated by organized hit squads. In addition to US intelligence sources, French, British, and German agencies have traced the trail of responsibility back to Tehran.[4]

Terrorism is not identical to human rights abuses, though the two often accompany one another. Whereas the international human rights community has been more careful to distinguish between them, the United States has tended to lump the two together in its critique of Iran. To that mix, it has added another: Iran's purported attempt to obtain nuclear weapons. In the words of former Assistant Secretary of State for Near East Affairs, Robert Pelletreau, "We have deep objections to several of Iran's policies, including its support for terrorism, pursuit of weapons of mass destruction, support for Hamas and other violent groups seeking to derail the peace process, subversion of other governments, and a human rights record which is deservedly condemned by the international community."[5]

The animosity between Iran and the United States directly shaped and continues to shape the human rights policies of the Iranian government. That does not mean that Iran's domestic policies are shaped by either American or international criticisms. Laws governing property, theft, marriage, and speech stem from the Koran and Islamic jurisprudence, and have little or nothing to do with the international community. Yet, even in the domestic sphere, the Islamic Republic of Iran contends with many of the same accusations that the Shah did.

Although the human rights violations of SAVAK were widely publicized and denounced by the Iranian opponents of the Shah's regime, once in power these same opponents have committed many of the same abuses. Since the 1979 revolution, Iran has been repeatedly censured for human rights abuses by the United Nations. For instance, in 1983, a UN Human Rights Commission report estimated that between 5,000 and 20,000 people had been executed since 1979. The same report documented electric shock torture, whippings, and mock executions in Iranian jails. The allegations were vehemently denied by the authorities in Tehran.[6] In 1987, the UN General Assembly adopted a resolution expressing "deep concern" over human rights violations in Iran, including persecution of religious minorities; the vote was 58 in favour, 22 against, and 42 abstentions.[7]

More recently, Amnesty International reported that "thousands of political prisoners" were being held in Iranian jails, many of them "without charge or trial." The report noted that "flogging and amputation" were common punishments for persons convicted of crimes such as theft or fraud. Political trials involving accusations of espionage or "propagating pan-Turkism" fell "far short of international fair trial standards." And the report also raised the issue of extrajudicial executions of prominent critics of the regime.[8]

In response to international criticism, members of the Iranian government have responded in several ways. They have denied that the alleged abuses have occurred; they have defended certain practices as sanctified by Islamic law; and they have attacked the United States for slandering the Islamic Republic and using international human rights regimes as yet another way to isolate and undermine a government that it wants overthrown.

Clearly, Iran does not possess a strong domestic legacy of human rights. Both the Pahlavis and the revolutionary government spoke of basic rights such as education, employment, housing, freedom of assembly, and fair trial. Yet both the Shah and the revolutionary clerics interpreted all of these human rights as secondary to the rights of the monarchy (under the Shah) or to the law of God and the Koran (under the revolution).

Until 1979, Iran had been governed for thousands of years by monarchs. With few exceptions, the rule of these monarchs was absolute. Traditionally, the clergy deferred to the monarchy; they supported the monarch as the source of order in society. Even if a particular king was brutal and corrupt, the clerics tended to believe that even a bad monarch was preferable to chaos. And they believed that, without a ruler, society would inevitably descend into chaos. At the turn of the twentieth century and for a brief period in the early 1950s, a constitutional movement flourished in Iran but, each time, traditional Iranian absolutism trumped constitutionalism, albeit with the help of outside powers. In 1907, both the British and the Russians supported the king against the reformers, and in 1953 the United States supported the Shah against Mossadegh.

With the advent of the Islamic Republic, Iran underwent a dramatic change. Suddenly, rights were at the centre of political debates. Not human rights per se, but rather Islamic rights. The Koran and the huge corpus of Muslim jurisprudence spoke volumes about the rights of individual believers in relation to the state and to the ruler. These rights, however, are secondary to the will of God. In the Islamic Republic, there have been and continue to be heated debates over rights, debates that are bounded by and complicated by the paramountcy of God, the Koran, and the legacy of Khomeini. Since the election of the moderate cleric Mohammed Khatami to the presidency in 1997, the internal debate over both human rights and Islamic rights has intensified. Though Khatami welcomes and even fosters the airing of different views and different perspectives, the Iranian government continues to exist within the framework established by Khomeini and the clerics who established the Islamic Republic.

Thus, neither in the past nor in the present does Iran have a tradition of absolute human rights. Rather, human rights are understood within the context of other rights. In the case of the revolutionary regime designed by Khomeini, human rights exist only within the framework of an Islamic Republic and Islamic law. Individual human beings have rights that Islam and God grant to them, not rights that attach to them simply because they are human beings.[9]

## II. National domestic factors

In terms of human rights, the two most significant factors in Iran today are Islam and Iranian attitudes towards the American government. Islam and how it is interpreted by the post-Khomeini regime are arguably the most important domestic factors in Iran. The revolutionary Shiite ideology of the Islamic Republic is unique, and it conditions the official attitude of the regime toward all questions. On human rights, the clerical regime asserts that Islam has its own standards; Iran therefore makes the cultural relativist argument about human rights and rejects many critiques of its record on the grounds that Western societies have no authority to impose their standards on Iran. At the same time, whenever they are criticized for human rights violation, the leaders of the Islamic Republic accuse the United States of using the international human rights movement to isolate Iran.

World Islamic revolution was both the ambition and the policy of the first Islamic Republic.[10] Various branches of the revolutionary government sponsored conferences on political Islam that amounted to primers on how to achieve power. Khomeini called on Muslims everywhere to rise up against their corrupt leaders and transform their societies according to God's law. These appeals struck a resonant chord amongst Shiite Muslims in Iraq and the Gulf states, as well as in war-torn Lebanon, where the Hezbollah Party is funded by Iran. The rhetoric was also revanchist, at times stridently so. Using a combination of repression and accommodation, Muslim states as disparate as Morocco and Pakistan, Saudi Arabia and Indonesia tried to stave off the potentially destabilizing influence of revolutionary Islamic ideology.

By 1988, however, the Iranian government no longer placed export of revolution at the top of the agenda. As is true for many states, the Iranian regime was not and is not unitary. Different ruling groups in Iran adhere to different lines on the export of revolution, on political pluralism, and on crime and punishment. Some retain the early revolutionary fervour, others are simply ambitious for power and influence and give only lip-service to Islam; some speak of ending Iran's international isolation;

others resist any rapprochement with the United States. With the death of Khomeini in 1989, no one individual appeared who could subsume the contradictory impulses.

Khomeini's successor as spiritual leader, the Ayatollah Ali Khamene'i, represents the powerful "hard line" of Iranian politics. Yet, though Khomeini until his death in 1989 and after that Khamene'i as supreme jurisconsult exercise extraordinary powers under the Iranian Constitution, the exact division of powers and jurisdictions of various branches and ministries has always been vague. This makes any discussion of Iranian human rights policy (or any other policy) difficult. In short, there is no single Iranian "human rights" policy.

It has long been accepted by students of American government that bureaucratic politics often lead not to a unitary policy, but rather to policies. The same is true for the post-Khomeini Iranian state. Not only is there a range of views, but it is not always clear who is determining policy, and quasi-official organizations such as the Mustazaffin Foundation may implement policies that are more extreme, more violent, and less respectful of international norms than the officials of the interior or other ministries.

On at least one issue, however, there is consensus: in the eyes of Iranian leaders, the United States is the primary threat to the Islamic revolution. For that reason, Iranian statements on human rights almost always include statements about the United States. In the eyes of Khamene'i, the most pernicious factor in world affairs in general and on Iran in particular is "the hegemony of the United States." He has repeatedly assailed the US government for "its influence and interference in Islamic countries."[11]

The Iranian government views the international system through the lens of its distrust of the United States. In the Iranian view, the international system is dominated by the United States. As the international hegemon, the United States makes the rules, and these rules are designed to keep any would-be competitors at a disadvantage. The Iranian revolution embraced an ideology that explicitly and virulently rejected the United States as a hegemon. This ideology was based on the principle that Islam is the only true path for Iran, and that the rules of Islam, as explicated by the supreme jurisconsult, are profoundly different from the rules of the "Great Satan," the United States. In the words of Khamene'i, "the Islamic Republic's system is standing against this hegemonic system."[12]

Believing that the US government is unalterably opposed to Iran, Iranian leaders interpret any international criticisms of Iranian human rights abuses in light of American attempts to undermine the revolution. In the words of former President Ali Akbar Hashemi Rafsanjani, "I think human rights is used as an instrument to exert pressure and also to achieve some goals that particularly the United States pursues. For example, you see in the U.S. an incident takes place, the mass killing in Waco, Texas of the Davidian sect ... but very soon, they just stifle the matter as if nothing has happened. But if a small incident takes place in Iran, it is blown way out of proportion and is publicized for years." Rafsanjani also castigated the treatment of prisoners in the United States and asserted that in Iran, contrary to the accusations of the US government, Amnesty International, and the Human Rights Commission, prisoners "visit with their families, and are treated with dignity."[13]

From Iran's perspective, the international human rights regime is part of that US-controlled hegemonic system. Condemnation of Iran's human rights record is, therefore, interpreted by the ruling clerics as an attack on Iran by the United States and its proxies. It does not matter whether the institutions criticizing Iran are American, European, Asian, or independent. It does not matter whether Iranian human rights abuses are publicized by NGOs such as Amnesty International, or United Nations groups such as the Human Rights Commission. All of them are perceived as part of a hegemonic system created and dominated by the United States.

For instance, in 1992, Iran reacted angrily to a harsh UN report by expelling all foreign Red Cross workers from the country on the grounds that the Red Cross had been complicit in helping UN authorities compile the report.[14] Justifying the expulsion, Iranian officials at the United Nations criticized Human Rights Commission envoy Galindo Pol for failing to do justice to the status of human rights in Iran under political pressure from Washington. Iran's deputy foreign minister accused Pol of copying the US State Department's report on human rights.[15]

These allegations were reiterated by Iran in 1996, when a UN special representative on human rights, Canada's Maurice Danby Capithorne, visited Iran. An editorial in the *Tehran Times* stated that:

> Criteria for human rights are respected by everyone; however, any judgement on the situation of human rights in a country should be harmonious with the nation's culture, religion and traditions. The special envoy should not surrender to direct and indirect pressures from the United States and other Western powers, whose aims are to use human rights as a leverage against Iran.... One can magnify minute flaws of any country in order to present it in a bad light. The consequences would be that countries which do, in fact, violate human rights in a major way take on a low profile, while countries with minor human rights violations enter the stage for the scrutiny of world public opinion.[16]

When Capithorne submitted his report in October, he noted that the condition of human rights in Iran had deteriorated, with many new instances of arrests of teachers and lawyers who had said or written things that the clerics found objectionable.[17]

The Iranian government's response to American condemnation of its human rights record is not without foundation. Successive US administrations have been highly selective about which countries they single out for human rights criticism. Until 1989, countries seen as allies in the Cold War infringed human rights with the impunity born of the knowledge that the United States and NATO would turn a blind eye. Even today, US policy on human rights is extremely varied and even contradictory. The case of China demonstrates these contradictions. The same abuses committed by the Chinese government, including torture, extended imprisonment without habeas corpus, press and political party restrictions, and extraterritorial attacks on dissidents, elicit condemnation when committed by Iran but muted objections when committed by China.[18]

Iran's belief that international politics are dominated by the United States and its allies is also hardly unfounded, nor is its suspicion that US and UN condemnations of human rights abuses are not always as neutral as they are purported to be. The United States points to the Iranian government as the fount of international terrorism, both in the Middle East and throughout the world, yet evidence for American accusations remains flimsy at best.[19] Certain branches of the Iranian government, and the Mustazaffin Foundation in particular, may be more complicit than others in funding international Muslim groups who use violence to achieve their aims. That much seems clear, but the more extreme allegations that inner circles of the Iranian government order and implement international terrorism are unproven.

Nonetheless, Iran often overstates the influence of the United States on international human rights issues. America dominates the Security Council, but it has rarely had its way in the General Assembly. And it is in the General Assembly that most human rights resolutions are debated and passed. Though the Islamic Republic may be correct that the international system is permeated by American hegemony, in the area of human rights American officials often struggle unsuccessfully to assert their agenda. A quick look at the history of international human rights law shows that Europe, particularly the Netherlands and Scandinavia, has been at the forefront, not the United States.

Furthermore, most human rights organizations have concluded that Iran has severe human rights problems. The fact that they may not be as severe or as extensive as the United States and the United Nations allege does not mean that the Iranian government respects human rights, its denials notwithstanding.[20] Neutral human rights organizations have documented mistreatment of prisoners, executions, torture, assassination of dissidents abroad, lack of political pluralism, and oppression of religious minorities. Although the rights record of the "second republic," as post-Khomeini Iran is sometimes called, has shown improvement, that record is still troubling, the election of Khatami to the presidency notwithstanding.[21] Faced with these charges, Iran does not simply deny that abuses are taking place. Rather, the Iranian government argues that it cannot and should not be judged by a set of standards alien to Islam. Unlike many autocratic countries, the Iranian government has an ideology that justifies policies that the international community labels human rights abuses.

Much of this ideology falls under the category of cultural relativism.[22] According to Iran's leaders, Islam is a complete system of law and morality distinct from secular, Western law and morality.[23] The individual in the Iranian revolutionary framework is not free to do as he wants. Rather, he is free to do God's will, much as the early Puritans in Massachusetts were free to live morally. Islamic law (sharia) defines the universe of rights. Under the sharia, a chronic thief should be punished with the loss of a hand. Hence, that is moral. That punishment is right. Similarly, the sharia does not speak of political pluralism as a right. In fact, according to Khomeini's theory of the supreme jurisconsult, human rights are adjudicated by the jurisconsult speaking for the Hidden Imam. Whatever the jurisconsult decrees is by definition right, assuming that his decrees are compatible with the Koran and the sharia.

Iran claims for itself an Islamic tradition of rights and responsibilities. In 1996, the head of the Iranian judiciary, Ayatollah Mohammed Yazdi, announced a new set of tougher punishments, in accord with "Islamic penal law." Under the revised code, "a robber or a thief found guilty of robbery or theft for a fourth time would not be entitled to leave nor to pardon when he is serving his sentence." He described the laws as "progressive."[24] A month later, commenting on international criticisms of Iran, he defended the "Islamic penal system" and said that, whether or not Western societies like Islamic proscriptions for punishment, that system "cannot be altered." It cannot be altered because, according to the clerics who govern the Islamic Republic, the Islamic penal system is the product of the sharia. It is God's law. Yazdi announced that, in order to leaven the Western bias in international human rights, Iran had established an "Islamic human rights commission."[25]

Also in 1996, the official radio station of the Islamic Republic launched a weekly programme on human rights called "Hidden Truth." According to the producers, the aim of the programme was "to unravel the real essence of the concept of human rights.... The program will look at the various philosophical and legal aspects of human rights, how the concept is used and abused by various countries and international organizations, and the situation of human rights in other countries." Much of the programme consisted of an attack on "Zionist" human rights abuses in the Occupied Territories and American inconsistency in condemning abuses in some places and not in others.[26]

In 1997, Dr. Mohammed Khatami won the Iranian presidential election to succeed Rafsanjani. Khatami was known as a cultural moderate, and his victory had not been expected. In Iran, his election was touted as a testament to the openness of Iran's political process. International monitoring agencies concurred that the actual voting had been conducted fairly and in an orderly fashion, though numerous potential candidates had been disqualified by a committee of experts who rule on the religious acceptability of potential office holders.

In speeches and interviews before the election, Khatami spoke about human rights. Time after time, he pointed to the rights that the Islamic Republic guarantees, yet he also indicated areas where the actual record fell short. On freedom of the press, he stated that "publications should be the eyes and ears of the people since their main role is to channel freedoms. A great transformation took place in our country's press after the revolution." He continued, "[u]nfortunately, self-censorship persists and there is still intolerance on the part of some officials and organizations with regard to publications." On the rule of law, Khatami commented that "one of the sources of pride for the system and the revolution which was brought about by the efforts and insistence of his eminence, the Imam [Khomeini] (may his soul be sanctified) was the compilation and ratification of the constitution, a mere eight months after the victory of the Islamic Republic so that we could all be aware of our rights and obligations within a legal framework."[27]

In another interview, Khatami championed multi-party democracy. "A dynamic and progressive society cannot strengthen itself without civilized institutions, which include parties.... This culture of participation and involvement ... should metamorphose naturally so that all the leanings, the factions, and the press can play a role." In the same interview, Khatami discussed the importance of independent universities – "the bulwarks of thought and wisdom in our society," the Constitution – "which has specified the rights and limits of individuals and the duties and powers of the government and each institution," the rule of law – "what is important is a society governed by law and order that is organized in such a way that each person is aware of his duties and performs them accordingly," and the status of women – "women constitute half of our society and every decision that is made regarding society should take that half into consideration.... Women in our society have been deprived of most of the rights that Islam has envisioned for them, and the social and external possibilities . . . have not been as extensive as those for men. We should therefore take steps so that this historical tyranny and deprivation is eliminated."[28]

In a dramatic break from the past, candidates during the 1997 presidential election freely and sometimes bitterly criticized the Rafsanjani government and the Ayatollah Khamene'i for infringing freedoms that were supposedly guaranteed under the sharia and the Constitution. One candidate stated that "at present there is no such thing as press freedom in the country. The Constitution of the Islamic Republic of Iran is not a ceremonial publication. The person in charge of the executive authority must feel duty-bound to implement the Constitution."[29]

This ideological framework allows the Iranian government to infringe "human rights" as defined by the West, particularly in the areas of penal law, court trial, restrictions on women, and political pluralism. But it also enjoins Muslims to, among other things, protect religious minorities (albeit with certain restrictions[30]) and orphans, because both of these obligations are laid out in the Koran and are therefore enshrined in the Iranian Constitution. In a long article published in a Tehran newspaper on Islam and rights, a professor at the Qom religious seminary (where future clerics are trained) spoke of freedom as "a right bestowed upon every human being by God, and no one is entitled to deprive any individual of this right. . . . Freedom is not something granted to people by rulers and legislators." With a logic that might have warmed Rousseau's heart, the professor asserted that all human beings are blessed with free will but, "as the result of living in society, man should limit his own free will . . . in relation to the free will and actions of others." That does not mean, this argument continued, that a human being should ever submit to the dominion of other human beings. "The acceptance of Islam," the professor continued, "and the call of the prophets does not mean unquestioning obedience to others. . . . God forbids any compulsion in religion." In short, faith makes men free, but no one can be forced to accept faith. As a result, the Koran forbids the establishment of a religious dictatorship, and society will most approximate the religious ideal when "freedom of thought and expression" is not restricted.[31]

It is impossible to listen to this Qom professor or to President Khatami without recognizing that there is an Islamic human rights ideal and that many Iranians in positions of power and authority take the question of human rights extremely seriously. In many respects, the Islamic ideal is compatible with the international human rights conventions. In some areas where it is not, such as political pluralism and freedom of the press, the restrictions are not absolute and may not be any more restrictive than certain limits in Western societies. For instance, the right of free expression is not absolute in the United States, and it is even more constrained in the United Kingdom by strict libel laws. The difference is that restrictions in Western societies do not stem from religious law. And, although a council of experts frequently invalidates the candidacy of parties and individuals who do not meet minimum criteria under the government's interpretation of "Islamic suitability," political pluralism is rarely without some restrictions in any country.

However, while Iran defends itself against certain allegations of abuses on the grounds of cultural relativism, in other areas, the government violates its own constitutionally and religiously enshrined norms. In short, the Iranian government frequently fails to live up to its own rigorous standards of human rights.

The most egregious example is the treatment of the Baha'is by the revolutionary government. The Baha'is are an offshoot of Shiite Islam that the revolutionary regime considers heretical. Although the Koran enjoins Muslims to protect religious minorities, it also reserves the deepest condemnation for apostates: The Baha'is are neither particularly numerous in Iran nor particularly powerful, but they have been hounded, arrested, beaten, tortured, and killed by mobs, by revolutionary police, and by the armed forces. The regime has frequently assailed the Baha'is as outside the fold of Islam and deserving of death as heretics.

Just as the war with Iraq provided the new Islamic government with an external enemy to focus the energies of the country, the Baha'is act as an internal enemy whose presence helps the regime establish legitimacy. The persecution of the Baha'is acts as a glue for an otherwise fissiparous Iranian populace. Iranians may be divided between rural and urban, radical and moderate, religious and ostensibly religious, but they are all one "us" in the face of the Baha'i "them." The Baha'is internally serve much the same regime-stabilizing function as does the United States externally.

Although the persecution of the Baha'is serves a purpose for the regime, it can be squared with the sharia only by calling the Baha'is apostates, and that is a highly questionable designation. A similar rationale underlay Khomeini's fatwa calling for the death of Salman Rushdie. The regime responds to critics internal and external by saying that it acts in accord with the sharia, but in the case of both Rushdie and the Baha'is, as well as with its extraterritorial assassinations of dissidents and its restrictions on press freedom,[32] the regime not only violates international human rights norms but also stretches the sharia to the limit.

In recent years, Iran has shown some improvement in human rights, though the pattern tends to be two steps forward, one step back. The revolution has long since lost the fervour of its early years and, like most revolutions, it has entered its Thermidor phase. Many Iranians yearn for economic stability and normalcy, and they are increasingly cynical about the religiosity of the regime and its clerics. As a result, they are no longer as willing to support and aid the government in mass arrests or suppression of political dissent, and the 1997 presidential elections were the most democratic Iran has ever seen. Though political parties and candidates still must be approved by a council of experts, the grip of the Iranian government has loosened, and human rights abuses have consequently decreased.

## III. Multilateral and bilateral policy

As we have seen, in its rhetoric the Iranian government adheres to a set of Islamic human rights standards. At times, Iranian officials claim that these standards are equivalent or even superior to international norms. At other times, Iranians defend themselves against criticism from the international human rights community on the grounds of cultural relativism. Its response to UN human rights deliberations and investigations is to deflect attention away from its own abuses and toward alleged abuses by the United States and US allies. Whether it is former President Rafsanjani pointing to events in Waco, Texas, or officials recalling the downing of an Iranian civilian airliner by the American naval frigate Vincennes in 1988,[33] Iran tries to shift the international focus away from its own abuses and towards unpublicized violations in Western countries.

Iran is also a leading advocate of Palestinian rights, and it has repeatedly attacked the United States for its double standard over Israel. In the words of Sirous Nasseri, Iran's representative on the Human Rights Commission, "[t]he United States justified Israeli violations of Palestinian human rights and invoked security reasons and the fragility of negotiations. They turned a blind-eye to atrocities committed by Israel and established a double standard."[34]

Suffering from a US trade embargo and recent US laws that penalize foreign companies for doing business with Iran, Iran tries to draw attention to the "double standard" whenever it can. As part of its continuing campaign against Capithorne's report for the Human Rights Commission, Iran assailed the hypocrisy of the West on the treatment of religious minorities.

> The largest religious minority in France and England – the Muslims – is without rights, employment, or social security. Germany, with its implicit support of racists, periodically attacks the Muslims in that country.... The nation of Iran has a Constitution. This law may not be satisfactory to those who are running the New World Order, but is it a violation of human rights to act on and implement what is given in the nation's constitution?[35]

Iran calls on other countries not to follow the US line on Iran. When Japan made a proposed loan dependent on official Iranian condemnation of terrorism, the Iranian foreign ministry urged Japan not to buckle under US pressure "to refrain from carrying out business with Iran." Officials remarked that, by support for terrorism, the US government seemed to have in mind Iran's support for fundamentalist groups such as Hamas, Hezbollah, and Islamic Jihad. Iran vigorously defends its relationship with these groups, which are, "in the opinion of the Islamic Republic of Iran, struggling to attain their just rights – there is a difference between their popular struggles and terrorism."[36]

In 1996, the US Congress passed the Helms–Burton bill, which penalizes foreign companies for doing business with Iran and Cuba, because of their alleged support of terrorism and violation of human rights. The *Tehran Times* urged the European Union "to take a firm stance against U.S. hegemony."[37] But though Iran attempts to shift the debate on human rights, its influence in international affairs is limited, and few countries follow Iran's lead. UN human rights resolutions introduced and supported by Iran, whether condemning the treatment of prisoners in the United States or the treatment of Palestinians in Israel, are routinely voted down.

In its bilateral relations with other countries, the Iranian government must balance the same competing interests that any country does. At times, pragmatic strategic interests determine policy, and at other times Iran focuses on human rights, especially in its interaction with other Muslim countries. In its support for insurgent groups such as Hamas in Israel–Palestine and Hezbollah in Lebanon, the Iranian government sought both to extend its sphere of influence and to spread a brand of Islamic revolution that the early Republic valued greatly. In its relations with the Islamic government of Sudan, Iran has been at best cool, sometimes competitive, and occasionally hostile. Vying for leadership of the international political Islamic movement, the governments of the Sudan and Iran have spoken well of each other in public, but relations have been frosty.

Iranian leaders frequently avowed their solidarity with the Muslims of Bosnia during the mid-1990s, and Iran was an advocate of international action to prevent the massacres of Bosnian Muslims by the Serbs. The government also criticized the European Union and the United States for their lack of action in Bosnia, and it often suggested that the unwillingness of the West to act in Serbia demonstrated a "human rights for me but not for thee" attitude.[38] The decision by the NATO powers to bomb Serbia in response to events in Kosovo was welcomed by some in Iran, although the dismal result for the Muslim Kosovars who were expelled from their homes was interpreted by Iranians as yet another sign of the West's disregard for the human rights of Muslims.

Iran has vehemently condemned human rights violations in the Gulf sheikhdom of Bahrain, assailing Bahraini restrictions on press freedom, freedom of assembly, and the religious freedom of Shiite Muslims.[39] In Algeria, after the military government annulled elections won by fundamentalists in December 1991, that country was plunged into a brutal civil war. Iran excoriated both the military junta and the West for supporting it. According to the *Tehran Times*, "[t]he ruling junta in Algeria is not serious about putting an end to the bloodshed in that Muslim country.... Those countries that shed crocodile tears for the people of Cuba, China and other parts of the world claiming these nations are suffering from a lack of democracy gave the green light to the Algeria ruling clique encouraging them to annul popular elections." The editorial claimed that, even though the Algerian government infringes the fundamental rights of its citizens, rights recognized by the UN Charter, the "so-called patrons of human rights" adopt "a double standard" in the policy toward Algeria.[40]

In neighbouring Afghanistan, the fundamentalist Taliban movement took control of Kabul in 1996. The Taliban are a puritanical Sunni group whose interpretation of the sharia differs significantly from the ideology of the ruling clerics in Iran, and Iranian official news sources have been highly critical. In the words of a *Tehran Times* editorial, "[a] brief survey of the Taliban's record will shed light on the nature and doctrine of this fanatical and reactionary group which is seeking in vain to seize total political power in Afghanistan." Among its other crimes, the Taliban militia "banned Afghan women from all kinds of social activities.... Women are not even allowed to walk freely in the streets.... The group also compels the men at gunpoint to take part in congregational prayers." The paper called on the United Nations to intervene, and it warned that if the United Nations did nothing it would be tantamount "to approving all the inhuman and barbaric acts committed by the Taliban fanatics ... and will seriously undermine the respect for human rights in Afghanistan."[41] The Iranian government took a position on human rights violations in Afghanistan that was noticeably more stringent than that taken by the Western powers. Iran may have had strategic reasons for opposing the Taliban, but there is no more reason to impugn the integrity of the human rights argument developed by Iranian leaders in the context of Islamic rights than there is to question human rights arguments put forth by the US State Department.

## IV. Conclusion

Though Iran has never embraced the Western notion of universal human rights, the Islamic Republic does believe in "Islamic rights." In some respects, these are identical to the human rights championed by the United Nations. The laws of Islam and the Iranian Constitution offer protection from poverty and arbitrary violence at the hands of either the state or other people; property rights are defined and respected; and the rule of law is respected. In other areas, such as the treatment of women and crime and punishment, the Islamic Republic adamantly defends practices that many Western countries view as human rights violations. And, like most countries, the actual practices of the government frequently contradict or fail to live up to these ideals. The rule of law is often trumped by arbitrary exercises of power, and in at least one case, the Baha'is, religious minorities are persecuted.

Iran also suspects the motives of the international human rights movement. Many of the governing clerics simply do not believe in liberalism or political pluralism as defined by the Western democracies. Though Khatami has spoken in favour of pluralism, he makes his case on the basis of Islamic jurisprudence, and he does not embrace Western liberal traditions. At the same time, there is more genuine intellectual freedom and political participation in Iran than in dozens of countries in the Arab and Muslim world. Iranian leaders then interpret the denunciation of the human rights community as an annoying but predictable aspect of the campaign waged against Iran by the United States.

Although there is a thin line between apology for and explanation of Iran's human rights record in the 1990s, the situation is neither as grim as the United States says nor as pristine as the Iranian government avers. The excesses and atrocities of the early years of the revolution have largely ceased and, as the revolution becomes more institutionalized and less fervent, the human rights situation has improved. However, as long as there is an Islamic Republic dominated by the clerics, Iran will continue to interpret human rights differently than the international mainstream.

## Notes

1. See for example, Mark Gasiorowski, "The 1953 Coup d'Etat in Iran," *International Journal of Middle East Studies* (August 1987), 261–286; Barry Rubin, *Paved with Good Intentions: The American Experience in Iran* (New York: Oxford University Press, 1980); Zachary Karabell, *Architects of Intervention: The United States, the Third World, and the Cold War, 1946–1961* (Baton Rouge: Louisiana State University Press, 1998).
2. Asadollah Alam, *The Shah and I* (New York: St. Martin's Press, 1991), passim.
3. Mohsen Milani, *The Making of Iran's Islamic Revolution: From Monarchy to Islamic Republic* (Boulder, CO: Westview Press, 1988), 180ff; James Bill, *The Eagle and the Lion: The Tragedy of American–Iranian Relations* (New Haven, CT: Yale University Press, 1988), chaps. 1–2.
4. Nicholas Bethell, "The Real Threat of Iranian Terrorism," *The Independent*, 20 August 1996, p. 14.

5. "Comments of Robert Pelletreau, at the CENTCOM Annual Southwest Symposium, Tampa, Florida, May 14, 1996," *U.S. Department of State Dispatch* 7/23, 3 June 1996.
6. Summary of the report in the *Washington Post*, 1 March 1983.
7. "Rights Abuses Distress U.N.," *New York Times*, 27 November 1987.
8. "Iran," *Amnesty International Report 1997* (Washington DC, 1997), 184–187.
9. Gudrun Kramer, "Islamist Notions of Democracy," *Middle East Report* (July–August 1993), 2–8; Sharough Akhavi, "Islam, Politics and Society in the Thought of Ayatullah Khomeini, Ayatullah Taliqani and Ali Shariati," *Middle Eastern Studies* (October 1988), 404–423; Gregory Rose, "Velayat-e Faqih and the Recovery of Islamic Identity in the Thought of Ayatollah Khomeini," in Nikki Keddie, *Religion and Politics in Iran* (New Haven, CT: Yale University Press, 1983), 166ff.
10. Anoushiravan Ehteshami, *After Khomeini: The Iranian Second Republic* (New York: Routledge, 1995), 126–168; Judith Miller, *God Has Ninety-Nine Names* (New York: Simon & Schuster, 1996), 429–445; Milani, *The Making of Iran's Islamic Revolution*, op. cit., 239ff; Said Arjomand, *The Turban for the Crown: The Islamic Revolution in Iran* (New York: Oxford University Press, 1988); Ahmed Hashim, *The Crisis of the Iranian State* (Oxford: Adelphi Papers No. 296, 1995), 30ff; "Iran vs. the World," special issue of *Time*, 17 August 1987; John Esposito and John Voll, *Islam and Democracy* (New York: Oxford University Press, 1996), 52–60.
11. Khamene'i speech on Tehran Voice of the Islamic Republic of Iran, Foreign Broadcast Information Service [hereafter FBIS], FBIS-NES, 6 May 1995.
12. "Ayatollah Khamene'i Delivers Speech to Students," Tehran Voice of the Islamic Republic of Iran, FBIS-NES, 1 November 1995, pp. 63–65.
13. Excerpts from Rafsanjani interview with George Nader, president of *Middle East Insight*, in *Washington Post*, 9 July 1995.
14. "Iran, Angry at U.N. Report, Expels Red Cross Workers," *New York Times*, 22 March 1992, p. 14.
15. "Iran Says U.N. Report on Iran's Human Rights Biased," Xinhua General Overseas News Service, 9 March 1992.
16. "Daily Says Human Rights Should Be Judged on Nation's Traditions," British Broadcasting Corporation, 6 February 1996.
17. John Lancaster, "Iranian Crusade; Suspecting Liberal Tendencies in Schools, Clerics Launch Islamization Crusade," *Washington Post*, 15 December 1996, p. A31.
18. Aryeh Neier, "The New Double Standard," *Foreign Policy* (Winter 1996–97), 91–102.
19. "Is Iran the Godfather?" *The Economist*, 17 August 1996, p. 33ff.
20. Reza Afshari, "An Essay on Scholarship, Human Rights, and State Legitimacy: The Case of the Islamic Republic of Iran," *Human Rights Quarterly* 18/3 (1990), 544–593.
21. "Iran: Law versus Pen," *The Economist*, 28 June 1997, p. 42.
22. See Jack Donnelly, *International Human Rights* (Boulder, CO: Westview, 1993), 36ff; Ali Mazrui, "Islamic and Western Values," *Foreign Affairs* 76/5 (September/October 1997), 118–132.
23. Moojan Momen, *An Introduction to Shi'i Islam* (New Haven, CT: Yale University Press, 1985), 282–299.
24. "Iran: Yazdi – New Penal Law Provides for Tougher Punishments," *IRNA*, 8 July 1996, FBIS-NES-96-133.
25. "Iran: Judiciary Chief Rejects Charges of Human Rights Violations," 27 June 1996, FBIS-NES-96-127.
26. "Iran: New Program Exploring Human Rights Begins Broadcasting," Tehran Voice of the Islamic Republic of Iran First Programme, 27 August 1996, FBIS-NES-96-169.
27. "Iran: Khatami on Obligations of Press, Other Issues," *Ettela'at*, 18 March 1997, FBIS-NES-97-086.

28. "Iran: Khatami Views Universities, Women's Role," 17 March 1997, FBIS-NES-97-057.
29. Comments of Heshmatollah Tabarzadi, in "Iran: Presidential Candidate on Lack of Free Press in Iran," *Kar va Kargar*, 11 March 1997, FBIS-NES-97-077.
30. "Iran: Restrictions on Minority Communities Quite Natural," *Iran News*, 23 June 1996, FBIS-NES-96-127.
31. Comments of Mohammad Taqi Fazel-Meybodi, in "Iran: Qom Academic Advocates Freedom of Expression," *Kiyan*, 1 October 1996, FBIS-NES-97-020.
32. Christopher Lockwood, "Iran Is Stepping up Its Campaign of Murder," *Daily Telegraph*, 28 June 1996, p. 16; "Iran: Law versus Pen," op. cit., p. 42.
33. "Iran: Iranian Embassy Release Recalls Vincennes Incident," *IRNA*, 5 July 1996, FBIS-NES-96-131.
34. Sirous Nasseri speaking at the UN Human Rights Commission, M2 Presswire, 19 March 1997.
35. "Iran: Human Rights Report Attacked," *Kar va Kargar*, 1 December 1996, FBIS-NES-97-045.
36. "Iran: Japan Makes Loan Conditional on Criticism of Terrorism," *Salam*, 6 July 1996, FBIS-NES-96-132.
37. "Iran: EU Urged to Take Firm Stance against U.S. Hegemony," *Tehran Times*, 13 July 1996, FBIS-NES-96-138.
38. "Khamene'i Delivers 'Id al-Fitr Sermon," Tehran Voice of the Islamic Republic of Iran, 3 March 1995, FBIS-NES.
39. "Iran: Editorial Criticizes Bahraini Ruling Elite, Human Rights," *Iran News*, 19 December 1996, FBIS-NES-97-003.
40. "Iran: Daily on Human Rights, Democracy Violations in Algeria," *Tehran Times*, 22 July 1996, FBIS-NES-96.
41. "Iran, Afghanistan: Daily Views Taliban Human Rights Record," *Tehran Times*, 22 January 1997, FBIS-NES-97-017.

9

# Human rights and foreign policy in Central Europe: Hungary, the Czech Republic, and Poland

*Gábor Kardos*

## I. Historical introduction

Hungary, Poland, and the Czech Republic share the cultural identity of Central Europe, which is intertwined with Habsburg rule and thus affected by Vienna. "Budapest, Prague and Cracow were not just suburbs of Vienna," but rather part of a cultural network strongly connected with that imperial city.[1] Political traditions are also common. In 1331 the kings of the three countries (Hungary, Poland, and Bohemia) met in Visegrád (Hungary) to facilitate their economic ties. Bohemia, Slovakia, and Croatia, all parts of Hungary at one time, were under the same rule for 473 years. Hungary and Poland were unified for 172 years, and Poland and Bohemia were officially joined for 183 years.[2] In 1991, the leaders of Hungary, Poland, and Czechoslovakia met in Visegrád and renewed their trilateral cooperation, including in the field of foreign policy, aiming at full membership in Western international institutions. All three states felt the need to give attention to human rights through their foreign policies, in part to meet the expections of their Western colleagues. But all three countries also contained some cultural aspects generating domestic pressures in favour of human rights – at least at home if not abroad. This chapter addresses the place of human rights in Hungarian foreign policy, with comparative attention to the Czech Republic and Poland.

As far as traditions affecting human rights are concerned, Central Europe always had some elements of social autonomy. In addition,

Western versions of Christianity were preserved, as were some separation of powers and a measure of constitutionality. But the role of the state was stronger and the economy was weaker there than in the West.[3] The geopolitical identity of these countries "was and is based on a fundamental duality, on the hope of being accepted into the West and on the fear of being dominated by the East."[4] Beside this fundamental duality there was a general understanding of the geopolitical situation: nothing good can be expected from the strongest powers in the neighbourhood. This feeling, however, was never great enough to unite Central Europe, especially not between the two world wars, in the shadow of the Third Reich and the Soviet Union, mainly because in the twentieth century the fulfilment of national aspirations was essentially at the expense of others in the region.

A metaphor frequently used to describe the geopolitical position of especially Hungary, but also of the other two states, is the "ferry-state." Culturally and politically Hungary was attracted to the West, but the strong currents of power relations pushed the country to the East. It found its path to the West twice, once after the withdrawal of the Turks in the seventeenth century, and again after the collapse of the Soviet empire in 1989. The Czech Republic and Poland, too, considered themselves Western but often found themselves within the sphere of influence of an Eastern power. In all three states there was considerable support for individual rights, but international – as well as domestic – politics prevented their full development.

A brief look at recent history indicates the main lines of political evolution as regards human rights in these three states in Central Europe. In the 1920s and 1930s Hungary was an authoritarian state with a parliamentary facade; real parliamentary democracy never existed.[5] Conditions for human rights were definitely less favourable in Hungary than in Czechoslovakia (the predecessor of the Czech Republic and Slovakia) and similar to or slightly better than those in Poland. In the interwar period, Czechoslovakia was a well-functioning constitutional democracy, which possessed a Constitutional Court with powers over primary legislation.[6] Both the rule of law and legal science were highly developed in Czechoslovakia, as reflected in the well-known school of jurisprudence in Brno.[7] Between 1921 and 1926 Poland was a parliamentary democracy; in 1926, however, Marshall Pilsudski returned to power with the help of a military *coup d'état*. Pilsudski curtailed political freedoms, although he preserved a (limited) multi-party system. In 1935, with the acceptance of a new constitution, Poland was similar to later authoritarian-bureaucratic states in Latin America.[8]

After a short and limited parliamentary democracy (1945–1947) in Hungary, the Stalinist period (1947–1963) was brutal and provoked a revolution and a national uprising (Budapest Autumn) in 1956. This was suppressed by the Soviet Union, followed by a cruel repression. In the 1970s and 1980s Hungary was regarded as a reformed communist country, mainly owing to the market-oriented reforms in the economy. As a reformed country, the state permitted certain freedoms in areas of economic activity, especially consumer patterns. These freedoms slowly expanded to include other spheres of society, although fundamental rights were never recognized as belonging to individuals. Fundamental rights should not be confused with benefits conditionally given upon the "benevolent understanding" of the party leadership.[9] The Hungarian democratic opposition played a crucial rôle in undermining the official communist ideology, while the populist opposition drew the attention of the international public to the violation of Hungarian minorities' rights in the neighbouring countries. Since there were sizeable Hungarian minorities in neighbouring states such as Slovakia and Romania, human rights in the form of minority rights loomed large in Hungarian foreign policy in the first decade after the collapse of European communism.

After the Czechoslovak communist *coup d'état* in February 1948 a similar period of "construction of socialism" started; 20 years later, in 1968, this socialism wore a human face for a brief time under Alexander Dubcek. The Prague Spring, and the effort to combine socialism with some civil and political rights, were followed by a Soviet-inspired military intervention by the Warsaw Pact states, and personal freedom was once again suppressed. The political opposition took the form of a small human rights movement, the famous Charter 77, which was linked to the 1975 Helsinki Accord and the Western ideas (and pressure) supporting it.

In Poland, the Catholic Church was able to preserve its integrity and major parts of its social role. Furthermore private ownership remained legal with respect to agriculture. Mass demonstrations shocked the ruling circles in 1956 and in 1970. Personal freedoms were never secure, however, as seen by the anti-Semitic campaign lauded by the party state apparatus in the aftermath of the Middle East War in 1967. In 1980–1981 the Communist Party was forced to accept the conditions laid down by the independent trade union, Solidarity. In 1981, martial law was introduced in the country, and as a result the authorities banned Solidarity. Between 1981 and 1989, however, underground activities were so widespread in Poland that it was justified to talk about the existence of a second society. After the end of martial law (1983) the Communist agenda to polish the image of the regime led to a Constitutional Tribunal (1985) and a Parliamentary Ombudsman in 1987. The latter proved to be truly useful for human rights practices, mainly because of Ewa Letowska, who filled the job.[10]

The Hungarian transition to democracy (1989–1990) was slow because of negotiations and a peaceful adjustment to the new era that were strictly legally guided. In this process the fact that Hungary is said to be a nation of lawyers definitely played an important role.[11] In October 1989, "the velvet revolution" occurred in Prague and it changed the political system. The Polish transition to democracy was also a negotiated process with certain crucial but tentative elements of compromise (e.g. the first parliamentary election was only partially free, with the Communist Party having reserved seats in the Sejm).

In sum, Hungary and also Poland have so far had a rather weak democratic culture. It existed, for example, amongst the nobility in the sixteenth to nineteenth centuries. In these two countries, the push for civil and political rights has reappeared at certain times – in 1956 in Hungary and periodically in the modern era in Poland. The Czech Republic, on the other hand, has had direct experience of a functioning liberal or quasi-liberal democracy for some two decades.

Even where democracy has been weak, as in Hungary and Poland, two principles have been reasonably well accepted, at least in intellectual circles: the idea of constitutionality and the idea of self-government. The first refers to the operation of the state according to constitutional statutes and its accountability.[12] The second was interpreted by some Hungarian intellectuals to include protection against state power, at least in the form of what we would now call federalism, if not individual human rights. József Eötvös,[13] an eminent thinker, wrote in 1851:

> In order to limit state power ... it should also be provided that the individual should not stand isolated against the state power. Consequently, the only means of protection, in our age, against the omnipotence of the state is the same which has been serving as protection against any kind of unlimited power for centuries, namely that villages, provinces and state organs, which link the individual to the state should be given certain spheres of independent activities thus limiting state power very strictly in practice.[14]

Summing up important social and political virtues, in the case of Hungary it is necessary to emphasize the importance of individual economic freedoms,[15] a preserved sense of legalism[16] or legal formalism,[17] and sensitivity to minority rights. As far as the Czech Republic is concerned, the tradition of liberal constitutionalism, along with the spirit of civic action, although damaged by 40 years of communism, is still the strongest in the former communist Central Europe. Elements of Polish political culture are supportive of many internationally recognized human rights,[18] and the sense of political pluralism was preserved in Poland because of the role of the Catholic Church and the "second society." In Poland the working class was a leading anti-communist force. Yet trade unionism is still the most important contributing factor to the "trap of inherited entitlements"[19] – the demand to maintain the material content of social rights, which is, of course, a phenomenon in Hungary and in the Czech Republic as well. All three countries became used to an extensive welfare state, which is difficult to reconcile fully with an increased emphasis on individual freedom, especially on the basis of private property in the economic sphere.

## II. Domestic factors

As a consequence of the fall of communism, today the people do have human rights in Hungary but this does not mean that old social habits, especially patterns of behaviour that reflect the experiences of the communist period, have totally disappeared. People, unlike laws, have memories and established patterns of behaviour. These can be changed only gradually, if at all.[20] To transform hearts and minds is much more difficult than to model constitutions and laws on those of Western democracies, as a Judge of the Constitutional Court of the Czech Republic pointed out.[21] In an essay written in 1986, a Hungarian political dissident compared everyday social life in Britain and in Hungary. Unfortunately he missed three important social virtues in Hungary: privacy – general respect for the private sphere; fairness – trust in social exchanges; and efficiency in the management of everyday businesses.[22] As of the late 1990s, trust and efficient social management are still serious problems. As far as privacy is concerned, in the past politics endangered it. Today private consumerism does something almost as irritating. One of the achievements of "liberalization" under late socialism was some domestic privacy in Hungary, assuming you did not happen to be a political dissident. Today, even the human body and its intimate biological functions are perfect targets for aggressive television advertisements, as the flood of commercials demonstrates.[23] The realm of personal privacy is threatened more by economic than by political abuse.

Analysing the mood of the public towards human rights in Poland, Professor Kurczewski comes to a conclusion that is equally valid in Hungary and the Czech Republic:

> First, it is difficult to imagine an interest in human rights if poverty, disorganisation and discontent would exceed a certain level. Visibility of crime, new types of crime, the influx of criminals abroad and the availability of weapons make crime problems the most vulnerable point in the barrier that divides societies friendly to human rights from those that put other considerations above human rights. The Polish police find strong organized crime and a large amount of crime in general, and in this climate very often ideas focus on that. This has the potential to endanger the proper respect and protection of human rights. Until now however, the problem has not achieved the scale that would lead to the real endangerment of the right in question.[24]

The fear of rising criminality is the reason Poland, at least theoretically, has preserved the death penalty. This is also why proposals in favour of capital punishment have re-emerged in Hungary[25] and in the Czech Republic.

People are becoming accustomed to the legal defence of their human rights, whereas it was natural for them to turn to the law when there was a conflict over inheritance, for example. This has implications for foreign human rights policy. In all three states, there is now the possibility of submitting an individual complaint about rights violations under the European Convention on Human Rights. Ratification of this treaty has resulted in a large number of petitions in each state. Apart from this development, the lack of test cases and the relative weakness of domestic human rights groups continue to thwart the human rights culture, which is why the role of transnational human rights NGOs (Amnesty International, Interights, etc.) is still rather important. This, of course, does not mean that the top Hungarian human rights groups do not engage in valuable work. Here it is necessary to refer to the activities of the following NGOs: the Hungarian Helsinki Committee, mainly dealing with asylum seekers and victims of the brutality of the police; the Society for Freedoms, focusing on the rights of mentally ill patients; the Raoul Wallenberg Society, concentrating on racial discrimination; the Martin Luther King Society, fighting discrimination against blacks and Asians; the Hungarian Centre for the Protection of Rights, the Roma Civil Rights Foundation, and the Bureau for the Protection of Rights of National and Ethnic Minorities, combating discrimination against Romanies; and the Shelter Society, providing help for asylum seekers. They collect evidence of the violation of human rights, publish reports and periodicals, organize protest activities, build networks which raise funds, and provide legal aid. These activities are becoming more and more professional.[26]

In Hungary, two scientific periodicals are exclusively devoted to human rights (*Acta Humana* and *Fundamentum*). As far as the general press coverage of human rights violations is concerned, police violence, skinhead brutality against Romanies, and racial discrimination issues in particular attract significant attention.

Another important factor influencing the mood of the public towards human rights issues, which is to a certain extent connected with the fear of criminality, is immigration. Reflecting the negative attitude of the public, the government has put obstacles in the way of asylum seekers.[27] The same is true in the Czech Republic.

The widespread desire for secure jobs, and for social security in the broadest sense, not only leads to the "trap of inherited entitlements" but heavily influences voting behaviour. The electorate voted for the former communists in Hungary in 1994 and in Poland in 1993 because the people wanted to enjoy social protection again. But in both countries the new socialist parties strictly followed the path of marketization and the devolution of the welfare system. The search for social security led to the return of a Solidarity government in 1997 in Poland, and could also easily cause the fall of governments in Hungary. The Klaus government, which was devoted to strict market capitalism,[28] fell in the Czech Republic, but more owing to scandal than simply to a rejection of its economic policies. All three countries under review here continue to struggle to find a stable synthesis between the desire for social security and the desire for individual freedom – especially in economic matters. The older Western democracies have found a general zone of consensus about how to combine individual freedom with a welfare state, even though different political parties compete to move public policy one way or the other. The new Central European democracies are still trying to establish that general zone.

During the first years of transition from communism to market democracy, the constitutional courts, especially in Hungary, played a surprising if indirect role in shaping foreign policy on human rights. The paradigmatic case was the decision of the Constitutional Court of Hungary concerning the unconstitutionality of the death penalty.[29] At the time of the decision, Hungary was not bound by an international commitment to remove the death penalty, but the judgment referred to, among others things, Protocol 6 to the European Convention on Human Rights – which required outright abolition. In his concurring opinion, the President of the Court, Judge László Sólyom, stated that it was appropriate for the Court to examine foreign practice and noted that the international trend had been towards the abolition of the death penalty.[30] This judgment pre-empted a debate about ratification of Protocol 6 to the European Convention and of Protocol 2 to the UN Convention on Civil and Political Rights.

If one evaluates domestic developments as regards the realization of human rights in Hungary, Poland, and the Czech Republic through the eyes of human rights NGOs, the general picture is mostly favourable. These countries are liberal democracies, no political or other extrajudicial killings occur, habeas corpus exists, trials are fair and public, and there are free elections, free speech, and freedom of peaceful assembly and association.[31] This does not mean that sometimes serious rights problems do not arise, but this situation obtains in all liberal democracies. In Hungary, the slow privatization of nationwide TV channels (which was completed in 1998), abuse by the police, conditions in police detention facilities, the ill-treatment of the Romany population, and inhuman repatriation of foreigners[32] are all serious. The Commission of the European Union (EU) emphasized two things: corruption and treatment of Romanies.[33] In the Czech Republic, one finds the problems of access to information by journalists, abuse by the police, the degradation of the Romany population, and an over-long application procedure for asylum seekers.[34] In Poland, much scrutiny has been directed to the vague legal formulation of the law allowing wiretapping, inadequate conduct by the police, the problems of the right of appeal against a negative decision on asylum, and the legal existence of the death penalty (although it has been under a moratorium since 1 November 1995).[35] Thus the problems are similar: the aggressiveness of the police, discrimination against Romanies, bad treatment of asylum seekers, problems with the right to information and the freedom of the media – to which can be added declarations of racial hatred by right-wing extremists. Instead of focusing on these defects, however, the typical man in the street is more likely to mention the inability of the state to serve its citizens: the state provides insufficient regulations on this or that social service (for example on the rights of physically disabled), or inadequate conditions in centres for mentally ill persons or in prisons; the authorities exceed deadlines; court decisions remain on paper, etc.[36] Until a rights culture is instituted at home, human rights are not likely to be a major issue in foreign policy.

Thus, with the exception of certain issues – the multilateral protection of minority rights in the case of Hungary, or bilateral relationships including human rights aspects (Hungarian minorities in Slovakia, Romania, and Yugoslavia; the Polish minority in Lithuania; the Sudetenland question between the Czech Republic and Germany) – the Hungarian, Czech, and Polish states do not have many other specific human rights priorities in their foreign policy other than to prove their sincere adherence to international, especially to European, norms and to the EU common foreign policy.[37] The common foreign policy goals – full membership in NATO and the EU – create a community of interests[38] in the field of human rights policy among the three countries.[39]

It was symptomatic that until 1998 in Hungary there was no separate unit for human rights in the Ministry for Foreign Affairs;[40] human rights issues belonged to different directorates (UN and European integration). There is, however, a Government Office for Hungarian Minorities Abroad, which is independent from the ministry. At the time of the preparation of "basic treaties" with Slovakia and Romania (1994–1996) there was an institutional competition between these two units. The office represented the stronger position on minority rights claims, but in both cases the ministry was the "winner." The ministry emphasized that it was more important to conclude mutually acceptable treaties – as preconditions of membership in NATO and in the EU – than to demand unacceptably strong provisions to protect Hungarians abroad. Thus human rights issues were enveloped in other Hungarian foreign policy objectives.

## III. Multilateral policy

As far as the adherence of Hungary, the Czech Republic (Czechoslovakia before 1 January 1993), and Poland to the two UN basic human rights Covenants is concerned, these states had already ratified both during the period of dictatorial socialism in the 1970s without reservations.[41] But, like other socialist states, they did not at that time ratify Optional Protocol 1 to the International Covenant on Civil and Political Rights, which allowed individual complaints before the UN Human Rights Committee.

In 1988–1989, as a reflection of the new domestic politics, Hungary became a very active ratifier of human rights treaties (the most active among the three and in the Warsaw Pact).[42] Hungary ratified Optional Protocol 1 to the Covenant on Civil and Political Rights and the (1977) Additional Protocols to the 1949 Geneva Conventions on Human Rights in Armed Conflict, and acceded to the 1951 Refugee Convention and its 1967 Protocol. After 1 January 1990, Czechoslovakia and Poland followed this general line as well – although Poland has failed to ratify Optional Protocol 2 to the Civil-Political Covenant on abolition of the death penalty. All three states publicly renounced their abstentions in the 1948 vote approving the Universal Declaration of Human Rights in the UN General Assembly. Thus all three are now on record as endorsing the International Bill of Rights.

Regional human rights activities are very important for all three states. Hungary, the Czech Republic, and Poland actively participate in the system for the protection of human rights of the Council of Europe, which activity is strongly interconnected with the widespread desire within each to prove their commitment to the "idea of Europe."[43] One proves that one is European by committing to regional standards on human rights. All three ratified the Convention for the Protection of Human Rights and Fundamental Freedoms (European Convention on Human Rights), with reservations of minor importance.[44] All three accepted Articles 25 and 46 of the Convention on the right of individual petition and on the compulsory jurisdiction of the European Court of Human Rights. As far as the Protocols attached to the European Convention are concerned, there is almost complete adherence by each of the three countries, with small differences. Year by year, individual complaints are getting more and more satisfactory (early applications from Central Europe were frequently unacceptable).[45] National courts in all three countries are becoming accustomed to basing their decisions directly on the European Convention on Human Rights;[46] previously they never relied directly on an international treaty. With regard to the European Social Charter, all three states signed it, and Poland and Hungary have ratified it; Czech ratification is on its way.

The European Committee for the Prevention of Torture and Inhuman or Degrading Treatment or Punishment, on the basis of its first periodic visits, criticized prison conditions in both Hungary and Poland. Such issues were raised as insufficient accommodation and recreational activities, or the censoring of correspondence.[47] The governments tended to accept these well-documented observations.[48] The experts of the Council of Europe criticized the Czech Citizenship Law of 1992 because it excluded from Czech citizenship Slovaks who had their permanent residence in the Czech Republic. That law created a number of stateless persons, and it was also used in a discriminatory manner against the members of the Romany community. In Slovakia, Romanies who had been arrested but not prosecuted were treated as not meeting the legal requirements of a clean criminal record in order to apply for citizenship.[49] The government had failed to respond to criticism of this practice by human rights non-governmental organizations, but as a consequence of a report by the experts of the Council of Europe in April 1996 the law was amended.

From the mid-1970s, the diplomatic process known as the Conference on Security and Cooperation in Europe (CSCE), which later became the Organization for Security and Cooperation in Europe (OSCE), proved important to all three states. Hungarian diplomacy in the 1980s under late socialism took CSCE humanitarian commitments more and more seriously and tried to use them to justify domestic liberal steps (in the field of travelling abroad, for example), but Budapest tried to avoid any open confrontation with the Soviet Union.[50] The ruling political parties in both Hungary and Poland attempted to improve a range of humanitarian issues, but without changing the existing features of socialism or the one-party state. A more rigid view existed in Czechoslovakia (and also in the majority of the socialist states), which saw the whole subject of human rights and humanitarian affairs as a disguised Western attempt to smuggle a Trojan horse into the socialist camp in order to destroy it. During the second half of the 1980s at the Vienna Conference on CSCE principles, Hungary became active on minority issues. In 1988, Hungary supported a Canadian protest against Romania's policy toward its Hungarian minority. For the first time in the Helsinki process, an ally of the Soviet Union crossed the line between East and West. In June–July 1990, Hungary was an important actor in the group of states stressing minority rights at the Copenhagen Conference on the Humanitarian Dimension of the CSCE.[51]

When in the 1990s the OSCE addressed human rights in armed conflicts and/or issues of the right to collective self-determination, Hungary continued its active diplomacy – once again motivated by concern for the Hungarian minority in foreign countries. Thus Hungary was active diplomatically regarding the Ossetian, Abkhaz, Chechen, and other conflicts, in order to send diplomatic signals to Bratislava and Bucharest in particular. The basic message was that major problems can be avoided later through correct minority protection now.

In general, Hungarian foreign policy has been sympathetic to the human rights activities of the CSCE/OSCE since the 1980s.[52] In 1995, László Kovács, the Hungarian Minister for Foreign Affairs, evaluated the human rights commitments of CSCE/OSCE thus: "The political commitments are more elastic than the legal ones, consequently the political commitments accepted in the context of the OSCE – thus, in the field of human rights – point further than conventions. Obviously this tendency enforces the authority of the OSCE."[53]

With regard to the international financial institutions, Hungary, the Czech Republic, and Poland are borrowing states. Thus their voices are far from being important in such institutions as the International Monetary Fund or the World Bank. Because of their general support for the principle of international protection of human rights, they are not against the injection of human rights considerations into the conditions of loans of these international financial institutions. All three countries are founder members of the European Bank for Reconstruction and Development, which was the first development bank explicitly to include human rights requirements in its founding Statute.[54]

Hungary, as a non-permanent member of the UN Security Council (1992–1993), actively participated in the management of such delicate issues as the peaceful transition to majority rule in South Africa, problems affecting the process of monitoring UN decisions on Iraq, the war on the territory of the former Yugoslavia, and the establishment of the Criminal Tribunal devoted to the violation of international humanitarian law there. In the case of South Africa, Hungary's representative compared the transition to democracy there to what happened in his country:

> The dramatic changes which have occurred recently in the eastern-central region of Europe, including Hungary, bear some similarity to those now taking shape in South Africa. The most critical challenge that those changes posed for our region was that of ensuring that the transition towards democracy would take place peacefully. The experience my country has gained in this matter suggests that changes to our system carried out in our region were helped enormously by the absence of violence. Those changes of system succeeded in becoming substantial and convincing in nature, to the extent that power was transferred exclusively by peaceful means, through negotiation mechanisms, by means of agreements concluded between political partners of opposing camps. That experience has also shown that one must avoid doing anything that might serve to unleash passions and to set in motion uncontrollable processes, thus jeopardising the success of the transition itself.[55]

Hungary clearly indicated its support for the punitive measures of the Security Council against Iraq in defence of the right to existence of small states:

A year ago, the forces of an international coalition pitted themselves against Iraqi aggression. They liberated Kuwait and thus re-established international legality by acting in accordance with the United Nations Charter. We would like the government of the Republic of Iraq and its high-ranking representatives who are with us today to understand how a small country such as Hungary was jolted and distressed – through the implications of this act for international relations in general – at seeing a country not only invade another but then deny the very existence of that country Member of the United Nations. Therefore, Hungary has expressed its full support for the measures taken by the Security Council since the outset of the Gulf crisis.[56]

In answer to the Iraqi accusation that the members of the Security Council committed genocide against the Iraqi people, the Hungarian representative stated: "In our view, that is not the best way to convince the international community of the need to ease the sanctions imposed on Iraq. It is because of Iraq's refusal to cooperate."[57]

In the Yugoslav crises, for example in connection with the expulsion of CSCE missions by the Belgrade government, the Hungarian representative tried to act as a protector of the rights of ethnic Hungarians living there:

The decision of the Belgrade Government was taken at a time when the situation in each of the three regions continues to be volatile. The international community has had well-founded reasons to concentrate its attention recently on Kosovo, where tension gives cause for serious concern. However, the situation is also very fragile in Vojvodina and Sandjak, where the human rights and fundamental freedoms of ethnic communities are far from being fully respected. We are particularly concerned about the situation of the Hungarian minority in Vojvodina, which is being continuously threatened and lives under conditions of intimidation and harassment. As a consequence of this, tens of thousands of Hungarians have had to leave and seek refuge abroad, mainly in my country. It is not by accident, either, that at the same time Serb settlers have been sent to Vojvodina in large numbers, moving into the homes of Hungarians who left the region. Although the methods are somewhat different, the objectives behind this scenario are all too familiar by now.[58]

After UN Security Council Resolution 827 (1993) unanimously approved the establishment of the Criminal Tribunal, the Hungarian representative underlined the connection between the settlement of the Yugoslav conflict and the punishment of perpetrators:

Hungary has firmly supported all resolutions of the Security Council concerning grave violations of international humanitarian law. Hungary is convinced that persons who commit or order the commission of grave and systematic violations of that law should not escape the hand of justice, and their acts cannot enjoy impunity. We are deeply convinced that it is impossible to envisage a lasting settlement of the conflict in the former Yugoslavia, including the Republic of Bosnia and Herzegovina, without the prosecution of those who massacre and burn children, women and elderly people; who, with diabolical regularity, shell innocent civilian populations; who practice "ethnic cleansing", the true tragic implications of which have not yet been fully appreciated; who cut off the water supplies of besieged communities; who deliberately destroy cultural or religious property, and so on.[59]

The Hungarian seat in the Security Council was first taken over by the Czech Republic (1994–1995) and then by Poland (1996–1997). The Czech delegate, in the debate over the UN Secretary-General's report on Bosnia and Hercegovina, proved to be almost as passionate as the Hungarian delegate in the previous quotation:

Some have described the Secretary-General's report as containing "shortcomings", as providing "insufficient evidence", as containing "arbitrary statements". They have argued that the "alleged" mass killings and disappearances furthered a "propaganda campaign" of the Bosnian Government, and even that it was renegade Muslims who slaughtered thousands of their co-religionists.... We would, most of all, delight in finding out that the Srebrenica thousands were not killed at all, that they had merely been forgotten – sequestered, perhaps, in some barn in a hidden mountain valley. However, we are not aware of any such factual evidence. We are not aware of any evidence better than that provided in the Secretary-General's report, and we agree with him that it is indeed undeniable.[60]

The Polish delegate, in connection with the UN role in the solution of another conflict, the Haitian problem, emphasized two things: the fact that the Polish delegation associated itself with the statement by the Italian delegation on behalf of the European Union, and the contribution of the UN mission to the strengthening of the fragile nature of Haitian democracy.[61] The identification with the EU's standpoints and commitments to international endeavours to promote human rights are common in the foreign policy of the Visegrád three. The voting behaviour of the Central European states in the Security Council during the years of almost completely unanimous resolutions is not a real indicator; they just followed the dominant line.[62]

Hungarian leaders delivering speeches in the UN General Assembly in the 1990s attached special importance to human rights questions. Géza Jeszenszky, the Minister for Foreign Affairs of the first freely elected (conservative) Hungarian government, emphasized that minority rights are a part of human rights:

> In our age, the power of human rights has become global and cannot serve any particular interests. The idea of free individuals in a free world transcends State frontiers and fulfils a mission which will ultimately lead us to a world without borders.... The Government of the Republic of Hungary devotes particular attention to the international protection of minority rights. Therefore, we welcome the growing awareness that the rights of national, ethnic, religious and linguistic minorities form an integral part of universally recognised human rights.[63]

In the same month (October 1991), Prime Minister József Antall, indicating Hungary's commitment to the principle of self-determination, took a step to correct one of the diplomatic misdeeds of communist Hungary. In 1975, as a country of the Soviet bloc, Hungary was in favour of the anti-Zionist resolution of the General Assembly.

> The principle of the self-determination of peoples cannot be applied selectively. Peace in the Middle East can be brought about, *inter alia*, on the basis of that principle. It is urgent, therefore, that the General Assembly revoke its resolution on Zionism adopted in 1975. Zionism is the Jewish people's philosophy of self-determination and the establishment of their own State. The resolution to which I have referred thus calls into question those fundamental rights of the Jewish people.[64]

In October 1994, László Kovács, the Minister for Foreign Affairs of the socialist-liberal government (elected in 1994), underlined the universal character of human rights:

> By the same token, we believe that the United Nations has not yet exhausted the means available for the international protection of human rights. We urge the international community to seek new and innovative means and methods to safeguard the rights and freedoms of our fellow human beings, wherever they may live.[65]

He indicated Hungary's readiness to participate in civic human rights monitoring.[66] In October 1997, Kovács described the Hungarian contribution to the fulfilment of one of the prerequisites of respect for human rights – international peace:

> It is in this context that in recent years Hungary has increased its participation in UN mandated peace-keeping operations in a variety of ways, including both infrastructural and logistical support and the deployment of military and police personnel, an example of which is the Hungarian contribution to IFOR and SFOR and the considerable increase in the number of Hungarian peace-keepers serving in UNFICYP. We are pleased that the performance and professional skill of my compatriots engaged in various such operations all across the globe are considered positively.[67]

Hungary took other clear positions on human rights issues in the General Assembly. Budapest welcomed the Vienna Declaration and Programme of Action accepted by the UN Human Rights Conference in Vienna in 1993. It endorsed the innovative procedures developed by various human rights treaty bodies – such as the Committee on the Elimination of Racial Discrimination, the Committee on the Rights of the Child, and the Human Rights Committee – with regard to preventive action, emergency situations, early warning, and follow-up.[68] Hungary condemned the violation of human rights in Serbia, Iraq, Cuba, Myanmar, and the Sudan.[69] Hungary, as well as Poland, attached special importance to the adoption of the resolution on the establishment of the Office of the United Nations High Commissioner for Human Rights[70] and identified itself with the EU statement in support of the High Commissioner's strategy.[71]

This identification with the EU's standpoint is the main characteristic feature of the voting behaviour of Hungary, the Czech Republic, and Poland in the General Assembly. In 1995–1996, for example, similarly to previous years, the voting behaviour of the three countries was identical and strictly followed the line of EU states.[72]

The participation of the three Central European states in the work of the UN Commission on Human Rights reflects their attitude towards leading human rights issues and initiatives. Their policies changed as a consequence of their transition from dictatorial socialism to market democracy. They became supporters of Western, especially European, policies rather than followers of Soviet voting patterns and supporters of draft resolutions introduced by radical developing countries.

The icebreaker of the unity of the socialist camp was Hungary, as already noted with regard to the Vienna Conference of the CSCE. Hungary focused on Romania's persecution of its Hungarian minority not only in that regional body but also in the UN's Human Rights Commission. During the era of European communism, the socialist countries adhered to a tacit agreement not to openly criticize each other's minority policies. Hungary broke with this tradition and co-sponsored a resolution on Romania in the UN Commission on Human Rights. The resolution on the human rights situation in Romania[73] noted:

> That the Romanian Government's policy of rural systematization, which involves forcible resettlement and affects long standing traditions, would if implemented, lead to a further violation of the human rights of large sectors of the population and expressed the Commission's concern at the imposition of increasingly severe obstacles to the maintenance of the cultural identity of Romania's national minorities.[74]

The socialist member states either abstained (Yugoslavia) or did not participate in the vote (Bulgaria, German Democratic Republic, Ukraine,

USSR). The co-sponsors of the original draft resolution,[75] with the exception of Hungary, were all OECD member states.[76]

If one reviews the policies of Hungary, the Czech Republic, and Poland in the UN Human Rights Commission during the 1990s, it is fairly easy to conclude that they followed the European, but not necessarily the US, position on issues touching upon Cuba,[77] Iraq, and Iran, or the question of the realization in all countries of economic, social, and cultural rights.[78] It is difficult, however, to identify the dominant human rights theme of the three states. The only exception is Hungary's clear emphasis on minority and ethnic questions. Thus Hungary was active in the preparation of the resolution on the Rights of Persons Belonging to National or Ethnic, Religious and Linguistic Minorities.[79] A Hungarian national was also active on similar issues in the Sub-Commission on Prevention of Discrimination and Protection of Minorities, which reports to the Commission but consists of private individuals rather than state representatives. On many issues before the Commission and Sub-Commission, such as the human rights of all persons subjected to any form of detention or imprisonment or human rights violations in different parts of the world (Burundi, Rwanda, Myanmar, etc.), Hungarian, Czech, and Polish diplomacy is supportive. But these three Central European states normally do not play a leading role in human rights initiatives; they are European "followers" or "partners."[80]

## IV. Bilateral policy

Hungary's bilateral foreign policy on human rights has been dominated by its concern for ethnic Hungarians living abroad. As shown above, this concern was not absent from its multilateral policy. But this concern looms even larger in bilateral relations with its immediate neighbours. Although there is some variation across Hungarian governments, bilateral policy on rights abroad made in Prague and Warsaw is quite different, owing to different factual contexts. Thus this section focuses heavily on Hungary – if only for reasons of space limitations.

Hungary's modern borders had been set in 1920 in the Trianon Peace Treaty and they were reaffirmed in the Peace Treaty of Paris of 1947. More than 3 million ethnic Hungarians remained in neighbouring states. Today, 2.0–2.4 million live in Romania, 600,000–700,000 in Slovakia, 300,000–350,000 in Serbia, and 150,000–200,000 in Ukraine.[81] Hungary is a country where the percentage of national and ethnic minorities (Slovaks, Germans, Serbs, Croats, etc.) is comparatively small. Consequently, there is an asymmetry between Hungary and its neighbours regarding the protection of minority rights.

In general, the legacy of Trianon, the "Trianon syndrome," proved to be highly difficult to overcome for Hungarian foreign policy, with concern for human rights as a modern attachment to this syndrome. The Trianon syndrome, with its many different meanings, has since the Paris Peace Treaties that concluded the First World War never ceased to be present in Hungarian thinking on foreign policy. Trianon has been identified first of all with incapacity in political and economic affairs, with its neighbourhood policy sentenced to failure, and, last but not least, with the experience that Hungary has become a victim of Great Power politics.[82]

The collapse of the Soviet Union and its empire brought considerable hope for improvement in the status of the Hungarian minorities. It presented a historic opportunity to pave the way to a durable solution to this problem, but as it turned out progress was not possible immediately. More time was needed to conclude bilateral treaties on this historically sensitive issue. After 1989, Hungary played the role of the kin-state, demanding protective guarantees. But the neighbouring countries showed a noticeable reluctance to respond affirmatively. The reasons they behaved this way are complex.

In states such as Serbia and Slovakia, the process of creating a modern nation-state placed great stress on national and even ethnic unity. In Romania the process was different but the outcome was largely the same. An overwhelming emphasis on national unity did not leave much political space for the concept of minorities and minority rights. In all three states, ruling circles tended to view multilingual usage, especially in the state administration, in schools, or on street signs, as unpatriotic. The same negative view prevailed regarding claims for local self-government and for the return of properties seized from the Hungarian community during the Cold War.

The conservative Hungarian government (1990–1994) contributed to these broad feelings. Prime Minister József Antall declared himself to be the leader of 15 million Hungarians, although Hungary has only 10.5 million inhabitants. Antall later said that he regarded himself as a spiritual leader of all Hungarians, but the damage had already been done: his words were taken as a clear sign of the rebirth of Hungarian territorial revisionism. Without underestimating the damage from this clumsy diplomacy, one can note that, objectively speaking, any kind of Hungarian territorial revisionism is completely unrealistic. In the most important case, that of Romania, the overwhelming majority of the ethnic Hungarians do not live in the vicinity of the common borders, and the majority of the population of Hungary is not interested in any kind of border revision.[83] Maybe what happened in former Yugoslavia gave the impression to certain policy-makers in the West that the same could occur between Hungary and Romania or Slovakia, but this danger was overexaggerated. It is also true, however, that it is very difficult to measure the seriousness of a conflict. The standpoint of the conservative government on the connection between neighbourly relations and minority issues was clearly indicated by Prime Minister Antall: "We never said that the minority question was the only factor in interstate relations, but we find it impossible to have good relations with a country that mistreats its Hungarian minority."[84]

As far as the violent conflict in former Yugoslavia itself was concerned (1991–1995), at an early stage Antall allowed himself to say that the Trianon Peace Treaty and the Paris Peace Treaty had given Vojvodina, partly inhabited by ethnic Hungarians, to the Kingdom of Serbs, Croats, and Slovenes, but not to Serbia.[85] This seemed to imply that Vojvodina rightly belonged to the former Federal Yugoslavia, but not necessarily to modern, rump Yugoslavia. This statement, and the selling of weapons to Croatia,[86] clearly gave the impression that the Hungarian government was fishing in troubled waters. Consequently, when the Hungarian Minister for Foreign Affairs spoke about the Hungarians living in Vojvodina as "hostages to the Serbian or Yugoslav army,"[87] his words, although reflecting political reality, did not repair the damage. In any event, Hungary was able to handle the mass influx of asylum seekers from Vojvodina, Croatia, and Bosnia-Hercegovina. Budapest did not get involved directly in the conflict. It basically coordinated its policy with that of leading NATO powers.[88]

In 1991 Hungary concluded a bilateral ("basic") treaty with Ukraine in which the parties denounced even the peaceful revision of borders. They included a declaration with a list of minority rights, framed after the Copenhagen Declaration of the CSCE. They added the right to autonomy, and a commission was to set up oversee compliance. Towards Romania and Slovakia the conservative Hungarian government kept such a declaration as an ultimate bargaining chip, to persuade the two governments to respect the rights of the ethnic Hungarians.[89]

In 1993 Hungary tried to use its political relationships, mainly the German connection,[90] to link Slovakia's and Romania's admittance to membership in the Council of Europe with their treatment of minorities. This effort failed in the sense that both states were admitted without preconditions. But the Council subsequently set conditions for their treatment of minorities, which was to be monitored (Hallonen procedure).[91] The bilateral relationship with the countries was strained by Hungary's stance.

The socialist–liberal government led by Gyula Horn, elected in 1994, committed itself to speeding up Hungary's integration into NATO and the EU, even at the price of lowering the importance of minority rights commitments in the Basic Treaties with Slovakia and Romania. Horn was prepared to offer a declaration that Hungary had no intention of modifying its borders, peacefully or otherwise. The process of negotiation was pushed by both the elaboration of the Pact on Stability in Europe and

President Clinton's plan to enlarge NATO eastward. Finally, the Hungarian–Slovak Basic Treaty was concluded in the spring of 1995, and the Hungarian–Romanian Basic Treaty in the autumn of 1996 (the signing partners were Prime Minister Vladimir Meciar of Slovakia and President Iliescu of Romania). Minority protection was achieved by transferring non-binding international commitments, drawn from the United Nations, the Council of Europe, and the CSCE, into the text of the treaties. Article 2 of the Basic Treaty between Slovakia and Hungary states:

> The Contracting Parties, in their mutual relations as well as in their relations with other states, shall respect the generally accepted principles and rules of international law, in particular the principles laid down in the Charter of the United Nations, the Helsinki Final Act, the Paris Charter for a New Europe and other documents adopted in the framework of the Organisation for Security and Cooperation in Europe.

Article 2 is vague, to be sure, but Article 15 (4) b is more specific:

> [I]n the interest of defending the rights of persons belonging to the Slovak minority living in the Hungarian Republic, as well as the Hungarian minority living in the Slovak Republic, [the parties] shall apply as legal obligations the rules and political commitments laid down in the following documents....

The section then lists three documents: the Document of the Copenhagen Meeting of the Conference on the Humanitarian Dimensions of CSCE, UN General Assembly Resolution 47/135 (Declaration on the Rights of Persons Belonging to National or Ethnic, Religious and Linguistic Minorities) and Recommendation 1201 (1993) of the Parliamentary Assembly of the Council of Europe on an Additional Protocol on Rights of National Minorities to the European Convention on Human Rights.

This "legislation" of political commitments is not completely unique in international law. For example, Article 20 of the Czechoslovak–German Treaty of 1992 also "legalizes" the Copenhagen Document.[92] Article 15 (4) of the Hungarian–Slovak Basic Treaty contains the "Most-Favourable-to-Minority Persons Clause" vis-à-vis the Council of Europe Framework Convention for the Protection of National Minorities:

> [A]s regards the regulation of the rights and obligations of persons belonging to national minorities living within their territories [Slovakia and Hungary] shall apply the Council of Europe Framework Convention for the Protection of National Minorities adopted and signed by the Contracting Parties on February 1, 1995, as from the date of the ratification of the present Treaty and of the abovementioned Framework Convention by both Contracting Parties, unless their respective domestic legal systems provide a broader protection of rights of persons belonging to national minorities than the Framework Convention.

Beside these regulations, specific minority rights were included in the Treaty, including a wide range of linguistic rights (Article 15 (2) g): the right to use one's own name, the right to be taught in the minority language, the right to establish minority schools, etc. Slovakia attached a unilateral explanatory note to the Treaty claiming that there is no commitment on the Slovak side to applying collective minority rights, particularly since Recommendation 1201 (1993) of the Council of Europe does not include such rights.[93]

The Basic Treaty between Romania and Hungary follows the same line. Article 1 (2) refers generally to the same documents, Article 15 (2) contains the Most-Favoured Clause vis-à-vis the Framework Convention, Article 1 (b) refers to international documents in the field of minority protection mentioned in the appendix as legal commitments (the appendix mentions the same three documents), Article 15 (3) deals with language rights. The Treaty has a "footnote" explaining that, according to the understanding of the parties, Recommendation 1201 does not generate "collective" minority rights.[94]

The implementation of these provisions has gone better in Romania under the Constantinescu government than in Slovakia, especially under Meciar governments. In Romania the political party known as the Democratic Alliance of Hungarians became part of the ruling coalition in 1997 and was thus able to achieve an improvement in the treatment of ethnic Hungarians via local governments, as well as a widening of schooling rights in the Hungarian language. Unfortunately, in Slovakia, tensions remained between the two countries concerning the great emphasis on the Slovak "state" language, the opposition to bilingual school records, the failure of local governments to allow the use of Hungarian, etc.[95] Since the fall of Meciar in autumn 1998, the situation in Slovakia is more promising.

There were, of course, other human rights issues in Hungarian foreign policy besides the minority question. In June of 1997, Budapest concluded a treaty with the Vatican on state support for the Catholic church in Hungary and on a schedule for returning former church properties.[96] In 1996 the Hungarian parliament passed a law on collective compensation for seized personal assets, and the government came to an agreement on details with Jewish organizations (this duty came from the Paris Peace Treaty of 1947, but under the Soviet system it was never put into practice).

It might be briefly mentioned that Poland and the Czech Republic also faced the question of minority rights and ethnicity in their foreign policies – but on a much smaller scale than Hungary. After the renewed independence of Lithuania, issues about the Polish minority in that state generated tensions between the two countries. For example, planned diplomatic visits were cancelled in protest. This tension was eased[97] with the help of the CSCE and the Council of Europe, and Polish language and educational rights became better protected in Lithuania. With regard to the delicate issue of ethnic Germans in the Czech Republic, a Basic Treaty was concluded between what was then East Germany and Czechoslovakia in 1973 containing a declaration of the acceptance of the existing borders. Nevertheless, the sad memory of the German occupation and of the ethnic cleansing of the Sudeten territory by the Czechs after the Second World War, when ethnic Germans were sent to Germany, had cast a shadow on the Czech–German relationship. Finally, in 1996 they concluded an agreement expressing mutual forgiveness.

## V. Conclusions

Hungary, the Czech Republic, and Poland, formerly part of the Soviet *Zwangsordnung*, as well as former parts of Vienna's empire, now have reasonably well-functioning liberal democracies. This is the fundamental reason for their sincere if imperfect commitment to international human rights standards – both at home and abroad. Domestic factors pushing toward greater attention to human rights are reinforced by key international factors – primarily the requirements for membership in NATO and the EU. The foreign policies of the three countries toward the international protection of human rights are generally supportive, although each state puts its own nationalistic stamp on developments.

Hungary, the former "ferry-state" between the East and the West, and closely linked to the Czech Republic and Poland, seems to be firmly harboured among the Western nations and their emphasis on human rights. Its foreign human rights commitments and its home performance are becoming similar to what one might observe in any core state of the Western world. Because a relatively large number of ethnic Hungarians are found in neighbouring countries, Hungary's multilateral and bilateral policies both emphasize the deepening and widening of the protection of minority rights. The conclusion of Basic Treaties with Slovakia and Romania, which include minority rights standards, is not simply a precondition for Hungary's membership in NATO and EU, but a starting point for a long process creating liberal and peaceful relations in the Carpathian basin. Something similar could be said of Czech and Polish foreign policies on rights, but with much less emphasis on questions of particular interest to Hungary.

## Notes

1. Jacques Rupnik, "Central or Mitteleuropa?" *Daedalus* 119/1 (Winter 1990), 253.
2. Historical data quoted by Andras Inotai, "Past, Present, and Future of Federalism in Central and Eastern Europe," *New Europe Law Review* 1/2 (Spring 1993), 516.
3. Timothy Garton Ash, "Reform or Revolution?" in Timothy Garton Ash, ed., *The Uses of Adversity: Essays on the Fate of Central Europe* (New York: Random House, 1989), 250.
4. Wojtek Lamentowicz, "Russia and East-Central Europe: Strategic Options," in Vladimir Baranovsky, ed., *Russia and Europe: The Emerging Security Agenda* (Oxford: SIPRI, Oxford University Press, 1997), 356.
5. Kalman Kulcsar, "Constitutionalism and Human Rights in the Transformation of the Hungarian Political System," in Marta Katona Soltesz, ed., *Human Rights in Today's Hungary* (Budapest: Mezon, 1990), 15.
6. Istvan Pogany, "A New Constitutional Disorder for Eastern Europe?" in Pogany, ed., *Human Rights in Eastern Europe* (Aldershot: Edward Elgar, 1995), 225–226.
7. Zdenka Polivkova, "Human Rights in Post-Totalitarian Czechoslovakia," *All-European Human Rights Yearbook*, vol. 1 (1991), 231.
8. Jacek Kurczewski, "The Politics of Human Rights in Post-Communist Poland," in Pogany, *Human Rights*, op. cit., 112.
9. Elemer Kankiss, *Kelet-Europai Alternativak* [East European Alternatives] (Budapest: KJK, 1989), 82.
10. Roman Wieruszewski, "National Implementation of Human Rights," in Allan Rosas and Jan Helgesen, eds., *Human Rights in a Changing East–West Perspective* (London: Pinter, 1990), 286–287.
11. Geza Herczegh, the Hungarian judge of the International Court of Justice, wrote in 1993: "Some days ago, I was asked about the reasons or the secrets of peaceful transition from a dictorial regime to a pluralistic society. My answer was that we Hungarians are a nation of lawyers. Jurists have always played a great role in the Hungarian society. We are proud that our King Andrew II issued the so-called Golden Bill in 1222, seven years after the English Magna Carta limited royal power and recognized some fundamental rights and privileges for the nobility. But those remote historical events are not the most important; far more important is the fact that during the period of communist dictatorship we could preserve, at least partially, our legal traditions and culture, and some of our institutions." Geza Herczegh, "The Evolution of Human Rights Law in Central and Eastern Europe: One Jurist's Response to the Distinguished Panellists," *Connecticut Journal of International Law* 8/2 (Spring 1993), 325.
12. Kulcsar, "Constitutionalism and Human Rights," op. cit.
13. Eötvös never regarded himself as a federalist, as the idea of the federalization of Hungary was favoured by Hungarian political thinkers only at the end of the First World War.
14. József Eötvös, *"XIX. szazad uralkodo eszmeinek befolyasa az alladalomra* [The Influence on the State of the Prevailing Ideas of the 19th Century] (Budapest, 1851), as quoted by Kulcsar, op. cit., 22.
15. According to some views, these experiences of individual economic freedoms without having true political rights somehow deformed the idea of citizenship in the eyes of the Hungarians and led to a kind of "leave me alone" or "everybody deals with their own business" mentality, which is frequently but not necessarily intertwined with political passivity.

16. It is interesting to note that, although the Hungarian legal system belongs to the European continental legal system, the first Civil Code of Hungary was adopted only in 1959, 11 years after the communist political takeover. Consequently, until that time Hungarian civil law was based mainly on judicial practice, considered and treated as precedents. Being unique in Central Europe, Hungary had a civil law culture "which concentrated on the solution of individual legal cases using legal principles and processing them cautiously." Csaba Varga, "Transition in Central and Eastern Europe," *Connecticut Journal of International Law* 8/2 (Spring 1983), 502.
17. In November 1956, in the shadow of the Soviet troops, Prime Minister Imre Nagy declared the neutrality of Hungary; he postulated a wished legal status as reality.
18. David P. Forsythe, *Human Rights and World Politics*, 2nd revised edn. (Lincoln: University of Nebraska Press, 1989), 226.
19. Kurczewski, "The Politics of Human Rights," op. cit., 125. In the former socialist countries, maternity benefit, for example, in practice was a consequence not of the constitutional protection of the family but of the population policy. Andras Sajo, *Jogosultsagok* [Entitlements] (Budapest: Seneca, Institute of Legal Sciences of the Hungarian Academy of Sciences, 1996), 7.
20. Istvan Pogany, "Constitution Making or Constitutional Transformation in Post-Communist Societies?," *Political Studies* 44/3 (Special Issue 1996), 571.
21. Vojtech Cepl, "Transformation of Hearts and Minds in Eastern Europe," quoted by Pogany, "Constitution Making," op. cit., 571.
22. Istvan Orosz, *Westminster Modell* [Westminster Model] (Budapest: Katalizator, 1993), 69.
23. Peter Gyorgy, "Absztrakcio es Realitas" [Abstractions and Reality], *Elet es Irodalom*, 7 November 1997, p. 4.
24. Kurczewski, "The Politics of Human Rights," op. cit., 133.
25. In Hungary, the Smallholders Party (sitting in opposition) in particular favoured capital punishment.
26. Mate Szabo, "A Katakombakbol a Professzionalismus fele" [From Catacombs toward Professionalism], *Fundamentum* 1/2 (1997), 124–127.
27. See Boldiszar Nagy, "Changing Trends, Enduring Questions Regarding Refugees in Central Europe," in Pogany, *Human Rights*, op. cit., 185–215.
28. In certain fields only in rhetoric, especially as far as the functioning of the bankruptcy legislation is concerned.
29. Constitutional Court records: 23/1990 (X.31.) AB hat.
30. See Stephen I. Pogany, "Human Rights in Hungary," *International and Comparative Law Quarterly* 41 (July 1992), 681.
31. See, for example, the yearly reports of Amnesty International or Freedom House.
32. See "Are Police Officers Punishable?," "Police against Citizens: Cases of Ill-Treatment and Forced Integration, 1 January–30 September 1996," " Rights Denied: The Roma of Hungary," "The Case of Elmas Hasan," "A Statement on Hungarian Refugee Policy and Aliens," "Policy Concerning the Refusal of the Recognition of Elmas Hasan as a Refugee," Reports by the Hungarian Helsinki Committee, 1996.
33. "Az Europai Bizottsag Velemenye Magyarorszag Europai Unioba torteno jelentkezeserol" [The Opinion of the Commission on the Application of Hungary to the EU], *Agenda 2000*, HUN (1997), 13.
34. See *Annual Report 1996* by the Czech Helsinki Committee; "Czech Republic: Roma in the Czech Republic – Foreigners in their Own Land," *Newsletter* 8/11 (1996), Human Rights Watch/Helsinki.
35. See "Human Rights in Poland" (January–September 1996) and "Update" (February 1997), reports by the Helsinki Committee in Poland.

36. This is the conclusion of a Hungarian sociologist after he had read the 1995–1996 "Report of the Hungarian Parliamentary Ombudsman." His observations are valid also in the case of the two other countries. See Endre J. Nagy, "'Hetkoznapi jogallamiatlansag' vagy egy jelentes diszkret szociologiai baja" [Everyday Lack of Rule of Law or the Discreet Sociological Grace of a Report], *Fundamentum* 1/1 (1997), 71–73.
37. The political steps in the Yugoslav war and in its aftermath show this very well.
38. President Aleksander Kwasniewski of Poland used this expression in his Budapest lecture to the Hungarian Society for Foreign Affairs on 21 January 1997. Aleksander Kwasniewski, "Lengyelorszag es Magyarorszag az euroatlanti integracio fele vezeto uton" [Poland and Hungary on the Road Leading to the Euro-Atlantic Integration], *Kulpolitika* 2/3–4 (Autumn–Winter 1996), 5.
39. The protection of human rights and the maturity of political democracy were the fields that gave Prime Minister Klaus of the Czech Republic the feeling that his country was superior to the other Central European states: "After the division of Czechoslovakia, the Czech Republic moved geopolitically closer to the Western part of Europe." Miroslav Had, "The Visegrad Cooperation: Czech Policy and Cooperation in Central Europe," in Peter Bajtay, ed., *Regional Cooperation and European Integration Process: Nordic and Central European Experiences* (Budapest: Hungarian Institute of International Affairs, 1996), 130.
40. But there has been a Human Rights Department in the Ministry of Justice since 1989.
41. Here it is worth recalling what Professor Vojin Dimitrijevic, a former member of the UN Human Rights Committee, wrote: "Hypocrites are the parasites of true values." See Vojin Dimitrijevic, *Human Rights Today* (Belgrade: Medjunarodna Politika, 1989), 5.
42. Lauri Hannikainen, "CSCE State Adherence to Human Rights Convention," in Rosas and Hegelsen, *Human Rights*, op. cit., 343.
43. The "idea" or "thought" of Europe is generally understood as government based on freedom and the realization of human rights. See the Statute of the Council of Europe.
44. In the case of Hungary, it did not guarantee the right to access to courts in proceedings for regulatory offences before the administrative authorities. In the case of the Czech Republic, it did not get rid of military penitentiary disciplinary measures that contravened Articles 5 or 6 of the Convention.
45. See, for example, Appl. 21647/93, 22049/93, 24407/94 from Hungary.
46. In Poland, the first such decision was the 21 November 1995 judgment of the Court of Appeal of Byalistok.
47. The *Reports* were published in January 1996 (on Hungary) and February 1997 (on Poland) (Strasbourg: Council of Europe).
48. As a consequence of the Report on Hungary, the detention centre in Kerepestarcsa in Hungary was closed.
49. *Report of Experts of the Council of Europe on Citizenship Laws of the Czech Republic and Slovakia and their Implementation and Replies of the Governments of the Czech Republic and Slovakia* (Strasbourg: Council of Europe, 1996).
50. Istvan Gyarmati, "Az Europai Biztonsagi es Egyuttmukodesi Ertekezlet/Szervezet es Magyarorszag" [The Conference/Organization of European Security and Cooperation and Hungary], in Pal Dunay and Ferenc Gazdag, eds., *A Helsinki folyamat: az elso husz ev* [The Helsinki Process: The First Twenty Years] (Budapest: Strategiai es Vedelmi Kutato Intezet, Magyar Kulugyi Intezet, Zrinyi Kiado, 1995), 170.
51. Alexis Heraclides, *Security and Cooperation in Europe: The Human Dimension 1972–1992* (London: Frank Cass), 123.
52. Gyarmati, "Az Europai Biztonsagi es Egyuttmukodesi Ertekezlet/Szervezet," op. cit., 172–174.

53. László Kovács, "As EBESZ a jelen es a jovo kihivasai elott" [The OSCE in Front of the Challenges of Present and Future], in Dunay and Gazdag, *A Helsinki folyamat*, op. cit., 8.
54. The preamble to the Bank's Articles of Agreement states that contracting parties should be "committed to the fundamental principles of multi-party democracy, the rule of law, respect for human rights and market economies."
55. S/PV. 3095, pp. 91–92.
56. S/PV. 3059, p. 58.
57. S/PV. 3139 (Resumption 1), p. 77.
58. S/PV. 3262, p. 6.
59. S/PV. 3217, p. 21.
60. S/PV. 3612, p. 9.
61. S/PV. 3638, p. 9.
62. See *Indexes to Proceedings of Security Council*, 1992, 1993, 1994, 1995, 1996 (New York: UN Dag Hammarksjöld Library).
63. A/45/PV.18, p. 57.
64. A/46/PV.16, p. 26.
65. A/49/PV.14, p. 13.
66. Ibid.
67. László Kovács, Foreign Minister of the Republic of Hungary, "Address at United Nations General Assembly Fifty-Second Session General Debate," New York, 1 October 1997, *Current Policy* (1997/6), 3.
68. A/C.3/48/SR.39, p. 5.
69. A/C.3/48/SR.49, pp. 3–4.
70. A/C.3/48/SR.58, p. 2.
71. A/C.3/50/SR.22, p. 4.
72. *Index to the Proceedings of General Assembly Fiftieth Session – 1995/1996, Part I, Subject Index* (New York: Dag Hammarksjöld Library), 379–391.
73. Resolution 1989/75.
74. E.CN.4/1989/L.86, p. 172.
75. E.CN.4/1989/L.76.
76. Australia, Austria, France, Sweden, and the United Kingdom.
77. See, for example, the critical human rights situation in Cuba (E.CN.4/1996/L.86). The Czech Republic and Hungary are co-sponsors.
78. In the past, the cornerstone of the apologetic socialist (etatist-positivist) concept of human rights was to play off economic, social, and cultural rights against civil and political rights.
79. Resolution 1993/24. The text of this resolution is annexed to General Assembly Resolution 47/135 of 18 December 1992, by which the Assembly adopted the Declaration on the Rights of Persons Belonging to National or Ethnic, Religious and Linguistic Minorities; the latter was also elaborated with an active Hungarian contribution.
80. There is an emerging widespread consensus in the Commission – see the resolutions and decisions adopted by the Commission at its fifty-second session (1996), about three-quarters of which were adopted without a vote.
81. The numbers of ethnic Hungarians in Slovenia, Croatia, and Austria are significantly smaller. There is disagreement about the numbers of ethnic Hungarians living in neighbouring countries. George Schopflin divides the available data into three groups: official or semi-official figures of variable credibility (1), highest credible figures (2), and highest available figures, generally not credible (3). Hungarians in Romania: 1,620,000 (1), 2,000,000 (2), 2,500,000 (3); Hungarians in Slovakia: 560,000 (1), 650,000 (2), 750,000 (3); Hungarians in Serbia: 300,000 (1), 350,000 (2), ? (3). George Schopflin, "Hungary and Its Neighbors," *Challiot Papers 7* (May 1993), 35.

82. Laszlo J. Kiss, "Historicher Rahmen und Gegenwart ungarischer Aussenpolitik," *Osteuropa* 43/6 (1993), 569–570.
83. Laszlo Valki, "Security Problems and the New Europe: A Central European Viewpoint," in Andrew J. Williams, ed., *Reorganizing Eastern Europe: European Institutions and the Refashioning of Europe's Security Architecture* (Aldershot: Dartmouth, 1994), 114.
84. MTI (Hungarian News Agency), 20 April 1991. Quoted by Edith Elate, "Minority Rights Still an Issue in Hungarian–Romanian Relations," *RFE/RL Research Report* 1/12 (1992), 16.
85. Alfred A. Reisch, "Hungary's Policy on the Yugoslav Conflict: A Delicate Balance," *Report on Eastern Europe* 2/28 (9 August 1991), 37–38.
86. See James Gow, "Arms Sales and Embargoes: The Yugoslav Example," *Bulletin of Arms Control*, no. 3 (August 1991), 3.
87. Geza Jeszenszky, "Europe at the Parting of the Ways," *Current Policy*, no. 36 (1991), 6 (statement delivered at the Paris Institute of International Relations, 19 September 1991).
88. Pal Dunay, "Hungary: Defining the Boundaries of Security," in Regina Cowen Carp, ed., *Central and Eastern Europe: The Challenge of Transition* (Oxford: Oxford University Press, 1993), 138–140.
89. Pal Dunay, "Minorities in Hungary, Hungarian Minority in the Neighboring Countries," manuscript (Budapest, 1995), 13.
90. Germany was (and is) the centre of political gravity for Hungary because of its economic ties, its geographical location, and the good personal relationship between Chancellor Kohl and Premier Antall, then later between Kohl and Premier Horn.
91. In the case of Romania, after the election of the new president Emile Constantinescu and the inclusion of the Hungarian political party (the Democratic Alliance of Hungarians in Romania) in the Romanian government in 1997, the monitoring procedure in practice came to an end.
92. Bart Driessen, "A New Turn in Hungarian–Slovak Relations? An Overview of the Basic Treaty," *International Journal of Minority Rights* 4 (1997), 11.
93. "The Government of the Slovak Republic emphasizes that it has never accepted and has not enshrined in the Treaty any formulation that would be based on the recognition of the principle of collective rights for the minorities and that would admit the creation of autonomous structures on ethnic principle. It insists that it has agreed to mention the Recommendation of the Parliamentary Assembly of the Council of Europe No. 1201 (1993) exclusively with the inclusion of the restricting clause: '... respecting individual human and civil rights, including the rights of persons belonging to national minorities.' In conjunction with other relevant provisions of the document, the Treaty consistently respects the recognized European standards based exclusively on individual rights of persons belonging to national minorities. Consequently, no other interpretation comes into question." Quoted by Driessen, ibid., 7.
94. In most cases, individual rights necessarily have collective dimensions, since how can you practise your right to assembly, to association, or to religion completely alone? Here, "collective" means collective subjects (minority organizations), not individuals belonging to a minority community.
95. One should also take into consideration Premier Meciar's frequently intolerant and aggressive policy-making.
96. It is interesting to note that Poland, an almost completely Catholic country, ratified its concordat after long debates only in January 1988.
97. See, for example, *The Joint Declaration of the Presidents of the Republic of Poland and the Republic of Lithuania*, Warsaw, 17 February 1995.

10

# Human rights and foreign policy in post-apartheid South Africa

*Tiyanjana Maluwa*

## I. Introduction

On 19 February 1997 a brief exchange took place in the South African parliament between Colin Eglin, an opposition Member of Parliament, and Alfred Nzo, the Minister of Foreign Affairs. The subject matter of this dialogue was the impact of human rights violations on South Africa's relations with other countries.[1] There were three separate but related questions, which may be briefly paraphrased as follows. First, do fundamental human rights, and violations thereof, have any influence on the South African government's relationships with governments of other countries and what criteria does the South African government employ in its assessment of violations of human rights by governments of other countries? Second, in respect of what countries has the violation of human rights influenced the government's relationships with the governments of those countries? Third, has the government raised the issue of the violation of human rights with the governments of any other countries; if so, which governments?[2] In essence, the exchange was concerned with the role of human rights in South Africa's foreign policy.

In responding to these questions, the minister offered an affirmation of the new South African government's position on the role of human rights in foreign policy. With regard to the second question, the minister stated, in part: "The question of human rights is one of a number of factors that impacts continuously on the relationship of Government towards all other governments since all countries are accused, to a greater or lesser extent, of being guilty of some human rights violations."[3] In response to the third question, he went on to state categorically that "[human] rights considerations are now *an integral part* of South Africa's foreign policy and are raised as a matter of course in discussions and negotiations with other governments."[4] To underscore the point, the minister provided some examples. Thus, it was stated that South Africa had imposed a moratorium on the export of armaments to Turkey in May 1995, primarily owing to concern over human rights violations in that country. It was also pointed out that at the conclusion of former Iranian President Rafsanjani's visit to South Africa in September 1996, "no joint communique was issued because South Africa could not, during bilateral talks, accept the Iranian standpoint on human rights."[5]

The timing of these questions was not accidental. Then President Mandela had just completed a visit to a number of East Asian countries. He had been reported in the local media as having declared in the course of his visit to Singapore that South Africa was not going to base its choice of friends or the conduct of its foreign affairs on the human rights records of other countries. Rather, that such matters were to be regarded as remaining within the exclusive domestic jurisdiction of those states.[6] Ironically, the exchange referred to above also took place shortly before rumours began to surface in the local media that South Africa had quietly lifted its self-imposed embargo on the export of armaments to Turkey. This was subsequently confirmed by both Aziz Pahad, the Deputy Minister of Foreign Affairs, and Kader Asmal, a cabinet minister who was also the Chairperson of the National Conventional Arms Control Committee. In the latter's words, the decision was taken "for political reasons in South Africa's interests."[7]

Given these developments, one is compelled to ask: to what extent has the *actual practice* of post-apartheid South Africa in incorporating human rights in the formulation and implementation of its foreign policy accorded with its *professed policy* on the matter? What contradictions have emerged in South Africa's attempts to combine ethical considerations, such as the protection and enhancement of human rights, with foreign policy objectives? How is South Africa's emphasis on the protection of national interests to be reconciled with the emphasis on the promotion of human rights abroad?

This chapter seeks to examine these questions. The thesis of this discussion can be simply stated. In its efforts to articulate a human-rights-oriented foreign policy, South Africa finds itself in the age-old dilemma in which the older liberal democracies of the West have from time to time found themselves.[8] This dilemma is often reflected in the apparent indecision about whether or not to elevate human rights over state sovereignty; whether or not to privilege human rights concerns in foreign countries over the advantages of carrying out trade with those countries; and whether or not to give priority to demands for the protection of human rights abroad over national strategic concerns at home. It will be shown that, in the final analysis, because of its failure to make clear choices on these competing demands, South Africa will likely continue to offer general platitudes on lofty principles that cannot be squared with its actual practice on the interaction of human rights and foreign policy. The most probable result is that foreign policy formulation and implementation will continue to be characterized by double standards and inconsistencies. As is argued in this chapter, this is a fairly common characteristic even among countries, especially in the West, that purport to place a high premium on human rights in the design and conduct of their foreign policy.

The above thesis acknowledges the fact that the role of human rights in foreign policy has always been a contested issue in international relations. History shows that the prominence given to human rights in foreign policy debates has tended to vary depending on the particular paradigm under consideration. It has been suggested, for example, that the history of East–West relations was in an important sense the history of a dispute about human rights.[9] Yet, Western countries have not always been necessarily consistent in their advocacy of a human-rights-oriented foreign policy as far as North–South relations are concerned. It is generally acknowledged that American foreign policy towards Africa under the stewardship of Henry Kissinger, for example, was marked by the deliberate exclusion of human rights considerations from foreign policy. What was more important in the United States' dealings with former President Mobutu's Zaire, apartheid South Africa, and assorted despotic and undemocratic regimes in various parts of the continent was the perception that these countries provided a bulwark against Soviet or communist expansionism in the region. Political repression and flagrant human rights violations did not feature prominently, if at all, as a restraining factor in the pursuit of American foreign policy interests in these countries.

The reasoning behind this approach was that the defence of the morality of state or national interests must override other concerns.[10] It was an approach that, therefore, deliberately subordinated human rights concerns to Cold War calculations and resulted in obliviousness, for example, to the claims of people on the receiving end of oppression and torture in various countries.[11] Mullerson has examined the inconsistencies and paradoxes of this approach and, not surprisingly, concludes that, with the end of the Cold War, the interaction of human rights and foreign policy is at a cross-roads. He accordingly observes that:

> During the Cold War, human rights issues in international relations were often used for political purposes which were far from a genuine concern for human rights. On the other hand, human rights were often forgotten for the sake of *raison d'etat*. [Human] rights seem to affect post–Cold War international relations more than before because there is no longer an overwhelming security threat; instead, there are multifarious threats to international security, many of which have their origin in the human rights situation of a particular country.[12]

The continuing relevance of human rights to post–Cold War diplomacy is not, of course, limited to relations between the major powers. It also pervades the interactions between the major powers and the smaller nations in North–South relations. Moreover, human rights considerations are increasingly playing a part in the foreign policy calculations and choices of the smaller and middle powers of the South even in their relations with each other, as the South African policy statements suggest. At least this much can be discerned from the rhetoric.

## II. Domestic factors

Previous South African governments never pretended to pursue a foreign policy based upon or informed by human rights considerations. The new government, by contrast, claims to have introduced human rights criteria into the conduct of its foreign policy. Yet, as will be seen in this discussion, in some cases the foreign policy of the post-apartheid government clearly contradicts these self-claims regarding the incorporation of human rights criteria into foreign policy-making. This can be noted, for example, in the area of arms sales, in the treatment of refugees and undocumented migrants, and in the context of relations with governments and regimes that are widely suspected of committing serious violations of human rights against their own populations.

To date there has not been any official foreign policy document (that is to say, a government "White Paper") in South Africa. Some critics have argued that this is an indication of a lack of a coherent foreign policy vision. Thus, commentators have observed that foreign policy-making has been characterized more by short-term, ad hoc, reaction than by long-term strategic visionary management. Indeed, it has been noted that it may take some time to refine the process of foreign policy formulation and implementation.[13] It cannot be denied that the Department of

Foreign Affairs (DFA) has been slow in articulating a comprehensive new vision to underpin South Africa's proposed international relations agenda. It was only in June 1996, a full two years after the assumption of power by the new government, that the DFA released what has been politely described in some academic circles as "a kind of draft white paper."[14] However, simply to state this would be to create the impression that no directions or principles have been enunciated by the policy makers in the DFA since the inception of the new government. It would also be to overlook the difficulties facing the DFA in its attempts to integrate and change the two distinct foreign policy traditions of the liberation movement and the previous apartheid government, and the consultative process it has to embark upon in this regard. To be sure, the foreign policy objectives of South Africa can be gleaned not only from the discussion document, but also from the various pronouncements that have been made by the Minister of Foreign Affairs and his deputy, and also by former President Mandela himself and the former Deputy President, Thabo Mbeki, in different forums and contexts.

In 1993, before assuming the presidency, Mandela outlined the pillars on which South Africa's foreign policy would rest. These were that:

- issues of human rights are central to international relations and that they extend beyond the political, embracing also the economic, social and environmental spheres;
- just and lasting solutions to the problems of humankind can only come through the promotion of democracy worldwide;
- considerations of justice and respect for international law should guide relations between nations;
- peace is the goal for which all nations should strive, and where this breaks down, internationally agreed and non-violent mechanisms, including effective arms-control regimes, must be employed;
- the concerns and interests of the continent of Africa should be reflected in [South Africa's] foreign-policy choices; and
- economic development depends on growing regional and international economic cooperation in an interdependent world.[15]

It has been noted that, of these, the greatest attention was given by Mandela to the issue of human rights and the promotion of South Africa's economic interests, but that developments within South Africa in the months that followed the publication of these views demonstrated just how difficult it is to combine these two as guiding criteria for a nation's foreign policy.[16] Shortly after the inauguration of the new government on 10 May 1994, the Minister of Foreign Affairs reiterated these themes in his first address to the South African parliament. He declared that South Africa's foreign policy was going to be based on the following guiding principles:

Firstly, a commitment to human rights, specifically the political, economic, social and environmental circumstances; secondly, a commitment to the promotion of freedom and democracy throughout the world; thirdly, a commitment to the principles of justice and international law in the conduct of relations between nations; fourthly, a commitment to international peace and internationally agreed mechanisms for the resolution of conflict; fifthly, a commitment to the interests of Africa in global affairs; and sixthly, a commitment to expanded regional and international economic co-operation in an interdependent world.[17]

However, it should be immediately noted that in further policy guidelines outlined to parliament some four months later, in August 1994, the minister emphasized that the achievement of South Africa's declared foreign policy objectives would be circumscribed by a number of considerations, for example: that the national interests of South Africa and the security and quality of life of South Africans, as well as justice and the international rule of law, peace, economic stability, and regional cooperation, would be paramount.[18]

These policy objectives and guidelines have been repeatedly articulated in subsequent parliamentary statements and debates, as was noted at the outset of this discussion. It is clear that, at least in official rhetoric, the promotion of human rights is seen as an integral component of the new foreign policy. How one implements this aspect of foreign policy is, however, not clearly spelled out. It is in the context of the actual process of conducting international relations that the ambiguities and inconsistencies surrounding the promotion of human rights through foreign policy begin to emerge. This has been acknowledged by the Deputy Minister of Foreign Affairs himself, Aziz Pahad, who observed in September 1996 as follows;

We start from the premise that South Africa is committed to human rights. The problem we face in this regard is the issue of possibilities and limitations on South Africa in the real world. How do we get human rights enforced and implemented in the international environment? There must be a possible [*sic*] contradiction between South–South cooperation and the values which we may want to project. There has to be interaction between theory and practice.[19]

The foreign policy of a country is intrinsically linked to domestic politics and framed by the prevailing global norms. Now, according to the pronouncements quoted above, adherence to human rights forms the foundation upon which post-apartheid South Africa's national politics are to be conducted. In suggesting that there must be a contradiction between South–South cooperation and the values that South Africa may project, Aziz Pahad was recognizing the dual path that the country has to tread. At least two issues ought to be borne in mind here.

First of all, South Africa is, on the one hand, an African country. As such, it is a member of the group of nations that comprise the so-called "South" and whose approaches to human rights do not always coincide with those of Western powers. On the other hand, South Africa is in certain respects "a part of the West in Africa," as Mills richly expresses it.[20] As such, it aspires to an approach to human rights that accords with the general tenor adopted by the longer-established Western liberal democracies. Secondly, South Africa is both an aid recipient and, in relation to some African states, an aid provider. Thus, both its domestic and foreign policies have to conform to the norms set by Western governments and, to a limited extent, international financial institutions (IFIs). It is to be noted, for example, that, although it is not yet the official policy of the World Bank and the International Monetary Fund to make human rights conditionality a systematic part of their policies, some Western powers have forced the Bank, but not the Fund very often, to look at human rights factors on a willy-nilly basis (for example, by insisting on linking ecological concerns or the issue of good governance to loans). Thus far, South Africa has not yet had to contend with such demands. In any case, given post-apartheid South Africa's comparatively commendable record, to date, of human rights observance and democratic governance, it is unlikely that such conditionalities would be relevant even if South Africa were to become a borrower state from the World Bank or other IFIs in the foreseeable future. The role of human rights in South Africa's relations with IFIs does not, therefore, call for any detailed examination in the present discussion.

And, so, we might ask: what are, or have been, the practical manifestations of the ambiguities of South Africa's foreign policy? How has the contradiction between "South–South cooperation and [South Africa's] values" anticipated by Deputy Foreign Minister Aziz Pahad been demonstrated? To date, the implementation of the human rights objectives has been evidenced through such acts as the signing of treaties, participation in multilateral forums dealing with human rights issues, the redefinition of the principles and practices relating to the export of arms and other military equipment, and South Africa's engagement with the question of human rights and democratization in a number of African countries, notably Lesotho, Nigeria, and the Democratic Republic of Congo (formerly Zaire). The ambiguities are more starkly evident in South Africa's relations with some Asian and Middle Eastern countries, where trade rather than human rights appears to be the paramount concern; in its relations with Cuba; in its treatment of refugees, especially those from other African countries; and in the way it seeks to implement its foreign policy, namely through "quiet diplomacy" or "creative engagement," for example in relation to Indonesia, as will be discussed later. It is instructive to look at some of these examples in both the multilateral and bilateral contexts. But, before turning to these examples, it is important to note that a variety of factors, as well as actors, in the domestic political sphere will continue to be critical in the process of shaping a human-rights-oriented foreign policy for South Africa.

South Africa, much more so than most other African countries, boasts a vibrant and activist civil society. A number of civic organizations played a crucial role in accelerating the pace of change and the collapse of the apartheid order in its final days: the church, youth groups, the labour movement, various civil rights campaigners and human rights organizations, and so on. Some of these groups have already shown that they intend to keep watch over the new government's conduct of foreign policy, insofar as compliance with the government's own declared human rights criteria is concerned. In general, most of these organizations have insisted that South Africa use its moral authority to promote respect for human rights around the world, and especially in Africa, and they urge the involvement of civil society in this process. Thus, organized labour, through the Congress of South African Trade Unions (COSATU), has been very vocal and insistent on the need for the South African government to press for democratic change in Nigeria and for the betterment of respect for human rights in countries such as Swaziland and Zambia. Indeed, COSATU went out of its way to pledge solidarity with locally based Nigerian pro-democracy campaign groups in organizing demonstrations and campaigns against the military regime of General Abacha after the execution of Ken Saro-Wiwa and eight of his fellow human rights campaigners in 1995.

Church groups and other civic organizations have also been critical of continued arms sales to rebel movements and governments engaging in gross violations of human rights or international humanitarian law. Human rights campaigners and academic scholars have called upon the government to adopt legislation (and not simply regulations or procedures internal to the government) incorporating human rights principles into its conduct of foreign affairs.[21] Partly in response to pressure emanating from civil society, in March 1998 the South African parliament finally adopted legislation barring the provision of military assistance to foreign bodies or regimes by private persons or organizations from South Africa. The Regulation of Foreign Military Assistance Act makes it a serious crime for South African citizens to become involved in mercenary activity of any kind, inside and outside of South Africa. The legislation also makes it illegal for foreigners to use South African soil as a springboard against other countries. The enactment of this law was provoked by the repeated allegations of involvement of a South African company, Executive Outcomes, in the provision and sponsorship of arms and mercenaries in countries as far field as Angola, Papua New Guinea, and Sierra Leone.

In brief, the most important domestic factor that will guarantee the government's compliance with its own self-declared commitment to human rights is without doubt the vigilance offered by civil society itself. South Africans are only too aware of the all-too-recent abuse of human rights by previous regimes in their country. The involvement of previous South African governments in large-scale destabilization campaigns and cross-border human rights violations in neighbouring countries – Botswana, Lesotho, and Mozambique – is still fresh in most people's memories. It is these memories that will, in part, ensure that pressure continues to be brought to bear upon the relevant authorities to ensure full respect for the human rights criteria that the post-apartheid government purports to follow in its foreign policy.

## III. Multilateral policy

The South African government has indicated that it proposes to approach the promotion of human rights abroad, and conflict prevention and resolution, within established multilateral frameworks and institutions.[22] It has been suggested that there are at least three reasons for multilateral schemes being better than unilateral or even bilateral approaches to these matters. First, a multilateral forum is said to have greater legitimacy than a state acting alone. Second, multilateralism increases the effectiveness of the initiative and the sanction by demonstrating that a large number of states are committed to a course of action in the pursuit of the common goal of human rights protection. Finally, it is argued, the employment of a multilateral approach, for example through international or regional organizations, in turn helps to consolidate the international human rights structures themselves, thereby contributing to the growth of an international human rights culture.[23] In order properly to assess these multilateral approaches, first one must look at how international human rights law is encoded within the municipal legal sphere of the given state; and, second, one should determine how this law guides, or ought to guide, the state's conduct of its relations with other states and other international actors.

### *Human rights in the Constitution of South Africa: Status of the International Bill of Rights*

The South African Constitution of 1996 was symbolically signed by then President Mandela on 10 December 1996, International Human Rights

Day, at Sharpeville. Sharpeville is, of course, tragically remembered as the scene of one of the most brutal massacres and human rights violations in South Africa's recent history. The Constitution entered into force on 4 February 1997. It had been drafted and adopted in terms of Chapter 5 of the interim Constitution of South Africa of 1993, which ushered in South Africa's first democratically elected government on 10 May 1994, when Nelson Mandela was sworn in as President.

The 1996 Constitution largely confirms the innovative approach that had earlier been embodied in the interim Constitution of 1993 in entrenching certain fundamental human rights in a justiciable bill of rights.[24] The Constitution is also unique among most modern constitutions in according international law, and in particular international human rights law, a constitutionally defined status within the municipal legal system and an explicit role in the interpretative process.[25] The Constitution thus creates a legal and political environment that aims to guarantee and protect the entire range of internationally recognized human rights for the benefit of all individuals in post-apartheid South Africa. This domestic protection of fundamental rights complements the international protection regimes established under international law and institutions.

A perusal of the rights protected in the South African Constitution of 1996 easily reveals that there is significant commonality with the rights stipulated in the principal founding instruments of international human rights law. These instruments, collectively termed the "International Bill of Rights", are: the Universal Declaration of Human Rights (1948), the International Covenant on Civil and Political Rights (1966), and the International Covenant on Economic, Social, and Cultural Rights (1966). There are other aspects of the South African Constitution that are also relevant to any discussion of the interaction between human rights and foreign policy in the new South Africa. In this regard, one needs to mention only two such aspects. First, the Human Rights Commission. This is a body established under the Constitution with powers, *inter alia,* to "promote the protection, development and attainment of human rights" and to "monitor and assess the observance of human rights" (Section 184). Second, the establishment of Parliamentary Portfolio Committees – the so-called "watchdog committees." This ensures internal scrutiny of all legislative acts by peer committees within parliament. The Parliamentary Portfolio Committee on Foreign Affairs is thus empowered to assess the conformity of legislation that impacts on the conduct of South Africa's foreign policy with the Constitution, including the bill of rights. This new system also allows non-governmental organizations (NGOs) to lobby parliament, through the portfolio committees, on proposed legislation or other government policy initiatives. Some commentators have suggested that this system is ineffective, not least because the DFA is not required to justify any decisions to parliament.[26] I would argue, however, that potentially this presents human rights NGOs with an effective, if indirect, mechanism to get involved in the legislative debates concerning human rights and foreign policy, among other subjects.

The constitutional and legal structures put in place in post-1994 South Africa are clear enough. As stated earlier, the principal objective is to create a political and constitutional order based on respect for human rights. It should follow from this that in all its actions – both administrative and legislative – the government is obliged to abide by the human rights standards and norms set out in the Constitution, relevant national legislation, and applicable international human rights instruments. There is nothing startling in the proposition that states must respect the human rights standards and criteria that they themselves have enshrined in their national constitutions and legislation. The critical question is whether, and to what extent, these criteria ought also to guide their foreign policy. The practical implementation of South African foreign policy to date has not accorded with this proposition.

### *Regional developments*

As already noted above, to most observers within and outside South Africa former President Mandela embodied the ideals of human rights and justice. His stature, with varying degrees of success, enabled him to assume the role of mediator in civil conflicts in Africa and to position himself to speak up against human rights abuses by his counterparts elsewhere on the continent. The common global expectation, going back to the inception of the new democratic order, was that South Africa, through the persona of Nelson Mandela, would champion human rights throughout Africa and elsewhere in the third world.

It is primarily within Africa that the South African government's attempts at fostering a climate in which human rights prevail can be seen. The restoration of the democratically elected government of Lesotho after it had been ousted in a *coup d'état* and South Africa's attempts to negotiate with the military rulers of Nigeria in order to secure the release of political prisoners (as well as its campaign to institute an investigation into allegations of human rights abuses in the country) are only two high-profile examples in this regard. To these may be added the involvement by South Africa in the failed mediation between Mobutu Sese Seko and Laurent Kabila, whose rebel forces drove the former out of power in the renamed Democratic Republic of Congo in May 1997. Unfortunately, Nigeria and the former Zaire also happen to be the two cases that have shown up the impotence of South Africa's self-proclaimed human-rights-oriented foreign policy. The strong position taken on Nigeria at the time of the Commonwealth Heads of State and Government Meeting in New Zealand in November 1995 was significantly softened not too long afterwards. Similarly, concerns over massacres of refugees by the soldiers of Kabila's Alliance des Forces Démocratiques pour la Libération du Congo-Zaire (AFDL) in the eastern part of the Democratic Republic of Congo were played down by the South African government, apparently in the misplaced belief that a softer attitude in this regard would guarantee the success of then President Mandela's mediation effort. Despite these setbacks, more recent developments suggest that South Africa is getting involved as a mediator in the long-running civil war in the Sudan. Both the Sudanese president and a representative of the major rebel movement, the Sudan People's Liberation Army (SPLA), were in South Africa at the beginning of August 1997 for exploratory talks with then President Mandela. Thus far, however, South Africa's role has largely been a diplomatic one. It has resisted calls to send troops to countries or regions afflicted by civil strife, usually citing the unpreparedness of its national defence force for such operations.

South Africa also has to walk the tightrope between enforcing human rights and being perceived as either a regional hegemon or a proxy doing the bidding of external powers, such as the United States, that may be seeking to police and dominate the continent. These perceptions partly explain the reluctance of most African states to heed South Africa's calls for concerted action in reaction to the violations of human rights in Nigeria. It is also largely because of this that South Africa now seems to prefer "quiet diplomacy," which essentially entailed using Mandela's moral authority to intercede in behind-the-scenes negotiations with foreign leaders on issues of human rights violations in their countries, rather than venturing into more overt tactics such as the unilateral imposition of sanctions or calls for the imposition of such sanctions, as was attempted in the case of Nigeria.[27] But, more importantly, South Africa has also come to appreciate that it is only within the space provided by the relevant regional organizations, the Southern African Development Community (SADC) and the Organization of African Unity (OAU), that it can most effectively pursue a meaningful human-rights-oriented foreign policy.

### *The Southern African Development Community (SADC)*

South Africa has been a member of the SADC since 29 August 1994. In this brief period, it has already proved to be a pivotal member of this regional grouping. This period has also witnessed important developments in the field of human rights promotion. In the first place, SADC established, on 26 June 1996, an Organ for Politics, Defence and Security, with the primary objective of coordinating policies and activities in areas implied in the title of the entity itself ("politics, defence and security"). But the Organ is also predicated on a number of guiding principles, among which are the "observance of human rights, democracy and the rule of law" and the "observance of universal human rights as provided for in the Charters of the OAU and the UN."[28] In fact, it may be noted that, prior to the establishment of this Organ, South Africa had already participated in a regional initiative to restore stability and democracy in a neighbouring SADC state, namely Lesotho.

The government of Prime Minister Ntsu Mokhehle in the tiny landlocked Kingdom of Lesotho had experienced months of instability, including an army mutiny, shortly after being elected in the country's first democratic election in almost a quarter century, held in 1993. In August 1994, King Letsie III dismissed the government and in effect implemented a *coup d'état.* The ousted government was finally restored to power only after some high-level diplomacy involving Botswana, South Africa, and Zimbabwe. These three countries undertook the initiative to enforce what had emerged as an "SADC regional consensus" on the need to resist unconstitutional usurpation of power and to protect democracy and human rights.

Alongside this development is the long-standing proposal, dating back to 1994, for the establishment of a human rights commission or court as part of the institutional machinery of SADC. It is felt that such a commission or court would ensure a more certain enforcement of human rights in the southern African region and complement whatever is provided for under existing UN or OAU machinery.[29] It seems apt to conclude that with its far-reaching domestic bill of rights, which, as we have seen, entrenches the most widely recognized fundamental human rights, and the emerging human rights jurisprudence from its Constitutional Court, South Africa stands in a unique position to contribute to, and enrich, this proposed regional human rights regime among SADC countries.

### *The Organization of African Unity (OAU)*

South Africa has also sought to play a very active role in promoting democracy, human rights, and conflict resolution within the institutional framework provided by the OAU since its admission to this continental body on 23 May 1994. South Africa has reiterated these objectives on a number of occasions. Thus, then President Mandela declared at the summit of the Assembly of Heads of State and Government on 8 July 1996 in Yaounde, Cameroon, that "South Africa would not shrink from its responsibility to help resolve conflict and advocate human rights on the continent."[30] South Africa's advocacy of human rights within the OAU was strengthened when it acceded to the African Charter on Human and Peoples' Rights on 9 January 1996. The African Charter was adopted by the Organization of African Unity in 1981 and came into force on 21 October 1986. It is the newest of the regional human rights conventions, with what is claimed to be a distinctly "African character." It draws upon other human rights conventions, and recognizes basic civil, political, economic, social, and cultural rights. In addition, it gives recognition to so-called third-generation (or solidarity) rights: for example, rights to development, a healthy environment, self-determination, peace, and so on. South Africa has also become involved in the African Commission on Human and Peoples' Rights, which was established to oversee implementation of the African Charter and to monitor human rights violations reported to it. The current chairperson of the South African Human Rights Commission, Dr. Barney Pityana, was voted into membership of the African Commission at the summit of the Assembly of Heads of State and Government in Harare, Zimbabwe, in June 1997. Another OAU institution in which South Africa is likely to play an important role is the proposed African Court on Human and Peoples' Rights. On 27 February 1998, the OAU Council of Ministers approved the draft Protocol on the Establishment of an African Court on Human and Peoples' Rights at its 67th Ordinary Session in Addis Ababa, Ethiopia, and recommended it for adoption by the Assembly of Heads of State and Government at its summit in June 1998 in Ouagadougou, Burkina Faso. South Africa has already indicated its commitment to the proposed court. In fact, the South African government hosted the very first meeting of government legal experts at which the draft Protocol was first elaborated and examined.[31]

### *The United Nations*

The previous apartheid regime in Pretoria had tended to view the United Nations and other international human rights organizations with both suspicion and disdain. This was hardly surprising, given the widespread condemnation that apartheid South Africa was subjected to in these organizations. Moreover, for a period of 20 years, starting in 1974, South Africa was not allowed to take up its seat in the UN General Assembly, although it continued to be a member of the organization. The advent of a new democratically elected government, therefore, marked a turning point for South Africa's relationship with the world body. Not surprisingly, Mandela's theme in his first address to the UN General Assembly since assuming the presidency was that of "democracy, peace and human rights." He reminded fellow member states that the great challenge of our age is to answer the question: "[What] is it that we can and must do to ensure that democracy, peace and prosperity prevail everywhere?"[32]

Without doubt, the most significant aspect of South Africa's participation in the United Nations, insofar as the question of human rights is concerned, was its election to chair the UN Human Rights Commission during its 54th Session (March–April 1998). South Africa took up its seat on the Commission on 1 January 1997. Here, again, the debate on human rights violations in Nigeria provided South Africa its first opportunity to translate into practice its verbal commitment to the struggle for human rights in Africa and elsewhere in the world. It was also an opportunity to promote, in the scheme of its international relations, the human rights culture that had been laudably incorporated into its national legal order. South Africa was thus the only African country to support the resolutions on Nigeria both in the UN General Assembly and (with the exception of Uganda) in the Commission, much to the chagrin of most African states and the OAU itself.[33] On other human-rights-related matters, South Africa has been quite content to follow the general line adopted by the United Nations. A case in point is the Western Sahara: progressive forces and some political groups at home and abroad have criticized the South African government for not taking a more proactive position and declaring its recognition of the Polisario Front's unqualified right to self-determination over the disputed territory. Clearly, the solidarity that the African National Congress (ANC) may have extended to the Polisario Front in its days as a liberation movement has not been translated into concrete support in the post-liberation era, nor has it persuaded the South African government to shy away from maintaining fairly close and cordial ties with Morocco. Like most other African states, South Africa is happy to accept the Saharan Arab Democratic Republic as a fellow member of the OAU while also acknowledging the legitimacy of the on-going efforts by the United Nations to negotiate a lasting solution to the dispute between Morocco and the Polisario Front over the Western Saharan territory.

## IV. Bilateral policy

Mention has already been made of South Africa's involvement in the resolution of the crisis in Lesotho. This was a regional initiative undertaken with the blessing of SADC. South Africa has also attempted to intercede in other situations on a bilateral basis, with mixed results. In 1996, Raymond Suttner, then an ANC Member of Parliament and Chairperson of the Parliamentary Portfolio Committee on Foreign Affairs, identified the principal obstacle here as being the fact that, although

South Africa may have decisive moral power in the world today, it has limited leverage. He argues that:

> It does not dispense much aid. Yet it does have some leverage, greater or less in the particular case, in relation to some states. [Bilaterally], in relation to a relatively powerful state like Nigeria located some distance from South Africa's borders, its influence is less than in relation to a state like Swaziland and possibly also Zambia. It is still less in relation to a power like China, even if South Africa were to have diplomatic relations.[34]

Since these words were written, experience has shown that South Africa's efforts to influence the cause of human rights in both Swaziland and Zambia have fared no better than in the case of Nigeria. Attempts to mediate between trade unions and other political groups agitating for democratization and human rights, on the one hand, and King Mswati of Swaziland and his government, on the other, have so far remained unsuccessful. Similarly, President Chiluba's government in Zambia was not impressed with South Africa's attempt to play a mediating role in the crisis sparked by what many viewed as an undemocratic decision by the Zambian government to bar former President Kenneth Kaunda from contesting elections for the presidency.[35] South Africa was accused of being partial and biased towards Kaunda, and therefore unsuited to the role of mediator. It is suggested that perhaps, here, as in the case of Swaziland, an SADC-led regional initiative might have proved more successful. It is obvious that South Africa's smaller neighbours are more likely to resist any attempt at unilateral initiatives by South Africa to intervene in their domestic affairs in the cause of human rights and democracy than they would be if such initiatives were undertaken as part of a regional, SADC-sponsored course of action. South Africa's comparative regional strength and its regional power status place it in a vantage position to promote human rights in the region. However, any perceptions of hegemonic aspirations in either bilateral or regional interactions with its neighbours are bound to arouse the kind of resistance witnessed in the reactions by both Swaziland and Zambia.

South Africa's ability to influence countries further afield than the SADC region is also extremely limited. Except for Nigeria and Kenya, it has very limited trading links with countries known to violate human rights in Africa, for example Sierra Leone, the Sudan, Chad, and Equatorial Guinea, to mention only a few cases. South Africa is also chiefly concerned with promoting trade and investment. Indeed, since 1994 it would seem that this concern, rather than human rights issues, has preoccupied its foreign policy agenda. The promotion of trade and investment is often in conflict with human rights concerns. This is clearly demonstrated in South Africa's relations with some Asian countries, in particular Indonesia. Known for its human rights abuses in East Timor, Indonesia remains a chief target for South Africa's investment portfolio. In June 1996, then President Mandela paid his first state visit to Indonesia (although it was his third visit to the country). Human rights advocates and activists criticized these new directions in South Africa's foreign policy. In response, Mandela is reported to have said that South Africa would not recoil from establishing ties with countries or regions in which human rights violations had allegedly occurred.[36] During this trip, Mandela also indicated that South Africa would remove Indonesia from the list of countries to which the sale of arms is prohibited. Such is the inconsistency that attends the foreign policy of a state that is not in a position to refuse trade from the major transgressors of human rights. Or, to put it another way, the contradiction embedded in the simultaneous pursuit of national interest and human rights. South Africa finds itself more in a relation of dependency on Asian countries than they are on it. In these relations the human-rights-based foreign policy is whittled down to Mandela simply imploring the leaders of these countries to "start thinking of behaving."[37]

A somewhat interesting postscript to the controversy over the Indonesian visit must be recorded, however. Shortly after his return to South Africa, it was revealed that, while in Indonesia, President Mandela had in fact requested, and been granted, a meeting with the jailed East Timorese leader, Xanana Gusmao. This extraordinary meeting took place at a state guest-house on 15 July 1997, with President Suharto's blessing. And, within a week of this revelation, Jose Ramos-Horta, exiled leader of the East Timorese resistance movement and joint winner of the 1996 Nobel Peace Prize, was in South Africa to hold talks with President Mandela on East Timor on 25 July. This visit was followed five days later by that of the Portuguese President Jorge Sampaio, whom Mandela had apparently already drawn into these consultations.[38] Some four months later, President Suharto paid an official visit to South Africa. At the conclusion of the visit, Mandela announced that he had made a breakthrough in his search for a lasting solution to the East Timor question. The details of this apparent breakthrough have, however, never been made public.[39] Talks between President Mandela and the Indonesian authorities seem to have continued behind the scenes in the ensuing period. Although very little is known about the substance of these talks, it is just possible that this could turn out to be the one instance of South Africa's "quiet diplomacy" that may well confound the sceptics and Mandela's critics.

South Africa's relations with Cuba, Libya, and Iran provide an insight into the importance of historical factors that negate a blanket condemnation and ostracization of all human rights abusers. These countries supported the liberation movement, hence the reluctance to implement or support sanctions against them for their human rights violations. South Africa did not bow to pressure from the United States to implement sanctions against Cuba and voted against two US-sponsored resolutions at the United Nations: one on the blockade against Cuba, and the other a motion seeking an investigation into alleged human rights violations in Cuba. The Cuba question has been a highly charged one in political debates in South Africa, and one that has sorely tested the political resolve of the South African government in the face of virulent and relentless criticism both from the United States government and from the local anti-communist lobby in South Africa. This is not the place to explore the complex political considerations that underlie this question. Suffice it to note that, on the face of it, South Africa's relations with Cuba seem to contradict the previously declared guiding principles of its foreign policy. As various commentators on both sides of the political divide have been quick to concede, the value of these relations is to be measured not in material benefits but in the historical and ideological relationship that exists between the Castro regime and the liberation movement in South Africa. Here, the ANC-led government is more concerned to show appreciation for the assistance given to it by Cuba than to remain faithful to its professed objective of pursuing a foreign policy based on the twin imperatives of human rights protection and democracy.[40]

Precisely the same kind of considerations arise in respect of South Africa's support for the lifting of the sanctions imposed on Libya for its suspected role in the Lockerbie air disaster. Similarly, Iran remains a friend of South Africa, despite the criticism voiced in some quarters in the West against the close diplomatic ties between the two countries. As was noted at the outset of this discussion, South Africa has openly acknowledged the existence of differences of opinion on human rights issues between the two countries, but this did not prevent President Mandela from defending these ties and declaring that the enemies of the West are not necessarily South Africa's enemies. Indeed, this is a refrain that has been repeated on a number of occasions whenever criticism has been raised by some Western governments against the initiation or maintenance of bilateral diplomatic or trade relations with countries designated as human rights abusers, such as Cuba, Libya, Iran, and Iraq.[41]

From the foregoing, it is possible to discern at least three overarching principles that underpin South Africa's bilateral foreign policy. First, there is the principle of sovereignty and protection of the national interest: here, South Africa insists on choosing its own friends and pursuing any bilateral relations that will best advance its national interest. Thus, relations with Iran are partly driven by the need to secure favourable trading terms for its importation of oil and petroleum products from this

Middle Eastern country.[42] Second, there is the principle of reciprocity: as indicated above, South Africa under the ANC-led government feels duty bound to reciprocate the assistance accorded to it by certain countries or regimes during the long years of the liberation struggle. Bilateral relations with Cuba and Libya are routinely defended on this ground. Third, there is the principle of equal treatment and universality. South Africa has argued that, because of its professed stance of non-alignment, it will maintain bilateral relations with all states, irrespective of their political, ideological, or religious orientation, as long as such relations fall within the overall framework of its foreign policy objectives. What all this implies is that one, or a combination, of these principles can expediently be used to explain away the awkward cases where South Africa finds itself dealing with countries whose human rights and democratic credentials may be found wanting by both international as well as its own domestic standards.

In the area of arms control we once again note the ambiguities of South Africa's foreign policy. In the first place, decisions were taken to accede to the Treaty on the Non-Proliferation of Nuclear Weapons and to sign the African Nuclear-Weapon-Free-Zone Treaty (the Pelindaba Treaty). At the time of writing, South Africa is one of only 11 countries to have ratified the latter treaty; it deposited the instrument of ratification with the OAU Secretary General on 27 March 1998. Secondly, there followed the restructuring of state-owned arms manufacturer Armscor, apparently heralding an attempt to make domestic changes in the arms manufacturing industry in order to foster the principles of human rights abroad. The Cameron Commission, appointed to investigate the structure, practice, and policies of Armscor, tabled its report in July 1995.[43] Many of the recommendations of this commission were taken up in the restructuring of the parastatal company. Among these was the call to respect the arms embargo drawn up by the United Nations, thereby ending South Africa's covert sales of arms. Armscor was also enjoined to uphold transparency and to embrace social values that incorporate the promotion of democracy, human rights, and international peace and security. The Cameron Commission noted: "The new criteria for [determining] which categories of weapons may be exported, and to which countries, should be based above all on South Africa's commitment to democracy, human rights and international peace and security."[44] Cock notes that, in the 1995 classification of arms client countries, a complete ban was placed on arms exports to 31 countries where instability or human rights violations meant that those arms might be put to illegitimate use.[45] Included in this category were Lesotho, Rwanda, the Lebanese Christian militia, and Nigeria. Another nine countries could receive only "non-lethal equipment" (for example, Angola and Mozambique), and lighter restrictions were placed on 15 more countries (for example, India and Pakistan). These restrictions were said to be even stricter than those of the United Kingdom.[46]

The question may still be posed, and Cock indeed poses it:[47] do the manufacturing and sale of arms not inherently contradict the promotion of human rights, international peace, and security, even if one screens one's clients? Violence, irrespective of the ends to which it is put, violates the most basic of human rights, namely the right to life. There is also no guarantee that those not currently on the embargo list will not at a later stage use the arms they acquire against their own populace, for example in the event of civil strife. It is also doubtful whether the arguments that are usually proffered, that the sale of arms abroad is necessary for the country's own security, and that it is a means by which to generate national wealth, can be supported at any cost to human rights considerations.

South Africa has already back-tracked on some of its earlier restrictions. A few months after it issued the list of clients for arms sales, it decided to resort to a case-by-case formula for deciding on prospective clients. It is this mechanism that allows the country to contemplate, and even defend, the exportation of arms to such countries as Indonesia, Syria, Rwanda, and Turkey despite the continuing violations of human rights in these countries and the real likelihood that some of these countries may use those arms to violate the human rights of their own citizens. South Africa's recent arms trade dealings with Algeria provide an instructive example.

As was noted above, South Africa chaired the 1998 session of the UN Human Rights Commission. The question of human rights abuses in Algeria was reportedly addressed during this session, by way of a statement from the chair.[48] It is interesting to note that South Africa had, prior to assuming the chairmanship of the Human Rights Commission, already issued a statement, on 28 January 1998, condemning "in the strongest terms acts of senseless violence," and affirming its support for the Algerian government "[to] help ensure that the current, systematic genocide of Algerian people is brought to an end." Significantly, this statement was issued only a day after South Africa and Algeria had reportedly concluded a deal relating to the latter's purchase of remote-piloted surveillance aircraft.[49] Despite these developments, it is generally agreed that South Africa was able to speak with an impartial and objective voice on the human rights situation in Algeria during its tenure as chair of the Human Rights Commission.

Perhaps the unstated cynical response in all these cases is simply that, if South Africa does not sell arms to these countries, somebody else will. Alas, this is a familiar response that even the so-called older democracies have invoked to justify controversial bilateral relations – whether in terms of diplomatic intercourse, trade, or arms sales – with some of the worst human rights offenders in the world today. The contradictory stances that some Western countries have tended to adopt in their dealings with the People's Republic of China, especially in the immediate aftermath of the Tiananmen Square massacre, bear witness to this.

## V. Concluding observations

It is obvious that high expectations have been placed on the post-apartheid government in South Africa to lead the way in championing respect for, and protection of, human rights, especially on the African continent. As noted earlier in this discussion, this is only to be expected. The 1996 Constitution, which underpins the new political and legal order, is predicated on respect for three fundamental values: equality, freedom, and human dignity. Indeed, these provide the foundational principles of the post-apartheid order. These values are also basic to any project aimed at realizing and protecting human rights in any society.

The reason for adopting an approach that was friendly to international human rights law in the new constitutional scheme in South Africa is not too hard to find. The apartheid order in South Africa represented a negation of some of the most fundamental principles of international law: self-determination, equality, non-discrimination, and so on. During this era, South Africa was also a major violator of human rights and refused to subject itself to either constitutional or international law restraints in the field of human rights. It is a commonplace that apartheid South Africa developed a remarkable degree of antipathy towards – if not an outright disdain for – international law and the international community, especially the international human rights movement. It goes without saying that any meaningful transition to a new democratic order in the country was one that required a commitment to the acceptance of the need to protect human rights by both national and international mechanisms. The entrenchment of a justiciable bill of rights and the explicit incorporation of international law into South African municipal law represent an obvious acknowledgement of this need.

The post-apartheid government has also moved fairly quickly to sign all the major human rights treaties. Among these are the two International Covenants of 1966, the Convention on the Elimination of All Forms of Discrimination Against Women, the Convention on the Rights of the Child, the African Charter on Human and Peoples' Rights, the UN Convention Relating to the Status of Refugees, and the OAU Convention Governing the Specific Aspects of Refugee Problems in Africa. A list of these treaties is given in the appendix to this chapter. This is a radical departure from the apartheid regime's policy, which refused to append its signature to any of these treaties.

There can be no doubt that, domestically, post-apartheid South Africa has laid down a firm foundation for the protection and promotion of all the internationally recognized fundamental human rights. But, most importantly, the constitution incorporates international law, including international human rights law, into the domestic legal system. The challenge for the South African government lies in both its willingness and its ability to translate these lofty constitutional ideals and values into practice. In the realm of foreign relations, the challenge is to ensure that the domestic commitment to human rights also informs all aspects of foreign policy formulation and implementation. One way of achieving this would be to adopt legislation that introduces human rights principles into the government's own actions, including its conduct of foreign policy. The difficulties, dilemmas, challenges, and, at times, inconsistencies that attend this process have been noted in this discussion. On the whole, however, it is fair to conclude that South Africa's efforts at incorporating human rights considerations in the design and conduct of its foreign affairs represent honest attempts at walking the tightrope between safeguarding national interests at home and fighting to ensure respect for human rights abroad. In this endeavour, South Africa has not fared any better or any worse than some of the older democracies in the West.

## Appendix: Human rights treaties to which South Africa is a party (through signature, accession, or ratification)

Slavery Convention (1926)
Convention for the Suppression of the Traffic in Women and Children (1921)
Convention for the Suppression of Traffic in Persons and Exploitation of the Prostitution of Others (1950)
Convention for the Suppression of the Traffic in Women of Full Age (1933)
Protocol to Amend the Convention for the Suppression of the Traffic in Women and Children of 1921 and the Convention for the Suppression of the Traffic in Women of Full Age of 1933 (1947)
Geneva Conventions (I, II, III, IV) (1949)
Final Protocol to the Convention for the Suppression of Traffic in Persons and Exploitation of the Prostitution of Others
International Agreement for the Suppression of the White Slave Traffic (1904)
Protocol Amending the International Agreement for the Suppression of White Slave Traffic of 1910 (1949)
Convention on Consent to Marriage, Minimum Age for Marriage and Registration of Marriages (1962)
Convention on the Rights of the Child (1989)
Freedom of Association and Protection of the Right to Organize Convention (1948)

Right to Organize and Collective Bargaining Convention (1949)
Convention on the Elimination of All Forms of Discrimination Against Women (1979)
Protocol Additional to the Geneva Convention of 1949 Relating to the Protection of Victims of International Armed Conflicts (Protocol I) (1977)
Protocol Additional to the Geneva Convention of 1949 Relating to the Protection of Victims of Non-International Armed Conflicts (Protocol II) (1977)
Convention Relating to the Status of Refugees (1951)
Protocol Relating to the Status of Refugees (1967)
OAU Convention Governing the Specific Aspects of Refugee Problems in Africa (1969)
Convention on the Political Rights of Women (1953)
Convention on the Nationality of Married Women (1957)
Convention against Torture and Other Cruel, Inhuman or Degrading Treatment or Punishment (1984)
International Covenant on Civil and Political Rights (1966)
International Covenant on Economic, Social and Cultural Rights (1966)
International Covenant on the Elimination of All Forms of Racial Discrimination (1966)
African Charter on Human and Peoples' Rights (1981)

## Notes

1. These exchanges, held on a regular weekly basis during parliamentary sittings, are formally known as "Interpellations, Questions and Replies." They provide Members of Parliament with the opportunity to pose questions to ministers for immediate, brief responses outside the normal debating sessions.
2. *Interpellations, Questions and Replies of the National Assembly*, First Sess., Second Parl., No. 1, 12 February – 13 March, 1997, col. 132.
3. Ibid., col. 133.
4. Ibid., col. 133 (emphasis added).
5. Ibid., col. 133.
6. President Mandela is reported to have responded to his critics thus: "[South Africa] will not avoid ties with regions where human rights abuses were reported" (*The Star*, Johannesburg, 6 March 1997).
7. See *Mail & Guardian* (Johannesburg), 9–15 May 1997, p. 4.
8. The terms "West" and "Western," as they are used in this discussion, refer to the unexamined conglomerate of the United States of America, Europe, and assorted offshoots that claim a shared tradition of political pluralism defined in terms of regular multi-party democratic elections and the observance of the rule of law.
9. R. J. Vincent, *Human Rights and International Relations* (Cambridge: Cambridge University Press, 1986), 61. See also W. Korey, *The Promises We Keep: Human Rights, the Helsinki Process, and American Foreign Policy* (New York: St. Martin's, 1993).
10. See discussion by H. Arnold, "Henry Kissinger and Foreign Policy," *Universal Human Rights* 2 (1980), 57. On the view that during the Cold War the United States undermined a number of elected governments and engaged in other anti-humanitarian interventions in order to increase its power vis-à-vis the Soviet Union, see chapter 2 in this volume; see also D. P. Forsythe, "Democracy, War, and Covert Action," *Journal of Peace Research* 29/4 (1992), 385–395.

11. Arnold, "Henry Kissinger," op. cit., 62–63; see also Vincent, *Human Rights*, op. cit.
12. R. Mullerson, *Human Rights Diplomacy* (London: Routledge, 1997), 3.
13. R. Henwood, "South Africa's Foreign Policy: Principles and Problems," in H. Solomon, ed., *Fairy Godmother, Hegemon or Partner? In Search of a South African Foreign Policy* (Pretoria: Institute for Security Studies, 1997), 16.
14. Department of Foreign Affairs, *South African Foreign Policy Discussion Document* (Pretoria: Department of Foreign Affairs, 1996); see discussion by G. Mills, "Leaning All over the Place? The Not-so-new South Africa's Foreign Policy," in Solomon, *Fairy Godmother*, op. cit., 22–24.
15. N. Mandela, "South African Foreign Policy," *Foreign Affairs* 73 (1993), 87.
16. See V. Shubin, *Flinging the Doors Open: Foreign Policy of the New South Africa*, Southern African Perspectives, No. 43 (Belville: Centre for Southern African Studies, University of the Western Cape, 1995), 8.
17. Republic of South Africa, *Debates of Parliament (Hansard)* (National Assembly), 27 May 1994, col. 216.
18. Ibid., 8 August 1994, col. 915.
19. Department of Foreign Affairs, *Proceedings of Foreign Policy Workshop*, Randburg, South Africa, 9–10 September, 1996, pp. 8–9.
20. Mills, "Leaning All over the Place?", op. cit., 19.
21. See, for example, J. Klaaren, "Human Rights Legislation for a New South Africa's Foreign Policy," *South African Journal on Human Rights* 10 (1994), 260.
22. See, for example, statement by Deputy Minister of Foreign Affairs Aziz Pahad, "South Africa and Preventive Diplomacy," *South African Media Circulation* (Pretoria), 13 July 1995. See also, Department of Foreign Affairs, *Policy Guidelines by the Minister and Deputy Minister of Foreign Affairs* (Pretoria: Department of Foreign Affairs, 1995).
23. V. Seymour, *Global Dialogue, Human Rights and Foreign Policy: Will South Africa Please Lead*, Southern African Perspectives, No. 55 (Belville: Centre for Southern African Studies, University of the Western Cape, 1997), 18.
24. For a more extended discussion of this, see T. Maluwa, "International Human Rights Norms and the South African Interim Constitution 1993," *South African Yearbook of International Law* 19 (1993/94), 14.
25. See, especially, the references to international law in Sections 39, 231, 232, and 233.
26. See Human Rights Watch (Africa), "Recommendations to the Truth and Reconciliation Commission" (New York: Human Rights Watch, January 1998). In this report, Human Rights Watch makes the categorical observation that "[the] new government of South Africa is still responsible for serious abuse of human rights, largely but not only because of the legacy of the past. Torture of criminal suspects by police continues, even without the active support of the political authorities, as do deaths in detention and summary executions." This is a rather hyperbolic charge that is not supported by any specific evidence anywhere in the report itself, other than the single reference to the death, after spending some hours in police detention, of a Burundian asylum seeker in Cape Town in June 1997 (p. 23). For a general account relating to the alleged abuse of undocumented migrants, asylum seekers, and refugees, see Human Rights Watch, *"Prohibited Persons": Abuse of Undocumented Migrants, Asylum Seekers, and Refugees in South Africa* (New York: Human Rights Watch, 1998).
27. Thus, for example, South Africa's unilateral attempt to impose sanctions against General Abacha's regime in Nigeria following the execution of Ken Saro-Wiwa and his fellow human rights activists in 1995 was not widely supported within either the Commonwealth or the Organization of African Unity. Indeed, some African leaders, including the Secretary General of the Organization of African Unity, publicly criticized then President Mandela for his government's position on the matter. See *Mail & Guardian* (Johannesburg), 17–23 November 1995.

28. Department of Foreign Affairs, *Communique on SADC Organ*, Pretoria, 28 June 1996.
29. The original proposal for the establishment of an SADC human rights commission or court has been replaced by a proposal to establish an SADC Tribunal, with a wider jurisdiction going beyond human rights issues per se. The new proposal, which was examined and adopted by a meeting of government legal experts in Lusaka, Zambia, 14–15 August 1997, was subsequently submitted to a meeting of the SADC Council of Ministers held in Port Louis, Mauritius, in September 1998. However, to date, no final decision has been taken on the actual establishment of the proposed tribunal.
30. See *Cape Times* (Cape Town), 9 July 1996.
31. The draft Protocol was first examined by a meeting of government legal experts convened by the Secretary General of the OAU, in collaboration with the government of the Republic of South Africa and the International Commission of Jurists, in Cape Town, South Africa, from 6 to 12 September 1995. The final version of the draft Protocol was presented to the OAU Council of Ministers for consideration and adoption during the Council's 67th Ordinary Session. See *Report of the OAU Secretary General on the Draft Protocol to the African Charter on Human and Peoples' Rights on the Establishment of an African Court on Human and Peoples' Rights*, Council of Ministers, Sixty-seventh Ordinary Session, 23–27 February 1998, CM/2051 (LXVII).
32. President Mandela's speech to the UN General Assembly, 3 October 1993. See excerpts in *The Argus* (Cape Town), 4 October 1994.
33. Seymour, *Global Dialogue*, op. cit., 20.
34. R. Suttner, "South African Foreign Policy and the Promotion of Human Rights," in *Proceedings of Workshop: Through a Glass Darkly? Human Rights Promotion in South Africa's Foreign Policy* (Braamfontein: Foundation for Global Dialogue, 1996), 17.
35. The crisis in Zambia arose when President Chiluba's government forced through a controversial constitutional amendment barring any Zambian national one or both of whose parents were not born in Zambia from standing for the presidency. This was generally seen as a ploy to prevent the former president, Kenneth Kaunda, whose parents were of Malawian origin, from making a political comeback and standing for presidential elections
36. See note 6 above.
37. Ibid.
38. *The Argus* (Cape Town), 30 July 1997.
39. President Mandela's last public statement on the matter was in the course of a press conference convened after President Suharto's visit to South Africa in November 1997, when he simply declared that he would not reveal the results of his discussions with the Indonesian ruler until he had formally briefed the UN Secretary-General.
40. Henwood, "South Africa's Foreign Policy," op. cit., 12; see also R. Suttner, *Some Problematic Questions in Developing Foreign Policy after April 27 1994*, Southern African Perspectives, No. 44 (Belville: Centre for Southern African Studies, University of the Western Cape, 1995), 11–14.
41. Henwood, "South Africa's Foreign Policy," op. cit., 13. Then President Mandela reiterated this position even more forcefully at a press conference held in Cape Town on 27 March 1998 during US President Bill Clinton's visit to South Africa.
42. R. Henwood, "South Africa's Foreign Policy and International Practice – 1994/95 – An Analysis," *South African Yearbook of International Law* 20 (1994/95), 283.
43. *Cameron Commission of Inquiry into Alleged Arms Transaction between Armscor and One Eli Wazan and Other Related Matters*, First Report, Johannesburg, 15 June 1995.
44. Ibid., 131.

45. J. Cock, "Arms Trade, Human Rights and Foreign Policy," in *Proceedings of Workshop: Through a Glass Darkly? Human Rights Promotion in South Africa's Foreign Policy* (Braamfontein: Foundation for Global Dialogue, 1996), 28.
46. See *Mail & Guardian* (Johannesburg), 28 July–3 August 1995.
47. Cock, "Arms Trade," op. cit., note 45.
48. Personal communication from Mr. Ahmed Motala of Amnesty International, London, United Kingdom, 28 February 1998.
49. *Reuters/AFP*, Pretoria, South Africa, 28 January 1998.

# 11

# Latin American foreign policies and human rights

*Cristina Eguizabal*

Human rights as found in international law are a relatively recent addition to the agenda of international affairs, dating mostly from 1945. Political antecedents, however, have been present in the international arena for a long time.[1] Moreover, political controversy is not a new feature of the international discourse on human rights.

Almost two hundred years ago, Napoleon's armies conquered Europe supposedly in the name of "liberty, equality, fraternity" – and thus arguably to spread the "rights of man" over the old world. During the height of colonialism in the nineteenth century, the Western version of human rights provided the foundation at home for the "white man's burden" abroad and its "civilizing mission" as articulated primarily by the British and French. The rights of man became part of the West's ideological arsenal in its fight against Nazism and Fascism during especially the 1930s and 1940s. The collective human right to the self-determination of peoples, championed by President Wilson as a guarantee for peace after the First World War, became a potent ideological weapon in the hands of African and Asian independence patriots after the Second World War.

During the Cold War years, the West saw itself as standing for liberal democracy and individual rights in the face of the totalitarian threat, even as the West was undermining those very same values in places like Guatemala from 1954. Much of the global South invoked the notions of social and economic rights as the rationale for their demands for a fairer international economic system. A majority of third world intellectual and political élites viewed international social justice as their right, while the West, led by the United States, fiercely resisted all efforts to produce a New International Economic Order.

In Latin America the human rights issue was seen by many on the political right as a useful rhetorical device in their anti-communist crusade, especially since the Universal Declaration of Human Rights mentioned the right to private property. Much of the political left in Latin America focused on social justice and denounced the concept of political rights as part of Western imperialism.

Today, although the concept of human rights is still seen by some as an ideological weapon in the hands of the West or global North, the debate over the universality of human rights appears embedded in a broader controversy of paradigmatic proportions over the changing notion of state sovereignty in the modern world. The sovereignty of the state is being challenged ethically, politically, and economically. From an ethical perspective, the peoples of the world are increasingly holding national governments accountable for the way they treat their citizens. Politically, most governments have accepted, at least on paper, to adhere to international standards in the treatment of their nationals, also accepting, at least in principle, the right of other governments and international institutions to hold them to these standards through international monitoring mechanisms. Last, but not least, the need for national economies to be directly linked to the global market has opened most societies to international financial and economic scrutiny. More recently, the international community, led by the World Bank, has begun demanding – at least spasmodically – good governance as linked to economic transactions.

Latin American societies have been permeated by these controversies over human rights. Their governments have been, at different historical junctures, more or less involved in the international debate over human rights issues. The Western hemisphere has the second-best regional system for the protection of human rights, second only to the Council of Europe. Historically, some Latin American states championed human rights – such as small Costa Rica. This was certainly true at the time the United Nations Charter was drafted. Today, with democratically elected governments ruling in most of Latin America, a positive foreign policy stand over human rights is fortunately becoming the norm, not the exception. Let us not forget, though, that in the not so distant past most Latin American foreign policies were devised, in the name of anti-communism, as shields destined to protect military dictatorships while they waged "dirty wars" against the people. Thus it is fair to ask whether or not Latin American states will continue to stress human rights issues in their foreign policies.

## I. Historical background: The asylum tradition

Latin American political élites felt very early on the need to forge principled foreign policy discourses. Although the concept of "nation" that swept the region during the nineteenth century excluded indigenous peoples and certain other ethnic groups, the theme of human rights appeared as a key component of the region's international relations. At home, the Latin American independent republics aspired to be liberal democracies. Abroad, the first Hispanic American conferences dealt extensively with a selected number of human rights issues such as slavery, continental citizenship, and asylum. The latter became an important part of the region's diplomatic tradition.

The exclusive concept of nation espoused by the Latin American founding fathers might explain the élitist conception of asylum that they forged, primarily offering protection to the cosmopolitan élites to which they belonged. During subsequent years, however, the region's asylum tradition evolved into a broader humanitarian practice protecting large numbers of individuals who had been obliged to abandon their homes because of political persecution (Chile, Argentina, Uruguay, and Brazil during the 1970s) and indiscriminate violence (Central America during the 1980s).

The first reference to the right of asylum and the codification of extradition appeared in the 1848 Latin American Confederacy Treaty. The right of asylum would later be codified by the 1877–1880 Treaty of Extradition – where for the first time a clear distinction between criminal and political offences was made – and subsequently by the 1889 International Criminal Law Treaty, the 1928 Havana Convention, and the 1933 Montevideo Treaty.[2] These documents essentially stated the inviolability of the right of asylum. They also established the concomitant obligation of the granting country to prevent the beneficiaries of its protection from engaging in activities targeted against their country of origin. At a time when national borders were still in flux, and political persuasions – conservative or liberal – were as strong as national allegiances, the practice of political asylum granted by friendly countries to their neighbours' political opponents was at its core a functional mechanism for the protection of the nascent civilian political élites. The consolidation of national armies at the end of the nineteenth century would change the nature of civilian politics; however, the practice of diplomatic asylum remained and over the years benefited broader categories of political opponents.

Countless opponents to military strongmen ruthlessly ruling in different Latin American countries during the 1950s – Trujillo in the Dominican Republic, Pérez Jiménez in Venezuela, Rojas Pinilla in Colombia, Stroessner in Paraguay, and Somoza in Nicaragua – found protection in

Latin American embassies and refuge in civilian-ruled Costa Rica, Mexico, and Brazil. Similarly, during the struggle against General Batista's dictatorship in Cuba, Latin American embassies in Havana offered protection to large numbers of Castro's supporters. Subsequently many of his opponents would be sheltered until 1961, when, following Washington's leadership, all Latin American governments, except Mexico, severed diplomatic ties with the revolutionary government of Cuba. In the 1970s, some countries became safe havens to thousands fleeing repression: Chilean, Argentinian, Uruguayan, and Brazilian intellectuals and artists were allowed to find new homes in the northern part of the subcontinent – particularly Costa Rica, Mexico, and Venezuela.[3]

The 1980s witnessed more than 2 million people forced to abandon their homes as a consequence of armed conflicts in Central America. Most of them became refugees in their own countries – displaced persons. But at least 200,000 received formal refugee status in neighbouring countries – Mexico, Honduras, and Costa Rica – where the United Nations High Commissioner for Refugees (UNHCR) established numerous camps. Opponents to the Central American military regimes had been granted political asylum by the Costa Rican, Nicaraguan, and Mexican governments since the beginning of the decade. Political preferences played increasingly important roles as the Mexican and Nicaraguan authorities welcomed mostly sympathizers of the leftist insurgencies, whereas the Guatemalan government allowed the foes of Sandinista rule in Nicaragua to settle in its territory.

In August 1987, after almost 10 years of civil strife, the Central American presidents committed themselves to seek political solutions to the armed conflicts that opposed them and divided their societies. Invoking the right of Central America to self-determination, they asked external powers – namely the United States and Cuba – to cease supporting their political allies on the ground. Among their multiple commitments to promote democracy, they agreed to respect the right of the displaced populations to return to their homes and asked for the international community's assistance. In September 1988, the Central American governments met in San Salvador with UNHCR and donor agencies' representatives and devised a reinsertion strategy to be known as CIREFCA (from the Spanish acronym for the International Conference for Central American Refugees). CIREFCA's Plan of Action (1989–1994) expanded the concept of refugee to include not only the internally displaced, but also those who had stayed, thus addressing in more general terms the socioeconomic consequences of being uprooted. The reinsertion process was conceived as an integral part of other efforts towards peace and democracy; respect for human rights was at the core of the whole endeavour.[4]

The very important part played by the international community in the solution of the refugee crisis in Central America and in the following peace process should not obscure the crucial contribution specifically made by Latin American diplomacy, and the extent of Mexico's leadership role. It is undeniable that the Mexican authorities were concerned about Central American unrest spilling over the border, fearing that violence would engulf their southern states – Chiapas, Tabasco, Quintana Roo, and Campeche. However, Mexico's foreign policy behaviour also stood out as symbolic of shared Latin American paradoxes in the conduct of foreign affairs. Mexico was active on matters that deeply affected other countries, but at home it tried to cling to a long-standing tradition of absolute self-determination. The ruling Institutional Revolutionary Party was highly reluctant to endorse any scheme that seemed to intrude on what was called the country's internal affairs. Be that as it may, within the conceptual framework of a Latin American "collective security regime," Mexico and other states were willing to provide crucial humanitarian and diplomatic initiatives – in this case high-profile diplomacy in favour of a political solution to the Central American conflicts.[5]

Thus we see that the long-standing tradition of honouring political asylum in Latin America led in contemporary times to great attention to refugee matters in foreign policy. This focus was combined with efforts to provide security in the region, especially in Central America in recent years. Increasingly, even in Mexico, international solutions were needed for humanitarian and political problems, which reduced the commitment to an expansive and absolute view of state sovereignty. The focus on human rights (as linked to security) was not forced on Latin American states by outside powers and organizations, but evolved through various state foreign policies in the region.

## II. Domestic factors: More political space for rights

Most Latin American states, having been victimized by outside intervention, historically defined the protection of state sovereignty and the endorsement of the traditional principle of non-intervention as their paramount goals in foreign policy. Repressive states obviously had an interest in these claims, to shield their repression from outside scrutiny. But more progressive Latin states also were highly nationalistic, because their experience suggested that the US government would join local and transnational business interests to block progressive social and economic change.[6] Against this background, it should not come as a surprise that the Latin American political left, including the moderate left, tended to see the renewed human rights discourse from the mid-1970s as another excuse for US intervention.

Although geopolitical considerations raised by the traditional US foreign policy establishment made many of President Carter's initiatives look vain at best, hypocritical at worst, his human rights foreign policy had an everlasting impact on Latin American perceptions of Washington's loyalties. It demonstrated to Latin American reformers that the alliance between the US government and right-wing sectors, although still possible (as the Reagan administration would prove in Central America), had ceased to be "automatic." President Carter showed that Washington could eventually tolerate reform in Latin America and to certain extent even promote it. Carter's emphasis on human rights in Latin America opened much-needed political space, which allowed activists – locally as well as internationally – to voice their demands for greater respect.

Latin American constitutions read well on paper, but actual respect for human rights had been inconsistent at best in most Latin American countries, particularly concerning the rights of the most vulnerable sectors of society such as indigenous populations, the working poor, racial and ethnic minorities, and women. Despite spasms of major repression, as in El Salvador in 1932 and in Colombia during 1948–1958, political repression in the region had been selective and largely buffered by the practice of diplomatic asylum. The 1973 military coup that overthrew the democratically elected government of Salvador Allende in Chile inaugurated an era of widespread and brutal repression. Indiscriminate abuses against the entire population were aimed particularly at decimating the new generation of political and intellectual leaders who had in large numbers supported President Allende's regime in the region's most stable democracy. Military coups soon followed in Uruguay that same year, and in Argentina three years later; repression worsened elsewhere.[7]

Long-standing international religious groups and human rights nongovernmental organizations (HRNGOs), such as the World Council of Churches, the International Commission of Jurists, the UN Quaker Office, the International League for Human Rights, the Fédération Internationale des Droits de l'Homme, and Amnesty International, were the first to denounce the abuses. They also had been active in denouncing repression by Franco in Spain, Salazar in Portugal, and the Greek military dictatorship. Along with a small number of Scandinavian and West European governments, they constituted what appears today as "the first generation" of activists denouncing human rights abuses by the Latin American military governments.

The *coup d'état* in Chile – and Washington's involvement – stimulated the creation of new human rights organizations in the United States (e.g. the Washington Office on Latin America, the Lawyers Committee for International Human Rights). Both joined the transnational human rights coalition early on. Private philanthropic institutions such as the Ford

Foundation were, as their main funders, instrumental in the creation and development of the transnational human rights coalition that would eventually include Latin American HRNGOs as well.[8]

In Latin America, the first HRNGO, the Argentinian League for the Rights of Man, had been created in 1937 in opposition to General Uriburu's military coup. The Paraguayan Commission for the Defence of Human Rights, created 30 years later, in 1967, was only the second one.[9] After 1973, the progressive worsening of the human rights situation in the region prompted the creation of multiple organizations in a relatively short period of time. Some resulted when victims of human rights violations or their families got together and demanded the truth (e.g. the Mothers and Grandmothers of the Plaza de Mayo in Argentina, the Myrna Mack Foundation, and the Group for Mutual Support in Guatemala). Other HRNGOs were established by religious organizations as vehicles for their pastoral work (e.g. Vicaría de la Solidaridad in Chile, Justice and Peace in Colombia, and the Brazilian Commission for Peace and Justice). A third type of HRNGO resulted from the gathering of concerned professionals, such as lawyers and journalists. Many such professionals, or their closest relatives, were victims of human rights violations themselves. This situation led to the creation of professional groups such as the Peruvian Institute for Legal Defence and the Colombian Commission of Jurists. Finally, several regional Latin American HRNGOs or coalitions of HRNGOs were established (e.g. the Andean Commission of Jurists and SERPAJ, the Latin American Service for Peace and Justice).[10]

A heterogeneous and informal human rights coalition emerged on a transnational scale that was capable of creating and mobilizing considerable political capital and of moving the issue of human rights from the periphery of the international community's concerns to the centre. In spite of formidable official opposition, Latin American HRNGOs, supported by their international counterparts, the international press, and progressive governments, were capable of creating political space for the region's democratic transition.

HRNGOs played particularly important roles where transitions to democracy resulted from internationally brokered and carefully negotiated political agreements. In Central America and Haiti, human rights observer missions worked closely with local groups, setting the context for fairness in internationally monitored elections that led to democratic governments. HRNGOs contributed decisively to investigating past abuses and establishing institutional and, when possible, personal responsibilities for them. They were also instrumental in pushing for a restructuring of the armed forces, the abolition of compulsory conscription, and the creation or re-establishment of civilian police forces.

Table 11.1 **Latin American countries' status vis-à-vis selected international human rights treaties**

| Country | ICCPR | Optional Protocol to ICCPR | Second Optional Protocol to ICCPR (abolition of death penalty) | ICESCR | Covenant against Torture and other Cruel, Inhuman, or Degrading Punishment |
|---|---|---|---|---|---|
| Argentina | X | X | | X | X(22) |
| Bolivia | X | X | | X | |
| Brazil | X | | | X | |
| Colombia | X | X | | X | |
| Costa Rica | X | X | S | X | |
| Dominican Republic | X | X | | X | |
| Ecuador | X | X | X | X | X(22) |
| El Salvador | X | X | | X | X* |
| Guatemala | X | | | X | |
| Haiti | X | | | | X* |
| Honduras | S | S | S | X | |
| Mexico | X | | | X | |
| Nicaragua | X | X | S | X | S |
| Panama | X | X | X | X | |
| Paraguay | X | X | | X | |
| Peru | X | X | | X | |
| Uruguay | X | X | X | X | X(22) |
| Venezuela | X | X | X | X | X(22) |

S: country has signed but not yet ratified.
X: country is a party, through either ratification, accession, or succession.
*: country either signed or became party in 1996.
(22): Declaration under Article 22 recognizing the competence of the Committee against Torture to consider individual complaints of violations of the Convention.

In the realm of foreign policy, very early in the transition process HRNGOs pushed for the prompt ratification of international human rights agreements such as the two Basic Covenants – the International Covenant on Civil and Political Rights (ICCPR) and the International Covenant on Economic, Social, and Cultural Rights (ICESCR) – as well as the inter-American human rights protection instruments (see tables 11.1 and 11.2). Although with reservations, most of the Latin American governments had signed the treaties; however, many had failed to ratify them. Human rights activists thought, correctly, that legislative ratification of these Covenants would serve as benchmarks and oblige govern-

Table 11.2 **Inter-American human rights regime**

| Country | Inter-American Convention on Human Rights (1985) | Inter-American Convention to Prevent and Punish Torture (1985) | Inter-American Convention on the Forced Disappearance of Persons (1994)[a] |
|---|---|---|---|
| Antigua and Barbuda | | | |
| Argentina | X(62) | X | X |
| Bahamas | | | |
| Barbados | X | | |
| Belize | | | |
| Bolivia | X(62) | S | S |
| Brazil | X | X | S |
| Canada | | | |
| Chile | X(62) | S | S |
| Colombia | X(62) | S | S |
| Costa Rica | X(62) | S | X |
| Cuba | | | |
| Dominica | X | | |
| Dominican Republic | X | X | |
| Ecuador | X(62) | S | |
| El Salvador | X(62) | X | |
| Grenada | X | | |
| Guatemala | X(62) | X | S |
| Guyana | | | |
| Haiti | X | S | |
| Honduras | X(62) | S | S |
| Jamaica | X | | |
| Mexico | X | X | |
| Nicaragua | X(62) | S | S |
| Panama | X(62) | X | X |
| Paraguay | X(62) | X | X |
| Peru | X(62) | X | |
| Saint Kitts and Nevis | | | |
| Saint Lucia | | | |
| St. Vincent and the Grenadines | | | |
| Suriname | X(62) | X | |
| Trinidad and Tobago | X(62) | | |
| United States of America | S | | |
| Uruguay | X(62) | X | X |
| Venezuela | X(62) | X | S |

S: country has signed but not ratified.
X: country is a party, through either ratification or accession.
(62): Declaration under Article 62 recognizing as binding the jurisdiction of the Inter-American Court of Human Rights (on all matters relating to the interpretation or application of the American Convention).
*a*. This Convention entered into force on 29 March 1996.

ments to guarantee certain standards of respect that otherwise the newly established civilian authorities might not be willing – or able – to assure.

With the exception of Cuba, by 1998 all the other Latin American countries were ruled by democratically elected civilian authorities. Democracy has conferred broad legitimacy on civil and political rights as valid guiding principles for Latin American polities. Once again the written constitutions endorse liberal democracy. Unfortunately, in spite of the generalization of fairly elected civilian governments throughout the continent, human rights violations continue on a larger scale than one might expect. Democratic institutions are still weak: legislators are ill prepared, courts are inefficient, corruption is rampant in all branches of government and at all levels, and the dominant political culture still reveals troublesome authoritarian dimensions. The drastic economic liberalization policies favoured by the international financial institutions – commonly known as structural adjustment programmes – have been relatively successful in reducing inflation and spurring economic growth. The goal of reducing deficits, however, has been pursued by sharply reducing social spending – which was never very high to begin with. Poverty has grown throughout the continent, and the gap between rich and poor, the greatest of any region, has widened.

Citizen security has become a constant preoccupation for all sectors of Latin American societies, as is true in the newly democratizing states of Eastern Europe. Common crime, once confined to the poor neighbourhoods of the cities, today is prevalent and does not spare anyone. Drugs and drug trafficking compound the problem. In some countries such as Venezuela and Brazil, not to mention Colombia, the levels of violence have attained alarming levels. Among the worst human rights offenders are often the police forces. This police brutality is reinforced by an extremely inefficient judiciary, and by the middle classes' penchant for confusing poverty with criminality. In Brazil, for example, police have become notorious for killing marginalized Brazilians such as street children and landless peasants. Most victims are young, poor, and black. In Venezuela, democratically elected governments during the past 35 years have not been able to curb abuses. In fact, the number of human rights violations is increasing. This context undermines an emphasis on human rights, as many middle- and upper-class elements stress law and order rather than rights.

During the past decade, state-sponsored violence has receded even in countries such as Colombia, Mexico, and Peru where guerrillas are still active. Colombia is the Latin American country where the worst violations of the right to life and to physical integrity are taking place. Political violence, common crime, and drug trafficking appear closely intertwined. Assassinations, extrajudicial executions, kidnappings, disappearances, and forced displacements abound. The situation for human rights continues to deteriorate in general. This generalization may be less true in Guatemala, Haiti, and Peru where human rights violations were widespread, but the situation in these three countries has improved – at least at the time of writing. In Guatemala and Haiti, progress can be partially attributed to the presence of international observers. In Peru, the apparent defeat of the Shining Path guerrillas has reduced their capacity of exerting violence. Moreover, extrajudicial executions and disappearances have diminished. However, the levels of political violence are still too high even compared with other Latin American countries, and a lack of due process is prevalent. The treatment of prisoners continues to be a major issue, and the democratic process has been severely restricted. Mexico is going through its worst political crisis since the 1911 Revolution and one of the worst economic crises of the twentieth century. Standards of living markedly deteriorated in the late 1990s, while common crime has alarmingly increased. Police are among the most lawless of Mexican authorities. They are notoriously corrupt and brutal. According to Amnesty International, the Mexican army and other security forces have extensively used torture in Chiapas in their fight against the Zapatista rebels.[11] Political murder was obvious in early 1998.

The human rights situation in Cuba merits a special mention. Undoubtedly, the Cuban revolutionary government has made a considerable effort to advance the Cuban population's economic and social rights and to maintain them despite the hardships imposed by the demise of the socialist bloc and the tightening of the US economic embargo. However, the constant violation of Cubans' freedom of association and of expression, and the right to due process, is notorious.[12]

It is not difficult to understand why human rights issues continue to be major concerns for most Latin American governments. However, by accepting international oversight, those Latin American governments most genuinely committed to improving their countries' human rights situation are using foreign policy as an additional instrument to try to consolidate liberal democracy. Along with information from HRNGOs, governments striving to be rights protective use international legal instruments as power resources in their struggle to control authoritarian circles and strengthen control over their reluctant armed and security forces.

## III. Multilateral human rights policy

### *Priorities in the global debate*

Since 1945 many Latin American states have shown shifting priorities in the global discourse on human rights. State foreign policies in the hemisphere have reflected a lively domestic debate about whether all rights are really interdependent, a view endorsed in numerous UN resolutions. Some believe priority should be given to the collective and mostly economic right to national development – a "right" approved by the UN General Assembly in 1986 but not codified in treaty law. Others believe that individual social and economic rights should take priority over civil and political rights. These two positions have been influenced by both Marxist theory and the rhetoric of third world solidarity. But others in Latin America endorse the traditional US position that civil and political rights are most important. Of course, military and other authoritarian governments have argued that it was necessary to suspend most human rights for the sake of "national security."

By the 1960s, a group of leading Latin American economists from the Economic Commission for Latin America (ECLAC) – a subdivision within the United Nations Economic and Social Council (ECOSOC) – had coined a new theory of development. According to their central hypothesis, underdevelopment was not a "stage" – as classical economic theory argued – but had historically constituted the "necessary condition" for the growth and development of the colonial and neo-colonial powers. The theory went on to state that the basic mechanism for this occurrence had been a net transfer of wealth from the underdeveloped South to the developed North, as the decreasing ratio between the international prices of raw materials and the prices of manufactured goods clearly indicated.[13] There followed the strategy of forming international price cartels by the Southern countries, among which the Organization of Petroleum Exporting Countries (OPEC) became the better known and (temporarily) the most powerful.[14] These events fit with the growing demand for recognition of the "third-generation" right to development as a collective human right.

At the United Nations, demands for greater "international social justice" became the third world countries' rallying cry. First there was the creation of the United Nations Conference on Trade and Development (UNCTAD), where the Group of 77 was formed with the mandate of articulating the concerns of the third world. Subsequently, at the General Assembly, the non-aligned countries became an important voting bloc. In both forums Latin American diplomacy – led frequently by Cuba, Mexico, and Venezuela – championed not only the right to development but also the idea of economic and social rights as a precondition for genuine respect of individual political and civil rights.[15]

In the framework of North–South contradictions, socialist countries considered themselves objective allies of the developing countries and supported third world demands at the United Nations. By doing so they naturally furthered Washington's initial impulse to view the whole debate on economic and social rights as a communist plot.

The idea that the right to development should be guaranteed by the rich countries as reparation for past grievances informs the current discussion concerning the indivisibility between civil and political rights – which are most commonly accepted as human rights – and economic, social, and cultural rights – which many continue to characterize as goals and aspirations. However, the history briefly noted above – with Latin American states deeply involved in international diplomacy – clearly constitutes an important antecedent to the current discussion on the need to promote development strategies that do not curtail the realization of the whole array of human rights. The current international discourse on "sustainable human development" reflects this concern that attention to civil and political rights not exclude the socio-economic context – defined in terms of both individuals and nations.

By the end of the 1970s, the same intellectuals who had first advanced the idea of socio-economic rights in various forms were now being persecuted as communist agents by the military dictatorships that ruled their countries. The need for protecting basic civil and political rights became a matter of life and death and mobilized important sectors of international public opinion, particularly in Europe. In the United States, President Carter had put the issue of human rights at the forefront of his administration's foreign policy – at least in terms of rhetoric. In reality, his administration undertook many initiatives for civil and political rights in Latin America, as in Nicaragua under the Somoza dynasty. In the long term, despite all its inconsistencies, Carter's rhetoric in favour of human rights, plus several initiatives such as the attempted protection of prisoners in places like Chile and Argentina, changed the correlation of political forces in the hemisphere to the detriment of the principle of the supremacy of state sovereignty – and to the detriment of the "national security state" as practised by military élites.

With the end of the Cold War, the old argument that branded economic and social rights as the creation of communist governments – led by the Soviet Union – has become irrelevant. However, the protection of social, economic, and cultural rights continues to be largely neglected, today in the name of free markets.[16] The remaining challenge is how to design a viable and politically acceptable human rights strategy that effectively promotes the interrelatedness of the two sets of rights.[17] The challenge is especially difficult because the United States does not accept socio-economic rights as true human rights.

Today, all Latin American governments have signed and ratified the most important international human rights treaties – the International Covenant on Civil and Political Rights, and the International Covenant on Economic, Social, and Cultural Rights. With the exception of Cuba – which once accepted the 1948 American Declaration of the Rights and

Duties of Man – all other Latin American and Caribbean governments have also ratified the Inter-American Convention on Human Rights.[18] Two Latin American governments, Costa Rica and Uruguay, were the first to propose, 50 years or so ago, the creation of a UN Human Rights High Commissioner. A Latin American diplomat, from Ecuador, became the first person to occupy the post created by the UN General Assembly in 1994 following the recommendation of the 1993 UN Vienna Conference on Human Rights.[19]

## *The inter-American human rights system*

If we look at political culture on a hemispheric or regional basis, and when we see that culture translated into regional international law, we can see that conflicts abound. The drive for democracy and rights-protective states, and even for a rigorous regional system for the protection of human rights, has been accompanied by many authoritarian governments and much brutal repression. The latter elements were frequently supported by Washington in the name of freedom from communism. Thus there has been a profound conflict in Latin America between liberal and illiberal elements. At the close of the twentieth century, liberal elements held the upper hand.

During February and March 1945, at the Inter-American Conference on Problems of War and Peace, the governments of the Americas declared their adherence to the principles of international law guaranteeing the essential rights of man and appointed a commission of jurists to draft an American Declaration.[20] The inter-American system of human rights protection and promotion formally materialized in 1948 alongside the Organization of American States (OAS), when the American Declaration of the Rights and Duties of Man was approved in Bogotá, Colombia.

At that time, most pro-fascist dictators had been replaced in Latin America by well-meaning civilian democrats who, confident in the virtues of liberal democracy, were genuinely interested in promoting rights-protective countries. To a great extent, the first steps to establish an inter-American system of human rights were taken as symbolic gestures signalling Latin American support for Western democratic values. Subsequently, liberal democracy and the accompanying belief in human rights would become pawns in the East–West superpower rivalry. Democracy became equated with anti-communism and the protection of human rights was superseded by national security considerations. Regional freedom from communism was accompanied by the suppression of individual freedom within many Latin countries.

The hemisphere went through its first Cold War crisis in 1954: Washington suspected President Arbenz of Guatemala of harbouring communist sympathizers and saw his reformist policies as threats to freedom in the Americas. The United States sought the support of Latin American governments for a series of diplomatic sanctions against the Arbenz regime, which it obtained in exchange for the Eisenhower administration's commitment to increased economic aid to the region. Despite the fact that Arbenz had been elected in relatively free and fair elections, the Central Intelligence Agency organized the overthrow of Arbenz and supported the establishment of brutal military government, a chain of events endorsed by most neighbouring states.

As is well known, a second Cold War confrontation in the Americas centred on Cuba, beginning with Castro's revolutionary triumph in Cuba in January 1959, and peaking in October 1962 with the missile crisis. In August 1959, when foreign ministers from the OAS member states convened in Santiago de Chile during their Fifth Consultative Meeting, Fidel Castro had neither openly adhered to Marxism–Leninism, nor declared his regime's allegiance to the socialist bloc. However, his pervasive anti-imperialistic rhetoric, wide-ranging populist measures, the arbitrary and harsh treatment meted out to former supporters of the deposed Batista regime, and the general absence of due process were considered ominous signs by Washington. This perception was shared by most other governments in the region. As in 1954, hemispheric governments elevated fear of reform movements and deference to Washington over tolerance of political diversity. There was also genuine fear that Castro would indeed move toward communism and an alliance with the Soviet Union. This fear allowed Kennedy to present a united regional front to Khrushchev during the missile crisis. Traditional Latin suspicions of Washington's intentions were somewhat appeased by President Kennedy's Alliance for Progress, which at least promised the foreign assistance Latin American governments had been demanding since the end of the Second World War.

In the midst of these Cold War tensions, hemispheric states created the Inter-American Commission on Human Rights in 1959. If the objective were to avoid radical political and social revolutions that would lead to "other Cubas," an international legal instrument guaranteeing the protection of human rights was widely seen as useful. The Inter-American Human Rights Commission was created by a plurality of votes, with the declared goal of offering legal options to counter tyranny and oppression. It is composed of independent experts rather than state representatives. As such, the Commission was seen as an interim solution – until an Inter-American Court of Human Rights could be created.[21] The 1969 Inter-American Human Rights Convention – legally in force for consenting states since 1978 – finally established the Inter-American Court of Human Rights. The Convention incorporated the Commission's role, without precluding the Commission from acting apart from the Convention.

To date, the Commission has been the most active organ of the inter-American regime for the protection of human rights. This is not only because of its independent membership, but also because, as part of the OAS, it has jurisdiction over human rights matters apart from the regional Convention on Human Rights. A number of states have failed to accept the compulsory jurisdiction of the Court. The Commission, although lacking supreme and binding authority, has nevertheless carried out many investigations and issued many reports. This was true, for example, of the Commission's response to complaints of human rights violations in Argentina (prior to Buenos Aires' ratification of the Convention in 1984); in Brazil (a few months before Brasilia's ratification of the treaty); and even in Cuba (whose membership in the OAS was suspended in 1963 and which today is the only country in Latin America and the Caribbean that has not ratified the Inter-American Human Rights Convention). Latin American governments, however, have never authorized the Commission to deploy human rights observer missions. The OAS currently sends electoral observers to member states, but has never established human rights observer missions.[22]

The inter-American human rights regime has not been as effective as its companion system under the Council of Europe. During the Cold War, the hemisphere manifested numerous governments that elevated suppression of "leftist" movements over defence of human rights – to a much greater extent than in Europe. Washington's security concerns in the hemisphere led it to support this repression – again to a much greater extent than in Europe. The inter-American regime, essentially an intergovernmental system with pockets of uninstructed officials, was ineffective at eliminating gross violations of human rights by its member states.[23] However, if the inter-American system of human rights protection had been less than fully effective as an instrument for enforcing compliance from governments, its diplomatic usefulness became clear when its reports helped denounce and isolate the governments with the worst human rights records. Indeed, among the finest hours of the Commission were the 1978 and 1980 reports presented at the respective OAS annual assemblies. Thus the Commission served as a focal point for all those circles resisting repression.

Between 1975 and 1989/90, of 267 cases cited in the Commission's annual reports, the governments of Chile, Argentina, Nicaragua, Peru, and Cuba were the most frequently named, closely followed by the governments of Bolivia, Haiti, Guatemala, El Salvador, and Paraguay – with more than 10 citations each.[24] The Commission has also acknowledged two complaints, in 1988 and 1989, by the National Action Party (PAN) against the government of Mexico, concerning the violation of political rights as well as their right to due process. A complaint from the Yanomani Indians against the government of Brazil concerning the violation of their rights has been recognized as valid too.[25] Although the Mexican government ratified the Convention in 1982, and Brasilia did 10 years later, neither government has yet accepted the jurisdiction of the Court.[26] Such situations highlight the continuing role of the Commission.

Ironically, with the spread of democratic government in the region, the caseload of the Commission and the Court has increased rather than declined. The Court has ruled 17 times on cases concerning Peru (4), Honduras (3), Argentina (2), Guatemala (2), Surinam (2), and Venezuela, Nicaragua, Colombia, and El Salvador (1 each). Peru, Honduras, Surinam, and Colombia have been condemned to reparations. Of the 17 rulings of the Court, 8 were issued between 1986 and 1992, and 5 were issued in 1995.

For its part, the Commission has remained highly active. For example, it organized extensive consultations on a Declaration of Indigenous Rights. The Canadian Bar Association, the American Anthropological Association, and the World Council of Indigenous Peoples, among others, were invited to discuss the draft, which should soon be presented at the OAS General Assembly for its approval. Concerning women's rights, the Commission has named a special Rapporteur to establish if domestic legislation and actual legislative and political practices truly guarantee the rights of women according to American legal instruments.[27] The Commission's report on the status of women's rights will make recommendations to the governments for improving their standards, particularly concerning the protection of women subject to domestic violence.

Hemispheric states also inject human rights in the summit diplomacy of the Americas, the other important multilateral forum in the Western hemisphere. Within the agenda put forward by the Plan of Action signed in December 1994 by the participating heads of state and government at the hemispheric summit in Miami, a Working Group on Democracy and Human Rights was established, coordinated by the governments of Brazil and Canada with the assistance of the OAS. This group concentrated on four key areas: developing democratic culture, encouraging greater transparency and the rule of law, strengthening electoral processes, and establishing priorities for the promotion of human rights. Thus the working group signalled the region's interest in improving the quality of democracy as the best way of protecting and promoting human rights.

Now that the hemisphere manifests more genuine or aspiring liberal democracies, the regional system is working better and may begin to approximate its European model. The key to regional protection is the absence at the national level of abusive regimes that refuse to be bound by the rule of law. Liberal democratic governments, in essence respectful of the rule of law and of their citizens' fundamental civil and political rights, are more amenable to accepting the regional – and global – human rights protection mechanisms and view them as compatible with domestic objectives. There is thus less tension between claims to human rights and claims to state sovereignty. The Latin American countries' commitment to the inter-American human rights system is made evident by the increasing – albeit still largely inadequate – budgetary allocations for the Inter-American Human Rights Commission and Court.[28] Furthermore, some governments are using these international mechanisms to strengthen democratic control over military and security forces. The policy of the Colombian government is a case in point. President Samper has requested the presence of an international human rights observer mission in an attempt to strengthen the executive's capacity to monitor and check human rights violations in its territory.

### *Latin American new political regionalism: Protecting democracy and improving its quality*

Democratically elected leaders are genuinely trying to close the gap between the internationally recognized human rights to which their countries have subscribed and actual governmental agencies' everyday practice.[29] As indicated above, this quest is made difficult by several factors: economic conditions, political history, and bastions of illiberalism, particularly in military circles. Awareness of domestic and regional deficiencies in the human rights field has caused most Latin American states to eschew an activist foreign policy on most global issues.

The region's historical economic weakness and lack of financial autonomy have reinforced the dominant pattern of "small-state" reactive diplomacy, basically concerned with keeping foreigners at bay. Following the realist paradigm, which the majority of Latin American foreign policy establishments have favoured, national interest has indeed been equated with the pursuit of state power – defined in terms of national autonomy. Latin American solidarity has been seen as an important foreign policy tool by most countries; collective diplomacy has been sought, as a means of defending common interests against foreign encroachment. Fear of Washington's intervention is legendary.

Consistent with this tradition, Latin American democratic regimes today have not established activist foreign policies on most global human rights issues. A state like Costa Rica may take some initiatives on human rights education in the UN Human Rights Commission, but most Latin and Caribbean states tend to focus their foreign policies on human rights on two subjects: application of international standards in the domestic legal order, and the workings of the regional human rights system.

Despite important progress, consolidating the rule of law is still an aspiration for most hemispheric societies, and the protection of human rights continues to be an important issue in domestic policies. Although only Cuba among hemispheric states is under the scrutiny of the UN Human Rights Commission, it has been well documented that countries such as Peru (which paradoxically has recently been elected by ECOSOC to the Commission[30]), Brazil, Mexico, and Colombia, *inter alia*, have serious problems of human rights abuses.[31]

Realistically aware of the remaining power of the armed forces, Latin American civilian leaders have tried to use regional institutions to protect liberal democracy in the various nations. Yet they remain trapped by their traditions. Although the OAS voted in September 1994 to support Father Aristide as the rightfully elected leader of Haiti in the face of military opposition, the OAS still could not bring itself to endorse a US-led use of force to guarantee democratic governance. Washington had to turn to the United Nations, rather than to the OAS, to secure a resolution authorizing "all necessary means" – meaning the use of force. Latin states were in favour of democratic government, but not in favour of legitimizing yet another use of force in the region by Washington. The same pattern had played out earlier when President Bush deployed force in Panama, arguably in favour of the elected Endara government and against the authoritarian Noriega government. With some justification, the OAS refused to endorse that use of force either. Thus the OAS has certainly gone on record in favour of liberal democracy, but not so clearly in favour of the use of force to secure or defend various manifestations of liberal or almost-liberal democracy.

The background to this tension merits summary. The OAS's 1991 Santiago Declaration committed hemispheric governments diplomatically to support any elected regime threatened by hostile forces. The Santiago commitment has since been reaffirmed by the Washington Protocol, which provides for the expulsion of a state from the OAS in the event of the overthrow of a democratic regime, and the Managua Protocol, which commits member states to the active promotion and consolidation of democracy and to preventive efforts against threats to democratic regimes. This evolving regime of democracy protection proved to be an effective deterrent in Guatemala in 1991 when the elected president himself sought the support of the armed forces against the elected Congress.[32] In a volte-face, Washington was a staunch opponent of this *auto-golpe*. The OAS was less successful in Peru in 1992 when President Fujimori attempted something similar. However, after condemning the coup, the OAS was able to send a fact-finding mission. Diplomatic pressure was instrumental in convincing President Fujimori to accelerate his original timetable and convene a Constituent Assembly that would restore democratic legitimacy to his government. Nevertheless, Peruvian democracy remains quite imperfect by liberal standards.

There are other examples of Latin diplomacy working for liberal democracy. In Central America, much Latin diplomacy has been directed not just to simple peace but to a liberal democratic peace. During the 1980s, the governments of Mexico, Colombia, and Venezuela, opposing the Reagan administration's policy towards Central America, formed the Contadora Group. They were soon joined by the governments of Peru, Argentina, Brazil, and Uruguay. According to most analysts, this Contadora diplomacy was instrumental in slowing down the militarization of the Central American conflicts. Although its mediation effort was not fully successful, it laid the groundwork for the subsequent Central American negotiated peace settlement – a settlement linked to the goal of liberal democracy in places such as Nicaragua and El Salvador. The eight Latin American foreign ministers of Contadora and its Support Group – along with the UN and OAS secretaries-general – formed the first verification commission of the Esquipulas II agreement.

The Rio Group, which succeeded Contadora, now includes all South American governments – plus Central American and Caribbean participation based on a rotation system. The Rio Group constitutes an important venue for Latin American and Caribbean multilateral diplomacy, where democratically elected heads of state and government periodically confer. The underlying theme of the high-level gatherings has been how to address their countries' current security concerns (drug trafficking, money laundering, corruption, common crime) effectively from a liberal democratic perspective.[33]

Mercosur, South America's regional integration treaty, has a "democracy clause" that automatically suspends any country's participation in the regional arrangement in the event of a military coup.[34] A timely intervention by Brazil's and Argentina's foreign ministers was crucial in avoiding a military coup in Paraguay in 1995.

The Ibero-American summits – the periodic gatherings of all Latin American and Iberian heads of state – have also made a practice of explicitly subscribing to the principles of representative democracy and explicitly evoking the rights of free speech, religion, and assembly. The summits have become important venues allowing Latin American governments to implement an activist stand in promoting human rights in Cuba. During the 1996 Ibero-American summit in Viña del Mar, by signing the final joint declaration, Fidel Castro committed himself to the respect of these rights. In the future his peers will undoubtedly try to hold him accountable for his promise.

Although the great majority of Latin American and Caribbean governments object to the US Helms–Burton legislation, which seeks to punish those parties using expropriated American property in Cuba in profit-making activity, and have opposed the broader US economic embargo against Cuba for several years, they are withholding full admission for Cuba into the most important regional integration arrangements in the name of the "democracy clause." Most Latin states, however, have resumed diplomatic and consular bilateral relations with Cuba.

## IV. Two examples: Costa Rican and Argentinian foreign policies and human rights

Historical background and domestic constraints only partially explain Latin American policy behaviour. International determinants are also important factors to take into account. Among them, US foreign policy has historically constituted the external variable *par excellence.* Insofar as human rights have been an important theme of the United States' foreign policy, Latin American governments have tended to address human rights first and foremost as a component of their overall relationship with Washington. As far as human rights are concerned, neither Costa Rica's nor Argentina's foreign policies, although quite different in content, constitute exceptions.

### *Costa Rica's principled diplomacy*

Economic conditions and the country's geographic isolation during the colonial era created the foundations for the establishment of a fairly democratic and stable political order during the republican era. Many Costa Ricans owned land – very small parcels in most cases – but private ownership and the ensuing shortage of labour helped blur class lines quite significantly. To a great extent, the economic system led to a greater tolerance of others and a suspicion of extremes in political affairs. Additionally, unlike many areas of the Spanish empire, where the Church acted as a repressive force, fostering social stratification, in Costa Rica the Church remained weak throughout the colonial era. When independence from Spain was declared, in 1823, basic forms of political, economic, and social institutions, allowing for evolution toward a form of capitalistic democracy in the nineteenth and twentieth centuries, were in place. There were problems of race, economic disparity, and social stratification, but they were relatively mild compared with other parts of Central America. The long and destructive struggles that plagued other Latin American governments never afflicted Costa Rica, thus reducing the core international powers' rationale for intervention.

Influenced by nineteenth-century liberalism, the leaders of the Costa Rican ruling class promoted many of their ideas in the Constitution of 1871, a very progressive document even by contemporary standards. Costa Rican élites shared a commitment to expanded education and political opportunities and the separation of church and state. They abolished capital punishment, created a tolerance for non-Catholic religions unparalleled in the region, improved educational opportunities, and allowed for journals and newspapers to thrive.

Costa Rica's democratic development quickened in the first part of the twentieth century. Direct election of the president was introduced in 1913. After General Rodrigo Tinoco's short-lived military dictatorship (1917–1919), reformers created a national agency to monitor elections (1925), established the secret ballot (1928), and made voting compulsory (1936). Electoral fraud was not fully eradicated until 1948, but elections became more meaningful.

The military was never a powerful institution, and its weakness removed another repressive force that undercut democratic development in other Central American republics. In 1918, Costa Rica's military had 5,000 soldiers and 700 policemen. By the mid-1940s, its military had shrunk to only 300 soldiers, with a police force of just over 1,100.

By 1940, when Costa Ricans abandoned the classic liberal political model and tried to implement a reformist agenda, the realities and myths surrounding Costa Rica's historical development had created a belief among most US observers that in its political, social, and economic institutions Costa Rica more closely resembled the United States than most countries in Latin America.[35] The Costa Rican government of Dr. Rafael Calderón Guardia enacted a very progressive labour code, and created social security and public health systems with the support of the local communist party without arousing major opposition from the Roosevelt administration.

Although Calderón's government enjoyed some autonomy in domestic policies, in international affairs it chose firmly to support the Allies throughout the Second World War, accommodating US demands on issues such as the handling of German and Italian nationals and the question of diplomatic recognition of Peronist Argentina. By the end of the war the Calderón government had placed more than 200 people of German and Italian descent in internment camps in the United States.[36] Costa Rica's policy towards other Central American republics had historically been ambivalent. Costa Rican élites, uneasy with the authoritarian practices favoured by their neighbours, had oscillated from cautious engagement to outright isolationism. Calderón Guardia's own authoritarian bent led him to establish a very close relationship with General Anastasio Somoza, the Nicaraguan strongman.

The results of the 1948 presidential elections, unfavourable to a second Calderón candidacy, were annulled. This was the last of a series of violent incidents that had marred the political scene since the end of the war. Under the leadership of José Figueres Ferrer (Don Pepe), the democratic opposition organized a successful armed uprising. Don Pepe's ideas had a profound impact on his country's policies and political culture.

In his book *Ideario Costarricense* (1943), Figueres had outlined a proactive engagement in favour of democratic movements fighting against the dictatorships in Latin America as the most important goal of the foreign policy implemented by a truly democratic government. The new Constitution, which was voted during his first term, was very much influenced by his social democratic ideology. The document acknowledged the state's responsibility for stimulating production and promoting the equitable distribution of wealth. It mandated the creation of autonomous government agencies to guide and regulate the economy and social services programmes and created a civil service. The Constitution also established the Supreme Electoral Tribunal, with the rank of "fourth branch of government," extended suffrage to women, and ended legal discrimination against blacks from the Limón area. In 1949, a constitutional amendment ratified the December 1948 Provisional Junta's decree abolishing the armed forces.

In December 1947, Figueres, along with exiled leaders from Nicaragua, Venezuela, and the Dominican Republic, had signed the Caribbean Pact and created the Caribbean Legion, a political alliance aimed at overthrowing the region's dictators. Despite Figueres' claims that Costa Rica constituted the weakest link in the dictatorial chain, the group chose to concentrate its efforts against the Dominican Republic's dictator. Only after Trujillo defeated an invasion in early 1948 did the Legion turned its attention toward assisting Figueres in Costa Rica.[37] José Figueres and his party Liberación Nacional would not forget their friends on the democratic left.[38]

Needless to say, Figueres' aid to the Caribbean Legion was a potent irritant to successive US administrations, which considered his alliance with the group and support of its activities as a threat to the region's status quo. The attacks on Washington's dictatorial allies in the Caribbean Basin diverted American attention and energy away from more important matters in Asia and Europe. Despite the pressures to abandon his friends, Figueres continued to assist the Legion's attempts to establish democratic governments in the region, justifying his work as "moral and necessary."[39]

According to the Costa Rican Constitution, foreign policy is the purview of the president of the Republic and the relevance of its profile has depended on the type of presidential leadership. As a general rule, Figueres and subsequent presidents from the Liberacion Nacional party have had more active foreign policies than other parties' presidents. In the absence of a professional diplomatic corps, the only other important figure in foreign policy decision-making has traditionally been the minister of foreign affairs.[40]

Figueres' successor, Otilio Ulate (1949–1953) abandoned the anti-dictatorial crusade and, like previous Costa Rican governments, backed Washington's initiatives at the United Nations as well as the OAS. It was during his administration that Costa Rican diplomats began explicitly referring to "absolute respect of human rights" as one of the goals of their country's foreign policy, and framing their anti-communist stance as well as their anti-colonialist and anti-apartheid policies in those terms.[41] At the OAS, Costa Rican diplomats played an important role in the creation of the Inter-American Court of Human Rights, which was recognized by the inter-American community when it decided to locate the Court in San José.

Without abandoning altogether their country's traditional position against military dictatorships, Francisco Orlich's government (1958–1962), Figueres' third administration (1970–1974), and Oduber's government (1974–1978) focused their foreign policy on North–South issues. At a time when most countries were ruled by military governments, Costa Rica would have been almost totally isolated. During his last administration, Figueres even abandoned his practice of withholding diplomatic recognition of de facto governments, but allowed his country to become a safe haven for South American and Central American political refugees. Daniel Oduber Quirós, who would later become a prominent leader of the International Socialists, along with presidents Luis Echeverría from Mexico, Carlos Andrés Pérez from Venezuela, and Alfonso López Michelsen from Colombia (the only remaining civilian leaders in Latin America at the time), set up an informal "foreign policy coalition." The goal of this informal group was to foster democratic solidarity while supporting the creation of a new international economic order more favourable to the third world.

The Nicaraguan insurgency revitalized Costa Rica's anti-dictatorial sentiments and Costa Rica became not only a safe haven but also a very important source of support for the Sandinista rebels. The day Somoza abandoned Managua, all the churches in Costa Rica tolled their bells. On 19 July 1978, every Costa Rican was a Sandinista. President Carazo's administration, although not a Liberación one, opted for an activist foreign policy along the lines established by his predecessor. For example, Costa Rica became an observer at the Non-Aligned Movement, recognized the Polisario Front, and established diplomatic relations with most of the African and Asian countries. The traditional human rights discourse was toned down in favour of more contemporary third world concerns.

President Monge (1982–1986) was the opposite. He inherited a disastrous domestic economic situation at a time when Washington had declared war on the Sandinista regime. President Monge allowed the United States to train anti-Sandinista combatants on the Costa Rican northern border and an increased militarization of the country's police forces. His government abandoned the social democratic alliance, which would henceforward be known as the Contadora Group, and opted for an unconditional diplomatic alignment with the Reagan administration. In compensation, the country's external debt was successfully renegotiated and aid from the US government flowed generously, which undoubtedly eased the pain inflicted on the middle classes and the popular sectors by stabilization and structural adjustment policies implemented by his government.

Not everyone in Costa Rica approved of Monge's foreign policy choices. Public opinion was extremely divided. An important section – including former President Figueres – strongly opposed them and proposed to declare Costa Rica's neutrality in order to reverse the country's increasing involvement in the Central American wars. According to them, this would allow for appeasement with the Sandinistas without having to condone Nicaragua's growing authoritarianism.

Oscar Arias (1986–1990) proposed a different foreign policy course to his countrymen. The Arias Plan sought to complement Costa Rica's non-involvement in the region's conflicts, not with traditional Costa Rican isolationism, but with an active search for regional peace and democracy. One of the most innovative aspects of the peace framework proposed by Arias, which the other Central American leaders accepted in the Esquipulas Accord, was their commitment to respect human rights and hold internationally observed elections. Guaranteeing respect for democracy and human rights was therefore made a regional priority.[42]

At home, President Arias instigated legal reforms giving the people new instruments to demand respect for their rights. He successfully proposed the creation of a new constitutional chamber of the Supreme Court where anyone could directly complain if they thought that their rights had been violated.

His successor, José María Figueres Olsen (Don Pepe's son), constructed his foreign policy around the theme of sustainable development and thus introduced the idea of environmental rights into the equation. The Central American presidents established a Sustainable Development Regional Alliance (ALIDES), which has become one of the cornerstones of the integration process. In the Alliance, the signing governments pledge themselves to a wide range of new policies that interpret sustainable development to include improved social equity, expanded democratic political participation, and increased respect for cultural, gender, and human rights, in addition to ecological sustainability.

## *Argentina's nationalism and foreign policy*

Argentina was also an isolated backwater in the Spanish American colonial empire. But unlike Costa Rica, which exported coffee and bananas, Argentina supplied Western Europe with the foodstuffs it needed. The pampas, among the most fertile lands in the world, were exactly what was required to produce the grains and meat the new industrialized countries needed to feed themselves. Great Britain, Argentina's principal customer until the 1950s, supplied the capital in the form of investment in the railroads, docks, packing houses, and public utilities. Foreign investment also came in the form of British firms that handled insurance, shipping, and banking. Like Costa Rica, Argentina was underpopulated. The badly needed workers came from southern Europe, primarily Spain and Italy. By 1914, approximately 30 per cent of the Argentinian population was foreign born (13 per cent in the United States).

The high degree of foreign economic involvement became a target for Argentine nationalists. Dependence on foreign resources also contributed to on-going Argentine self-doubt about the country's capabilities of achieving a more self-sufficient economy and an authentic "national" culture. This self-doubt has permeated Argentina's foreign policy until very recently.

The 1912 electoral reform gave all Argentine males over 18 years of age the right to vote. At the time only 1 million qualified. The electoral laws excluded women – women would be given the right to vote in 1946 by Perón – and also left outside the political system at least half of the male adult population who had not undergone naturalization. Voting was mandatory, and voter participation was generally high: 70–80 per cent of eligible voters cast ballots in presidential elections.[43] Unfortunately, electoral fraud and demagoguery were widespread.

In 1930, the slow progress achieved since the 1912 electoral reform was halted and civilian democracy was overthrown by a military coup. Under the leadership of General José F. Uruburu, a first attempt at establishing a corporate state was made. It was not completely successful this time, and civilian politics had to be partially reinstated.

As the war spread in Europe in the early 1940s and the Axis armies seemed invincible, the Argentine military longed for a steady, sure leadership in their own land. Congress was dissolved in 1943, the end of political parties was decreed in 1944, and very few civilians were allowed to serve in the government. In 1946, General Juan Domingo Perón, former Labour Secretary and Minister of Defence of the military governments, won the elections by a landslide.

Internationally the Argentine military refused to join the US military-led effort, opting for a "neutrality" that would allow them to continue selling essential foodstuffs to Britain while withholding their political and military allegiance during the hostilities. Argentina finally declared war on Germany barely a few months before the Third Reich armies were crushed by the Allies.

Perón reorganized the state following corporatist principles. He also reduced foreign influence in the economy. In 1946 he reorganized the Central Bank so as to increase control over all foreign-owned monetary assets. In 1948 his government nationalized the British-owned railways, still the heart of the national transportation system. Also nationalized was the leading telephone company (US-controlled ITT) and the French-owned dock facilities. In July 1947, Argentina had paid off its entire foreign debt, which according to Perón amounted to a "declaration of economic independence." He was re-elected in 1951, thanks to the overwhelming support of newly enfranchised women voters and of the working classes.

In 1953, Perón's second term was abruptly terminated by his fellow officers outraged by his government's increasing reliance on labour, the most radical sector of his movement.

A new attempt at ending military rule began with the 1958 presidential election. The victor was Arturo Frondizi, who had mounted an aggressively nationalistic campaign and had been able to attract some Peronist support. He was ousted by the military two years before the end of his term. Arturo Illía, elected in 1963, after a previous election had been annulled by the armed forces, was also ousted by the military three years later. Apart from a three-year Peronist hiatus (1973–1976), the armed forces would govern Argentina for the next 13 years. The military would prove to be the worst human rights abuser in the history of the South American country.

In spite of their very narrow margin of autonomy vis-à-vis the military, the two civilian presidents, Frondizi and Illía, were able to conduct fairly independent foreign policies. There were two basic foreign policy themes: the right to self-determination and economic nationalism. Neither support for human rights nor buttressing democratic regimes was compatible with the principle of non-intervention. Frondizi invoked only the right to self-determination during the main foreign policy crisis of his administration: the Cuban revolution. The Argentines abstained in the OAS when Cuba's membership was suspended in 1962 at the VII consultative meeting of ministers of foreign affairs of the OAS member states. A few months later, however, Frondizi was obliged to severe diplomatic ties with Havana, pressured by the Argentine armed forces, which were interested in accessing US military aid at the time. President Illía would invoke the same principles during the Dominican crisis. Like most other Latin American governments, rather than condone US unilateral intervention in the Caribbean island, the Argentinian government voted for the formation of an inter-American force, but the Argentine military did not participate.[44] In 1964, the Argentinians became observers at the Non-Aligned Movement, the principal third world forum.

The second important theme of both civilian presidents' foreign policy was that of economic nationalism. Argentine diplomacy was an articulator of the region's stance at the first UNCTAD as well as a proponent of the OAS's Latin American Economic Commission. Social and economic claims were integral components of the policy, but they were stated on behalf of the collective – the nation – not of the individual.

During the military dictatorship, the main goal of foreign policy was to conceal from the outside world and/or to justify the excesses committed in the name of "national security doctrine." The tense relations with Washington following President's Carter decision to suspend US military aid, loan guarantees, and donations were little by little replaced by a "pacific coexistence." The business community lobbied hard in both countries for more flexibility from both ends.[45] The Argentine military agreed to allow the OAS Commission to send a fact-finding mission. In exchange, Washington authorized a multi-million credit from the Eximbank for the purchase of US-made turbines for the hydroelectric project of Yacitерá.

In a gesture of defiance, the Argentine military had refused to join the US-sponsored trade embargo against the USSR following the invasion of Afghanistan. Moscow had become one of Argentina's main trading partners and also one of Buenos Aires' main supporters in the United Nations in favour of its claims for non-intervention. In spite of the increasingly close relationship between Argentina and the USSR – and despite President Reagan's staunch anti-communism – his administration made the Argentine military its South American closest ally. The Argentine military were sent to Central America as advisers in counterinsurgency. Most observers agree that it was the warm relationship the Argentine military government had developed with the Reagan administration that led General Galtieri to suppose he would have at least Washington's tacit support after invading the Malvinas/Falkland Islands.

The Argentine armed forces' débâcle precipitated the demise of the military regime. Rául Alfonsín, the Radical Party's candidate, surprisingly won by a landslide. Domestically his priority was to consolidate democracy, particularly by establishing firm civilian control over the military.

The new regime faced serious problems. First was the commitment to prosecute the military personnel and police who had killed or disappeared more than 10,000 suspects. Alfonsín owed his election to this commitment and to the Argentinian people's demands for justice. The new civilian government had to face impossibly thorny questions: Where did the criminal responsibility end? How many officers should be brought to trial? and the biggest unknown of all: Would the civilian government survive such an attempt? The second major problem was the economy. The country could not make the payments on its huge foreign debt and in 1983 inflation had reached 400 per cent. Despite the repression, the Peronist labour unions still yielded considerable power, so economic policy based on "shock therapy" was impossible to implement. The third major problem for Alfonsín was to build a strong power base that would allow him to confront the two other challenges faced by his government.

Foreign policy was a key element of Alfonsín's survival strategy. Risking the loss of the much-needed US government support to conclude successful negotiations with the international financial institutions, he chose to set an independent course for Argentina concerning the Central American wars that was closer to European and other Latin American foreign policies than to Washington. Alfonsín and his foreign minister, Dante Caputo, thought that a firm international stand in favour of democracy, pluralism, human dignity, and human rights achieved through political negotiations was the best way to use foreign policy as a tool in their quest to strengthen civilian control over the military. Concerning human rights specifically, the Argentine Congress ratified the International Covenants on Civil and Political Rights and Economic, Social, and Cultural Rights in 1986.

Alfonsín's government charged the nine military commanders-in-chief for crimes ranging from murder to rape. Five were convicted and given prison terms. Three of the four acquitted were later tried by military justice and sentenced to prison. However, a military revolt in 1987 protesting against the impending prosecutions forced Congress to exempt all officers below the rank of General and several attempted coups convinced Alfonsín of the need to implement appeasement strategies vis-à-vis the military or risk a bloodbath.[46]

Alfonsín's successor, Carlos Menem, chose to concentrate domestically on the economic restructuring that would inevitably pitch him against the still powerful trade unions. He decided to pardon the military. He needed the political space to attack the economic paralysis. Several months after taking office he issued sweeping pardons for participants in previous military revolts and in December 1990 he pardoned the former leaders of the military government and commuted their sentences. One of the goals of these measures was to change his country's international image to one of a mature democracy and for that he needed a functioning economy.

In his foreign policy, Menem chose to abandon Argentina's traditional non-interventionist stance and distance from US foreign policy and, on the contrary (like Costa Rica), chose to align himself closely with Washington's policies. His government dropped all militaristic aspects of foreign policy. The Argentine military participated in the UN-endorsed Persian Gulf war effort and since have participated extensively in peace-keeping operations and international observer missions. The Menem government also signed and ratified the Treaty of Tlatelolco – declaring Latin America a nuclear-free zone – and has thus abandoned Argentina's nuclear policy.

President Menem actively supported the UN embargo against the military dictatorship in Haiti, and Argentina is the only major Latin American country that has not objected to the Helms–Burton legislation against Cuba. In exchange for Argentina's support, President Clinton declared the South American country a major non-NATO ally, a distinction long coveted by the Menem administration. Argentina's alignment with Washington's policies and its belonging to the West is not questioned any more. However, human rights have not become a primary concern for the Menem government. Once very active, the domestic human rights movement has been declining since the 1990s, which might explain why the government's domestic record is not as good as it should be.

While human rights abuses have not completely disappeared (although they continue to diminish), in the economic realm the structural adjustment and stabilization policies have taken a very heavy toll on the standards of living of most Argentinians. Journalists reporting on government corruption are still being intimidated – the assassination of one photo-journalist prompted massive popular demonstrations demanding a thorough investigation and full disclosure. In 1997, Amnesty International cited reports of torture and ill-treatment of detainees in police custody, and of killings by the police suggesting possible extrajudicial executions. According to the same source, widespread demonstrations against government economic policies were routinely forcibly dispersed by police who beat and ill-treated demonstrators.[47] Increased police accountability and a more efficient judiciary are considered to be pressing needs by the vast majority of the Argentine public.

Contrary to the region's foreign policy tradition, in the 1940s Costa Rica's reformist leaders chose to protect their state-centred political model from outside intervention by espousing some of the most important US foreign policy concerns. Faced with such an overwhelming power asymmetry, they soon realized that the only way of shielding themselves from outside intervention was by becoming a preferred US ally – certainly the best Central American one.

Argentines, who for a long time cherished regional power ambitions, confronted with the superpower's own hegemonic designs chose to protect themselves from foreign powers, championing the cause of non-intervention in the internal affairs of the American republics. For most of the twentieth century Argentina's diplomacy tried to enshrine the principles of non-intervention and the right to self-determination in the inter-American system, but, lacking the power resources to impose them, Argentina's foreign policy makers never transcended the legal and rhetorical dimensions. Today, Argentine civilian governments, particularly President Menem's, have adopted a foreign policy strategy very similar to the one favoured by Costa Rica's leaders during most of the twentieth century. Argentina's economic privatization reforms and its peace-oriented foreign policy, along with a very friendly attitude towards most of Washington's diplomatic initiatives, have earned the country the status of a non-NATO major ally of the United States. The Argentine government was an early supporter of international intervention in Haiti, and the country's armed forces have been part of a great number of UN peacekeeping operations. Clearly breaking with the past, Argentina has been one of the most outspoken Latin American critics of Cuba's human rights violations. Ironically, Costa Rica has kept a lower profile in its criticism of Castro's regime, and has recently established a desk at the Spanish Embassy in Havana, uncharacteristically opting to distance itself from US policy.

## V. In sum

In the post–Cold War era, a process of conversion from the imperative of state security to an aspiration for human security is slowly taking shape in Latin America. The region's traditional perception of its extreme vulnerability to foreign intervention is being gradually replaced by a more confident relationship with the international system. Most of the countries seem quite comfortable in an interdependent world and a wide spectrum of sectors in Latin American societies are willing to accept a diminished sovereignty in exchange for enhanced human security. Instead of seeing the international system as a source of threats, following in the footsteps of HRNGOs the region's democracies are increasingly considering it a source of power and learning to use it to their advantage. For example, civilian governments often invoke the international human rights covenants and ask for assistance – human rights monitors, electoral observers – from the international community in order to eradicate the authoritarian pockets still remaining in Latin American societies and polities.

Latin American human rights foreign policies are being conceived as key components of democratic consolidation. They are used either as devices to extract power resources from the international system for strictly domestic purposes, or as elements of a multilateral and regional strategy for maintaining representative democracy as the region's preferred form of governance.

# Notes

1. Elaine Pagels, *Adam, Eve and the Serpent* (New York: Random House, 1988).
2. More recently the 1984 Cartagena Declaration concerning Central American refugees further codifies the practice.
3. Ligia Bolívar, "Los Organismos de Derechos Humanos en Venezuela," in Hugo Frühling, ed., *Derechos Humanos y Democracia. La Contribución de las Organizaciones no Gubernamentales* (Santiago, Chile: Instituto Interamericano de Derechos Humanos, 1991), 225.
4. In December 1984, an international conference met in Cartagena de Indias (Colombia) to look for viable solutions to better address the problem of refugees and displaced persons in Central America and Mexico. In their final declaration, the governments represented at the conference (22, including 10 Latin American ones not directly implicated in the conflict) had already accepted a broader responsibility of the international community concerning the populations in distress: refugees, internally displaced, and people without documents.
5. Mexico accepted more than 50,000 Central American refugees, primarily from Guatemala's indigenous communities, and through the Mexican Commission for Refugee Assistance (Comisión Mexicana de Asistencia al Refugiado - COMAR) provided them with comprehensive support. The Mexican government was one of the key participants in the Contadora Group and thus played a very positive mediation role in the Isthmus during the decade.
6. US direct intervention in the Dominican Republic, 1967, and Grenada, 1982; and more or less indirect interventions in Guatemala, 1954, Brazil, 1964, Chile, 1973, and Nicaragua and El Salvador, 1979–1989.
7. Hugo Frühling, "Las Organizaciones no Gubernamentales. Nuevos Actores en la Protección a los Derechos Humanos en Américan del Sur," in Frühling, *Derechos Humanos y Democracia*, op. cit.
8. Kathryn Sikkink, "The Emergence, Evolution and Effectiveness of the Latin American Human Rights Network," in Elizabeth Jelin and Eric Hershberg, eds., *Constructing Democracy. Human Rights, Citizenship, and Society in Latin America* (Boulder, CO: Westview, 1996) 59–97.
9. Frühlig, *Derechos Humanos y Democracia*, op. cit, 14.
10. Carlos Basombrio, *... Y Ahora qué? Desafíos para el Trabajo por los Derechos Humanos en América Latina* (Peru: Diakonía, 1996), 20–23.
11. Ibid., 83–104.
12. United Nations Economic and Social Council, Commission on Human Rights, "Report on the Situation of Human Rights in Cuba Submitted by the Special Rapporteur, Mr. Carl Johan Groth, in Accordance with Commission Resolution 1996/69 and Economic Council Decision 1996/275," E/CN.4/1997/53, 22 January 1997.
13. Whereas these structural economists recommended a reformist strategy of protected markets and import-substituting industrialization as a way of reversing the deterioration in the terms of exchange, their more radical successors, the dependency theorists, argued for the establishment of strong ties with the socialist bloc as the only way of shielding their economies from the pernicious influences of capitalistic development.
14. Other price cartels included copper, banana, sugar cane, and coffee producers.
15. Most of the Latin American countries joined the Group of 77, but only a minority (Cuba, Panama, and Sandinista Nicaragua) became non-aligned active members. Latin American governments preferred to maintain an observer status.
16. David P. Forsythe, "Human Rights and US Foreign Policy," in David Beetham, ed., *Politics and Human Rights. Political Studies* 43 (Special Issue, 1995), 116–120.

17. Aryeh Neier, "The New Double Standard," *Foreign Policy*, no. 105 (Winter 1996–97), 91–101. Philip Alston, "Economic and Social Rights," in L. Henkin and J. L. Hargrove, eds., *Human Rights: An Agenda for the Next Century* (Washington, D.C.: American Society of International Law, Studies in Transnational Legal Policy, No. 26, 1994), 137–166, and Danilo Türk, "Development and Human Rights," in ibid., 167–181.
18. Other important American human rights legal instruments include the 1985 Cartagena de Indias Inter-American Convention to Prevent and Punish Torture; the 1988 San Salvador Amendment to the Inter-American Convention on Economic, Social and Cultural Rights; the 1990 Asunción Amendment on the Abolition of the Death Penalty; the Convention on the Forced Disappearance of Persons: the Covenant on the Prevention and Sanction of Torture; and the Inter-American Covenant on the Prevention, Sanction and Eradication of Violence against Women, adopted in 1994 at Belem do Pará.
19. Ambassador José Ayala Lasso was replaced by Mary Robinson, Ireland's former president. Sonia Picado, a Costa Rican lawyer and diplomat, had made the shortlist to succeed the Ecuadorian diplomat.
20. In 1938, preoccupied by the deteriorating situation in Europe, the governments of the Americas had adopted the Declaration on the Defence of Human Rights at the Eighth International American Conference, in Lima, Peru.
21. Led by Rómulo Gallegos, former president of Venezuela and one of Latin America's leading intellectuals of all times, the Inter-American Human Rights Commission began its activities on 3 October 1960. At the creation of the Court, its mandate was expanded and its legitimacy enhanced. The Commission's legal standing was further reinforced by the Buenos Aires amendment to the OAS Charter (approved in 1967 and effective in 1970), which adopted the human rights body as an integral part of the hemispheric organization.
22. In Nicaragua, the OAS International Commission for Support and Verification of the Esquipulas II (CIAV-OAS) peace accords was set up with the basic mandate of monitoring former Sandinista foes' reinsertion into civilian life. Needless to say, the CIAV-OAS has had an important human rights observation component.
23. Tom Farer, *The Grand Strategy of the United States in Latin America* (New Brunswick, NJ: Transaction Books, 1988), 77.
24. Instituto Latinoamericano de Servicios Legales Alternativos (ILSA), "El Sistema Interamericano para la Protección de los Derechos Humanos: sus Logros y Limitaciones," unpublished manuscript, 1992, chap. 5.
25. The Commission based its decision on Articles 1, 8, and 11 of the 1948 Declaration (rights to life, freedom, and personal security; the right to circulate freely; and the right to the preservation of health and welfare).
26. Héctor Faúndez Ledesma, *El Sistema Interamericano de Protección de los Derechos Humanos. Aspectos Institucionales y Procesales* (San José, Costa Rica: Instituto Interamericano de Derechos Humanos, 1996), 603–605.
27. Twenty-two governments have already ratified the 1994 Belem do Pará Covenant on the Prevention, Sanction and Eradication of Violence against Women. Elizabeth A. H. Abi-Mershed and Denise L. Gilman, "La Comisión Interamericana de Derechos Humanos y su Informe Especial en Derechos de la Mujer: Una Nueva Iniciativa para Examinar el Estatus de la Mujer en las Americas," in CLADEM–IIDH, *Protección Internacional de los Derechos Humanos de las Mujeres. Primer Curso Taller* (San José, Costa Rica: IIDH, 1997), 166.
28. By 20 per cent or more every year since 1994 according to the Working Group on Democracy and Human Rights. Michael Schifter and Sean Neill, "Implementing the Summit of the Americas: Guaranteeing Democracy and Human Rights," North–South Center Working Paper, Miami, November 1996.

29. Brazil's exhaustive Programa Nacional de Dereitos Humanos, Ministério da Justiça, at http://www.mj.gov.br/pndh/default.htm.
30. Maurice Lemoine, "Morts vivants et morts tout court," *Le Monde Diplomatique* (June 1997), 3.
31. *New York Times*, 8 August 1997.
32. Jorge Serrano Elías resigned his presidency and left the country. He received diplomatic asylum from the Panamanian government and lives in Panama.
33. Francisco Rojas Aravena, "El Grupo de Rio y la Seguridad Regional en América Latina," in Olga Pellicer, ed., *La Seguridad Internacional en América Latina y el Caribe. El Debate Contemporáneo* (México D.F.: Instituto Matías Romero de Estudios Diplomáticos/Universidad de las Naciones Unidas, 1995), 173–202.
34. Brazil, Argentina, Uruguay, and Paraguay are Mercosur's founding members. Chile and Bolivia have received associate and observer status, respectively. Venezuela and Peru are seeking admission.
35. Longley Kyle, *The Sparrow and the Hawk. Costa Rica and the United States during the Rise of José Figueres* (Tuscaloosa: University of Alabama Press, 1997), 7
36. Ibid., 34.
37. Charles D. Ameringer, *The Democratic Left in Exile: The Antidictatorial Struggle in the Caribbean, 1945–1959* (Coral Gables: University of Miami Press, 1974), 63–75.
38. Venezuelans fighting Pérez Jiménez and Cubans fiighting Batista would later join the Caribbean Legion.
39. Kyle, *The Sparrow and the Hawk*, op. cit., 92.
40. Since 1948, three presidents had previously served as foreign ministers: Mario Echandi, Daniel Oduber, and Calderón Guardia. Gonzalo Facio, twice Figueres' foreign minister, lost Liberación's 1974 and 1978 primaries.
41. A. Volio, "Lighting the Path to a Better World," *United Nations Bulletin* 13 (1 December 1952).
42. President Arias was awarded the 1987 Nobel Peace Prize for his efforts in promoting peace in Central America and continues to be actively involved in pursuing demilitarization throughout the third world.
43. Thomas E. Skidmore and Peter H. Smith, *Modern Latin America* (New York: Oxford University Press, 3rd edn., 1992), 86.
44. The Costa Rican government sent a platoon of civil guards.
45. *Clarín*, 10 March 1979.
46. Three coups were attempted during Alfonsín's administration (April 1987, January 1988, and April 1988). They were unsuccessful because the Argentine people took to the streets, making clear their total support for the democratic regime. The last military insurgency was against Menem as late as December 1990.
47. Amnesty International, *Report 1997* (London: Amnesty International Publications, 1997), 74–75.

# 12

# An overview

*Jack Donnelly*

The preceding chapters have surveyed the international human rights policies of several diverse countries. Although the selection is not entirely representative – in particular, countries that even today largely overlook human rights in their foreign policy have been ignored, for obvious reasons – it is sufficiently broad to allow some preliminary conclusions about the state of human rights in post–Cold War foreign policy. Many states in the post–Cold War world include respect for internationally recognized human rights as part of their national self-images and as an objective in their foreign policies. Few, however, make more than occasional, modest sacrifices of other foreign policy interests in the name of human rights. In this concluding chapter, I will try to draw attention to both the reality and the limits of states' concern with international human rights.

Realists, who still dominate the intellectual and policy-making mainstream in most countries, properly emphasize the characteristic unwillingness of states to sacrifice material interests. Nonetheless, the fact that human rights are a bounded or secondary interest makes that interest no less real than those with higher priority. If the impact of limited interests is limited, that is still an impact. Even where human rights do not decisively tip the decision-making balance, they still may have some weight. And when a decision does hang in the balance, even the small additional weight of human rights considerations may prove to be decisive in determining national policy.

Human rights advocates properly emphasize the growing prominence of human rights in the foreign policy rhetoric, and even practice, of most states. Human rights today have become firmly entrenched on the foreign policy agendas of many, perhaps even most, states. The clear influence of human rights norms and values, as well as the importance that states give to verbal and symbolic dimensions of foreign policy, suggest further limitations in realist theories. Many states simply do not define their national interests entirely in terms of power, or even material interests.

Nonetheless, although in the late 1990s more and more states talk about human rights, probably with greater sincerity than in the past, few consistently do much more. And no state places human rights at the top of its agenda. In few are international human rights even near the top. This concluding chapter attempts to expand on this summary account of limited (but real) progress and impact, drawing heavily on the preceding case-studies. In addition, it highlights important elements of diversity in the international human rights policies and practices of contemporary states.

## I. Human rights and national identity

This volume has argued that for states, as for individuals, what one does is shaped by who one is. National interests are not given simply by objective factors such as geography, history, or position in the balance of power. Furthermore, national identity, like personal identity, is significantly a matter of ideals and aspirations. The national interest is a matter of what a state values, which is determined in part by how that state sees itself, both nationally and internationally. The international human rights policies of most states are in significant measure identity based; that is, they reflect the extent to which (national and international) human rights values have shaped or re-shaped understandings of who they are and what they value. The clear evidence of the preceding chapters is that many – almost certainly most – states today identify more strongly with internationally recognized human rights than even a decade, let alone half a century, ago.

### *Alternative identities*

The characteristic identification of late-twentieth-century states with human rights, however, must be seen in historical context. Iran, whose reluctance to identify itself with human rights seems so anomalous today, is much closer to the cross-cultural and trans-historical norm. Human rights have become central to the self-images of most states only in the past several decades – in many cases, only in the past decade or two.

Claims of superior civilization – for example, Roman, Christian, Muslim, European, and Chinese – have been a much more common basis for foreign policy than identification with a common humanity. In Western and non-Western societies alike, the right to rule has more often rested on a divine mandate, or simply superior power, than on popular sovereignty. Tradition and the demands of social order have justified many more governments than the rights of the citizenry have. The rights of a few, determined by birth, wealth, power, religion, virtue, age, race, or ethnicity, usually have been seen as superior to the rights of many or all.

Almost all societies have believed that rulers ought to treat their subjects fairly and seek to realize their interests. Few, however, have recognized *rights* of subjects (citizens) that can be exercised against their rulers. For example, Qing emperors and medieval European princes recognized a divinely ordained duty to rule justly. This heavenly obligation, however, was not accompanied by rights of the subjects to enjoy such rule. With such internal rights conceptions, it was inconceivable that human rights would have a place in international relations.

Even where rights of the ruled have been recognized, they have typically been seen as special, rather than general or universal, rights. For example, England's Magna Carta arose from a struggle between the king and the nobility in which the rights of the ordinary Englishman were never even considered. Even Britain's "Glorious Revolution" of 1688 was only about the rights of Englishmen. As Edmund Burke a century later noted so forcefully, these are very different from the rights of man.[1]

## *The rise of human rights identities*

The United States was the first country to place natural rights – the rights of man, or what we today more inclusively call human rights – at the heart of its national self-definition.[2] Many Americans have attributed this to superior virtue. Others, more plausibly, have pointed to the relatively flexible class structure made possible by the lack of a hereditary nobility, by massive immigration, and by the vast supply of "vacant" land. We should also note that Americans were among the first to have the language of natural rights readily available in their political struggles.[3] Soon after, inspired by both the general idea and the American example, others, beginning in France in 1789, advanced similar claims of rights.

Human rights were part of the founding self-image of the states of Central and South America, when they threw off Spanish (and Portuguese) colonial rule. But the tortured fate of human rights in most of Latin America since independence – Costa Rica over the past half century has been the exception that proves the rule – makes India a much more interesting case. Indian independence in 1947 gave considerable additional impetus to the post–Second World War surge of decolonization. And, as Sanjoy Banarjee emphasizes in chapter 7, India's identification with the human rights values of self-determination and racial equality was (along with its relatively great power) central to its leadership efforts in the third world during the Cold War era.

Countries without human rights in their founding myths have in recent decades increasingly incorporated human rights into their national self-conceptions. In South Africa, for example, human rights became a central part of the national self-image through a revolutionary (although not especially violent) political transformation that brought the end of apartheid. Russia and Hungary might be interpreted in the same light.[4]

The United Kingdom and the Netherlands represent the path of evolutionary transformation. Although one can point to no decisive turning point, by the end of the Second World War both countries had come to identify themselves with the cause of universal human rights – at least at home. And once they had dismantled their colonial empires, in part through the influence of human rights ideas (in both metropolitan and colonized political communities), human rights emerged as an increasingly prominent part of national identity and foreign policy.

Dutch relations with Indonesia provide a striking example. Immediately after the Second World War, the Netherlands fought to maintain colonial rule. In the 1960s, massive Indonesian human rights violations were met by little more than muted verbal condemnation. By the early 1990s, however, as Peter Baehr shows in chapter 3, the Netherlands was willing to accept modest but real economic and political costs, and face the stinging charge of neo-colonialism, to press concerns over Indonesian human rights violations.

### *National and international dimensions*

In all these cases, national and international ideas and values interacted dynamically. The international dimension has been perhaps most striking in cases of revolutionary transformation, going back at least to Tom Paine's pamphleteering on behalf of the American and French revolutions.

In India, Gandhi learned from his earlier South African experiences and, like many later nationalist leaders in Asia and Africa, effectively used the "Western" language of self-determination and equal rights against colonialism. The struggle against apartheid in South Africa had an important international dimension that ultimately changed the foreign policies of most Western countries, turning even American conservatives such as Newt Gingrich against support for continued white rule. Beyond any material costs associated with economic sanctions, this weakened the sense of legitimacy and resolve of many white South Africans.

In the Soviet bloc, the Helsinki Final Act and the follow-up meetings of the Conference on Security and Cooperation in Europe (CSCE) provided important support for human rights activists, especially in Russia and Czechoslovakia, and contributed subtly but significantly to the delegitimation of totalitarian rule.[5] Gábor Kardos in chapter 9 even suggests that the most important human rights activity of post-Soviet regimes has been to incorporate international norms into national law and practice.

The international dimension is also clear where human rights have been incorporated into national self-images by more evolutionary means. In most of Western Europe, participation in the Council of Europe's regional human rights regime has placed national rights in a broader international human rights perspective. Britain's decision in 1997 to incorporate the European Convention directly into British law is a striking example of the inter-penetration of national and international rights conceptions. A very different kind of international impetus was provided, in Europe and elsewhere, by Jimmy Carter's 1977 decision to make human rights an explicit priority in American foreign policy. It is no coincidence, for example, that the 1979 Dutch White Paper followed closely on the US example.

International human rights ideas have penetrated even Iran. As Zachary Karabell indicates in chapter 8, Iranian authorities and associated scholars, in addition to criticizing international human rights norms, have argued that these values are both prefigured by and largely incorporated in Islamic law. We should also note that the Iranian revolution that overthrew the Shah was a broad-based social movement that included human rights advocates who have been forced underground, but not eliminated. One might even suggest that recent "reformers" within the Iranian government, and their (apparently quite numerous) supporters in Iranian society, have been at least indirectly influenced by international human rights norms.

Independent human rights activists with prominent transnational connections – for example, Aung San Suu Kyi in Burma and Jose Ramos-Horta in East Timor – are an increasingly prominent feature of the political landscape. In addition, ordinary citizens have more and more come to frame their political and economic aspirations in terms of respect for human rights. Such individuals, and the groups that they represent and participate in, are nodes for an increasingly transnational process of normative transformation that is reshaping notions of political legitimacy and national identity – and, through these mechanisms, national foreign policies.

## II. Self and other, inside and outside

Human rights are held by all human beings, regardless of who or where they are. Thus authoritative international documents characteristically use formulations such as "Everyone has the right" and "No one shall be." To identify with human rights is to identify with all human beings, regardless of nationality (or other status). To identify with human rights is to deny (at least some) fundamental moral differences between ourselves and others.

Talk of national identities, however, underscores the continuing power of particularistic, differentiating self-images. In addition to seeing ourselves as human beings, and thus part of a cosmopolitan moral community, we see ourselves as citizens – Indians, Costa Ricans, Hungarians, South Africans, Americans – as well as members of diverse ascriptive and voluntary groups, such as women, Asians, Europeans, Muslims, Catholics, workers, teachers, electricians, farmers, fathers, sisters, children, football fans, hackers, environmentalists, and human rights activists.

Although national identities may be neither as flexible nor as varied as individual identities, they have multiple elements, which we have seen may change over time. No country's national self-image is exhausted by a commitment to human rights. For example, although Baehr, with little exaggeration, calls human rights a "sacred subject" in contemporary Dutch policy, he also emphasizes the continuing importance of a competing mercantile national self-image. Sergei Chugrov, in chapter 6 on the Russian Federation, argues for a deep cultural split that leads to a simultaneous identification with and rejection of "Western" human rights. In this section, I will explore some of this multiplicity by examining dominant conceptions of the boundaries between self and other and between inside and outside.

### *Nationalist and internationalist identities*

Are nationals and foreigners, "self" and "other," seen as fundamentally different or alike? Imagine an ideal-type continuum. One end point would be marked by a purely national identity that denies any significant similarities between nationals and foreigners. Nazi Germany perhaps approximates this nationalist extreme. The distinction between civilized and barbarian peoples, drawn for example by classical Greeks, Qing Chinese, and nineteenth-century Europeans, also lies toward the nationalist end of the continuum.[6] The other end point would be a purely cosmopolitan identity that completely denies the moral or political significance of national (and other) differences. Religious figures such as Jesus

Christ, Mohammed, and the Buddha provide the clearest examples. Movements, both religious and secular, that profess and seek to spread a universal model of social organization and values provide an approximation in political practice.

Most of the countries considered in this volume fall near the middle of this continuum. The persisting centrality of national (and subnational) identities precludes a deeply cosmopolitan self-image in all contemporary states. But extreme isolationist nationalism is rare. Therefore, I will refer to (relatively) nationalist and (relatively) internationalist self-images, which help to shape states' choices of which rights receive special foreign policy attention, in which areas of the world.

Iran presents by far the least internationalist human rights vision among the countries surveyed in this volume, and one of the least internationalist (along with countries such as Burma and Saudi Arabia) in the contemporary world. In its foreign policy, Iran identifies primarily with co-religionists. Iran is committed to what it sees as universal (Islamic) values, but in a particularistic way that largely ignores the rights and interests of foreign non-Muslims. Difference rather than similarity is emphasized in dealing with what the rest of the world – and sometimes even Iran, as in the case of Bosnian Muslims – calls human rights issues.

Russia has endorsed the language of internationally recognized human rights. Nonetheless, most of post-Soviet Russia's bilateral human rights diplomacy, as Chugrov notes, has been directed toward Russian minorities in the "near abroad." Although minority rights certainly are important human rights, this near-exclusive focus on discrimination against co-nationals represents a self-identification that emphasizes the difference between self – Russians or, more broadly, Slavs (e.g. in Bosnia) – and other.

India's recent emphasis on issues of intolerance and terrorism is in some ways similar. Human rights issues tend to be viewed through the lens of national and regional concerns: communal strife throughout the subcontinent, plus the volatile combination of political and communal conflict in Kashmir and Sri Lanka. But India's focus has been more on a class of violations than on the particular characteristics of those whose rights are violated. Furthermore, the traditional Indian emphasis on self-determination and racial equality has involved a substantially more internationalist commitment to common values shared despite other, often dramatic, differences. Although less nationalist than Russia, India's international human rights policy has largely been restricted to these rather narrow sets of rights. Its much broader domestic commitment to human rights has not been significantly expressed in its international human rights diplomacy.

The orientation of the Netherlands is more fully internationalist, involving a fairly comprehensive foreign policy commitment to *international* human rights. Although focusing on violent abuses of rights to personal security in prominent bilateral human rights disputes (Indonesia and Surinam), Dutch international human rights policy has stressed both civil and political rights and economic, social, and cultural rights. For example, development assistance is seen as an integral part of Dutch international human rights policy, in contrast to the largely tactical linkage characteristic of US policy. In addition, although former Dutch colonies do receive special consideration, and commercial interests are hardly ignored, the bulk of Holland's development assistance goes to countries chosen on the basis of shared values, need, and geographical diversity – in sharp contrast to, for example, France and the United States.

The United States lies closer to India than to the Netherlands. The American definition of human rights, which denigrates economic and social rights, is highly selective. Nonetheless, the American focus on civil and political rights is somewhat broader than that of India. And the global scope of American human rights initiatives, especially in the post–Cold War world, involves an unusually close identification of national and international human rights interests.[7]

## *Openess to international society*

States differ not only in the ways in which they associate themselves with human rights violations and struggles abroad, but also in their openness to international human rights pressures.[8] The Netherlands lies at the internationalist end of this spectrum as well. Holland freely submits itself not only to regional and international human rights scrutiny but to multilateral guidance. For example, Dutch non-discrimination law has been substantially reshaped through the Council of Europe's regional human rights regime, individual petitions to the Human Rights Committee, and decisions by the European Union's Commission and Court of Justice. In the Netherlands, the commitment to *international* human rights is for local as well as foreign consumption.

The United States, by contrast, is extremely reluctant to open itself to international scrutiny – although somewhat less reluctant than even 20 years ago. For example, when the United States finally ratified the International Covenant on Civil and Political Rights in 1992, it refused to accede to the (first) Optional Protocol, which authorizes the Human Rights Committee to receive individual petitions. More recently, the United States has resisted allowing Americans to be subjected to the independent authority of the proposed international criminal tribunal.

Iran's attitude is even more hostile to international scrutiny, as reflected in its paranoid, conspiratorial vision of American hegemony. India's more moderate sensitivity to outside human rights pressure is much closer to that of the United States. Although a leader in aggressive international human rights campaigns against apartheid, racism, and colonialism, India has consistently rebuffed international campaigns directed against its own practices. And, like the United States, it has refused to participate in the Optional Protocol's system of individual communications.[9]

Banerjee, in discussing this pattern of Indian foreign policy, distinguishes between assertive and defensive international human rights diplomacy. This formulation usefully points to a characteristic style of "addressing" international human rights concerns, namely, ignoring them or denying their legitimacy. But when he writes of India and China undertaking "joint defensive diplomacy on human rights, each remaining silent about the other's human rights violations,"[10] a decision to ignore human rights violations (or subordinate them to other national interests) is perversely described as a defensive human rights policy.

Targets of bilateral and multilateral international human rights initiatives do increasingly face the need to respond. Political alignment and appeals to sovereignty and self-determination provide less insulation than during the Cold War. Responses, however, can be defensive and nationalist, as is typical of countries such as India, Iran, and the United States, or open and internationalist, as is often the case in the Netherlands and Costa Rica.

India and the United States nonetheless remind us that nationalist defensiveness need not reflect a poor human rights record. India has for 50 years had one of the better domestic human rights records in the third world. Likewise, US opposition to international scrutiny is more principled than evasive, reflecting a deeply rooted sense of "exceptionalism" and an unusually stringent conception of sovereignty.

In discussing international norms, it is essential to recall that, in addition to human rights, sovereignty and non-intervention are vital norms of international society. All states, in fact, have a deeper and more enthusiastic commitment to sovereignty than to human rights.

We must not overestimate either human rights or sovereignty in their characteristic struggles. Although somewhat less jealous of their sovereignty than the United States or India, even Costa Rica and the Netherlands are not even close to giving it up even in the limited domain of human rights. For example, Costa Rica, when faced with an adverse ruling on the rights of journalists from the Inter-American Court of Human Rights in an advisory opinion that it had itself requested, simply ignored the Court. But the centrality of sovereignty to all states should not obscure the fact that they have very different understandings of its appropriate scope and implications, which reflect relatively nationalist or internationalist self-images. The Netherlands, for example, sees itself more thoroughly as part of international (and European regional) society than does the United States; it participates in international society less selectively and less conditionally. The Netherlands is more willing to accept awkward or inconvenient (international and regional) norms and obligations, especially when there is a general commitment to a particular field of international activity (as in the case of human rights). As Baehr reminds us, we should not idealize Dutch policy. Nonetheless, Dutch international human rights policy rests on a comparatively deep commitment to international human rights norms and full participation in global and regional human rights regimes. The Dutch often see the range of sovereign prerogative as significantly limited by international human rights law. India and the United States, in contrast, see a greater tension between sovereignty and international human rights – at least when it comes to their own sovereignty. Not just on human rights, but in most other issue areas as well, India and the United States are very reluctant to accept the idea that they should bring their own divergent practices into conformity with international norms. They are much more likely to remind others of their sovereign right to pursue their own interests, as they see them, even when those interests conflict with international norms.

It is worth re-emphasizing that this has little to do with widespread systematic deviations from international norms. India, Costa Rica, and the Netherlands have few significant substantive disagreements about international human rights norms. The United States asserts its sovereign right not to be scrutinized almost as forcefully for civil and political rights, where normative differences are minor, as for economic and social rights. Openness to international scrutiny is a matter of national values and attitudes that are in principle (and in these cases in practice) independent of the substance of national human rights ideas and practices.

### *National attitudes towards international human rights*

The two dimensions of attitudinal variation discussed above can be combined in figure 12.1. This diagram maps the space occupied by the countries considered in this volume, which in this regard accurately represent the range of international attitudes (although the sample over-represents the top-right quadrant). The vertical axis, however, is severely truncated from what is theoretically possible. Figure 12.1 excludes cosmopolitan conceptions, of which there are no examples among contemporary states. Even within the realm of internationalist (as opposed to cosmopolitan) openness, considerable vacant but theoretically possible space at the top is not represented.

I want to draw attention to three features highlighted by figure 12.1.

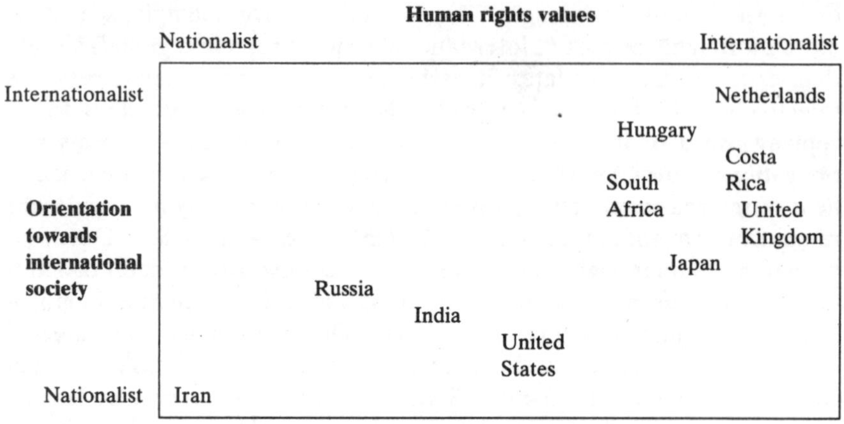


Fig. 12.1 **National attitudes towards international human rights**

First, although many states today accept substantial international monitoring, even the most internationalist reserve a near-exclusive national right to implement and enforce internationally recognized human rights. Even where international monitoring is accepted, states reserve a right to implement the findings of supervisory committees. The global human rights regime is largely a system of national implementation of international human rights norms. (The European regional regime is the exception that proves the rule. And even the European Court of Human Rights relies ultimately on the willingness of states to give national legal force to its findings.)

Second, the fact that countries are arrayed along a single diagonal reflects the tendency for internationalist (or nationalist) orientations to apply both when adopting international norms and when deciding whether or not to open oneself to international monitoring. Although states are at liberty to endorse internationalist norms but assert a sovereign right not to be scrutinized by other states or multilateral bodies – as many European states did in the 1950s – adopting more internationalist human rights norms seems to exert a strong pull toward greater openness to international scrutiny.

Third, were we to compare the distributions 25 and 50 years ago, for both our subset of case-study countries and the full universe of states, we would see a clear progression towards greater internationalism on both dimensions. This is another way of noting that human rights have become a much less controversial and more firmly established subject on international agendas.

## III. The intensity of human rights commitments

International human rights policies are (at most) one part of national foreign policies, which all states consider to be driven primarily by the pursuit of the *national* interest. Therefore, unless we implausibly assume that international human rights take priority over all other national interests, human rights must sometimes be sacrificed to other interests and values. How often and in what circumstances are states characteristically willing to subordinate international human rights concerns? *How much* do states value international human rights? Answers to these questions are less encouraging (from the viewpoint of human rights advocates), and considerably less internationalist, than the analysis so far might suggest.

### *Tradeoffs*

Consider another ideal-type continuum. A state might in principle put international human rights at the bottom of its priorities (unwilling to sacrifice any other interest in the pursuit of international human rights objectives) or at the very top (willing to subordinate all other interests that conflict with its international human rights concerns). The chapters in this volume suggest that most contemporary states lie toward the minimalist edge of this continuum. Human rights typically (but not always) lose out in conflicts with most (but not all) competing foreign policy objectives.

Imagine a simple foreign policy model with four interests: security, economic, human rights, and other. The chapters above provide no examples of states sacrificing significant perceived national security interests for human rights. Security conflicts may have somewhat moderated in number and intensity in many parts of the globe in the post–Cold War era. Therefore, human rights may be less often "trumped" by national security. But this is a change in the frequency of conflicts, not in the relative rankings of international human rights and national security.[11]

The chapters above do show states occasionally giving human rights priority over economic interests. For example, although Baehr emphasizes the limits of Dutch sanctions against Indonesia in the early 1990s, the Netherlands did accept modest but real economic (and political) costs. Such behaviour, however, is the exception rather than the rule, even for the Dutch.

International responses to the 1989 Tiananmen Square massacre illustrate the range of responses characteristic even in high-profile cases.[12] Most states that had substantial economic relations with China did adopt aid, trade, or investment sanctions. Japan did so with considerable reluctance, great inconsistency, and for the briefest possible period – yet with real costs to Japanese firms. The United States, by contrast, responded with sufficient vigour that economic sanctions were the central issue in US–Chinese relations until 1994, and a major irritant into 1997. The Netherlands and the United Kingdom took something of a middle course, in the context of a broader European response.

India, however, remained largely silent and thus indirectly, but intentionally, supportive of China. Russia, which also shares a border with China, largely restricted itself to verbal criticism. Japan's reluctance to pursue sanctions had important security as well as economic dimensions. Even the United States never consistently applied the military and political sanctions it announced.[13] Tiananmen thus illustrates both the characteristic subordination of human rights to national security and the occasional willingness of states to subordinate economic interests to human rights.

The residual category of "other interests" is so broad that little of general interest can be said. It is worth noting, though, that in most countries human rights could be usefully separated from the "other" category only relatively recently. And in most countries today there are more interests in the "other" category that human rights (at least occasionally) effectively compete with than even 10 years ago.

### *Choice of means*

So far we have measured the intensity of states' commitment to human rights by the interests they are willing to subordinate. We might call this the foreign policy opportunity cost of human rights initiatives. Intensity of commitment can also be measured by the direct costs a state is willing to bear, as seen in the means characteristically used to pursue international human rights objectives. When other interests do not override international human rights, how far are states willing to go?

Although there is a close relationship between these two measures of intensity of commitment – the higher the ranking of an interest, the more likely a state is to use strong means to realize it – the analytical distinction is sometimes useful. For example, even if human rights remain below security concerns, we still need to know which means a state is typically willing to use when security interests do not preclude action. To take an example from a different issue area, one of the striking changes in international relations over the past century has been the decline in the willingness of states to use force on behalf of economic interests, despite the fact that economic interests have not dropped significantly on the foreign policy agendas of many, if any, states.

International human rights interests are almost never pursued with military force. Only when faced with genocide or severe humanitarian emergencies have states used force to pursue international human rights bilaterally (e.g. India in East Pakistan [Bangladesh]) or multilaterally (e.g. Rwanda, Bosnia, Somalia).[14] Furthermore, over the past half-century, most such massive and severe emergencies have not mobilized international armed force. Even in the post–Cold War era, forceful responses have not been universal. Consider, for example, the refusal to use force to halt the genocidal civil war in the Sudan. We should also emphasize that even a country like the Netherlands is reluctant to risk the lives of Dutch soldiers when it does participate in peacekeeping operations, such as those in Bosnia.

Moving down the ladder of strength of means we find occasional uses of trade and investment sanctions, most notably in the international campaign against apartheid in South Africa in the 1980s. But strong economic sanctions, as we have already noted, remain exceptional. States will sometimes pay more in money than in lives, but not all that often.

Aid is more regularly used to pursue international human rights objectives. Although aggregate data show only a modest relationship between foreign aid allocations and the level of respect for human rights in recipient countries,[15] aid allocations have in many particular instances been altered in response to human rights violations. Although the United States provides the greatest number of examples, the Netherlands and, to a lesser extent, the United Kingdom have also used aid regularly in the past decade or two to attempt to influence international human rights practices. Even Japan, which has historically been extremely reticent about linking aid and human rights, has included human rights considerations (at least formally) in allocating development assistance since 1992.

We should note, however, that aid and (especially) trade have been used primarily punitively to pursue international human rights objectives. The Netherlands (along with so-called "like-minded countries," such as Sweden, Norway, and Canada) has made a fairly concerted effort over the past two decades to direct aid to rights-protective regimes, not just away from rights-abusive regimes.[16] In recent years, other countries have begun to give greater consideration to aid as a positive instrument in the pursuit of human rights – an inducement and reward, rather than just a punishing sanction.[17] Nonetheless, most states remain much more willing to use aid to punish bad human rights performance – and even then with little consistency – than to reward good performance.[18]

Verbal rather than material sanctions and inducements provide the heart of most international human rights initiatives. Condemnations of violations and praise for good or improved performance are the most common means used by all states to further their international human rights objectives. Although words may be cheap, rarely are they free, especially in the world of diplomacy. In any case, verbal policy is an important and appropriate means for pursuing human rights, like other, interests. Furthermore, as I will argue in more detail below, verbal policy may help to alter or maintain the international normative environment within which states act.

States also regularly engage in symbolic action such as recalling ambassadors, suspending educational, cultural, or sporting exchanges, endorsing international investigations, and voting for condemnatory resolutions in international organizations. Even aid sanctions are often largely symbolic. For example, Dutch aid to Indonesia in the early 1990s was less than 2 per cent of the world total, and Japan responded to Holland's cuts by increasing its own assistance to Indonesia.

A growing number of states also provide direct and indirect support to local human rights activists and non-governmental organizations doing human-rights-related work. Such support may cross over from symbolic to material action. Even here, though, the material action is relatively indirect, channelled through local human rights advocates, rather than direct bilateral or multilateral action against another state.

In summary, we can say that international human rights initiatives are almost always subordinated to security interests, and usually subordinated to economic interests as well. Although virtually all foreign policy instruments have been used by states in pursuing international human rights objectives, from private diplomatic initiatives up to the use of force, the means used are usually verbal and symbolic. Nonetheless, international human rights initiatives are an increasingly common part of the foreign policy of most states. When human rights concerns coordinate rather than compete with other foreign policy interests – for example, in India's opposition to genocidal massacres in East Pakistan (Bangladesh) or US policy toward post-Tiananmen China – relatively forceful responses become possible. And the case of Rwanda, however tardy and weak the international response, suggests that in at least some extreme cases states will agree to use force to protect internationally recognized human rights even in the absence of supporting security or economic interests.[19]

## IV. Evaluating international human rights policies

Most states in the contemporary world are more concerned with human rights at home than abroad. Liberal democratic regimes in particular regularly tolerate international human rights practices they would not even consider accepting nationally. Although cosmopolitan moralists may condemn this "inconsistency," it is an inescapable consequence of a world of sovereign states. States have a special legal and political responsibility for the rights and interests of their own nationals. National foreign policies are *supposed* to treat the interests of nationals and foreigners differently.

Not all differences, however, will be acceptable to states that have included international human rights among their foreign policy interests. Which are deemed acceptable and which are not raises important issues of moral and policy consistency that may influence the efficacy of international human rights policies.

## *The purposes of human rights policies*

Before we can say much about the consistency (or efficacy) of states' international human rights policies, we need to know what they are attempting to achieve. The "obvious" goal of altering the behaviour of the country targeted by a particular initiative requires little comment. But many, perhaps most, international human rights initiatives have other purposes as well. Therefore, they cannot be evaluated simply – perhaps not even primarily – by success or failure in altering the human rights practices of targeted states.

An immediate and tangible impact need not even be among the goals of well-designed human rights initiatives. For example, India did not expect to change South African policy by supporting UN resolutions condemning apartheid. Holland did not imagine that suspending aid to Indonesia would alter the policies of the Suharto regime. No reasonable American expected that sanctions imposed after the Tiananmen massacre would establish democracy in China, or even return the country to the level of political openness it had reached in the late spring of 1989.

In these examples there was some hope of contributing to eventual changes. But, even here, the kinds of changes aimed for are varied. Deterring similar violations in the future may justify pursuing initiatives for which a state expects no tangible impact in the target country. A level of pressure that cannot be expected to alter behaviour in the immediate target may have a tangible impact on a weaker or more dependent country. Even in the immediate target, it may reduce or forestall repeat violations. Having previously been called to task, even states that refuse to remedy past abuses may be willing to moderate, or even eliminate, future abuses. International pressures on Chile and Argentina in the 1970s and El Salvador and Guatemala in the 1980s suggest the possibility of moderating future violations even by relatively recalcitrant regimes.

Even where there is no long-run expectation of altering behaviour in the target state, international human rights initiatives may reasonably be undertaken. For example, the aim may be to "punish" rather than to "reform." Even if competing interests or limited resources preclude altering behaviour in the target, states may reasonably choose to impose costs on those who violate internationally recognized human rights. Given the reluctance of states to use strong means on behalf of international human rights, such "punishment" most often is sadly, even ludicrously, weak. Nonetheless, imposing some costs on rights-abusive regimes is usually preferable to imposing none.

A more diffuse objective of international human rights initiatives may be to contribute to maintaining or transforming the international normative environment. Rather than seek to alter particular practices in any country, the aim may be to influence dominant conceptions of political legitimacy. Post-communist governments in Hungary, Poland, and Czechoslovakia, for example, saw themselves as beneficiaries of such a normative transformation, and their enthusiasm for strengthening the Organization for Security and Cooperation in Europe reflected their desire to contribute to its maintenance. American and European pressures for multi-party elections, especially since the end of the Cold War, have often been directed at influencing broader standards of legitimacy, beyond any impact they may (or may not) have in the immediate target country.

The "precedents" of international human rights policies, however, may have an internal rather than an external target. Their aim may be to establish or support a pattern, or future stream, of foreign policy initiatives. When the Carter administration suspended US aid to Guatemala in 1977, the purpose was at least as much to set a new precedent for American policy as it was to alter Guatemalan human rights practices. Baehr suggests that the precedent established by strong Dutch sanctions against Surinam in the 1980s helped to tip the balance in favour of sanctions against Indonesia in the 1990s. Sanctions that had little discernible short- or medium-term effect in Paramaribo seem to have had a significant medium- and long-term impact in The Hague.[20]

Finally, irrespective of any immediate or long-term impact – direct, indirect, or diffuse; internal or external – states may undertake international human rights initiatives because they are legally, politically, or morally demanded. The US Congress has required the President to impose sanctions for certain human rights violations, perhaps most notably in the Jackson–Vanik Amendment's requirement that trade preferences be denied to countries that restrict emigration. Internal (and even international) political pressure may leave foreign policy decision-makers little choice but to act, as illustrated by both American and Japanese sanctions against China after Tiananmen. Occasionally, a response to international human rights violations is even seen by states as morally demanded, irrespective of legal or political pressure. Rwanda and Somalia seem to have fallen into this category in the foreign policies of a number of states.

Hard as it may be for realists to comprehend, states sometimes find it important to stand up for what they value, independent of any other pressures or expected impact, at home or abroad. Such symbolic acts of "witness" – acting out of respect for and to give voice to one's values – may influence the international normative environment, have a long-run impact on the target (or another) state's human rights practices, or sustain a desirable pattern of foreign policy practice. But even if they do not, they may be demanded for their own sake.

We cannot understand many international human rights initiatives without considering the fact that they are perceived as morally desirable, perhaps even demanded. As we have seen, states are much more likely to "do the right thing" when the costs are low or other interests provide additional incentives. Nonetheless, international human rights initiatives occasionally are undertaken primarily because they are right. And even when self-interest is a large part of the motivation, international human rights initiatives often do reflect a solidaristic identification with the rights or well-being of foreigners.

### *Selectivity and consistency*

This appeal to morality, however, raises the tawdry image of trading moral values off against material interests. If human rights are moral values, how can they be appropriately or "consistently" sacrificed to non-moral interests? How can we "put a price" on life, liberty, and suffering?

Such questions rest on a contentious conception of morality. For example, utilitarianism and other consequentialist moral theories see morality as centrally concerned with calculating relative costs and benefits, rather than rigidly following a moral law. But even if we conceive of morality as a matter of categorical imperatives, challenges to the "consistency" of international human rights policies often confuse foreign policy and moral decision-making.

Realists rightly remind us that foreign policy decision-makers are required by their office to take into account the national interest, which is (at most) only partly defined by morality. Moral perfectionism is an inappropriate standard for foreign policy. Many realists, however, go too far when they categorically denigrate morality in foreign policy. The national interest may – and today for many states does – include a moral dimension. Moral interests are no crazier an idea than economic or security interests. The task of the statesman is to balance competing national interests, whatever their character.

Nonetheless, the realist tendency to contrast material and moral interests does point to a significant problem. The differences between human rights and, say, national security seem to be matters of quality, not mere quantity. How then are we to treat like cases alike – consistently – in the absence of a common metric? To pursue the balancing metaphor, how much does one unit of national security (whatever that might mean) weigh relative to a unit of human rights?

But is the problem all that much more severe for human rights than for, say, economic interests? As I am writing this, controversy is raging over Chinese launches of American satellites. Beyond partisan politics, of which there is much, the dispute involves fundamental disagreements about the relative weights that ought to be assigned to the security and economic interests involved. Such disputes seem very similar to those over the place of human rights in Sino-American relations.

Consider also the choice of means. How many American (or Pakistani, or Canadian) lives was it worth to save hundreds of thousands of Somalis from starvation in 1992? To save a smaller number of Somalis from factional warfare among their leaders in 1993? There is no apparent qualitative difference between such calculations and those involved in, for example, the Gulf War. How many American (or British, or Dutch) soldiers was it worth to expel Iraq from Kuwait? To overthrow Saddam Hussein? The problem of competing incommensurable interests is a general problem of foreign policy, not one restricted to human rights and other moral interests.

Issues of consistency do have a special force in moral reasoning. The "golden rule" of doing unto others as one would be done by underscores the fact that morality in significant measure means not making an exception for oneself (or those one is aiding). But, even from a purely moral point of view, only comparable human rights violations require comparable responses. Human rights may be "interdependent and indivisible," but that does not require an identical response to every violation of every right.

Even from a purely moral point of view, considerations of cost may be relevant. Few would consider the United States to be morally bound, all things considered, to risk nuclear war in order to remedy human rights violations in China simply because it acted relatively strongly to remedy similar violations in, say, Guatemala. Conversely, the fact that no state is willing to threaten the use of force to free Tibet from Chinese domination, thus risking nuclear war, does not mean that considerations of moral consistency preclude the use of force in, say, East Timor. That option is precluded instead by competing economic and security concerns. Balancing competing values *requires* taking account of all the values involved. And consistency requires treating like cases alike *all things considered*, not just looking at similarities in human rights violations.

Furthermore, to address only moral (in)consistency is to address but one part of the relevant foreign policy. In addition to the authoritative international human rights standards of the Universal Declaration and the Covenants, which can be taken as a rough approximation of an international moral standard, states must consider their own often much more limited international human rights objectives, as well as other aspects of the national interest. Even if a state's actions or policies are morally inconsistent, they may be consistent from a foreign policy point of view.

For example, George Bush extended most-favoured-nation trading status to China in 1990 but denied it to the Soviet Union. Looking solely at human rights behaviours – Tiananmen versus perestroika, glasnost, new thinking, and the collapse of the Soviet empire – this seems wildly inconsistent. But considering all the interests involved, it is plausible, if controversial, to find no *foreign policy* inconsistency. Bush argued, not implausibly, that his actions properly balanced a complex set of competing security, economic, and human rights interests.

Consider again the "precedent" of Surinam for Dutch policy toward Indonesia. Would it have been "inconsistent" not to have suspended aid? Perhaps. But it might instead have reflected a reasonable and consistent calculation that the economic and security costs in Indonesia were sufficiently great to justify, perhaps even require, subordinating Dutch international human rights concerns.

We can know whether different responses to comparable human rights violations represent inconsistent foreign policy only if we know all the interests involved and the values (weights) attached to them. Alleged inconsistencies in international human rights policies may be – and I would suggest often are – consistent policies based on a relatively low weighting of international human rights interests. It may be inconsistent, from an abstract human rights point of view, for Hungary to undertake international initiatives on behalf of the Hungarian minority in Romania, but not on behalf of Russian minorities in Lithuania or Ukraine, or of the Tamil minority in Sri Lanka. But there is no evident conflict with the Hungarian national interest.

Hypocrisy, error, and inattention are no less common in foreign policy than in other human endeavours. But, in considering the issue of consistency, we must not confuse the standards of international human rights norms, nationally defined international human rights objectives, and the national interest more broadly conceived. Furthermore, all three must be distinguished from foreign policy actions that reflect a relatively low evaluation of a state's international human rights interests.

Human rights, as we have seen, usually have only a secondary place in the scheme of foreign policy interests. Human rights policies are at best a part – most often a rather modest part – of the foreign policy of most states. Therefore, it is unavoidable that even well-designed foreign policies will treat comparable human rights violations differently.

### *Towards more effective international human rights policies*

Inconsistency may indeed reduce the efficacy of even well-meaning and otherwise well-planned initiatives. I would argue, however, that, although little in the preceding chapters speaks directly to this issue, much of the real and remediable (more than moral) inconsistency in international human rights policies arises from inattention and lack of coordination. Foreign policy, whether addressing human rights or other interests, tends to be made on a case-by-case basis, with relatively little coordination or strategic vision. Balances are struck not by omniscient rational actors but in more or less intuitive ways by usually harried decision-makers grappling with the particularities of pressing issues.

Bureaucratic politics also play a role. The frequent conflicts between human rights and national security officials are well known. Regional branches within the foreign ministry may operate with very different baseline assumptions and expectations. Those working with international financial institutions may come to the table with a very different perspective than those working with human rights institutions.

Bureaucratic organization thus may be significant to the success of a state's international human rights policy. For example, during the Carter administration, human rights concerns were infused more broadly through the foreign policy bureaucracy by devices such as the creation of a Bureau of Human Rights and Humanitarian Affairs within the US State Department and the inter-agency "Christopher group," as well as by congressionally mandated reporting (which required local embassies to give greater attention to human rights issues). The recent reorganization of the Dutch foreign ministry reflects a similar effort to integrate human rights concerns more into day-to-day work, rather than as a separate consideration added relatively late in the decision process.

The other principal source of inconsistency, I would suggest, is a tendency to overly grand policy pronouncements. Perhaps the classic example is Jimmy Carter's claim that human rights were the "heart" of American foreign policy. Having thus raised unrealistic expectations, many observers came to judge American actions as heartless and inconsistent.

Both kinds of inconsistency, however, are rooted in a relatively low valuation of international human rights. Excessively grand rhetoric is a sign of an interest having a lower value in practice than policy pronouncements suggest. And the higher an interest is valued, the more a state is likely to struggle against the tendency toward bureaucratic fragmentation. The biggest "problem" is that foreign policy decision-makers often value human rights less than human rights advocates would like them to. In most countries, the single greatest contributor to more effective international human rights policies would be to increase the priority of human rights relative to other foreign policy objectives.

Consistency is a matter of correctly adding up the various prices and values already assigned to foreign policy interests. Sometimes just calculating correctly will be enough to get "better" human rights policies (judged from the standpoint of human rights advocates). This is especially true in foreign ministries where realist rhetoric has special force or in countries where national security and economics ministries dominate the decision-making process. But a much greater contribution – again, measured from the perspective of human rights advocates – could be made by "getting the prices right," by increasing the price states are willing to pay in order to achieve their international human rights objectives.

This is one final way to restate the central argument of this chapter. Human rights have a greater prominence in the contemporary foreign policy of more states than at any other time in the past. The end of the Cold War has removed, or at least moderated, many impediments to more effective international human rights policies. But, while international human rights are working their way up the foreign policy agendas of a growing number of states, in few if any have they come even close to the top.

## Notes

1. In addition, of course, the rights of English women (and many other groups) were not at issue in either of these charters of rights. "Englishmen" meant, at best, propertied male citizens – and not even all of them were able to enjoy these rights equally.
2. From a vast literature see especially Michael H. Hunt, *Ideology and U.S. Foreign Policy* (New Haven, CT: Yale University Press, 1987); Hunt is particularly good on the combination of US confidence in its positive leadership with its racism. T. Davis and S. Lynn-Jones, "City upon a Hill," *Foreign Policy*, no. 66 (1987), 20–38; these authors place the chauvinistic rhetoric of Ronald Reagan in proper historical context. Richard Rosecrance, *America as an Ordinary Country: US Foreign Policy and the Future* (Ithaca, NY: Cornell University Press, 1976); Rosecrance compares lofty American expectations with the early demise of the "American century." The journalist Thomas L. Friedman notes that even foreign circles of opinion, in Lebanon for example, looked to a magnanimous and altruistic United States to save them from their own political deficiencies, in *From Beirut to Jerusalem* (New York: Anchor Books, 1989).
3. The idea of human rights – rights that one has simply as a human being and may exercise against one's own society and state – was almost completely absent from political debate prior to the more radical stages of the English Civil War of the 1640s. It did not enter the mainstream of political debate in any country prior to the mid-eighteenth century.

4. Such a reading would view Marxism–Leninism–Stalinism as a rejection of ostensibly universal but in fact bourgeois "human rights" in favour of, initially, the dictatorship of the proletariat, and, ultimately, a form of socialism that transcends individual rights. An alternative interpretation, advanced by many Soviet bloc theorists in the 1970s and early 1980s, would say that the Soviet model rested on an alternative (and more genuine) conception of human rights. Although I reject this reading (see, e.g., Jack Donnelly, "Human Rights and Human Dignity: An Analytic Critique of Non-Western Human Rights Conceptions," *American Political Science Review* 76 (June 1982), 303–316), it would imply that in 1989 the dominant conception of the substance of human rights changed, following on a more evolutionary transformation that occurred during the Khrushchev, Brezhnev, and post-Helsinki eras.
5. See, for example, Sandra L. Gubin, "Between Regimes and Realism – Transnational Agenda Setting: Soviet Compliance with CSCE Human Rights Norms," *Human Rights Quarterly* 17 (May 1995), 278–302.
6. We should note, however, that the Greeks and Europeans also recognized very important differences, such as those between Athenians and Spartans or Germans and French, among "civilized" peoples. Furthermore, China saw civilization as accessible (through emulation and extended tutelage) to those who were not Han Chinese.
7. Ironically, Iran, for all its substantive differences from the United States, presents a similar combination of the aggressive promotion of allegedly universal values with a very strong nationalist twist. For completeness, we can place Japan and the United Kingdom somewhere between the United States and the Netherlands. South Africa, which as chapter 10 indicates is still struggling to determine how internationalist a vision it wishes to pursue, belongs in the same range of the spectrum. Hungary lies in this middle range as well: its special attention to Hungarian minorities in neighbouring countries would seem to place it much closer to the United States than to the Netherlands, but its identification with Europe pulls in the opposite direction. Costa Rica falls near the Netherlands, close to the internationalist boundary of contemporary international human rights policies.
8. Kathryn Sikkink draws a very similar distinction in "The Power of Principled Ideas: Human Rights Policies in the United States and Western Europe," in Judith Goldstein and Robert O. Keohane, eds., *Ideas and Foreign Policy: Beliefs, Institutions, and Political Change* (Ithaca, NY: Cornell University Press, 1993).
9. Of the countries considered in this volume, as of 28 May 1998 Costa Rica, Hungary, the Netherlands, and Russia were parties to the (first) Optional Protocol. India, Iran, Japan, South Africa, the United Kingdom, and the United States were not. (Information taken from the United Nations High Commissioner for Human Rights' Web site http://www.unhchr.ch, at http://www.un.org/Depts/Treaty/final/ts2/newfiles/part_boo/iv_boo/iv_5.html).
10. See page 181 above.
11. This assessment may be too harsh and static, as a result of assuming a fairly conventional definition of national security, which, for all the talk of common security, peace building, and the like, remains the understanding most commonly held by contemporary states. For an introduction to alternative ways of conceptualizing the relationship between human rights and security, see David P. Forsythe, *Human Rights and Peace: International and National Dimensions* (Lincoln: University of Nebraska Press, 1993) and, much more briefly, Jack Donnelly, "Rethinking Human Rights," *Current History* 95 (November 1996), 387–391. For example, an emphasis on personal security for citizens would make human rights and national security in many instances complementary rather than competing concerns. On the broader issue of reconceptualizing security in a

multilateral context, see Emanuel Adler and Michael Barnett, eds., *Security Communities* (Cambridge: Cambridge University Press, 1998), especially Emanuel Adler, "Seeds of Peaceful Change: The OSCE's Security Community-Building Model."

12. For a brief overview, see Jack Donnelly, *International Human Rights* (Boulder, CO: Westview Press, 2nd edn., 1998), chap. 6.
13. The other countries considered in this volume either were preoccupied with internal issues or had no significant economic relations at stake.
14. Some might want to add the inclusion of human rights into UN peacekeeping missions in countries such as Guatemala and Angola. In such cases, however, the willingness to use force on behalf of human rights was modest and entirely conditioned on human rights issues falling within a broader international peace and security mandate. The same is even more clearly true of humanitarian operations in northern and southern Iraq; the human rights of the Kurds were an afterthought, and those of the southern Shiites an even later (and more modestly felt) thought.
15. There is a fairly substantial quantitative literature on human rights and aid in US foreign policy. David Carleton and Michael Stohl, "The Foreign Policy of Human Rights," *Human Rights Quarterly* 7 (May 1985), 205–229, present a classic finding of no linkage. David L. Cingranelli and Thomas E. Pasquarello, "Human Rights Practices and the Distribution of U.S. Foreign Aid to Latin American Countries," *American Journal of Political Science* 29 (August 1985), 539–563, argue for a modest but statistically significant relationship. Some of the most sophisticated recent work has been done by Steven Poe and his colleagues. See, for example, Steven C. Poe and James Meernik, "US Military Aid in the 1980s: A Global Analysis," *Journal of Peace Research* 32 (November 1995), 399–411; Steven C. Poe and Rangsima Sirirangsi, "Human Rights and U.S. Economic Aid during the Reagan Years," *Social Science Quarterly* 75 (September 1994), 494–509; Steven C. Poe, Suzanne Pilatovsky, and Brian Miller, "Human Rights and US Foreign Aid Revisited: The Latin American Region," *Human Rights Quarterly* 16 (August 1994), 539–558; and Steven C. Poe, "Human Rights and U.S. Foreign Aid: A Review of Quantitative Studies and Suggestions for Future Research," *Human Rights Quarterly* 12 (November 1990), 499–512.
16. See, for example, Olav Stokke, ed., *Western Middle Powers and Global Poverty: The Determinants of the Aid Policies of Canada, Denmark, the Netherlands, Norway and Sweden* (Uppsala: Almquist & Wiksell International, 1989).
17. Proposals to establish trade preferences for rights-protective regimes, however, have not been seriously considered, at least in the United States, GATT, and the WTO. For one interesting academic proposal, focusing especially on labour rights, see George DeMartino, "Industrial Policies versus Competitiveness Strategies: In Pursuit of Prosperity in the Global Economy," *International Papers in Political Economy* 3 (No. 2, 1996), 1–42, at pp. 28–34.
18. The rationale for this approach might be that respect for internationally recognized human rights should be routinely expected from all states, rather than treated as an internationally praiseworthy achievement deserving reward. Although I have considerable sympathy toward this view, it ignores the political realities of achieving progress in implementing human rights, especially when starting from a record of substantial, systematic violations. Working positively to support governments making human rights progress may be a far more effective strategy than using aid punitively, if only because systematic violators are unlikely to be swayed by the modest amounts typically involved in aid sanctions. Conversely, international financial support for governments making real progress is not only powerful symbolism but may in some cases have a real political impact.

19. NATO bombardment of Yugoslavia in response to repression and ethnic cleansing in Kosovo, which began as I was completing final revisions on this chapter, also suggests a growing willingness to overrule arguments of sovereignty in the face of severe humanitarian crises, at least in a regional context. Although security interests have been appealed to in justifying the attacks, that rationale seems weak and poorly thought out. The real driving force does seem to be humanitarian crisis. But the continuing reluctance to impose sanctions on Turkey for its systematic human rights violations in Kurdish areas of its country nicely illustrates the enduring priority of security concerns over human rights even in the Western/NATO region.
20. A different sort of primarily internal orientation is represented by the efforts of newly democratic governments in Argentina, Chile, and a number of countries to associate themselves with international human rights norms and initiatives in order to strengthen *national* human rights initiatives and to mobilize national support for human rights.

# Postscript: The Kosovo crisis

*David P. Forsythe*

As this book was being completed during the spring and summer of 1999, the Kosovo crisis erupted in the Balkans. It is highly relevant to the subject of human rights and foreign policy in comparative perspective. We did not want to delay the book project by rewriting various chapters, but we did want to make the book as timely as we possibly could. Hence the decision was taken to add this postscript, even though at the time of writing the full outcomes are not entirely clear.

It is still true in general, as Jack Donnelly noted in his concluding chapter, that although most states now talk a great deal about human rights in foreign policy, they are still reluctant to incur heavy costs in blood or treasure to protect rights beyond their borders. Relatively painless diplomacy for rights is one thing, but military intervention or disruption of important trade is another. As I noted in chapter 2, after the Cold War there was a clear pattern showing reluctance by the United States to take costly action abroad for internationally recognized human rights: in the armed conflicts in former Yugoslavia 1992–1995; regarding the arrest of those indicted for international crimes in that area from 1993; in Somalia from the autumn of 1993; in Rwanda in 1994; in what became Democratic Congo during 1995; and so on. Although other states like Britain and France were willing to take some casualties through participation in United Nations military operations in places such as Bosnia, they too showed little eagerness to intervene to stop atrocities in places such as Rwanda and Democratic Congo, not to mention Algeria and Sri Lanka. As Peter R. Baehr showed in chapter 3, even states like the Netherlands that pride themselves on commitment to internationally recognized human rights were not anxious to take casualties in defending supposed safe areas like Srebrenica in the Bosnian war. Japan had been willing to exercise diplomatic leadership for a liberal democratic peace with human rights in Cambodia. But it eschewed forceful action to dislodge the Khmer Rouge from its sanctuary, and it was well known that the Japanese were averse to taking any casualties for the sake of human rights in Cambodia.

The Kosovo crisis deviates to some degree from this pattern. The crisis shows, among other things, the difficulty of precisely predicting the future based on history. It takes only one major case to alter or refine an evident historical pattern. The general problem has regularly reappeared in social science analysis. Reference to another sequence is instructive.

A persuasive case can be made that Nikita Khrushchev was acting on rather clear history when he tried to place attack missiles in Cuba in 1962. John Kennedy had not been forceful in interaction with the Soviet First Secretary during their debates at the world fair, the US President had not reacted strongly when the Berlin Wall went up, and Kennedy had not been decisive and determined when he called off plans for the United States to provide air cover for the otherwise doomed Bay of Pigs invasion of Cuba. If the West could place missiles in Turkey aimed at the Soviet Union, why could not the East have missiles in Cuba aimed at the United States?

From this view, it was rational for Khrushchev to think that Kennedy would not react strongly to the introduction of missiles in Cuba that, although they could strike parts of the United States mainland, did not change the strategic balance between the two superpowers in any meaningful way. Soviet submarines could already strike much of the United States with their missiles. Soviet missiles in Cuba were more a political than military issue. Yet Kennedy did react strongly to Soviet initiatives in 1962 regarding Cuba, to the point of threatening strategic nuclear war over the missiles and letting the Soviet leadership choose whether to back down or fight. So a historical pattern may yield to new calculations. Kennedy had indeed appeared weak up until October 1962, but he toughened considerably – wisely or not – during the Cuban missile crisis.

The Kosovo crisis represents that rare situation in international relations in which a group of important states altered the immediate past pattern and decided to risk at least some significant things for matters that were primarily and significantly related to human rights – although more traditional geo-political considerations were not totally absent. The actions of the Western liberal states, through the North Atlantic Treaty Organization (NATO), constituted as principled a major use of force that one can identify in the post–Cold War period, and relatively more principled than some past uses of force that were accompanied by claims to humanitarian intervention. I refer to uses of force by India in Pakistan/Bangladesh (1971), by Vietnam in Cambodia (1979), by the United States in Grenada (1982), etc. Ironically, however, the NATO use of force in 1999 remained controversial in many quarters, and not just in Federal Yugoslavia.

I see no reason to doubt NATO's many statements that the trigger for systematic air strikes in Federal Yugoslavia was widespread persecution and repression of ethnic Albanians in the previously autonomous region of Kosovo, combined with the refusal of the government of Slobodan Milosevic to negotiate a peaceful settlement of the ethnic conflict acceptable to the international community. Just as Milosevic had brought about the breakup of Communist Yugoslavia through his assertions of Serbian power at the expense of other ethnic groups, and just as he had actively supported ethnic cleansing and other gross violations of human rights in Bosnia during 1992–1995, so he had organized systematic persecution and repression of the ethnic Albanians in Kosovo. As a result, more and more ethnic Albanians in Kosovo had become radicalized and had joined the armed opposition – the Kosovo Liberation Army. Organized and systematic Serbian repression had been primarily responsible for a low-level guerrilla and civil war in Kosovo, in which violations of the laws of war such as the killing of civilians and captured combatants were carried out by both sides.

What was primarily at issue in Kosovo in 1999 was the nature of Europe. Was it to be rights protective under the banner of liberal democracy, or was it to encompass a chauvinistic and brutal leader like Milosevic? What was primary to NATO were humane values, not protection of strategic resources or alliance partners. Serbian persecution of ethnic Albanians was all the more uncomfortable for NATO because it had passively watched the gross violations of human rights in Bosnia during 1992–1994 carried out primarily by Serbian parties. In Bosnia, Europe was once again the scene of ethnic cleansing and concentration camps. NATO had not reacted quickly or decisively in Bosnia and the situation had become worse. When the United States and NATO became more active and forceful in 1995, the Dayton peace agreement resulted. Milosevic had proved flexible in the face of NATO air strikes, and after Dayton the situation clearly improved in relative terms, even if falling far short of the consolidation of a stable democratic peace. NATO tried to apply these lessons to Kosovo in 1999. It was at least a shift from previous policy, although not a total break with it.

True, commitment to human rights within Europe was not the only issue involved in the Kosovo crisis. President Clinton spoke about the stability of neighbouring states like Albania and Macedonia. There was a fear that continuing Yugoslav repression would drive many of the ethnic Albanians of Kosovo into those neighbouring states – or even into the Yugoslav province of Montenegro – in such numbers that they would prove destabilizing. Indeed, this was the short-term result of NATO's air strikes, as Yugoslavia actually intensified its repression of the Albanians. But, in the long term, NATO was able to coerce Milosevic into allowing a more autonomous Kosovo, and allowing most Albanians who wanted to do so to return to their towns of habitual residence.

Then there was the issue of NATO itself. Recently enlarged, what was the point of NATO if not to guarantee liberal democracy within Europe? Given the weakness of the Russian Federation and its dependence on Western assistance and investment, NATO was certainly not needed for its original purpose of protection against traditional inter-state attack from the East. If NATO could not act "out of area" in such places as the Balkans in the name of human rights and democracy, there would be increasing calls for its dissolution. Doing away with NATO might be good or bad, but as long as it existed it needed a practical mission.

Moreover there was also the concern that Greece might be drawn into the general conflict in ways that proved disruptive to a NATO alliance that included Turkey. Greece had an ethnic Albanian minority, had already engaged in conflict with Macedonia on various issues, and had seen fit to cooperate with the Serbs on still other issues. Surprisingly enough, the Greek government held relatively firm during the weeks of NATO's bombing, despite its public opinion that was decidedly pro-Serbia. But continued instability in the Balkans was definitely not in the interest of NATO, which already was dealing with Greek–Turk friction on its southern flank.

Once engaged, if NATO did not follow through expeditiously and prevail, its future power would be questioned. Likewise, if the United States led NATO into action in the Balkans but did not prevail, United States leadership in Europe would be suspect.

So there were a number of essentially political questions at issue in NATO's involvement in the Kosovo crisis. Yet the main reason given for the air attacks was genuine: the desire to protect ethnic Albanians from persecution by an illiberal Milosevic regime. If ever there were an essentially humanitarian intervention, at least in motivation and intent, this was it. Other claims to strictly humanitarian intervention had not measured up to that standard. India had partitioned arch-rival Pakistan in 1971; Vietnam had set up the friendly Hun Sen puppet government in Cambodia in 1979; the United States had ousted the leftist government of Maurice Bishop in Grenada in 1982; and so on. Particularly in the last case, arguments about humanitarian intervention – namely the rescue of

American medical students – were essentially a smoke screen for geopolitical and ideological strategy.

Serbian repression and intransigence explain the remarkable NATO unity, based on Western public opinion, in support of the 1999 intervention. All 19 NATO members stuck with the air attacks, despite various controversies, throughout the bombings. True, some states seemed less committed than others. Italy expressed a desire for an early end to the violence. Germany floated a peace plan during the second week of attacks. Greek support was clearly suspect. And so on. But despite debate about various aspects of NATO's approach to Kosovo, the West showed exceptional unity. This was because the West held much of the high moral ground in the face of clear and major violations of human rights by the Milosevic regime – against the background of similar violations encouraged by Milosevic in Bosnia. Eventually trainloads of ethnic Albanians dumped by Serbia on the borders of neighbouring states conjured up memories of other European trains – carrying Jews to the concentration camps of Hitler's Third Reich.

To say that NATO had primarily a largely disinterested or altruistic or humanitarian motivation to its action in Kosovo is not to say that the air strikes were uncontroversial. Legally speaking, NATO did not make a strong argument for justification. The UN Security Council had not explicitly authorized the use of force. The West, fearing Chinese and/or Russian vetoes, did not want to put the question of using force to a vote. If a resolution authorizing force had been presented and vetoed, although the onus for blocking action would have been on Beijing and/or Moscow, it would have proved more difficult to go ahead with the bombing. Federal Yugoslavia had not militarily crossed an international frontier at the time the air strikes commenced. Thus it was difficult to argue that NATO was acting in self-defence or in response to a threat to the peace or breach of the peace.

NATO did not argue explicitly, clearly, and forcefully for the concept of humanitarian intervention: the right of outside parties to use coercion to try to protect the rights of those persecuted or repressed within a state. Such a concept was not part of the UN Charter, was disliked by much of the global South, which feared Great Power intrusion into their "domestic" affairs, and might be misused against Western interests in the future. The claim to humanitarian intervention was a fairly radical claim, and NATO lawyers seemed to prefer the more cautious – but mostly unconvincing – claim that previous UN Security Council resolutions had implied authorization for the use of force in Kosovo. Four states of the West had taken this same line in 1991 when forcefully intervening in northern Iraq to protect Iraqi Kurds.

So in 1999 NATO allocated to itself the right to enforce protection of human rights in Kosovo, which made rather large parts of the world nervous. But the counter-option was even more unattractive: to stand aside, as in Bosnia, and observe ethnic cleansing and something on the verge of genocide transpire in the midst of Europe.

Thus Federal Yugoslavia, supported by states such as Russia and China, argued that NATO was engaged in aggression. The argument went as follows: Yugoslavia was acting within its own territory; thus the concept of state sovereignty prevailed; a state had the right to suppress an armed uprising; outside states had no right to compel Belgrade to take any particular course of action regarding the ethnic Albanians. According to the UN Charter, international peace should prevail, especially when the core issue relates to outsiders' conceptions of "justice." Peace was to prevail over a contested version of justice. Under the UN Charter, the only just war is a defensive war.

There were other complications for NATO. We have already noted that for a time its air strikes produced exactly what it said it wanted to prevent: increased repression of the ethnic Albanians, and increased pressures on neighbouring areas from hundreds of thousands of forced migrants. Furthermore, the air strikes clearly killed and wounded a number of innocent civilians, while appearing to some to be disproportionate to the original human rights violations. On the first point, international law had never been clear on the amount of "collateral damage" to civilians that was permitted while engaging in attacks on permissible military targets. On the second point, regarding proportionality, it was difficult to say with precision whether sustained bombing of the military capability of Yugoslavia, including much of its industrial and communications infrastructure, was legitimate. Some of this bombing produced considerable environmental damage – as when NATO bombed a chemical plant near Belgrade. Some observers, and not just in Yugoslavia, believed NATO's course of action, whatever its intentions, was worse – doing more harm – than the original situation. The cure was supposed to be better than the disease. There was, after all, such a thing as the hell of good intentions.

It is relevant to note that the main reason NATO engaged in air strikes – supposedly to deter Milosevic from further actions against the ethnic Albanians – was precisely the assumption that Western public opinion would not tolerate body bags coming home from a military operation that did not involve the core or vital national interests of the NATO states. This lesson was learned not just in Vietnam but also in Lebanon in the early 1980s and Somalia in the early 1990s – and in Bosnia as well. Western public opinion, and related legislative opinion, while backing NATO's controversial course of action during the bombing, did not demand a costly ground war. In this sense there was considerable continuity between the West's response in Kosovo and previous dilemmas in Rwanda and Bosnia.

After two weeks of military action, including the capture by Yugoslavia of three American military personnel, public opinion hardened – at least in the United States. A similar trend had occurred in particularly France when Serb parties had held Western personnel hostage in Bosnia and used them as human shields. Thus for a time there was increased talk in the West of committing ground forces in Kosovo, and the Clinton administration moved toward a call-up of the military reserves. But Milosevic's decision to accept NATO's terms for halting the bombing settled the military issues.

Kosovo was not Rwanda, or Algeria, or Chechnya. In Kosovo, NATO took the decision to engage in forceful intervention largely for human rights reasons. This, after all, was Europe, and NATO had been profoundly embarrassed by its lack of action in the very nasty Bosnian war. The most recent and local lesson of history seemed to be that Milosevic would yield to force, and that use of force was the only way to stop another huge tragedy. But Kosovo was far more important to Milosevic than Bosnia had been, and events in Kosovo had far greater impact on his personal power than events in neighbouring areas in the past. So he stood firm during the early weeks of NATO attacks, was prepared to engage in truly massive and open and gross violations of human rights, and thus exposed evident weaknesses of NATO military strategy. Yet in the end NATO prevailed, with the help of Russian mediation.

At least in Europe, in 1999 the member states of NATO were indeed prepared to undertake significant, costly action to try to protect the rights of others. NATO put its prestige on the line and spent a considerable sum of money, even if it adopted high-altitude bombing to minimize Western casualties. The realists continued to object, arguing that real national interests lay in improved relations with China and Russia and in more attention to terrorism, especially when linked to weapons of mass destruction. Kosovo, even with gross violations of human rights, was far down their list of priorities. For NATO, however, what was at stake in Kosovo was not just the rights of ethnic Albanians but the moral and political composition of Europe. And in that the Western states came to believe they had a vital national interest. NATO's grand strategy was liberal – to create a rights-protective Europe – even if its military strategy and tactics were decidedly realist – to prevail by force of arms.

# Contributors

**Ms. Chiyuki Aoi**
Ph.D. candidate, Columbia University, New York, USA

**Dr. Peter Baehr**
Professor Emeritus, Netherlands Institute of Human Rights, University of Utrecht, The Netherlands

**Professor Sanjoy Banerjee**
Associate Professor, International Relations, San Francisco State University, USA

**Dr. Sergei Chugrov**
Senior Researcher, Institute of World Economy and International Relations, Moscow, Russia

**Professor Jack Donnelly**
Andrew Mellon Distinguished Professor, Graduate School of International Studies, University of Denver, USA

**Dr. Cristina Eguizabal**
Ford Foundation, New York, USA

**Professor David Forsythe**
Charles J. Mach Distinguished Professor, Political Science Department, University of Nebraska, USA

**Dr. Zachary Karabell**
Research Fellow, Miller Center, University of Virginia, USA

**Professor Gábor Kardos**
Department of International Law, Eotvos Lorand University, Budapest, Hungary

**Professor Tiyanjana Maluwa**
Department of Public Law, University of Cape Town, South Africa

**Dr. Sally Morphet**
Research Analyst, British Foreign and Commonwealth Ministry, London, UK

**Professor Yozo Yokota**
Department of Law, University of Tokyo, Japan

# Index

Abacha, General (Nigeria) 257
Abdallah, Farooq (Kashmir) 197
Abkhazia, dispute with Georgia 169–170, 234
Aceh, human rights violations 70, 71, 72
Act of Settlement (England) (1700) 89
*Acta Humana* 229
Advisory Committee on Human Rights and Foreign Policy (Dutch) 53, 58–59, 74
  report 63
Advisory Council on Foreign Affairs (Dutch) 59, 60
Afghanistan
  appointment of Rapporteur 105
  Taliban movement 220
  and UK aid 107
  USSR invasion 303
Africa: and Japanese aid 135
African Charter on Human and Peoples' Rights 263, 270
African Commission on Human and Peoples' Rights 263
African Court on Human and Peoples' Rights 263
African National Congress (ANC) 264
African Nuclear-Weapon-Free-Zone Treaty (Pelindaba Treaty) 268
Ainu people (Japan) 120, 124
Aiyengar, Srinivasa (India) 187
Alatas, Ali (Indonesia) 72
Albania
  and national minorities 67
  US democracy assistance programme 43
Albright, Madeleine (US Secretary of State) 26
Alexander II, Tsar, Emperor of Russia 150
Alfonsín, Rául (Argentina) 303–304
Algeria, human rights abuses 269
Allende, Salvador (Chile) 281
Alliance des Forces Démocratiques pour la Libération du Congo-Zaire (AFDL) 261
Alliance for Peace 290
American Anthropological Association 292
American Bar Association 28
American corporates: and human rights 25
American Declaration of the Rights and Duties of Man 29, 288–289
American hegemony 211, 213, 219, 318
American individualism 22–3, 28

American national self-image 45
Amnesty International 57, *58*
  Argentinian human rights violations 305
  Indian human rights violations 198, 199
  and Latin America 281
  and Pinochet case 108
  reports on Iranian human rights abuses 208–209, 212
  reports on Mexico 286
  role in Eastern Europe 229
  Russian cooperation 160–161
  and sanctions against Iraq 186
  and UK 92, 98, 99
Amnesty International-USA 24
Amritsar massacre (India 1919) 187
Andean Commission of Jurists 282
Andrés Pérez, Carlos (Venezuela) 299
Angola
  and arms sales 258, 268
  UN peacekeeping operations 64
Annan, Kofi (UN Secretary-General) 36
Antall, József (Hungary) 237, 240, 241
Anti-Apartheid Movement 90
anti-humanitarian interventions, US 23
anti-personnel land mines ban 36
anti-Semitic campaign, Poland 226
Anti-Slavery Society (human rights NGO) 99
Antigua and Barbuda, Inter-American human rights regime *284*
Arbenz Guzmán, Jacob (Guatemala) 289–290
Argentina
  economy/foreign trade and investment 301, 302, 304
  human rights issues 278, *283*, *284*, 288, 291, 292, 306
  hydroelectric project 303
  invasion of Falkland Islands (Malvinas) 303
  military regimes 57, 281, 302–303
  nationalism and foreign policy 301–306
  politics 301–302
  relationship with USSR 303
  UK policy towards 111
  and UN peacekeeping operations 305, 306
  US alignment 305, 306
  and World War II involvement 302
Argentinian League for the Rights of Man 282
Arias Sánchez, Oscar (Costa Rica) 300
Aristide, Jean-Bertrand (Haiti) 294
Armenia, CIS agreement on assistance to refugees 168
arms sales
  and human rights issues 269
  and South Africa 251, 257–258, 266, 268
  UK embargoes 93, 107, 108
Armscor (South Africa) 268
Article 19 (human rights NGO) 99
Ashibe, Professor Nobuyoshi (Japan) 117
Asia
  attitude to human rights 125–126
  security concern 126
Asia Watch (HRNGO) 198, 199
Asia–Pacific Economic Cooperation network 126
Asian Development Bank (ADB) 126, 128–129, 130
Asian Development Fund (ADF) 129
Asmal, Kader (South Africa) 251
Assam: insurgency 190
Association of South East Asian Nations (ASEAN) 125
  Regional Forum 126, 127
asylum seekers 229
  in Russia 168
  South American tradition 278–280
Aung San Suu Kyi (Myanmar) 139, 314
Ayodhya mosque destruction 190, 192
Azerbaijan: CIS agreement on assistance to refugees 168

Baby, M.A. (India) 195–196
Baha'is group (Iran) 217, 221
Bahamas: Inter-American human rights regime *284*
Bahrain: human rights violations 220
Bahujan Samaj Party (BSP: India) 192
Baltics, the: and Russia 166–168
Bangkok Declaration on Human Rights (1993) 125, 126, 127
Bangladesh 189
Barbados: Inter-American human rights regime *284*
Batista, Fulgencio (Cuba) 279
Batista regime (Cuba) 290
Bay of Pigs (Cuba) invasion 336
Bayly, C.A. 188
Belarus
  CIS agreement on assistance to refugees 168

and Russian foreign policy 164, 165–166
Belize: Inter-American human rights regime *284*
Bellona (Norwegian environmental foundation) 155
Bengal famine 188
Berlin Wall 336
Bharatiya Janata Party (BJP) 182, 190, 192, 194, 197
bilateral policies
Dutch 55, 68–75
and human rights 13–16
Japan 134–140
US 39–40
Bill of Rights (England) (1689) 88, 116
Bishop, Maurice (Grenada) 338
Bohemia 224
Bolivia
human rights *283*, *284*, 291
UK aid policy 93, 106
Bolshevik revolution (1917) 149
Bosnia
and Dayton Accord 33
and ethnic cleansing 340
human rights violations 337
Muslims 219
NATO action 219–220
and US foreign policy 44
and violation of Genocide Convention 157
Botswana
and human rights violations 258
and Lesotho instability 262
Boutros-Ghali, Boutros (former UN Secretary-General) 65
Brazil
asylum provision 279
crimes of violence 285
human rights issues *283*, *284*, 291, 294
and political persecution 278
Brazilian Commission for Peace and Justice (HRNGO) 282
Breed Mensenrechten Overleg (BMO: Netherlands) 58
Brezhnev leadership: and Helsinki Agreement 151
Britain *see* United Kingdom
British Broadcasting Corporation (BBC) 183
British colonialism, effects on India 188–189
British Commonwealth 105–106
*British Policy towards the United Nations* (FPD: 1978) 91
British Refugee Council (NGO) 99
British Secret Service 206
Broek, Hans van den (The Netherlands) 60, 66
Brussels Treaty 100
Buddhism: in Russia 154
Bureau of Human Rights and Humanitarian Affairs (US) 330
Bureau for the Protection of Rights of National and Ethnic Minorities (Hungary) 229
Burgers, J. Herman (The Netherlands) 57
Burke, Edmund 312
Burma
and development assistance programmes 69, 108
and European Union 66, 102
and international human rights 316
and US foreign policy 44
Burton, Dan (US Congressman) 201
Bush administration
and human rights treaties 28
and Iran 207
and Santiago Declaration 30
Bush, George (US president) 137, 185, 294
and human rights 24
and Somalia 43
and trade with China 329
and US intervention in Panama 40

Calderón Guardia, Rafael 297
Cambodia
1997 coup 130
and development assistance programmes 40, 69
and Japanese 127, 134, 141, 336
OCR loans 129
and UN peacekeeping missions 34–35, 64
Camdessue, Michel (IMF) 162
Cameron Commission (1995) 268
Canada
Inter-American human rights regime *284*
and NAFTA 31
and national self-image 2
protest against Romania 233
Canadian Bar Association 292

capital punishment issue 160
in Costa Rica 297
in Eastern European countries 229
in Russia 154
*see also* death penalty
Capithorne, Maurice Danby (Canada) 212–213, 218
Caputo, Dante (Argentina) 304
Carazo Odio, Rodrigo (Costa Rica) 299
Caribbean Legion and Pact 298
Carter administration
and human rights issues 28, 29, 39, 330
and Latin America 30, 288, 326
and UK governments 93, 110
Carter, Jimmy (US president) 29, 207
and Argentina 303
and human rights issues 281, 288, 314, 330
and Iran (1980) 40
caste system (India) 188, 194
Castro, Fidel (Cuba) 290, 295
Catherine the Great, Empress of Russia 150
Central African Republic: UK policy towards 111
Central America
and human rights 278, 282
refugee crisis 280
Central Europe: history 224–228
Chad: human rights violations 265
Charities Aid Foundation (NGO) 99
Chechnya: conflict and human rights violations 154, 161, 162, 234
children's issues
Brazilian street children 285
child labour in India 200–201
mortality rate in Iraq 185
right to education 169
rights in Japan 120
UN Convention on the Rights of the Child 105
UN Principles Relating to the Protection and Welfare of Children 62
Chile
and development assistance programmes 69, 134
human rights issues 37, 278, 288, 291
Inter-American human rights regime *284*
military regimes 57, 281
UK aid policies 93, 106, 111
Chiluba, Frederick (Zambia) 265
China
and American corporates 25
and European Union 66, 102
G7 five-year trade agreement 138
and human rights issues 9, 12, 25, 37, 126, 197
Russian stance 159
and Japanese aid/investment policies 133, 135, 137, 141
nuclear tests 138
OCR loans 129
Tiananmen Square incident 107, 141, 270
and US foreign policy 44
World Bank loans 137–138
Chirac, Jacques (France) 66
Christian Democratic party (CDA: Dutch) 59
Christianity 89, 225
Christopher group (US) 330
Citizens' Advisory Council on Human Rights (Netherlands) 6
Civic Assistance Committee (Russian HRNGO) 169
civil–political rights 37, 101, 288
Dutch policy 52, 54
Russia 152–153
Clinton administration
and Dayton Accord (1995) 31
and economic and military aid 39–40
and human rights issues/treaties 27, 28, 29, 38
and Iran 207
and Kashmir issue 200
and NATO military intervention in Kosovo 341
and OAS 30
Clinton, William Jefferson (US president) 27, 305
and Denver summit (1997) 23
and human rights 24
and Kosovo crisis 337–338
and UN criminal court 36
and US intervention in Haiti 40
Cock, J. 268, 269
Cold War
crisis in Guatemala (1951) 289–290
Cuban crisis (1959–1962) 290
and human rights issues 184, 252–253, 276, 291
Russian approach to human rights 156
UK bilateral policies 106–109

collective human rights 53
  and Russian foreign policy 158–159
collectivism 150
Colombia 278
  guerrilla violence 285
  human rights violations 292, 293
  Inter-American human rights regime *284*
  and international human rights treaties *283*
  and liberal democracy 295
  repression 281
Colombian Commission of Jurists 282
colonialism
  and Gandhi 313
  and human rights 276
Commonwealth Heads of State and Government
  Declaration of Commonwealth Principles (1971) 105
  meeting (1995) 261
  meetings (1971, 1981, 1991) 105–106
  Working Party on Human Rights 105–106
Commonwealth Human Rights Initiative (NGO) 99
Commonwealth of Independent States (CIS) 163
  and Constitutional Court (Russia) ruling 169
  and enforced migration/refugees issues 168, 169
Communist Party: Czechoslovakia/Poland 226, 227
Conference on the Humanitarian Dimension of the CSCE, Copenhagen (1990) 233
Conference on Security and Cooperation in Europe (CSCE) 29, 30, 67
  Conference on the Human Dimension (CHD) 103–104
  and Eastern European countries 156, 233, 314
  Follow-up Meeting (Vienna 1989) 103
  review conference (Madrid 1980) 103
  UK participation 87, 91
  *see also* Organization for Security and Cooperation in Europe (OSCE)
Congress of South African Trade Unions (COSATU) 257
Constitutional Court of Hungary 230
Constitutional Tribunal (1985: Poland) 226
constitutions 89
  Japan 116–118
  Russia 153–154
consumerism: and personal privacy 228
Contadora Group (Costa Rica) 300
corporate sector: roles in liberal democracies 7–8
Costa Rica
  asylum provision 279
  and capital punishment 297
  and Caribbean Pact 298
  Constitution 297, 298
  human rights issues 6, 12, 277, *283*, *284*, 289, 312
    and foreign policy 296–300
  military forces 297
  and religious tolerance 297
  and US foreign policy 305
Council of Europe (CE) 2, 10, 96, 277, 291, 317
  British input 100–101
  Dutch involvement 67–68
  Framework Convention for the protection of national minorities 100–101
  House of Commons (UK) debate 110
  Ministerial Conference on Human Rights (1985) 100
  participation of Eastern European countries 160, 232, 241
Country Reports on Human Rights Practices 93
crime: in Latin America 285
Crimean Republic: and ethnic Russians 164–165
criminal offences/political offences: distinction 278
Crisis Management and Humanitarian Assistance directorate (Dutch) 76
Croatia 33, 67, 68, 224
Cuba
  and human rights issues 295
    violations 159, 238, 286, 291, 294, 302
  Inter-American human rights regime *284*
  politics and military regimes 279, 285
  relationship with South Africa 256, 266–268
  UK policy 111
Cuban crisis (1959–1962) 290
cultural relativism: and Islamic ideology 214
Current Digest of the Soviet Press 183

Czech Citizenship Law (1992) 233
Czech Republic
  citizenship 233
  history 224–228
  and human rights issues 228–231, 233, 244
  and IFIs 234
  multilateral policy 232–239
  politics 225, 227, 229–230
Czechoslovakia
  Constitutional Court 225
  Russian invasion (1968) 151

D66 (Dutch radical liberal party) 59
Dayton Accord (1995) 31, 33, 337
De Witt, Johan 50
death penalty
  and European Convention on Human Rights (Protocol 6) 230
  in Hungary 230
  Japan 123
  and Latin America countries *283*
  in Poland 229, 231, 232
  US policy 38
  *see also* capital punishment issue
Declaration of Independence (US) (1776) 89
decolonization, and India 312–313
Democratic Alliance of Hungarians 243
Democratic Republic of Congo *see* Zaire
democratization: and human rights 256
Denmark: and Chinese human rights violations 37
Denver summit (1997) 23
Department of Foreign Affairs (South Africa) 253–254
Department for International Development (UK) 95, 96
developing countries: and human rights violations 54–55
Development Assistance Committee (DAC) 139
development (national): rights and theory 62–63, 287
developmental loans policies: and Germany 10
Dili (East Timor) massacre 71–72
discrimination
  against girls and women (India) 191
  racial 37, 229
Doctors Without Borders (Médecins San Frontières) 25
domestic factors
  and foreign policy-making 8–9
  Russia 152–155
Dominican Republic 278
  and Caribbean Pact 298
  Inter-American human rights regime *284*
  and international human rights treaties *283*
  relations with Argentina 302–303
  US intervention 40
Donnelly, Jack: on India 187
drug trafficking 285
Dubcek, Alexander (Czechoslovakia) 226
Dupuy, Professor Pierre-Marie 116
Dutch Labour Party 74

East Asia: and Japanese aid 135
East Pakistan (Bangladesh): and human rights violations 324
East Timor 328
  invasion by Indonesia and human rights violations 70, 71, 140, 266
East–West relations 157
  détente 151
Eastern Europe
  bilateral policies 239–244
  domestic factors 228–231
  geopolitical identity of countries 225
  and IFIs 234
  and Japanese 122, 131, 140, 141
  minorities' rights 100–101, 239
  multilateral policies 232–239
  public sector resources 42
  transition from communism 230
Echeverría, Luis (Mexico) 299
ecological concerns, and IFIs 32, 256
Economic Commission for Latin America (ECLAC) 287
economic relations: and human rights 55
economic sanctions *see* sanctions
Ecuador
  Inter-American human rights regime *284*
  and international human rights treaties *283*
  and UN Human Rights High Commissioner 289
education
  in India 200–201
  and International Bill of Rights 169
Egeland, Jan (Norway) 49, 77–78

Eglin, Colin (South Africa) 250
Eisenhower administration
  and Guatemala 290
  and human rights treaties 28
El Salvador 44
  EU action 101
  human rights issues and violations *283*, *284*, 291, 292
  repression and political murders 24–5, 281
  UN involvement 34–35, 37
  US foreign assistance and studies 30, 39
environmental damage from NATO air strikes in Kosovo 340
Eötvös, József (Hungary) 227
Equatorial Guinea
  foreign aid 93
  human rights violations 265
  UK policy 111
Esquipulas Accord 300
Esquipulas II agreement 295
Estonia
  Law on Citizenship 167
  and national minorities 67, 166–168
Ethiopia: UK aid policy 93, 106, 111
ethnic cleansing: in Yugoslavia (former) 337, 340
ethnic cleansing, *see also* genocide
European Airbus company 66
European Bank for Reconstruction and Development (EBRD) 33, 131, 234
European Charter of Human Rights (ECHR) 100
European Commission of Human Rights 66, 67
European Committee for the Prevention of Torture and Inhuman or Degrading Treatment or Punishment 233
European communists: and human rights 30–1
European Convention on Human Rights (ECHR) (1953) 69, 90, 110, 167
  Article 3 170
  and Eastern Europe 229, 232
  Protocol 6 230
European Convention for the Prevention of Torture and Inhuman or Degrading Treatment or Punishment 100
European Convention for the Protection of Human Rights and Fundamental Freedoms 67
European Council of Ministers 66
European Court of Human Rights 10, 67, 90, 100, 320
  acceptance by Eastern European countries 232
  and British citizens 97, 100–101, 109
  and Russian Constitution 154
European Court of Justice (EU) 10
European Economic Community (EEC) *see* European Union (EU)
European Human Rights Commission 109
European Parliament 66
European Social Charter (1965) 90, 100, 104
  acceptance by Eastern European countries 232
European Union (EU) 2, 10
  and British involvement 91, 101–102
  and civil and political rights 101
  Declaration on Human Rights 102
  and economic sanctions 75–76
  and economic, social, and cultural rights 101
  membership 68, 87
  and right to development 101
  Working Group on Human Rights 102
Executive Outcomes (South Africa) 257
Eximbank 303
Export-Import Bank 140
extradition 108, 170–171, 278
Extradition Act (UK) (1989) 108

Falkland Islands (Malvinas): Argentinian invasion 303
Fédération Internationale des Droits de l'Homme 281
Figueres Ferrer, José (Don Pepe) (Costa Rica) 298–299, 300
Figueres Olsen, José, María (Costa Rica) 300
Finnemore, Martha 99
Ford Foundation: and human rights 281–282
Foreign and Commonwealth Office (FCO) (UK) 91, 92, 95
foreign democratic development: and liberal democracies 14
Foreign Policy Bureau (FPO) (Japan) 121
foreign policy-making and domestic factors 8–9
freedom
  of conscience 62, 152, 154
  Gandhi's conception 187

freedom (cont.)
  of the press 89
  of residence 169
  of speech 152
French Declaration of the Rights of Man and of the Citizen (1789) 116
French Revolution: Russian hostility towards 150
Frondizi, Arturo (Argentina) 302
Fujimori, Alberto K. (Peru) 140, 294–295
fundamentalist groups 219, 220
*Fundamentum* 229

Galtieri, Leopoldo (Argentina) 303
Gambia, the
  curtailment of British aid (1991) 109
  development assistance programmes 69
  Japanese aid policy 140
Gandhi, Indira: assassination 178, 182
Gandhi, Mahatma 186–188, 313
Gandhi, Rajiv: assassination 190, 201
General Agreement on Tariffs and Trade (GATT) 200–201
Geneva Conventions on Human Rights in Armed Conflict (1949) 11, 232
genocide 35, 157
  *see also* ethnic cleansing
Genocide Convention (1948) 28
Georgia: dispute with Abkhazia 169–170
Germany: and developmental loans policies 10
Gingrich, Newt (US) 314
Glasnost Fund 161
Gorbachev, Mikhail (Russia) 151, 152, 154
Government Communications Headquarters (GCHQ) (UK) 105
Government Office for Hungarian Minorities Abroad 231
governmental repression: and IMF policies 32
Greece: human rights issues 37
Greece
  and Kosovo crisis 338
  military junta 57, 281
Grenada
  Inter-American human rights regime *284*
  US intervention 40
Grotius, Hugo (1583–1645) 50, 89
Group of 7 (G7) 106
  Summits 137, 138
Group of 77 287
Group for Mutual Support (Guatemala) 282
Guatemala 37, 294
  developmental assistance programmes 69
  and human rights 276, *283*, *284*
    violations 286, 291, 292
  and Nicaraguan refugees 279
  and US foreign policy 30, 40, 44
Gulf War 179, 328
  Argentinian participation 305
  and India 181
Gusmao, Xanana (East Timor) 266
Guyana: Inter-American human rights regime *284*

Habeas Corpus Acts (English) (1640, 1679) 88
Hague, The: as international legal capital of the world 65
Haiti
  human rights issues 34, 37, 69, 282, *283*, *284*
    violations 184, 286, 291
  military dictatorship 34, 305
  US and international intervention 40, 236, 294, 306
Hamas fundamentalist group 219
Hastings, Warren 188
Havana: severence of diplomatic ties with Argentina 302
Havana Convention (1928) 278
Helms, Senator Jesse 28–29, 36
Helms–Burton bill (US) 219, 305
Helsinki Accords (1975) 102–103
  Basket Three 30, 31
  Charter 77 226
  and Soviet bloc 151, 314
Helsinki Commission 25
Helsinki Watch (HRNGO) 30
Hercegovina: Yugoslav violation of Genocide Convention 157
Hezbollah faction (Lebanon) 207
Hezbollah fundamentalist group 219
Hezbollah Party 210
High Commissioner on National Minorities (OSCE) 67
Hindu nationalism 180, 182, 192, 203
Hindu–Muslim issue 188–189, 190, 192
Honduras
  human rights issues *283*, *284*, 292
  and refugees 279

Horiguchi, Yusuke (IMF) 162
Horn, Gyula (Hungary) 241
House of Commons (UK) 98, 103
  Council of Europe debate 110
  and human rights 106–107
House of Lords (UK) 98, 108
human rights *see* international human rights; *see also under* named countries
Human Rights Commission (Russian) 168
Human Rights Commission (South Africa) 259
Human Rights Declaration 90
*Human Rights in Foreign Policy* (UK FPDs 1991, 1996) 91–94, 101
Human Rights, Good Governance and Democratization directorate (Dutch) 76
Human Rights Policy Department (HRPD) (UK) 95–96
Human Rights and Refugee Division (Japan) 120, 121
Human Rights Watch (NGO) 24, 99, 161, 184, 186
Humanist Committee on Human Rights (HOM) 58
humanitarian intervention 10–11, 40–41
Hun Sen (Cambodia) 127, 130
  government 338
Hungarian Centre for the Protection of Rights 229
Hungarian Helsinki Committee 229
Hungarian–Romanian Basic Treaty 241–243
Hungarian–Slovak Basic Treaty 241–243
Hungary
  bilateral policy/treaties 239–244
  and communism 151, 225–226
  history 224–228
  and human rights issues 9, 228–231, 230
  and international aid 140, 234
  and minority rights 67, 231
  multilateral policy 232–239
  politics and transition to democracy 226–227, 229–230
Hussein, Saddam 185, 328

Ibero–American summits 295
*Ideario Costaricense* (Figueres) 298
Iliescu, President (Romania) 242
illegal immigrants: and education 169
Illía, Arturo (Argentina) 302
Index on Censorship (NGO) 99
India
  and arms sales restrictions 269
  Constitution (1951) 186
  development/investment potential 10, 191–192
  discrimination
    against girls and women 191
    caste system 188, 194
  economic issues 179, 191, 203
  education issues 191, 200–201
  human rights issues 198–199
    child labour 200–201
    and domestic factors 190–194
    and foreign policy 178–186, 194–203
    historical origins 186–190
    international scrutiny 318–319
    intervention policies 11
    violations 181, 182, 200
  independence and partition 186, 189, 312–313, 338
  international institutions 194–196
  and international terrorism issues 316
  and Kashmir issue 180–181, 196–198
  military interventions 178
  political issues 5–6, 179, 186, 190, 192
  poverty 191
  relations with China 181
  relations with Soviet bloc 189–190
  relations with the West 181
  religion and philosophy 187, 189
  and self-determination 316
  *see also* Hindu nationalism; Pakistan; Tiananmen Square incident
Indian National Congress 187, 189
Indian Peace Keeping Force (IPKF) 201
indigenous peoples 12, 124
  in Latin America 281, 291–292
Indo-China: political instability 126
Indo-Sri Lankan Accord 201
Indonesia
  and the Dutch 51, 69–72, 77, 317, 321
  and East Timor 71–72, 140, 266
  human rights violations 69–72, 266
  and Islamic ideology 210
  Japanese aid and trade 126, 129, 139
  and South Africa 256–257, 269
  Suharto regime 57, 70
  UK aid 93, 106
Institutional Revolutionary Party (Mexico) 280

Inter-American Commission on Human Rights (1959) 290
Declaration of Indigenous Rights 292
Inter-American Conference on Problems of War and Peace (1945) 289
Inter-American Convention on the Forced Disappearance of Persons (1994) *284*
Inter-American Convention on Human Rights (1985) 29, *284*, 289
Inter-American Convention to Prevent and Punish Torture (1985) *284*
Inter-American Court of Human Rights 10, 284, 290, 299, 318
Inter-American Development Bank 33
Inter-American Human Rights Commission, Working Group on Democracy and Human Rights 292
Inter-American Human Rights Commission and Court 293
Inter-American Human Rights Convention (1969) 290, 291
Inter-American human rights regime *284*
Inter-Governmental Group on Indonesia (IGGI) 70, 93
intergovernmental organizations (IGOs) 1, 13
International Alert (HRNGO) 99
International Bill of Rights 3, 9, 15, 16, 29, 123
and education 169
endorsement by Eastern European countries 232
and Japan 122–125
and Russia 156
and South Africa 258–260
US ambivalence towards 22, 27–29, 33, 43
International Commission of Jurists (NGO) 58, 92, 99, 281
International Committee of the Red Cross 38
International Conference for Central American Refugees (CIREFCA) 279
International Court of Justice 28, 65
International Covenant on Civil and Political Rights (ICCPR) 4, 9, 27, 196, 232
on the Abolition of the Death Penalty 62
Conscientious Objection to Military Service 62
and Japan 123, 124, 132
and Latin America countries *283*, 288, 304
and South Africa 259
and Soviet Union 156, 169
and UK 87, 90, 91
and US 28, 317
International Covenant on Economic, Social, and Cultural Rights (ICESCR) 3, 27, 29, 33, 75, 196
and Japan 123, 124
and Latin America countries *283*, 288, 304
and South Africa 259
and Soviet Union 169
and UK 87, 90, 91
International Criminal Court 35, 95
international criminal justice 11–12, 35
International Criminal Law Treaty (1889) 278
International Criminal Tribunal for former Yugoslavia 65
International Federation of the Red Cross 140
international financial institutions (IFIs)
and human rights 10
and Japan 128–131
and US 31–33
international human rights 310
and arms sales 269
and bilateral policies 13–16
effectiveness and evaluation of policies 324–331
initiatives 323–324
moral inconsistencies 327–331
purposes 325–327
instruments 9–10
intensity of commitments 321–324
and national attitudes 319–320
and national domestic factors 4
and national identity 311–314
national initiatives 16
NGOs' role in Eastern Europe 229
observer missions 282
and political issues 5–6
scrutiny 317–319
treaties 27–8, 271–272
and use of force 322–323
International Labour Organization (ILO) 89, 96, 121
international law
development 110

first world conference (1899) 150
and human rights 213, 276, 314
and military interventions 340
and South African apartheid 270
International League for Human Rights 281
International Monetary Fund (IMF)
and Eastern European countries 234
and human rights issues 32, 256
and Japan 128
support of Russian monetary policy 162
and US 44
international monitoring 320
international politics: and ending of Cold War 184
International Red Cross
and Chechnya conflict 161
expulsion of workers by Iran 212
International Socialists 299
internationalism 24, 319, 320
Interrights (HRNGO) 99, 229
Iran 3
bilateral/multilateral policies 218–220
Constitution and monarchy 211, 215, 221
and fundamentalist groups 219, 220
human rights issues 66, 221, 311, 316, 317–318
and domestic factors 210–218
historical background 206–210
and Islam 209, 210, 214, 219, 220–221
monarchy and revolution 207, 209, 210, 314
and Muslims 210, 219–220
religious law 216–217
and South Africa 266–268
and terrorism 207–208, 213, 219
UK policies towards 107, 111
and US 40, 207–208, 211–212, 219
Iraq
human rights issues 66, 238
Russian foreign policy 158
UK arms exports 107
and UN 34, 235
sanctions issues 158, 179, 181, 184–185
and US media 25
Irian Jaya 51, 70, 71
Ishiwara, Takashi (Japan) 138
Islam 211
ideology 154, 210, 214
law (sharia) 214, 314
Islamic Jihad fundamentalist group 219
Israel 33, 37
Ivan IV (the Terrible) of Russia 150

Jackson–Vanik amendment (US) 39, 326
Jamaica: Inter-American human rights regime *284*
Japan
bilateral/multilateral policies 122–134, 134–140
bureaucratic system 119–120, 128, 141–142
and China 130, 133, 135, 137, 138, 141
colonial and military history 127
Constitution 116–118
foreign aid and trade 122, 126, 131, 134–140
policy 115, 133, 137, 141
human rights issues 6, 11, 115, 120, 134, 141
domestic factors 119–121
regional development 125–128, 130–131
violations 116, 138, 141
Human Rights and Refugee Division 120, 121, 123
and IFIs 128–131
imperial system 115–117
and International Bill of Rights 122–125
and Iranian terrorism 219
legal system 123–124
as mediator between East and West 126–127
and Myanmar 138
Official Development Assistance (ODA) Charter 119, 122, 135–140
politics 6, 119–120, 123
and United Nations 122–123, 131–134
Jeszenszky, Géza (Hungary) 236–237
Jiménez, Pérez (Venezuela) 278
John Paul II, Pope 155
Jubilee Campaign (UK NGO) 99
Judaism: in Russia 154
Juliana, Queen of the Netherlands 70
Justice and Peace (HRNGO: Colombia) 282

Kabila government (Zaire) 40
Kabila, Laurent (Democratic Republic of Congo) 260
Kaifu, Toshiaki (Japan) 131, 140

Kashmir 196–198, 203
 and human rights issues 180–181, 182
 human rights issues 183, 202
 and political conflict 190, 193–194, 316
Kaunda, Kenneth (Zambia) 265
Kazakhstan
 and development assistance programmes 69, 168
 and protection of national minorities 67
 and Russian foreign policy 164, 166
*Keizai Doyu Kai* (Japan Association of Corporate Executives) 138
Kennan, George 23
Kennedy administration, and human rights treaties 28
Kennedy, John F. (US president) 290
 and Cuban crisis 336
Kenya: Japanese aid policy 140
Khamene'i, Ayatollah Ali (Iran) 211, 216
Khatami, Dr Mohammed 209, 214, 215, 216, 221
Khobar (Saudi Arabia): bombing of American soldiers 207
Khomeini, Ayatollah Ruhollah 207, 209, 210, 211, 215
Khrushchev, Nikita 164, 290
 and Cuban crisis 336
Khurshid, Salman (India) 194–195, 197
Kissinger, Henry (US) 30, 252
Klaus government (Czech Republic) 230
Kooijmans, Professor (UN Special Rapporteur on Torture) 63
Koran 209, 214, 216, 217
Korea 126, 127
Kosovo crisis 335–341
Kovács, László (Hungary) 234, 237
Kovalyov, Sergei (Russia human rights activist) 154
Kozyrev, Andrei (Russia) 167–168
Kozyrev, Minister of Foreign Affairs (Russia) 172
Kreca, Judge (Russia) 157
Kurczewski, Professor Jacek (Poland) 228
Kurdish problem 69
Kuwait: Iraqi invasion 184–185
Kyrgyzstan
 and assistance to refugees 168
 protection of national minorities 67

Labour Party (PvdA: Dutch) 59
Latin America
 economic weakness 285, 293
 foreign policies 8, 286–296
 human rights issues 8, 277, 280, *283*, 286, 287
  inter-American system 289–293
  policies 280–286
  women's rights 292
 Japanese aid 135
 non-intervention principle 280
 as a nuclear-free zone 305
 politics and democracy 6, 278–279, 285, 293–296
 and US 39, 280
Latin American Confederacy Treaty (1848) 278
Latvia: and national minorities 67, 166–168
Lauterpacht, H. 88
Law on Citizenship (Estonia) 167
Laws of Manu (India) 188
laws of war 35
Lawyers Committee for International Human Rights (US) 24, 281
League of Nations 89, 90
least developed countries (LDCs): Myanmar 139
Lebanese Christian militia: arms embargo (1995) 268
Lebanon, and human rights violations 64, 159
Lesotho
 human rights issues 256, 258
 instability 262, 264, 268
 restoration of democracy 260
Letowska, Ewa (Poland) 226
Letsie III, King of Lesotho 262
Levi Strauss: and human rights issues 25
Liberación Nacional party (Costa Rica) 299
liberal democracies 49–78
 corporate sector roles 7–8
 and human rights issues 4–5, 230
 and loan decisions and development 14, 32
Liberal Democratic Party (LDP: Japan) 119, 121–122
Liberal Party (VVD: Dutch) 59–60
Liberation Tigers of Tamil Eelam (LTTE) 201
Libya 158, 266–268
Licensing Act (England) (1695) 89
Lithuania: and minority rights 67, 166–167, 243–244

Locke, John (1632–1704) 89, 116
Lockerbie air disaster 267
López Michelsen, Alfonso (Colombia) 299
Luard, Evan (UK) 91, 110–11
Lukashenko, Alexander (Belarus) 165–166

Maastricht Treaty *see* Treaty on European Union
MacArthur, General Douglas 116
Macedonia 67, 338
Magna Carta (England) (1215) 89, 96, 116, 312
Maintenance of Public Order Act (Japan) (1925) 116
Malawi: and aid issues 69, 109, 140
Mali: and development assistance programmes 69
Managua Protocol 294
Mandela, Nelson 258–259
  address to United Nations General Assembly 263–264
  and human rights issues 254–255, 260, 261, 262–263, 267
  as mediator 260, 261
  and South African foreign policy 254
  visits to East Asia and Indonesia (1966, 1997) 251, 266
Mandelbaum, Michael 26
Martin Luther King Society 229
Mauretania: and development assistance programmes 69
Mbeki, Thabo (South Africa) 254
Meciar, Vladimir (Slovakia) 242
Médecins San Frontières 25
media 1
  American 25, 183, 200
  British 99, 183
  in Hungary 230
  in Iran 215
  Islamic Republic radio station 214–215
  press freedom 89, 215, 220, 318
  Russian 163, 166
Menem, Carlos (Argentina) 304–306
mentally-handicapped rights: Japan 120
Mercosur: South America regional integration treaty 295
Mexico
  and human rights issues 5, 31, *283*, *284*, 294
  political and economic crisis 285, 286, 295
  and refugees 279, 280
Middle East 135
  peace process 158–159
Mierlo, Hans van (Dutch Foreign Minister) 68, 76
migration: enforced 169–170
military
  conscientious objection 62
  interventions 30
  regimes 277, 278–279
  UK Military Assistance Training Scheme 95
Milosevic regime: and Serbian repression 338–339
Milosevic, Slobodan (Yugoslavia) 337, 338, 340
Ministry of Foreign Affairs (Dutch) 60
Ministry of Foreign Affairs (Japan) 119–120, 137
minority rights 67
  Baha'is 221
  in Baltic states 167
  in Eastern Europe 100–101, 226, 231, 239, 241–244
    Romania 226, 233, 238
  Japan 123
  in Latin America 281
  Russian 167, 169–170, 316
Minority Rights Group (NG0) 99
Mobuto government (Congo) 40
Mobutu Sese Seko (Democratic Republic of Congo) 252, 260
Mokhehle, Ntsu (Lesotho) 262
Moldova 67, 170
Monge Álvarez, Luis Alberto (Costa Rica) 300
Montenegro: and Kosovo crisis 338
Montevideo Treaty (1933) 278
Morocco 210, 264
Mossadegh, Muhammad (Iran) 206, 209
Mothers and Grandmothers of the Plaza de Mayo (Argentina) 282
Mozambique
  and human rights violations 258, 268
  Japanese aid policy 141
  UN peacekeeping operations 64, 134
Mswati, King of Swaziland 265
Mullerson, R. 252–253
Muslim League 189
Muslims
  and Bosnia conflict 219–220
  Indian 197

Muslims (cont.)
  massacre in Srebrenica 64–65
  Shiite 210, 217
Mustazaffin Foundation (Iran) 211, 213
Myanmar (Burma) 127
  human rights issues 133, 238
  and Japanese aid 135, 138, 139, 141
  State Law and Order Restoration Council (SLORC) 133
Myrna Mack Foundation (Guatemala) 282

Namibia: and UN peacekeeping missions 34–35, 64
Nasseri, Sirous (Iran) 218
National Action Party (PAN: Mexico) 291
National Alliance of Women's Organizations (NGO) 99
national attitudes to international human rights *320*
National Conventional Arms Control Committee (South Africa) 251
National Endowment for Democracy agency (US) 41
National Human Rights Commission (India) 193, 199
National Institute for War Documentation (RIOD: Dutch) 64
national self-images 2–4, 310, 314, 315, 319
  American 21, 22, 23, 45
  and human rights 311–314
  and internationalist identities 315–317
nationality law: Japan 124
Nazi Germany: and national identity 315
"near abroad" (Russian) 164, 171, 316
Netherlands Jurists Committee for Human Rights (NJCM) 58
Netherlands, The
  Advisory Committee on Human Rights and Foreign Policy 74
  bilateral policy 68–75
  and colonialism 50–52
  Constitution 51, 61
  foreign development aid 15, 53–55, 69, 329
  human rights issues 75, 313, 316–317
    development aid 53–55
    NGOs 57–58
    policies 52–57, 64–65
    violations 55–57
  and Indonesian issues 69–72, 313, 326, 329
  and international institutes 65–68
  international trade 37, 50, 70
  multilateral policy 61–68
  national self-image 3, 319
  parliament and politics 59–61
  UN peacekeeping operations 323
New International Economic Order 277
*Nezavisimaya Gazeta* (Russian Independent Newspaper) 163
Nicaragua 278, 300
  and Caribbean Pact 298
  human rights issues *283*, *284*, 287, 291, 292
  insurgency 299
  and US foreign policy 30
Niger: development assistance programmes 69
Nigeria
  arms embargo (1995) 268
  bilateral policies 13–14
  and democratic change 257
  EU and UN action and resolutions 66, 102, 264
  and foreign aid 109, 140
  human rights issues 256, 260, 261, 265
Non-Aligned Movement 299, 303
non-governmental organizations (NGOs) 1, 30, 90, 281–4
  American 24
  British 98–99
  Dutch 57–58, 70, 76
  Japanese 141
  and Russia 153
  South African 259–260
  and Turkey 69
  and Universal Declaration of Human Rights 183–184
North American Free Trade Agreement (NAFTA) 31
North Atlantic Treaty Organization (NATO)
  action in Bosnia 219–220
  expansion 42–43, 161, 242, 338
  and human rights 31
  and Kosovo crisis 338–340
North Korea, Japanese aid policy 140
North–South issues/relations 253, 287, 299
nuclear tests and weapons 138, 208
Nzo, Alfred (South Africa) 250

Oceania, Japanese aid 135
Oduber Quirós, Daniel (Costa Rica) 299

Office of the UN High Commissioner for Human Rights 238
Office of the UN High Commissioner for Refugees 38
Official Development Assistance Charter (ODA) 122, 125, 128, 135–140
Ogata, Sadaka (Japan) 132–133
Ohira, Masayoshi (Japan) 135
Open Society Institute (George Soros Foundation) 163
Ordinary Capital Resources (OCR) loans 129, 130
Organ for Politics, Defence and Security (South Africa) 262
Organization of African Unity (OAU) 261, 262–263
  Assemblies of Heads of State and Government 262–263
  Convention Governing the Specific Aspects of Refugee Problems in Africa 270
Organization of American States (OAS) 13, 29, 30, 289, 291
  General Assembly 292
  human rights programme 30
  Latin American Economic Commission 303
  Santiago Declaration (1991) 294
  US democracy assistance program 41
Organization of the Islamic Conference 198
Organization of Petroleum Exporting Countries (OPEC) 287
Organization for Security and Cooperation in Europe, *see also* Conference on Security and Cooperation in Europe (CSCE)
Organization for Security and Cooperation in Europe (OSCE) 2, 10, 68
  British input 102–104
  Dutch initiatives 67
  and Eastern European countries 233, 326
  Russian input 156
  and US 29, 31, 41
Orlich, Francisco (Costa Rica) 299
Ossetian conflict 234
Owen, David (UK) 103

Pahad, Aziz (South Africa) 251, 255, 256
Paine, Tom 313
Pakistan 268–269
  human rights issues 181, 202
  and India 178, 199, 202
  and Islamic ideology 210
  and Kashmir issue 180–181, 182, 196–198
  politics 202–203
Pakistan movement 189
Pakistani Muslim League 203
Palestine
  human rights 158–159
  Iranian support 218
Palestine–Israeli agreements 159
Panama
  EU action 102
  human rights issues *283, 284*
  US intervention 40, 294
Papua New Guinea: and South African arms sales 258
Paraguay 278
  and human rights issuess *283, 284*, 291
Paraguayan Commission for the Defence of Human Rights 282
Paris Peace Agreement: Cambodian violation 127
Paris Peace Treaties 239–240, 241
Parliamentary Assembly of the Council of Europe (PACE) 160
Parliamentary Foreign Affairs Committee (UK) 98
Parliamentary Human Rights Group (UK) 98
Parliamentary Ombudsman (Poland) 226
Parliamentary Portfolio Committees (South Africa) 259
parliaments
  British 88, 98
  Dutch 60–61
  European 66
Peace of Westphalia (1648) 89
Pelindaba Treaty 268
Pelletreau, Robert (US) 208
Penal Reform International (NGO) 99
perestroika: and Mikhail Gorbachev 152
Permanent Court of Arbitration 65
Permanent International Criminal Court 65
Perón, Juan Domingo (Argentina) 301–302
Peru
  guerrilla violence 285
  human rights issues *283, 284*
    violations 286, 291, 292, 294
  Japanese aid policy 139, 140

Peruvian Institute for Legal Defence 282
Peter I (the Great) of Russia 150
Petition of Right (England) (1628) 116
philanthropic institutions: and human rights 281–282
Philippines
 OCR loans 130
 and World Bank aid 134
Physicians for Human Rights (US) 24–25, 186, 198
Pilsudski, Józef (Poland) 225
Pinilla, Rojas (Colombia) 278
Pinochet, Augusto (Argentina) 108, 134
Pityana, Dr. Barney (South Africa) 263
Pol, Galindo (United Nations envoy to Iran) 212
Poland
 and death penalty 232
 foreign aid 140, 234
 history and politics 224–230
 and human rights issues 228–231
 multilateral policy 232–239
Polisario Front (Western Sahara) 264, 299
political issues 97–98, 211
 and human rights 5–6, 52, 330
 repression in South America 278, 280, 281, 285–286, 299
 treatment of prisoners 70, 71, 139, 260
political–criminal offences: distinction 278
Porter, Bruce D. 163
Portugal
 Salazar repression 281
 and UN General Assembly 33
post-Cold War era
 and human rights 184
 and international human rights regime 186
poverty 54, 191, 285
Prague: "velvet revolution" 226, 227
Primakov, Foreign Minister (Russia) 168
prisons/prisoners: conditions and treatment 70, 71, 139, 233, 260, 288
privacy (personal): and consumerism 228
private for-profit corporations, and economic sanctions 2
Pronk, Jan (The Netherlands) 54, 55, 69
 and Indonesian problem 70, 71, 72
*propiska* (residence permit) system 168–169
Protestants: special rights in England 89
public opinion
 and human rights 4
 and NATO military intervention in Kosovo 340–341
 US 24
public sector resources: and human rights 42, 44
Punjab insurgency 182, 190, 203

Qom religious seminary (Iran) 216

Race Relations Action (UK) (1965) 90–91
racial discrimination 37, 229
Rafsanjani, Ali Akbar Hashemi (Iran) 211–212, 216, 218
 visit to South Africa (1996) 251
Ramos-Horta, Jose (East Timor) 314
 meeting with Nelson Mandela (July 1997) 266
Rao, Naarasimha (India) 197
Raoul Wallenberg Society (Hungary) 229
Reagan administration
 and human rights 28, 37, 39
 and Iran 207
 and Latin American policies 281, 295, 300, 303
Reagan, Ronald (US president) 303
refugees 38
 expansion of concept 279
 Indo-Chinese 120
 international treaties 168
 Latin America 279
 South African approach 256
regional development banks 128
Regulation of Foreign Military Assistance Act (South Africa) 257
religious issues
 freedom and tolerance 26, 63, 89, 120, 220, 297
 Indian policy 189
 in Latin America 281, 297
 Roman Catholicism 226, 227, 243
 in Russia 154–155
religious organizations as HRNGOs 282
reports and studies 17, 39, 63
Republican Party (US) 29
Reuters World Service 183
Reza Pahlavi, Muhammad (Shah of Iran) 206
Rhodesia: trade with UK 106
rights
 of asylum, first reference 278
 of children 62

- of the citizen 312
- civil and political 37, 52
- collective 53
- economic, social, and cultural 37, 101, 104, 288
- economic, social, and political rights 52, 54
- freedom of conscience 62
- freedom of expression 216–217
- of the handicapped 123
- of the individual 53
- of journalists, Costa Rica 318
- of the mentally ill 229
- religious 63
- socio-economic 32
- to development 62–63, 101, 287–288
- to rule 312
- to self-determination 306
- *see also* minority rights

Rights and Humanity (NGO) 99
Rights of Persons Belonging to National or Ethnic, Religious and Linguistic Minorities (UN) 239
Robinson, Mary (UN High Commissioner) 36
Roma Civil Rights Foundation (Hungary) 229
Roman Catholicism in Eastern Europe 226, 227, 243
Romania
- creation of nation-state 240
- and ethnic Hungarians 240
- EU action 102
- membership of Council of Europe 68
- minorities
  - persecution 233, 238
  - rights 67, 226, 231
- pro-democracy policies 41

Romanies, discrimination and violence against 229, 230–231, 233
Ron, James 183
Roosevelt, F.D. (US president) 110
Rousseau, Jean-Jacques 116
Rushdie, Salman 217
Russia
- American aid policies 155
- and the Baltics 166–168
- and Belarus 165–166
- bilateral policy 163–171
- capital punishment issue 154
- civil-political rights 151, 152–153
- Constitution 153–154
- cultural traditions 149
- domestic factors 152–155
- East–West relations 151, 153, 157, 172
- human rights issues 151, 159, 316
  - and foreign policy 3, 156–161
  - historical background 150–152
- and IFIs 162–163
- institutions 153–154
- and International Bill of Rights 156
- isolationism 152
- and Kazakhstan 166
- legal system 150, 153–154, 155, 170–171
- media 163, 166
- multilateral policy 156–163
- the "near abroad" 164, 171, 316
- and NGOs 153
- political culture 152–153
- and refugees 168–171
- regional developments 161–162
- and religious groups 154–155
- socio-economic rights 152–153
- and the Ukraine 164–165
- and UN arms embargoes 157
- *see also* Soviet Union

Russian Federation: membership of Council of Europe 68
Russian Orthodox Church 154, 155
Russian Public Television (ORT) 166
Rwanda 132
- arms sales and embargoes 268, 269
- and human rights violations 12, 61, 184
- and international criminal court 35
- and international sanctions 327
- UN peacekeeping operations 64
- and US 25, 38, 44
- *see also* Uganda

Saharan Arab Democratic Republic 264
St Kitts and Nevis *284*
St Vincent and the Grenadines *284*
Saivetz, Carol R. 163–164
Sampaio, Jorge (Portugal) 266
Samper, President (Colombia) 293
sanctions
- against China 326
- against Cuba 267
- against Iraq 158, 179, 181, 184–185
- against Libya 267
- against Rwanda and Somalia 327
- busting 9
- and European Union 75–76
- and international human rights 55, 323

sanctions (cont.)
  and private for-profit corporations 2
  and Serbia 185
  and South Africa 111
Sandinista regime (Costa Rica) 299–300
Santiago Declaration 30
Saro-Wiwa, Ken (Nigeria), execution 257
*sati* (widow immolation: India) 188
Saudi Arabia
  and international human rights 316
  and Islamic ideology 210
  and Kashmir issue 198
  and Universa Declaration of Human Rights (1948) 9
  and US liberal democracy support 43
SAVAK (National Security & Intelligence Organization: Iran) 206–207, 208
Schlessinger, Arthur M., Jr. 23
Schoo, Mrs (Dutch Minister) 73
self-determination 237, 306, 313, 316
Serbia
  creation of nation-state 240
  human rights violations 185, 238
  and Milosevic regime 338–339
  and sanctions 185
Serita, Professor Kentaro 116
SERPAJ (Latin American Service for Peace and Justice) 282
Seshan, T.N. 193
Sevastopol (Crimean Republic) 164–165
SFOR 35
Shah of Iran (Muhammed Reza Pahlavi) 206, 209, 314
Sharpeville massacre (South Africa) 259
Shelter Society (Hungary) 229
Sheremet, Pavel (Russia) 166
Shiite Muslims 210, 217
Siberian peasants: forced move 150
Sierra Leone
  human rights violations 265
  and South African arms sales 258
Sikhs 182, 190
Singapore: visit of Nelson Mandela (1996) 251
slavery: US policy 23
Slovakia 224
  creation of nation-state 240
  and minority rights 67, 226, 231, 233
Society for Freedoms (Hungary) 229
socio-economic rights 32, 288
  and Russia 152–153
  and South-East Asia 130
  and US 42
Solidarity movement and government (Poland) 226, 230
Sólyom, Judge Lásalo (Hungary) 230
Somalia 132
  British project aid 108
  and international criminal court 35
  and international sanctions 327
  and United Nations Security Council 2
  and US 25, 43, 44
Somoza, Anastasio (Nicaragua) 30, 278, 297
South Africa
  apartheid policies 57, 90, 91, 189, 313–314
  and arms sales 251, 257, 266, 268
  bilateral policy 264–270
  civic organizations 257
  Constitution 258–260, 270
  and economic sanctions 111, 314
  human rights issues 37
    and domestic factors 253–258
    and foreign policy 251–252, 253–254
    treaties to which South Africa is a party 271–272
    violations 250–253
  and Hungarian transition to democracy 234
  and Lesotho instability 262
  multilateral policy 258–264
  non-governmental organizations (NGOs) 259–260
  Organization of African Unity (OAU) 261, 262–263
  post-apartheid 250–272
  regional developments 260–261
  and SADC 261–262
  trade and investment 265–266
  UK arms exports/embargo 93, 106
  and United Nations 33, 263–264, 269
South African Human Rights Commission 263
South America
  historical background to human rights 278–280
  political violence 285–286
  *see also* Latin America
South–South cooperation 256
South-East Asia: and socio-economic rights 130
Southern African Development Community (SADC) 261–262, 264, 265

Soviet Union
  and African countries 252
  collapse 163, 240
  and Helsinki Accords 151, 314
  and human rights 30–1
  *see also* Russia
Spain: Franco repression 281
Srebrenica (Bosnia) 336
  and Dutch involvement 64–65, 77
Sri Lanka
  and development assistance programmes 69, 70
  political conflict 316
  relations with India 178, 199, 201
Starovoitova, Galina (Russia): assassination 155
START-2 Treaty 158
State Law and Order Restoration Council (SLORC) (Myanmar) 133
states
  and acceptance of international human rights provisions 9–10
  sovereignty 125–126, 280, 288
Stoel, Max van der (High Commissioner on National Minorities) 67
Stolypin, Peter (Russia) 150
Stroessner Matianda, Alfredo (Paraguay) 278
structural adjustment programmes (SAPs) 32
Sudan
  civil war 323
  foreign aid and development assistance programmes 69, 108–109, 140
  human rights violations 101, 238, 265
  relations with Iran 219
Sudan People's Liberation Army (SPLA) 261
Suharto, President (Indonesia) 70, 71
  visit to South Africa (1997)
Suharto regime: Indonesia 70
Supreme Electoral Tribunal (Costa Rica) 298
Surinam
  and the Dutch 69–72
  human rights issues 77, *284*, 317
    violations 63, 292
  suspension of Dutch aid 72–4
Sustainable Development Regional Alliance (ALIDES) 300
Suttner, Raymond (South Africa) 264–265
Swaraj (self-rule: India) 187–188
Swaziland: human rights issues 257, 265
Syria
  and arms sales 269
  and development assistance programmes 69
  and US liberal democracy support 43

Tajikistan 167, 168, 170
Takeshita, Noboru (Japan) 135, 137
Taliban movement (Afghanistan) 220
Tamil Tigers 201
Tarasssov, Judge (Russian) 157
Taters (Crimea); deportation and resettlement 164–165
*Tehran Times* 219, 220
terrorism (international)
  Indian condemnation 195, 198, 316
  and Iran 207–208, 213, 219
Thailand
  Japanese aid policy 139, 140
  OCR loans 129
Tiananmen Square incident
  and aid to China 130, 135–136
  and Chinese human rights diplomacy 181
  international responses 270, 321–322
    British reaction 107
    Indian reaction 181
    Japanese reaction 126–127, 133, 138
  and sanctions against China 326
  and US policy towards China 324
Tibet: use of UN military intervention 328
Tinoca, Rodrigo (Costa Rica) 297
Toleration Act (England) (1689) 89
trade unions: legalization in UK 89
Trans-Dniester conflict 170
Treaty of Amsterdam 75
Treaty on European Union (Maastrict: 1991) 66, 75
Treaty of Extradition (1877–1880) 278
Treaty on the Non-Proliferation of Nuclear Weapons 268
Treaty of Rome (1957) 101
Treaty of Tlatelolco 305
Treaty of Versailles (1919) 89
Trianon Peace Treaty 239–240, 241
Trinidad and Tobago: Inter-American human rights regime *284*
Trujillo, Rafael (Dominican Republic) 278

Turkey
  and arms sales 269
  and human rights violations 68–69, 76
  and Kosovo crisis 338
  and South African arms exports 251
  and US foreign policy 44
Turkmenistan: CIS agreement on assistance to refugees 168

Uganda
  UK aid policy 93, 106, 111
  *see also* Rwanda
Ukraine
  bilateral treaty with Hungary 241
  and ethnic Russians 164–165
  membership of Council of Europe 68
  and OSCE protection of national minorities 67
  and Russian foreign policy 164
Ukrainian–Russian treaties 165
Ulate, Otilio (Costa Rica) 299
Ul-Haq, General Zia (Pakistan) 202
United Kingdom
  aid to Indonesia 93
  arms exports and embargoes 93, 108
  bilateral policies 106–109
  and China question 37–38
  colonial inheritance and decolonization 90, 109
  and the Commonwealth 105–106, 110
  and Council of Europe 100–101
  and CSCE/OSCE 87, 91, 102–104
  EU involvement 87, 91, 101–102
  foreign aid policies 93
  foreign assistance programmes 15
  Foreign Policy Documents (FPDs) 91–94, 102, 107, 108
  human rights issues 91–96, 313
    and domestic factors 8, 96–99
    historical context 88–91
    and politics 5, 6, 94–95, 105, 110–11
    violations 97, 100
  ILO involvement 96
  incorporation of European Convention into British law 314
  and International Criminal Court 95
  and international criminal prosecutions 11
  multilateral policies 99–106
  NGOs 98–99
  politics and Parliament 88, 97–98
  religious freedom 89
  trade and investment in Argentina 301
  UN participation 87, 91, 92, 104–105
  US relationship 109–110
United Kingdom Military Assistance Training Scheme 95
United Nations
  arms embargoes 157
  criminal court negotiations 35–36
  and Dutch 61–68
  international tribunals 132
  and Japan 131–134
  peacekeeping operations 34–35, 132, 134, 157, 306
    Hungarian involvement 237–238
    in Yugoslavia 64–65
  and South Africa 263–264
  UK participation 104–105
  and US 33–38, 41, 43
United Nations Centre for Refugees in Moscow 168
United Nations Charter (1945) 9, 27, 90, 277
  British involvement 110
  Chapter VII 10, 11, 34, 35, 36, 43
  and NATO intervention in Kosovo 339
United Nations Commission on Human Rights 123
  Dutch input 61–62
  and European Council of Ministers 66
  Japanese involvement 127
  resolution on China 76
  UK involvement 92
United Nations Committee for the Elimination of Racial Discrimination 110
United Nations Committee on Human Rights, Geneva 28, 29
United Nations Conference on Human Rights, Vienna (1993) 3, 289
United Nations Conference on Trade and Development (UNCTAD) 287, 303
United Nations Convention against Torture and Other Cruel, Inhuman or Degrading Treatment or Punishment (1984) 105, 160–161, 170–171
United Nations Convention on Civil and Political Rights (Protocol 2) 230
United Nations Convention on the Elimination of All Forms of Discrimination against Women 105, 124
United Nations Convention on the Elimination of all Forms of Racial Discrimination (1995) 90–91, 123

United Nations Convention Relating to the Status of Refugees (1981) 123, 170, 270
United Nations Convention on the Rights of the Child 99, 105, 110
United Nations Declaration on the Elimination of All Forms of Intolerance and of Discrimination Based on Religion or Belief 154
United Nations Economic and Social Council (ECOSOC) 96, 104, 287
United Nations Food and Agriculture Organization 185
United Nations Friendly Relations Declaration (1970) 102
United Nations General Assembly 11–12, 104
  American influence 213
  British Foreign Secretary's speech (1976) 105
  Indian input 194
  Japanese involvement 127, 132
  and The Netherlands 49
  resolution on Iranian human rights abuses 208
  and South Africa 263
  Third Committee 96
  and US 33, 34, 36
United Nations High Commissioner for Human Rights (UNHCHR) 36, 94, 105, 132, 289
United Nations High Commissioner for Refugees (UNHCR) 12, 132, 168, 279
United Nations Human Rights Commission 12, 27, 36–37
  Drafting Committee 104
  Indian input 194
  Iranian human rights abuses 208, 212
  Japanese involvement 132
  and Kashmir issue 197
  and Netherlands 49
  South African participation 264, 269
  and UK 93–94
  and US 34
United Nations Human Rights Committee 99, 132, 238
United Nations International Bill of Human Rights 110
United Nations Protection Force in Yugoslavia (UNPROFOR) 77
United Nations Quaker Office 281
United Nations Refugee Convention (1951) 232
United Nations Register of Conventional Arms 95
United Nations Security Council 339
  and Eastern European countries 234, 236–237
  and Indonesia 51
  and Japan 132, 134, 141
  and Somalia 2
  summit (1992) 34
  and US 33–34, 36, 213
United Nations Special Rapporteur on Torture 63
United Nations Sub-Commission on the Prevention of Discrimination and Protection of Minorities 63, 123, 132, 239
United Nations Transitional Authority in Cambodia (UNTAC) 134
United Nations Universal Declaration of Human Rights 156
United States
  bilateral agreements with India 199
  Bill of Rights 28
  Bureau of Democracy, Human Rights, and Labor 6, 26
  Central Intelligence Agency (CIA) 206, 290
  Congress 25–26
  Constitution 22, 28
  debate on activist foreign policy 23
  democracy assistance program 41
  Foreign Assistance Act (1973) 207
  foreign assistance programmes 15, 39–40
  and foreign democratic development 14
  foreign policy 24–7, 44, 252
  Helms–Burton bill 219, 296
  and human rights issues 9, 22, 25–26, 34, *284*, 312, 317
    international scrutiny 317, 318–319
    legislation 207, 219, 296
    multilateral policy 27–38
    NGOs 281
    policies 27–38, 213
    and politics 5, 6, 7
    public opinion 24
    violations 200
  and humanitarian intervention 11, 40–41
  and IFIs 31–33

United States (cont.)
  and IMF 44
  and international criminal prosecutions 11
  and internationalism 24
  and Islamic revolution 211
  and military dictatorships 277
  military interventions 26–27, 30
  and national self-image 3, 21, 22, 23, 45
  and NATO expansion 42–43
  public sector resources 42
  relations with Iran 207–208
  and religious freedom 26
  Russian aid policies 155
  Senate Foreign Relations Committee 28, 29
  and socio-economic rights 21, 22, 42
  and UN 33–38, 43
  and World Bank 44
Universal Declaration of Human Rights (1948) 9, 27, 58, 90, 104, 183, 277
  Eastern European countries 232
  and India 194–195
  Japanese commitment 125
  and South African Constitution 259
universal human rights: UK and The Netherlands, 313
Uno, Prime Minister (Japan) 138
Uruburu, José F. (Argentina) 301
Uruguay
  Inter-American human rights regime *284*
  and international human rights treaties *283*
  military coup 281
  and political persecution 278
  UK policy 111
  and United Nations Human Rights High Commissioner 289
US–Chinese relations 322
US–Pakistani alliance 202
Uttar Pradesh state elections (1993) 192
Uzbekistan
  CIS agreement on assistance to refugees 168
  extradition of human rights activists 171
  and Russian minorities 167

Vajpayee, Atal Behari (BJP leader: India) 182, 192, 197
Vatican: treaty with Hungary 243
"velvet revolution", Prague 227
Venezuela 278
  asylum provision 279
  and Caribbean Pact 298
  crimes of violence 285
  human rights violations 285, 292
  Inter-American human rights regime *284*
  and international human rights treaties *283*
  and liberal democracy 295
Vicaría de la Solidaridad (HRNGO: Chile) 282
Vienna Conference 233
Vienna Declaration (1993) 156, 160
  and Programme of Action 238
Vienna Final Act 38
Vietnam
  OCR loans 129–130
  protest movement 57
  and UK aid 107
Vietnam War 189
Virginia Bill of Rights (US) (1776) 89, 116
Vitoria, Duke of (1792–1879) 89
Voorhoeve, J.J.C. 51–52
Vorontsov, Yuli (Russia) 170

Wales, Prince and Princess of: proposed visit to China (1989) 107
Warsaw Pact 232
Washington Office on Latin America 281
Washington Protocol 294
welfare systems: Eastern European countries 229–230
Western New Guinea *see* Irian Jaya
Western Sahara: human rights issues 264
Wilson, Thomas Woodrow (US President) 23, 90, 276
Women's Conference, Beijing (1995) 99
women's rights
  Japan 120, 121, 123
  in Latin America 281, 292
  and Taliban militia in Afghanistan 220
  UN Convention on the Elimination of Discrimination against Women 105
Woo-Cumings 129
World Bank 130, 277
  and donor countries' concerns 134
  and Eastern European countries 234
  and human rights issues 10, 32, 33, 256
  Inspection Panel 33
  and Japan 128

loans to China 137–138
and Pakistan 203
support of Russian monetary policy 162
and UK 95
and US 44
World Conference on Human Rights, Vienna (1993) 38, 57, 58, 125, 126, 156
Asia Regional Preparatory Meeting, Bangkok (1993) 125
World Council of Churches 281
World Council of Indigenous Peoples 292
*World of Difference, A* (Pronk) 54
*World in Dispute, A* (Pronk) 55
World War II
aftermath 90
and Argentina 302

Xinhua General Overseas News Service 183

Yaciter (Argentina) hydroelectric project 303
Yanomani Indians (Brazil) 291–292
Yazdi, Ayatollah Mohammed (Iran) 214
Yeltsin, Boris (Russia) 154, 155, 170, 171
Yugoslavia (former) 132
conflict 241
and Dutch military involvement 64–65
and human rights violations 184
and international criminal court 35
and NATO intervention 335, 337, 340
and OSCE/US policies 31
and Russian foreign policy 157
and UN 12, 34, 235–236
violation of Genocide Convention 157

Zaire 132
and development assistance programmes 69
and European Union resolution 66
and human rights issues 256
and US 25, 40
*see also* Democratic Republic of Congo
Zambia: human rights issues 257, 265
Zapista rebels (Mexico) 286
Zhirinovsky, Vladimir (Russia) 160
Zimbabwe: and Lesotho instability 262